Join the Conspiracy

JOIN THE CONSPIRACY

How a Brooklyn Eccentric Got Lost on the Right, Infiltrated the Left, and Brought Down the Biggest Bombing Network in New York

Jonathan Butler

AN IMPRINT OF FORDHAM UNIVERSITY PRESS

NEW YORK 2024

Fordham University Press also publishes its books in a variety of electronic formats. Some content that appears in print may not be available in electronic books.

Visit us online at www.fordhampress.com/empire-state-editions.

Library of Congress Cataloging-in-Publication Data available online at https://catalog.loc.gov.

Printed in the United States of America

26 25 24 5 4 3 2 1

First edition

CONTENTS

Friday. April 26: I wake up at 8:55 and run to the crew bus and leave for MIT. From Cambridge I call my home in Marlboro. My mother asks me, "Are you on the side of the law-breakers in this thing?" For ten minutes we exchange mother talk and revolutionary rhetoric. She points out that neither Gandhi nor Thoreau would have asked for amnesty. I admit I haven't read them. But Gandhi had no Gandhi and Thoreau hadn't read Thoreau. They had to reach their own conclusions and so will I.

—James Simon Kunen, *The Strawberry Statement*

PROLOGUE

IN 2019, CASTING ABOUT for a screenplay idea, I picked up a copy of *Bill Graham Presents*, the autobiography of the legendary concert promoter. Known primarily for his championing of Bay Area psychedelic bands like the Grateful Dead and Jefferson Airplane, Graham expanded to New York in early 1968 with the opening of the Fillmore East in a former Yiddish theater on Second Avenue and Sixth Street. The 2,600-capacity venue immediately became the must-play spot on the East Coast for a generation of genre-defining classic rock acts like The Who, Jimi Hendrix, and the Allman Brothers and brought even more attention to a neighborhood that was undergoing a once-in-a-generation culture shift. The injection of thousands of white hippies, runaways, and anarchists into what Abbie Hoffman called the "cultural fruit salad" of the Lower East Side had boosted crime rates and drug use in the neighborhood and exacerbated resentments among the Eastern Europeans, Puerto Ricans, and Blacks who were already competing for finite amounts of space and political power there.

Graham's entrance into the neighborhood was not as smooth as he might have hoped. In addition to the normal delays and cost overruns often associated with opening a new business, he faced pushback from some members of the community over his commercial success. In his book, the unapologetic Graham cites a run-in with a local group of anarchists and artists called the Motherfuckers who demanded that he turn the club over to the community for one night a week of free programming. Graham, a self-made entrepreneur who'd survived the horrors of the Holocaust as a child, did not take kindly to being told what to do, let alone being threatened with violence. But after a late-night shouting match on the stage with Motherfucker-in-chief Ben Morea following a nude theater performance, Graham grudgingly gave in to the radicals' demands, and the free-for-all evenings proceeded for the next two months until the fire department shut them down, giving the promoter a convenient out.

As a lifelong New Yorker with a degree in history, I couldn't believe I'd never heard of the Motherfuckers. The catchy and at-the-time unprintable name was short for "Up Against the Wall, Motherfucker," a line from "Black People" by the Black poet Amiri Baraka and a refrain that would echo through the antiwar and civil rights movements in the last couple years of the decade. It figured on placards at protests, in Mark Rudd's kiss-off letter to Columbia University president Grayson Kirk, and in the refrain of Jefferson Airplane's song "We Can Be Together," among others. These guys—and they were mostly guys—were wild. In addition to running crash pads for teenage runaways and free meal programs for the poor, the self-proclaimed anarchists staged mock assassinations of famous poets, shut down the Museum of Modern Art, and transported mounds of uncollected garbage from the Lower East Side to the fountains of Lincoln Center. Talk about cinematic!

The plot kept thickening. Another group I hadn't heard of that kept coming up as I dug deeper into the radical scene in the East Village was the Melville Collective. This loose-knit group of disaffected twenty- and thirty-somethings set off bombs in a half dozen high-profile locations in New York between July and November of 1969 before being brought down by an undercover informant, a blue-collar worker from Brooklyn named George Demmerle who'd belonged to a few right-wing organizations in the mid-1960s before he started popping up at socialism workshops and leftist demonstrations. How was it that I'd never heard of any of this stuff? Why had so little been written about it?

The opening twenty pages of *Days of Rage*, Bryan Burrough's 2015 book about the Weather Underground, provides a detailed description of the final weeks of the Melville Collective's bombing campaign. As far as I could tell, it was compiled largely from two first-person accounts: *Chief!*, the 1974 autobiography of NYPD detective Albert Seedman, which devotes one of its dozen chapters to the Melville case, and *Growing Up Underground*, the autobiographical account of Jane Alpert, the girlfriend and accomplice of bombing mastermind Sam Melville. (While I was researching and writing my book, Sam Melville's son, Joshua, published his own account of tracing and coming to terms with his father's legacy.) I also quickly found my way to the writings of Jeremy Varon, a professor of history at the New School, and in particular to his book called *Bringing the War Home*. Varon's work yielded not only details about Robin Palmer, the character link between Melville and Demmerle, but also insight into the mindset of the radical left leading up to the creation of the Weather Underground.

None of these books, however, included more than a passing mention of George Demmerle. A closer examination of the alternative newspapers at the time—the *East Village Other* and the *Rat Subterranean News*, most relevantly—yielded a few more crumbs, leading me finally to the only two interviews with Demmerle in print: a 1970 conversation with a conservative radio host that was transcribed in the *Berkeley Tribe*, and a 1995 profile in a Dallas weekly newspaper.

With just this simple sketch of Demmerle, I had enough to know I was on to a great story. I started to work on a draft of my screenplay and filed a Freedom of Information Act request with the FBI. I also combed through newspaper archives and books about the New Left, the civil rights movement, and the various factions that made up the antiwar coalition during the second half of the decade. Around the time that a four-hundred-page file arrived in my inbox from the FBI, it occurred to me that although Demmerle had died in 2007 at the age of seventy-six, his fourth and final wife might very well still be alive. With the help of a friend skilled in the art of internet sleuthing, I came up with a name as well as an email address. Twenty-four hours later I was on the phone with Carol Barnes Price. *Did she have any papers from George's time undercover?* I asked. *Yes, she did! A big collection, in the back of a closet somewhere*. Less than a week after contacting Carol, a banker's box full of photos, flyers, legal documents, and unpublished interview transcripts arrived at my home in Brooklyn.

Amid the papers were four issues of *Crazie*, the DIY magazine put out by a radical group called the Crazies that Demmerle was involved in founding in early 1969. The language, LSD-fused protest-era patois, was irresistible and pulled me in even further:

> Crazies are pigs' heads, nudity and mind fucking exhibitions for the benefit of liberal bullshit artists. . . . Crazies have bushy hair, long hair, crew cuts, grey hair and sometimes no hair at all. Crazies are anarchistcommunist-marxistmaoist-individualistreturntonatureist heavy revolutionaries. Crazies are N.L.F. flags and helmets at a street action. Crazies are a well-placed stone through a Chase Manhattan bank window. Crazies are a kick in the balls to a pig trying to vamp

on a brother. Crazies are brothers and sisters to each other. Crazies are Freedom, Peace and Power to the People.

Between the FBI files and this gift from Carol, it became obvious to me that the story I had stumbled onto deserved to be a book; the screenplay could wait. Not only was this an important piece of American history, but the participants who were still alive (and many were already dead) were also in their seventies and eighties and would not be around forever to tell their stories. Indeed, one of the most important sources both in terms of content and personal connection, Walter Teague, died as I was finishing the book. So began the two-year process of research, interviews, drafts, and revisions that resulted in the book you hold in your hands today. At times I felt like Carrie Mathison, the fictional lead character in the Showtime thriller *Homeland,* who, in a bipolar blur, finds herself staring at a wall of photos, flyers and scribbled notes, trying to fill in blanks, connect dots, and uncover secrets.

Along the way I received invaluable help and encouragement from Jeremy Varon, the New School professor, who not only reviewed my first draft but also generously provided me with several hours of interviews he had done almost thirty years earlier with Robin Palmer, one of the four most important characters in my account and another figure notably absent from the history books. My requests for interviews with other Movement members were generally well received. Old paranoias and resentments die hard, though, and some key players—most notably and regrettably Melville Collective members Jane Alpert and Wolfe Lowenthal—refused to talk. The great majority, however, seemed happy, relieved almost, that their stories might be preserved for posterity. After all, they were not just telling tales of youthful indiscretions—though I certainly heard plenty of anecdotes about drug use, pranks, and sexual escapades—but sharing with me the most meaningful experiences of their lives; the decisions many of them made as earnest young men and women in the sixties set them on lifelong paths of service, whether as public defenders, environmental activists, mental health professionals, or advocates for social justice.

Every source I talked to was generous with his or her time and had surprisingly detailed memories of their years in the Movement, as the agglomeration of antiwar and civil rights groups was referred to. Still, it's important to remember as a historian and as a reader that the events they were recalling happened more than fifty years ago, and that memories, even recent ones, are subjective. In recognition of that fact, this book is heavily footnoted, and the accounts of some of the era's tentpole events—the march on the Pentagon, the Columbia rebellion, the Democratic National Convention in Chicago, Nixon's inauguration, and the Days of Rage, in particular—are the result of an exhaustive effort on my part to triangulate first-person accounts with contemporaneous news stories and the in-depth reports that were prepared after the fact by task forces of journalists or government commissions.

While three of the main characters in this book—Demmerle, Palmer, and Melville—had been dead for years by the time I started on their trail, a few central players in the Movement were still alive and receptive to my advances. The most important of these for me was Teague. I spent several hours on Zoom with the eighty-six-year-old founder of the U.S. Committee to Aid the National Liberation Front of South Vietnam before driving down to spend the night at his house outside Washington, DC, in the final days of 2022, where I was given access to his voluminous library of photos, government documents, and Vietnamese publications. Though he was clearly ailing by the time of my visit, Teague's memory for people and events remained as sharp as his political convictions. It was difficult not to be impressed by his dedication and hard not to have his passion seep into the pages of this book. It was also impossible not to be moved when he died during the editing process just a month after giving me the rights to use dozens of his photos to help tell my story. Though neither of us believed in God, there was something that felt providential about my arriving in his final weeks to record his life's story and document his role in my tale of true believers, undercover agents, and over-the-top outlaws.

And for what? Beyond being a sexy tale full of subterfuge, excess, and exploding buildings, why tell this story? The central narrative itself, about an eccentric working-class man who'd bought into the anticommunist fear tactics of the McCarthy era and who infiltrated a group of left-wing bombers who'd swallowed a different batch of Kool-Aid, shows the extent to which normal citizens were willing to go and the sacrifices they were willing to make to further a cause they believed in. For someone like me, born in 1969, just days after the final bombing attempt by Melville, and coming of age amid the relative privilege and conservatism of the Reagan era, the chance to get inside the heads of people with this kind of passion and devotion was irresistible.

I began writing the first draft of this book within months of the murder of George Floyd by a white policeman in Minneapolis and within weeks of the storming of the U.S Capitol by right-wing extremists, both of which served as reminders of how little progress we had made over the past half century in healing the racial, class, and philosophical divisions that marked the conflicts of the sixties. While the politics and rationalizations of the people storming the Capitol on January 6, 2021, could not have been more different (or, in my opinion, abhorrent), some of the visuals were jarringly reminiscent of scenes from the Pentagon on October 21, 1967, a free-for-all where the QAnon shaman would have fit right in alongside the costumed leftists levitating and in some cases penetrating the ultimate symbol of U.S. military might. Even some of the iconography—in particular, the yellow "Don't Tread on Me" Gadsden flags with their image of a coiled rattlesnake—was the same. The xenophobes and racists of today's right and the activists of the 1960s radical left had one thing in common: a belief that the soul and future of their nation was on the line. Other than the Black Lives Matter movement in recent years and the 9/11 attack on the World Trade Center in 2001, there's been nothing in the lifetime of a Gen-Xer like me to take on such existential weight. (The slow burn of the climate crisis, while undeniably existential, has unfortunately failed to mobilize the same kind of widespread passion and panic.)

Another motivation to write this book: the more I researched the student, antiwar, and civil rights movements of the late sixties, the clearer it became that there was a gaping hole in the historical record, at least as far as secondary sources were concerned, when it came to many of the most radical groups. While plenty had been written about Students for a Democratic Society, the Yippies, and the Black Panthers—not coincidentally the three groups featured prominently in Aaron Sorkin's 2020 movie *The Trial of the Chicago 7*—there was shockingly little documentation about local groups such as the Motherfuckers and the Melville Collective that really set the tone and wrote the playbook, respectively, for the apotheosis and in time the undoing of the radical left, the Weathermen. There was almost nothing written either about important earlier organizations like the Veterans and Reservists to End the War in Vietnam and the U.S. Committee to Aid the National Liberation Front of South Vietnam, which played such instrumental roles in staging the smaller demonstrations and marches at the beginning of the war and challenging orthodoxies around what was acceptable behavior in the name of human rights. The same went for the Free School and the Alternate U., the leftist hubs in Lower Manhattan that hosted classes on everything from imperialism to psychedelic drugs and served as meetings places for the myriad political groups that formed as the war went on. It was hard to find a book that had more than a paragraph about any of them.

Questions about the motivations and morality of undercover informants like George Demmerle, who often crossed the line from being observers to coercive active participants, also fascinated me. And what about the FBI and other arms of law enforcement that not only collaborated with informants but often encouraged them to foment trouble? Just as the memories of those bearing witness are necessarily tinged by the passage of time and the implicit biases each of us carries, so are even the best-intentioned chronicles of history colored by the human being compiling them. Though it has sometimes felt like a weakness or at least a way around having to take a stand, I have always felt alienated by dogma, usually seeing gray spaces where others see black or white. Whether this account suffers for the lack of a strong point of view on which players were right or wrong or who went too far in furtherance of their deeply held beliefs is for the reader to judge. As an occupier of gray space, I've had to balance a great respect for the many characters in this book who seemed so sure of themselves in their willingness to sacrifice so much in pursuit of their idealism with the 20/20 hindsight of where their actions went either strategically or morally off course.

As the 2002 documentary film *The Weather Underground* shows so clearly, surviving members of the subset of radicals who, out of a sense of impotence and desperation, came to the conclusion that they had no choice but to "bring the war home" with street violence and bombings tend to look back on those days with mixed feelings: they remain steadfast in their critique of the United States and its racist, imperialistic tendencies but question and in many cases fault the morality and efficacy of their extreme tactics. When asked at the end of the documentary why he has been so reticent to speak about his time in the Weather Underground, Mark Rudd cites his "feelings of guilt and shame" that plague him to this day. "These are things I am not proud of and I find it hard to speak publicly about them and to tease out what was right from what was wrong," he says.

Finally, a word of thanks to some of those who helped along the way: In particular, my literary agent, Deirdre Mullane, and my editor at Fordham University Press, Fredric Nachbaur, both of whom were not fazed by my lack of credentials and believed in the story from the get-go. The same goes for Clara Platter at New York University Press and Stephen Wesley at Columbia, who read the manuscript early on and introduced me to Deirdre and Fredric, respectively. I owe deep thanks to Jeremy Varon, Carola Hoffman, Lew Friedman, Carol Barnes Price, Mimi Melegrito, Elizabeth Salzberg, and Patrick Jones, all of whom shared invaluable archives of interviews, publications, and photographs that enabled me to take such a completist approach to this project. And last to my wife, Kira von Eichel, a great writer and editor herself, for the countless dinner table discussions, stylistic critiques, and line edits over the past two years and a lifetime of supporting and saying "yes" to my sometimes harebrained schemes, like quitting my Wall Street job to write a blog, starting a goofily named food festival in a fledging neighborhood of Brooklyn, or writing a four-hundred-page nonfiction book after having not distinguished myself in any particular way as a history major at Princeton three decades earlier. Oh, and to my kids, who evolved from being high schoolers to vague sketches of adults during the writing of this book and were happy to indulge my absent-minded-professorness in the process. Thanks to all for believing in me.

INTRODUCTION

HIS TRADEMARK PURPLE CAPE and orange-plumed centurion's helmet jettisoned in favor of a less conspicuous set of work clothes, George Demmerle tried to remain calm as he paced the worn wooden floorboards of the East Second Street studio apartment that had served as the stash house over the past four months for the Melville Collective, a loose-knit group of journalists, professors, and agitators led by a mercurial thirty-four-year-old dropout named Sam Melville.

The apartment had been nicknamed the "Bomb Factory" by its transient tenants, and with good reason. Since making off with several crates of dynamite from a Bronx warehouse in July, the group had been on a bombing tear, setting off explosions at high-profile corporate and government sites all over Manhattan and in the process penning the playbook that the Weathermen, the Symbionese Liberation Army, and other radical groups would draw from in the coming years. Members of the collective had two more targets in their sights for this November night. Demmerle, whom Melville had brought into the fold just days earlier, was along for what was supposed to be the final ride. With signs mounting that the law was closing in, Melville planned to leave town the next day with his twenty-three-year-old girlfriend and accomplice, Jane Alpert.

A day earlier, the collective had made its biggest splash yet, earning ink on the front page of the late city edition of the *New York Times*. Flanked by a photo of Richard Nixon and other snapshots of the tumultuous time ("Enemy Steps Up Attacks Sharply: Offensive Is Seen," "Memphis Negroes

Dispersed by Gas," "Protest Erupts as Fort Dix Rioter Gets Three Years Hard Labor") was a headline the group of Lower East Side radicals could be proud of: "Bombs Go Off at G.M. Building, Rockefeller Center, Chase Plaza." As with all the collective's actions, Tuesday morning's explosions had been preceded by phone calls aimed at avoiding collateral damage; in fact, just one person, a service elevator operator at 30 Rockefeller Plaza, had been injured during the three-pronged attack. Perhaps the greatest inconvenience was borne by a group of late-night revelers at the Rainbow Room who, in their black ties and evening gowns, were forced to descend more than sixty flights of stairs into the late autumn night.

As the day progressed, hundreds of copycat threats poured into the NYPD switchboard, plunging a shell-shocked city into further chaos: Lincoln Center, the New York Stock Exchange, and the New York Times Building, among others, were evacuated. The next afternoon, as the public leafed through images of the wreckage in the New York dailies, a collective member and frequent collaborator of George's named Robin Palmer, accompanied by Melville, slipped out of the Bomb Factory and headed to the Criminal Courts Building on Centre Street in Lower Manhattan. Sneaking past security, he rode the elevator to the fifth floor, where he left a small bag in the janitor's closet.

Although he had seemed reluctant to play an active role in the group's earlier attacks, Palmer's radical bona fides were hardly in question. Since moving to the West Village in the early 1960s, the former paratrooper and Korean War objector had worked as an English teacher, deep sea diver, and porn actor while becoming more and more involved with antiwar and civil rights causes. His eighteen arrests included clashes with the police at the Pentagon in 1967 as well as rampaging through the streets of Chicago at the Democratic National Convention in the summer of 1968, a spree that landed him on the list of unindicted coconspirators in the Chicago Seven trial.

Although his group had seemingly gotten away with seven bombings in the city to date, and with an eighth device already set to go off that night, Melville wanted more. After rendezvousing with Melville at an East Village bar on Wednesday afternoon, Demmerle was still in the dark about that night's exact target when he showed up at the Bomb Factory around 8:00 o'clock, as instructed. There had been some disagreement among group members about the negative publicity that might surround setting off an explosion just three days before the huge antiwar march in Washington, DC, but, as he had done many times before, Melville brushed aside the concerns of his fellow collective members, as well as their instincts to steer clear of Demmerle, and plowed ahead. He wasn't much for collaborating, whether with his small group of fellow bombers or in any number of radical organizations that had sprung up downtown in the past four years.

Impatient and impetuous, Melville had spent hours jawboning with Demmerle at the Woodstock Music Festival in late August, each one-upping the other with revolutionary rhetoric and references to Movement heavies. Demmerle had become practiced at that sort of puffery, eager to prove his mettle as a true believer with the contacts and chops to back it up. For the past couple of years, the thirty-nine-year-old had become, if not a father figure, then at least a goofy uncle in radical circles on the Lower East Side, albeit one whose over-the-top antics and desperate need for attention elicited disdain from many of the more experienced and cautious members of the scene.

In addition to being older than most of the militant Movement members at the time—Melville, himself on the old side relative to most collective members, was five years younger than Demmerle—both men had recently left a wife and child. Sam, who married in 1957, moved out for good in 1965 when his son was three; George, already living on his own for a couple of years, parted ways with his wife of almost two decades and adopted teenage son when he moved into his own place in the East Village in late 1967. In search of adventure and meaning, Melville had abandoned a stable middle-class trajectory as a well-compensated draftsman with a four-bedroom apartment on the Upper West Side; Demmerle's quality-of-life adjustment was perhaps less dramatic, for he remained a welder in Brooklyn long after moving to Manhattan to be close to the action. And while many fellow Movement members were already in Washington for the march organized by the National Mobilization Committee to End the War in Vietnam (the "Mobe," as it was commonly known by then), the two loners had stayed behind to make their own mark on history.

Now, on the kitchen table in front of them, lay four Baby Ben alarm clocks, synchronized to the current time of 8:55 p.m. and connected by wires to a dozen red sticks of dynamite, all that remained from the group's summer heist. Sam put two of the bombs in George's backpack and two in his own duffel bag before grabbing a handgun from the kitchen drawer and donning his well-worn Army jacket. Demmerle, a good six inches shorter and thirty pounds lighter than Melville, tried his best to act confident as the bombing mastermind shooed him out the door. He couldn't blow it now.

For George Demmerle, this was the culmination of a three-year campaign to be accepted by the most radical of the radicals. For the past year he'd been talking to anyone who would listen about blowing things up. He had tried to convince Abbie Hoffman to receive a shipment of stolen Navy explosives and had pitched Hoffman's Yippie cofounder Jerry Rubin on a plan to bomb the Brooklyn Bridge, though George insisted later it had been the Manhattan Bridge he had in mind. And over the summer, at a dinner party in San Francisco, he had even tried to sell Alpert on a scheme to short-circuit the Wall Street power grid by pouring chemicals into the manholes that dotted the streets of Lower Manhattan.

Despite this bravado, Demmerle had never followed through on any of his big ideas. Accompanying Robin Palmer as he threw rocks at police cars in Chicago and using his karate skills to break up fights in his Brooklyn neighborhood were the extent of his violent acts to date. Disturbing the peace was one thing—George was known for leaping up at the end of Yippie meetings and shouting, "Who wants to go get arrested?"—but taking part in plans that could get people killed was quite another.

After all, George Demmerle, or Prince Crazie as he had successfully rebranded himself by this time, worked for the FBI.

Part I

INITIATION

Chapter 1

Born Under a Bad Sign

GEORGE EDWARD DEMMERLE'S HARD luck started before his birth. Conceived within weeks of the stock market crash of 1929, he was born at Greenpoint Hospital in Brooklyn on August 30, 1930, to Louise and Joseph Demmerle and brought home to a small walk-up apartment at 195 Grove Street in Bushwick, where his toddler brother Joe was waiting. Before a third son, Walter, joined them in early 1933, his father Joseph, not much of a breadwinner in the best of circumstances save for an occasional lucky night of cards, deserted the family. The boys' mother, a heavy smoker and drinker, was subsequently declared unfit by the Child Welfare Agency; one of George's younger sisters recalled that they were on welfare and had food in the house only 50 percent of the time. The three boys were packed off to a foster home in Harrison, New York.

Life with the first host family, the Howells, wasn't so bad. They took the brothers to the beach several times and even once to the movies to see *The Wizard of Oz*. "There was an element of gentleness, and kindness, and I had a sense of serenity there," George reflected as a grown man. Mr. Howell would sometimes take the boys up to the attic and play songs for them on a bugle or make toy guns for them out of clothespins and rubber bands.[1] That sense of belonging was shattered when the foster father died of lung cancer in 1936, a victim of mustard gas exposure in World War I.[2]

The three boys were sent next to live with a family in Rye, New York. This stint was far less successful. "It was the beginning of a bad, bad nightmare," George said later. "The foster parents were in it for the money."[3]

In the Gilbert household, there was rarely enough food to go around, at least for the foster children, and spankings were doled out for just about anything, including the failure to have a bowel movement before leaving for school in the morning. His teachers weren't much nicer. George's one memory from attending public school at that time, likely first or second grade, was of being forced to stand at the front of the classroom with his nose bubble-gummed to the blackboard in penance for some petty crime—perhaps being caught smoking a scavenged cigarette butt, a lifelong habit that he picked up at this unthinkably young age of seven. All he could do was hope for something to change.

In 1931, the year after George was born, Edwin Gould, scion of railroad magnate and notorious robber baron Jay Gould, had used his vast fortune to establish the Edwin Gould Foundation for Children on the site of an abandoned Salvation Army orphanage in Spring Valley, New York, thirty miles north of the city. Having lost a son himself, the financier and industrialist built the stately brick residence hall and the adjacent Lakeside Grammar School as more than a vanity project. "He moved furniture, he cleaned up the lawns and pulled the weeds . . . and he did it as if he was having the time of his life," recounted one of the early young boarders. Gould died just two years later, leaving the foundation half of his estate.[4]

By the time eight-year-old George and his two brothers arrived at Gould in 1938, the 150-acre campus housed close to a hundred children from broken homes, many of whom were, according to a foundation publication, "deeply troubled and anxious" and required psychiatric counseling and care. Madeline Sward, who arrived at Gould as a preschooler shortly before World War II, described life at the institution many years later in an essay: "They had their own laundry, their own farm and crops, school up to and through the eighth grade, their own swimming pool and just a self-sufficient small city," she wrote. "I learned how to pick corn, beans, and strawberries. The days were full of routine chores, school, and the 23rd Psalm at bedtime."[5] The young residents worked in the laundry and the cannery, and, according to George, were also "rented out" to neighboring businesses to pick string beans or load gravel into trucks; sometimes they would get paid ten or fifteen cents an hour, sometimes nothing.

The tone for the next few years of George's life was set on his initial journey to the school, when George asked the driver what they'd have for dinner when they arrived. "Toenails," the surly man replied. Young George was initially placed in third grade, but saddled with undiagnosed dyslexia, he was forced to repeat the year. In contrast to his brothers' cheerful

1. George Demmerle (bottom right), 8th grade class photo, 1945. Estate of George Demmerle.

recollections and class photos from the time, in which the students look well-fed and well-dressed (figure 1), George described the school as a place of practically Dickensian misery. Small for his age and separated from his brothers, he was a magnet for bullying by other students.

The faculty dished out its fair share of cruelty as well, at different times locking George in a windowless bathroom in the basement for hours and frequently forcing him to sleep under his bed. One day, when George was ten, he lined up on the stage with his fellow classmates and, with the whole school watching, waited for his turn as the headmaster told each child individually what he or she might grow up to be: *a lawyer, a firefighter, a nurse.* Then came George's turn. "George Demmerle," the headmaster's voice thundered, "will never amount to a damn thing!"[6]

A letter George received from a former classmate in 1999 suggests he wasn't the only one who had a rough time at the home. "I must tell you that I and many others have had similar gut-wrenching and negative feelings about our incarceration at Lakeside," a former classmate wrote three decades later. "Personally, it left me jarred and shattered without the subconscious psychological emotional support system that those people have who come from nurturing parents and families."[7]

George suffered similarly. "My self-esteem was always battered," George recalled. "I have a terrible habit of blocking unpleasantries out of my life. I guess there are maybe too many [that] I would be crushed by it all." One way George dealt with his unhappiness at Gould was to run away, something he tried a dozen times over the seven or so years he lived there. After finishing elementary school at Lakeside and attending three months of ninth grade at the local high school in Spring Valley, George fled for the last time in December 1945. The group home had had enough. "They said, 'You don't like it here? Fine," George said in a 1999 community television interview. "They gave me a dollar and a change of clothes, declared me an emancipated youth, and said, 'You're on your own.'"[8]

Though he'd seen his parents on only a handful of occasions during his time at Gould, George made his way back to Brooklyn, where he stayed off and on at his mother's apartment as odd jobs presented themselves in the city. While working as a messenger boy for Roosevelt Hospital on West Fifty-Ninth Street, George underwent a routine physical that revealed a congenital issue with his lungs that would plague him his entire life, a problem that would not be helped by his addiction to cigarettes. After doctors recommended he spend time in the country, he moved to a convalescent hospital in Connecticut, where he earned his keep working in the garden until, George claimed, the gardener became so frustrated with him that he threatened him with a pitchfork.[9] George also spent several months over the next year and a half in Connecticut, employed first at an old age home in Greenwich and later at a farm in Torrington.

The inability to hold down a job for more than a few weeks would plague him forever. "I was not prepared for the outside world when I left the institution," he said.[10] His time in foster care had not only left him short on life skills but also had a deep psychological impact, one that renewed contact as a teenager with his still down-on-her-luck mother did little to repair. Despite claiming to have achieved a level of congeniality with his mother, George never really felt loved by her, a consistent theme throughout the first decades of his life. He recalled Louise as "a good friend who happened to be my mother."[11] The lack of warmth George felt from his mother makes sense when you consider that one of her grandchildren said he'd never seen her smile and described her as "an authoritarian from way back—Hitler could have taken a few lessons!"[12]

In August 1947, two weeks before his seventeenth birthday, Demmerle signed up to work on the S.S. *Karla Dan*, a Danish tramp ship that was leaving for a series of cargo runs in the Caribbean and Central America. Although he was the youngest crew member and the lowest-ranked man on the staff, for the first time in his life he enjoyed some moments of camaraderie among the other sailors. For example, when fellow deckhands discovered he was a virgin, they persuaded a prostitute in one port of call to give him a freebie; this ruse worked so well that they kept repeating it at each stop, with young George thanking his coconspirators each time by buying them a round of drinks. The fun ended, however, after two months when the boat docked in Panama, and George was put under house arrest for not having a passport.[13]

Not knowing what to do with the underage paperless seaman, authorities in Panama finally put Demmerle on an American ship called the S.S. *John Ireland* that left for Egypt by way of Morocco on October 28, 1947. Upon arrival in Alexandria, where authorities at this time were on high alert for Israeli spies, he was arrested again for improper documentation and held until a U.S. diplomat named Norman Pratt could sort the situation out.[14] Ultimately, George was given a Seaman's Identification Certificate (figure 2) and, as a sort of apology for his detention, was invited to attend a 250-person dinner thrown by King Farouk before he boarded a ship back to the United States in late December.[15]

Upon returning by boat from Egypt to Brownsville, Texas, in the early days of 1948, George made his way back to Brooklyn. In search of work in early March, he literally stumbled into the next phase of his life. "I was walking around on the street in the cold and passed this recruiting station and I ducked in the doorway to get out of the wind and snow," he recalled. "The guy invited me in for a cup of coffee . . . and the next thing I know I was signed up for five years."[16] Despite his painful interactions with institutions and governments to date, young Demmerle clung to an unwavering faith in the United States and the leaders who represented its values and interests. He was a patriot, no questions asked, and, as someone who had never felt much familial embrace, he desperately wanted to belong to something.

George enlisted in the Air Force on March 24, 1948, and was first stationed at Lackland Air Force Base in San Antonio, Texas, before being transferred at the end of June to Keesler Air Force Base in Biloxi, on the Gulf Coast in Mississippi, to train as a radar technician. Hindered by dyslexia, the recruit flunked his communications exam. "I couldn't separate the dots and dashes right," he remembered. "But tests showed that I was quite intelligent so I could learn electronics. I did very well in the shop. I

SEAMAN'S IDENTIFICATION CERTIFICATE.

(To be issued only to seamen claiming American citizenship.)
(See General Instruction No. 474, July 22, 1916.)

Consulate of the United States of America at Alexandria, Egypt
(Name of office.)

I, Norman K. Pratt Vice Consul of the United States of America at Alexandria, Egypt, hereby certify that George Edward [illegible] the seaman to whom this paper is issued has sworn to and signed before me the statement concerning his birthplace, residence (naturalization) and occupation as seaman hereunto annexed, and that his photograph (or thumb print) has been placed hereon in my presence.

The personal description of the holder is as follows:

Age, 17; height, 5 feet 7 inches; color of eyes, hazel; hair, brown; complexion, fair; special characteristics, none

This paper is issued for purposes of temporary identification only, until the holder is able to apply for, and obtain, a regular American passport, upon producing the necessary documentary evidence.

In witness whereof I have hereunto affixed my signature and the seal of this office this 27th day of December, 1947
(Month and year.)

(Signature of officer.)
Norman K. Pratt

2. George Demmerle's Seaman's Identification Certificate, 1947. Estate of George Demmerle.

was near the top of the class."[17] After completing his technical training in Mississippi, George returned to New York on furlough.

The next few months were marked by a swirl of the kind of self-inflicted disasters that seem to have punctuated George's entire life, a chronologically confusing tale of AWOLs and arrests triggered, he claimed, by an initial incident in which his mother's boyfriend stole the money he needed to get back to base in California. He finally ended up at Stewart Air Force Base in Newburgh, New York, in September 1949, where he spent close to three months in the guardhouse before being sent home to Brooklyn on a bad conduct discharge in January 1950.[18] "I don't look for trouble," he said of this period. "It just seems like I don't know how to respond to what happens sometimes."[19]

While George had been at sea and in the service, the anticommunism movement had shifted into high gear at home. In the wake of President Truman's March 1947 signing of Executive Order 9835, which targeted "the presence within the Government service of any disloyal or subversive person [that] constitutes a threat to our democratic processes," Wisconsin Senator Joseph McCarthy and the weaponized House Un-American Activities Committee (HUAC) searched out "subversives" in the federal government and Hollywood before expanding their witch hunt to academia, the military, the Democratic Party, and even the church.

The fight to contain and root out communism, which shattered numerous lives and ruined countless careers, also became the north star of U.S. foreign policy, dragging the nation into its first—but certainly not its most consequential—proxy battle in the Cold War. When the United States stepped in to defend South Korea against a takeover by communist North Korea on June 25, 1950, Truman's rationalization for the invasion foreshadowed Dwight Eisenhower's domino theory: "If we let Korea down, the Soviet[s] will keep right on going and swallow up one [place] after another. If we were to let Asia go, the Near East would collapse and no telling what would happen in Europe."[20] While by no means a big follower of current events at this stage of his life, the Red Scare rhetoric left its mark on the impressionable, directionless young man.

Within a year of being discharged, Demmerle married a family friend from Ridgewood, Queens, Barbara Lynn Conner. Back in Brooklyn, though, he failed to get any professional traction. "I went through a lot of horrible, boring jobs," George recalled. "I'd get bored to death real quick, operating a machine and doing the same thing 8 hours a day, 5 days a week." He worked on a barge and then at a power press making tin can parts for about a year. While employed at the Detecto Scales Company, a maker of industrial scales, he learned some basic welding skills and then cycled through a succession of factory jobs—one making wrought iron furniture, another auto parts—none of which lasted more than a few months. He even worked briefly for an uncle in Brooklyn, welding oil tanks. "He just demanded far too much of me and I'm not perfect, you know," George rationalized after the fact.[21]

As George pursued a civilian life, the hits kept coming. One night after seeing a movie with Barbara, he had parked the car and was on the sidewalk having a smoke when, mistaking his cigarette for a joint, a pair of policemen accosted him and hauled him down to the station. The interrogation turned into a beating, according to George's telling, while he continued to maintain his innocence. As he was collecting his personal belongings in preparation to leave the station, George says he was hit over the back of the head and knocked out. Next thing he remembered, he woke up in an alley several blocks from the precinct, all his money gone.[22] How much truth or exaggeration lay in stories like this is impossible to know.

While George Demmerle may have been broke and directionless, the country around him was booming. The tremendous mobilization in manufacturing during World War II, combined with the pent-up demand from the Great Depression, had primed the U.S. economy for an unprecedented expansion, one that would lift millions of (mostly white) Americans into a new middle-class existence. Taking steps to try to get his life back on track and catch this wave, Demmerle passed his GED in the summer of 1953. That fall, he gave community college a try, attending a few months of classes at the New York City College of Technology in Downtown Brooklyn. School did not stick, however, and his personal life was not going well either. Around this time, George's wife had an affair with a Puerto Rican man and got pregnant.[23] Although she was shunned by her family, she and George remained married and living together at 1066 Myrtle Avenue on the border of Bedford Stuyvesant and Bushwick in Brooklyn while raising her son, whom they called Georgie but who now goes by Jorge.[24] In a 2023 interview, Jorge described his relationship with George as "business-like" and guided by a sense of obligation on one hand but also one of caring in which George imparted a strong moral compass and work ethic in his adopted son. "He instilled in me a drive to do things, a sense of independence and individual power," Jorge said. "I wouldn't have accomplished many of the things I have without that."[25]

In 1954, George began what would end up being a two-year stint—an eternity for him—at the Todd Shipyards, which had operations in both Brooklyn and Hoboken. As was his norm, when this job ended, he bounced to another. Demmerle's inability to fit into traditional organizational structures like school, the military, and the workplace were at odds somewhat with his unshaking deference to the institutions that formed the bedrock of postwar society in America. Attending church, for example, was one of the few constants in the first forty years of his life, but otherwise he seemed to be in a state of perpetual simmer. On the advice of his minister, in 1958 George began two years of therapy at the New York Foundation of Religion and Psychiatry on West Twenty-Ninth Street in Manhattan. Given the stigma attached to undergoing psychiatric treatment at the time, his trust in his minister's advice suggests how lost he must have been feeling in his late twenties. His therapist, who described George as being "sick, frustrated and disillusioned" and noted that he "blamed all his troubles on other people," administered an IQ test on which George received a well above average score of 127.

Regardless of the reasons, as the 1950s drew to a close, George Demmerle was angry and adrift, unsure of what or who to trust. "I started to read," he recalled of this time, "and the more I read, the more dissatisfied with life I became. It became apparent to me that the reality of American history was not consistent with what I was taught in the institution. My belief system was demolished."[26] His loyalty to country remained intact, but he was starting to have a sneaking suspicion that perhaps everything that he'd taken for granted about the country and its leaders was not as black and white as the self-declared patriots claimed.

Chapter 2

Right-Wing Seduction

IN 1964, THE SAME YEAR that Barry Goldwater became the Republican nominee for president, an unknown writer named John Stormer self-published the anticommunist, anti-elitist rant *None Dare Call It Treason*, later described by historian Richard Hofstadter as "a masterful piece of folkish propaganda."[1] Although by now the high-profile histrionics of the McCarthy era were in the rearview mirror, the book (which would end up selling seven million copies) still struck a chord with a certain segment of conservative America, eventually serving as not only a sort of bible but also a recruitment tool for fringe groups such as the John Birch Society.[2]

Named after an American killed by communists in China, the John Birch Society had been founded in 1958 by a wealthy manufacturer of such popular candies as Sugar Daddys and Junior Mints, Robert Welch, to counter what he saw as the encroaching threat of communism, from the Soviet Union in particular. At various points, the group, whose membership allegedly approached 100,000 at its peak in the early 1960s, accused Harry Truman, John F. Kennedy, and Dwight Eisenhower, among many others, of being part of a communist conspiracy and opposed the civil rights movement.

George Demmerle was living with his wife and son in Bushwick when a member of his church gave him a copy of the book.[3] It resonated immediately with his increasingly misguided sense of paranoid patriotism, and he accepted his acquaintance's invitation to sit in on a meeting and then to join. "From what I was reading, it looked like we were about to surrender

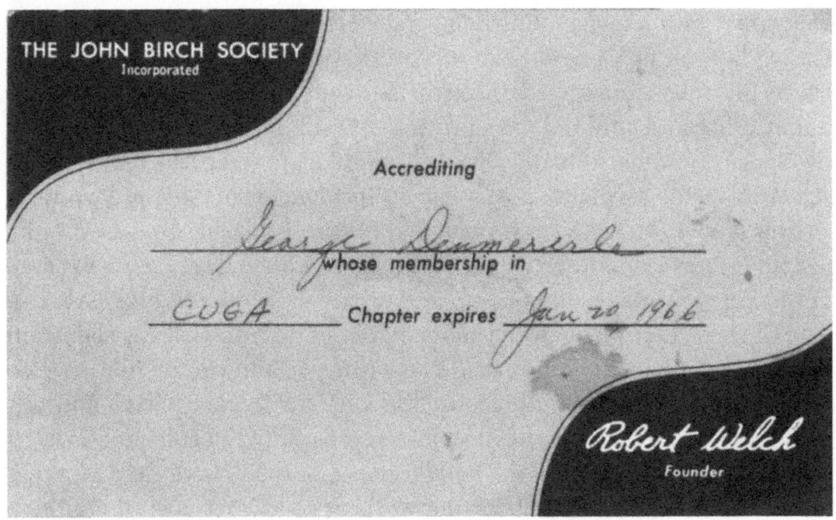

3. George Demmerle's John Birch Society membership card, 1966. Estate of George Demmerle.

to Russia," he said later. "It got me very upset because I started to think that the communists were going to take over the country unless something was done."[4]

Joining the John Birch Society (figure 3) gave George a sense not only of purpose but also of belonging. "[The acquaintance] brought me inside and introduced me to everyone and everybody cheered and applauded. You know, they made you feel welcome," he said. "I was just sucked into it."[5] George was such a true believer that he would bring his son to meetings and make him wear a "Better Dead than Red" button.[6] He might not have known it, but by 1964 the John Birch Society was working in concert with the New York Police Department, which helped keep track of all the communists in the city using a card-file system.[7]

While Demmerle and his fellow right-wing radicals had been preparing themselves for armed confrontation with the forces of communism, the left had been undergoing a transformation that would lay the groundwork for its own violent conflict on American soil. The classical worker-centric Marxist ideology that had formed the philosophical foundation of the Old Left since before World War II had been on the wane since the mid-1950s, and by the beginning of the 1960s a pronounced generational shift was becoming visible. Among those displacing the old guard were contributors to the journal *Studies on the Left* and members of the Ann Arbor–headquartered Students for a Democratic Society (SDS), who were more concerned with reinvigorating democratic ideals, fighting racism, and later ending the war in Vietnam than they were with the plight of the proletariat. As the 1960s progressed, these themes were increasingly placed neatly under a broader umbrella of anti-imperialism, with, as the progressive theologian Rosemary Ruether wrote, a particular "sympathy and sense of solidarity on the revolutionary nationalist movements in the 'third world.'"[8]

This New Left, as the agglomeration of earnestly and often awkwardly named groups came to be called, was centered on college campuses and, in the popular imagination, composed of largely white, middle-class students.[9] "New Left ideology put more emphasis on capitalism as alienation and consumerism than on naked class struggle and production," wrote the historian John Lynn. "It focused less on the working class, and this made the New Left more relevant and approachable to college-educated youths—not the masters of the middle class, but their children."[10] Not that the New Left didn't care about the working class, they just didn't think white workers could free themselves. As historian Richard Ellis pointed out in *Review of Politics*, the New Left, while writing off the "coopted" working class, "still clung tenaciously to the Marxist dream that in the struggle of the downtrodden lay the salvation of all." The main difference, Ellis said, "was that the savior was now the poor rather than the proletariat."[11] So while Marx was still a foundational text for the New Left members, they tended to be attracted to the early "soft" Marx rather than the "hard" Marx of *Das Kapital*.[12]

The closest thing to a New Left manifesto, the Port Huron Statement, written primarily by a young Tom Hayden and presented at the group's conference at an old United Auto Workers union camp in Port Huron, Michigan, in the summer of 1962, called for a "participatory democracy" that emphasized honesty and love and looked to universities at catalysts of social change.[13] "In participatory democracy, the political life would be based in several root principles," Hayden wrote. "That decision making of basic social consequences be carried on by public groups; that politics be seen positively, as the art of collectively creating an acceptable pattern of social relations; that politics has the function of bringing people out of isolation and into community."[14] The document was also noteworthy in calling for a new kind of alliance—between students, Blacks, and existing liberal organizations and publications—to bring about a progressive "realignment" of the Democratic Party.

For the first half of the 1960s the galvanizing political issue for white college students was without a doubt civil rights. They risked arrest and sometimes their lives to test the laws and social mores of the Jim Crow

South, joining sit-ins at lunch counters, going on Freedom Rides across state lines, and showing up for marches and demonstrations. During this period, the Black civil rights movement, through groups like Martin Luther King Jr.'s Southern Christian Leadership Conference (SCLC) and the Student Nonviolent Coordinating Committee (SNCC), welcomed their help.

By 1963, estimates historian David Farber, a million people had taken part in some nine hundred nonviolent campaigns of direct action but not much had changed in practice if you were a Black person, especially in the South. It was not until the SCLC-organized campaign of mass civil disobedience in Birmingham, Alabama, in the spring of 1963 and the shocking film footage of Black children being sprayed with firehoses that the political sands began to shift on a national level. On June 11, 1963, after deflecting entreaties from King and other Black leaders since taking office, President Kennedy announced plans to introduce a civil rights bill that would enforce desegregation in public facilities and schools and make it a crime to interfere with anyone's access to the polls based on race. A few hours later, thirty-seven-year-old Mississippi NAACP head Medgar Evers was shot entering his home in Jackson. Ten weeks after that, buoyed by the support of both King and President Kennedy, more than a quarter of a million people joined the March on Washington for Jobs and Freedom where King delivered his historic "I Have a Dream" speech.[15]

White students continued to work side by side with Black civil rights activists over the next couple of years. In particular, the SDS program known as Economic Research and Action Project (ERAP), which launched in September of 1963 with a pilot program to organize the unemployed in Chicago, became the driving force in students' efforts to find a practical application for their ideals. In its bid to create an "interracial movement of the poor," ERAP represented an evolution in thinking within SDS about civil rights. "We were convinced that the ultimate problems of racism could largely be solved if more money could be put into the hands of the Negroes," wrote Richard Rothstein, one of the SDS members to take part in the inaugural effort in Chicago.[16] While Lyndon Johnson, who had assumed the presidency and control of the Democratic Party after Kennedy was assassinated in late 1963, was working on passing the Civil Rights Act of 1964 in the summer of that year, many SDS members took part in ERAP programs in cities like Baltimore, Boston, Cleveland, Oakland, and, most famously because of Tom Hayden's involvement, Newark.[17]

The attitude toward the role of whites shifted drastically in 1966 as SNCC leadership passed from John Lewis to Stokely Carmichael, the "tall, slender, charming—and razor sharp" recent graduate of Howard

University, who subscribed to Malcolm X's more militant view of the world.[18] Popularizing the phrase "Black Power," Carmichael's ascendence "reflected a transformation in Black consciousness from interracialism and civil rights to a politics based on Black political and economic autonomy," wrote sociologist Becky Thompson.[19] As for whites, Carmichael's message was clear: stick to organizing in your own communities and trying to influence the lawmakers that look like you. "The question is, how are white people, who call themselves activists, ready to start to move into white communities?" Carmichael said in a speech at Berkeley in March 1966. "[By] building new political institutions to destroy the old ones and [by supporting] the concept of white youth refusing to go into the army."[20]

This shift was a bitter pill to swallow for the many whites who had devoted, in some cases, years of their lives to organizing, riding, and sitting in alongside Blacks in the fight for civil rights. "A lot of people's feelings were hurt," said Hayden. One such snubbed SNCC loyalist was Abbie Hoffman, the mile-a-minute Massachusetts native who threw himself into the fight first for civil rights and then against the war—and he wasn't just hurt, he was mad. "It's the kind of anger one might feel in, say, a love relationship, when after entering honestly you find that your loved one's been balling with someone else, and what's worse, enjoying it," he wrote in the *Village Voice* in December 1966. "Trust is a sharing thing and as long as Stokely [Carmichael] says he doesn't trust white people I personally can't trust him."[21]

The jettisoning of class as the left's central issue—a propensity that *Studies on the Left* contributor and motorcycle-riding Columbia professor C. Wright Mills termed, derogatively, the "labor metaphysic"—can be attributed not only to the improving economic status of the working class in the post–World War II boom but also to the working class's embrace of both anticommunism during the McCarthy era and, later, its perceived support for the Vietnam War. "Ultimately, what discredited the Old Left and caused it to lose moral authority in the eyes of a younger generation was the cold war and its anticommunist legacy," wrote John Patrick Diggins in *The Rise and Fall of the American Left*.[22]

Organized labor, foreseeing the inevitable boost in demand for goods and munitions that a war would bring, had been generally supportive of the Vietnam War early on. "Large sections of the labor movement saw the war as a solution to the pressing problems for which the unions had no other remedy," according to historian Philip Foner. "Early in the history of American involvement in Vietnam, guns brought jobs, which brought butter to many hitherto unemployed or underemployed and lulled them into support of, or at least indifference to, a war without which, it appeared they would return to the ranks of the unemployed." This boost in employment was largely limited to white workers, Foner notes; most Blacks, woefully underrepresented in union ranks, failed to see similar gains.[23]

By the middle of the decade, however, it was becoming clear that the rank and file did not share leadership's enthusiasm for the war. The August 1965 issue of the Local 140, Bedding, Curtain and Drapery Workers' Union newsletter noted that, "While registering our satisfaction with the gains we have made, we cannot at the same time forget that our country is at present involved in a war in Viet Nam, which if not stopped soon, might lead to a third world war, an Atomic war." The *Guardian*, a much more widely read left-wing newspaper based on New York's Lower East Side (and not to be confused with the Manchester, England, daily), made a point of highlighting dissension among union members. In a lengthy article in October 1965, the paper pointed to an appeal for peace to U.N. Ambassador Arthur Goldberg signed by members of twenty-two unions and a speech by United Auto Workers secretary Emil Mazey at a three-thousand-person rally in Ann Arbor in which he said, "We were lied to by Ike on the U-2 over the Soviet Union, lied to by the Kennedy administration on the Bay of Pigs, and now LBJ says we are in Vietnam to defend democracy."[24]

Antiwar rhetoric remained mostly absent from labor's highest ranks, though, even as the headlines worsened. AFL-CIO head George Meany pledged labor's support for the war, "no matter what the academic do-gooders may say, no matter what the apostles of appeasement may say."[25] A few factory workers coming out in favor of peace probably would not have mattered much to the most extreme antiwar activists towards the end of the decade anyway. "Even those [working class people] who didn't [support the war] still wanted the USA to come out okay, which in radical eyes made them *good Germans*," said Carola Hoffman, who left her New Jersey suburban home for New York City at age sixteen, becoming involved in numerous protests and antiwar groups in the late 1960s. As far as the members of the New Left were concerned, she said, "[the factory workers] were sitting back, watching TV and drinking beer, while their government perpetrated a holocaust."[26]

Despite having advanced one of the most progressive and pro–civil rights legislative agendas in modern history, President Johnson's decision to send in 3,500 Marines to Vietnam in March 1965 after a year of aggressive bombing by U.S. planes obliterated any remaining support he may have still had with the New Left and set off an era of mass demonstrations against the war. It was quite a reversal in his standing with the young and educated. Before the mobilization of troops, Johnson was a hero to many of the idealists who would later come to revile him. A case in point was leftist radical rabble-rouser Robin Palmer, who three decades later reflected on the president's standing before deciding to send U.S. soldiers to Vietnam. "Johnson seemed to be pulling out all the stops and just doing the right thing. It was even more inspiring that he had come from [a southern racist background] and was now on the vanguard of the civil rights movement."[27]

Just five weeks after the Marines landed at the U.S. airbase in Da Nang in March 1965, upward of twenty thousand people gathered on Easter Sunday at the Washington Monument for an SDS-sponsored rally. Historian Van Gosse argues that this was the moment that put the student group on the map as a national force to be reckoned with. "[The march] made SDS famous," he wrote, "and signaled the end of the control exercised by anticommunist liberals and socialists over the New Left."[28] Paul Potter, president of the student group at the time, put words to how many on the New Left were feeling in his speech that day: "The further we explore the reality of what this country is doing and planning in Vietnam the more we are driven towards the conclusion . . . that the United States may well be the greatest threat to peace in the world today."[29] Addressing the administration's central rationalization for its escalating commitment in Southeast Asia, Potter reluctantly concluded: "I would rather see Vietnam Communist than see it under continuous subjugation or the ruin that American domination has brought."[30] But the rising troop levels were good for one thing—SDS membership. In the three months following the demonstration in Washington, the number of SDS chapters tripled to more than a hundred, and the number of individual members swelled to "several thousand,"[31] while, over the next six months, more than a hundred colleges and universities held teach-ins on the war.[32]

At the annual SDS national convention, held outside the small Michigan town of Kewadin in June 1965, Vietnam may have been front of mind for most attendees, but arguably the most important outcome for the organization's future was a small change to its constitution. With perhaps only a dozen members of the Progressive Labor Party (PL), a Maoist sect that spun out from the Communist Party early in the decade, in attendance, National Secretary Clark Kissinger (no relation to Henry) proposed and was able to pass two amendments that were meant to enlarge the SDS tent but had the practical effect of removing the organization's anticommunist ban. As Todd Gitlin, who was there, wrote, "SDS stripped itself of its strongest line of defense at just the moment PL was moving in."[33] The foxes had been handed keys to the henhouse.

The revulsion and cynicism toward the war machine on the part of not only the middle-class white students but also older longtime antiwar figures like A. J. Muste and Dave Dellinger—who, along with the influential Black activist and Martin Luther King Jr. advisor Bayard Rustin, were founders of the pacificist journal *Liberation*—was well grounded in reality. By the spring of 1965 it was already clear to those in positions of power in the U.S. government and military that Vietnam was a lost cause, even if they would continue for years to sell a different story to the press and the public. In fact, just two days after ground troops arrived, Assistant Secretary of Defense John McNaughton estimated that 70 percent of the reason for staying in the war was to "avoid a humiliating US defeat."[34]

One of the first things that the National Mobilization Committee to End the War in Vietnam (popularly, and hereafter, referred to as "the Mobe") did after forming in August 1965 was to designate October 15–16 as the "International Days of Protest." In addition to antiwar demonstrations at dozens of colleges and cities across the nation and major protests in Tokyo, London, Stockholm, and Mexico City, the umbrella organization (the Mobe counted as members SDS, the May 2nd Movement, and the W. E. B. Du Bois Clubs of America, among many others) had planned a March for Peace on October 16, 1965, in New York City.

The parks commissioner denied organizers a permit of assembly, and so the march began on Fifth Avenue just above the Guggenheim Museum and ended on Sixty-Ninth Street between Park and Lexington Avenues. Speakers included Parade Committee chairman Dellinger and the heads of the SNCC and the Socialist Workers Party; there were also performances from the Rev. Gary Davis and other musicians. Many of the marchers were from left-wing groups like SDS, Progressive Labor (PL), and Youth Against War and Fascism (YAWF), but labor unions were also represented, with a hundred or so rank-and-file members of Local 1199 of the Drug and Hospital Employees Union turning out in their matching white and blue caps.[35] "The demonstrators marched in ranks of eight carrying banners and placards that declared 'Stop the Vietnam War Now,'" reported New York-based socialist newspaper *The Militant*. "Some carried reproductions of Vietnam war photos. One group carried a huge flag with dollar signs and skulls replacing the stars. Banner and placard-decorated floats displayed grim black coffins."[36]

One of the few hundred right-wing hecklers on hand was George Demmerle. The diminutive John Birch Society member, who'd recently moved out of the family apartment following further infidelity by his wife, arrived at the event expecting to find a mass of dirty hippies and goateed Russian intellectuals.[37] Instead he was shocked to see, depending on which report you read, somewhere between ten thousand and thirty thousand "normal looking" people parading past the Metropolitan Museum of Art and the Frick. There were plenty of children and strollers as well. Demmerle's mind was blown at what he saw as evidence of infiltration that went far beyond what he had assumed: "So here they came down Fifth Avenue, men, women, children . . . and I started screaming obscenities at them. I thought, 'What is happening here? There cannot be this many communists here!' I left that parade totally devastated, so scared that the communists were going to really win."[38] These realizations were catching George, who'd recently spent a few weeks in the Creedmoor Psychiatric Center in Queens, at a vulnerable time, and proper perspective was impossible.[39] In reality there were no more than a few thousand Communist Party members in the United States by this point, down from a peak of sixty thousand or so at the end of World War II.[40]

In addition to being subjected to George's epithets, marchers were pelted by reactionaries with eggs, tomatoes, and paint, though no one was injured seriously. Four of the counterdemonstrators, whose ranks included members of the conservative group Young Americans for Freedom and a neo-Nazi group called the National Renaissance Party, were arrested for disorderly conduct. Not all of the prowar activism was confrontational, though: one World War II veteran, decorated with six combat ribbons, marched quietly in circles nearby with a sign that read, "Support our men in Vietnam; Don't stab them in the back."[41]

More confrontation between the antiwar and prowar factions ensued less than a month later at a Veterans Day protest in Union Square organized by YAWF. Having learned their lesson from the run-ins at the Peace Parade in October, the New York Police Department had barricaded the entire north side of the park and brought in some hundred and fifty police officers to manage a crowd composed of roughly five hundred mostly young protesters and seventy-five or so counterdemonstrators. Distrustful that the police would stop the hecklers, who once again included Nazi sympathizers from the National Renaissance Party, from disrupting the antiwar speeches, YAWF also had its own "defense guard" of more than seventy young men on hand. Although there were a "few small scuffles," according to *Newsday*, the counterdemonstrators did not do much more than chant slogans like "Liquidate the Communist Scum" and "Down with Democracy." And since the hecklers were contained across the street, the shouting had little impact on the rally's featured speaker, former World War II paratrooper Fayette O. Richardson. "I think the Vietnam War is a dirty war against people fighting for their independence," Richardson said. "Who the hell are you to tell us to send our sons to fight in a war we never declared, never decided on, never honestly had a chance to discuss."[42]

That same evening, one of the first and certainly boldest voices to express not only antiwar but, in a new twist, pro-Vietnamese sentiment spoke at Columbia University to the Bertrand Russell Humanist Club. "Our job is to give [the Viet Cong] a voice—to present their side—now that they are being bombed and killed by the United States," Walter Dorwin Teague III (figure 4) said that night.[43] Decades later, Teague explained some of the early thinking that guided his antiwar strategy: "What I saw in the peace movement in 1964 and 1965 was that many good people were afraid to be

4. Walter Teague in the offices of the U.S. Committee to Aid the National Liberation Front of South Vietnam, 1966. Walter Teague Collection.

identified with the Vietnamese too much. . . . So I would say, 'In 1776, we fought against the British Empire [and now] the Vietnamese are fighting an American empire.'"[44]

Though descended from a wealthy industrialist and possessing the confident manner of someone to-the-manor-born, Teague had come to his leftist leanings via a hand-to-mouth childhood spent with his mother in Jim Crow–era Virginia. Rejected and largely ignored by his wealthy father and prolific industrial designer grandfather, Teague joined the Air Force in 1957 and spent three years in Okinawa before returning to New York City in 1960 with his first wife and their infant son.[45] A strong speaker with impressive organizing skills, Teague grasped early on the importance of symbolism in a protest movement and seized upon the idea of appropriating the Viet Cong flag in his work with the awkwardly named group he had started at the end of 1964, the U.S. Committee to Aid the National Liberation Front of South Vietnam (USCANLF, also called "the U.S. Committee"). In fact, two weeks after Teague's Columbia speech, he and some of his committee members were down in Washington, DC, selling Viet Cong flags from a pop-up booth they had erected at the Mobe convention that took place over Thanksgiving weekend.[46]

Increasingly desperate about the communist threat in the wake of the Fifth Avenue Peace Parade, George Demmerle soon grew fed up with the bureaucracy and inaction of the John Birch Society. "Meeting after meeting after meeting. They gave you stuff to study and learn. . . . We'd go to rallies and stuff like that, wave the flag, make a lot of noise and then go home. The next day you'd say, "Gee, went there, waved the flag, 'Yah, America!', but what happened? Nothing. Everything just stayed the same. And I started getting vocal. Let's bring about change, educate people." Disillusioned, Demmerle began to look for other outlets. FBI documents mention his association with the conservative-libertarian Young Americans for Freedom around this time but provide no further details about his involvement.[47]

Enter the Minutemen (figure 5). Founded in the early 1960s by a Missouri entrepreneur named Robert DePugh, the organization was composed of right-wing militants in a state of constant preparation for the imminent invasion of the United States by communist forces; when this

5. Minutemen promotional leaflet, mid-1960s. Estate of George Demmerle.

invasion happened, they believed, millions of homegrown sympathizers hiding in their midst would rise to overthrow the U.S. government. In addition to writing and distributing lengthy technical manuals related to waging war and fighting terrorism, the Minutemen held guerilla training camps for its members around the country. "They were armed to the teeth!" said Demmerle.[48] Just about every John Birch chapter had a Minutemen member lurking in it. After a Bircher meeting toward the end of 1965, one such lurker approached George and invited him to sit in on a Minutemen meeting. It was an easy pitch for the restless Demmerle. "I wanted to do something. I wanted to save my country. Protect it from those damn commies and get rid of those traitors in Washington, get us out of the U.N."[49] George was more prepared for action than he might have looked. According to his son, who once watched his father take out three much bigger muggers on their block in Brooklyn, George was quite good at karate at this point and could handle himself in a fight.[50]

Demmerle's involvement with the Minutemen started on an exciting note. "These guys were gung-ho, showing me their weapons, stuff like that," he said. "They were ready to take on the commies." On one occasion, George was among a group of two dozen Minutemen recruited by an army captain to take part in a training exercise at Fort Dix, New Jersey. The goal of the mock mission was to take over a power plant from real Green Berets. While the Minutemen stunned their professional adversaries by completing the mission in a matter of minutes, George was "shot"—by a paint gun—in the process.[51] Despite his stated enthusiasm, one of the early worksheets Demmerle filled out for the Minutemen—which was seized by officers of the New York State Police and the NYPD in a raid of the Minutemen headquarters on October 30, 1966—suggests that he had some reservations about being all-in with the radical right: "I feel that after your training program I would serve our cause better as a trained reserved agent to be activated at the right time with minimum contacts and association with other members."[52] This initial whiff of hesitation toward extremism was echoed by a later FBI report that attributed his departure from the John Birch Society in December 1965 not only to his boredom with the lack of action but also to a genuine concern about the group's radicalization. "He found that the Society . . . was so radical right and he also began to question the motives of the Society's founder, Robert Welch," the report stated.[53]

As 1965 turned into 1966, George continued attending Minutemen meetings and trainings, amassing a copious collection of the group's in-house manuals in the process: *How to Put Together a Rifle*, *How to Wage Guerilla Warfare*, *How to Prepare for Chemical and Biological Warfare*. Meanwhile, in the wake of his eye-opening experience at the Fifth Avenue Peace Parade, he embarked on what would be the first step in his plan to better understand—and defeat—the homegrown communist threat by visiting the independent bookstores and folding tables that dotted Lower Manhattan to collect pamphlets, flyers, and books that might help him know his enemy better. Whether he realized it or not, he was finding his calling.

In the spring of 1966, Demmerle, who had been promoted three times within the Minutemen's hierarchy in less than four months, abruptly left the group after incurring the wrath of his troop commander. The Milkman (the commander's code name as well as his profession) had announced plans to burn down a facility in New Jersey that he claimed was a communist training camp. Having missed the group's nocturnal scouting trip, George attended a daytime event open to the public to try to map out where the propane tanks were, where the electrical lines came in, and the like. In the process he realized that the target was in fact a forestry school; the watchtowers were not for use in military defense but for students to learn how to spot fires. After George reported the mistake to the state coordinator, the furious Milkman accused him of being a communist spy. "He plotted to have me killed because I made a fool of him," Demmerle said. Fearing for his own safety, he quit the group.[54] A few months later, he would also chalk up his departure from the Minutemen to the same feelings he'd developed toward the John Birch Society: both organizations were too radical and they "were not doing any good for the U.S."[55] Nonetheless, he remained as concerned as ever about the spread of communism in the United States and doing his part to prevent it.

In late 1965, in an effort to broaden its reach beyond its strictly pacifist base, the War Resisters League endorsed and gave meeting space to a new group of veterans who were not just for peace but for an unconditional end to the war in Vietnam—Veterans to End the War in Vietnam.[56] At the group's first meeting, a young Mike Spector, who along with his college pal Lew Friedman had signed up with the Army Reserve to avoid getting drafted, asked to be included. "So that was it, they had to change the name because of us," chuckled Friedman more than half a century later.[57] The Veterans and Reservists to End the War in Vietnam ("V&R" or "Veterans & Reservists"), as they called it, was born. An early flyer defined the organization's raison d'être:

> We who served in the armed forces, and reservists who may soon be called to fight in Viet Nam, are joining to protest our government's immoral and illegal actions in that country. We demand an immediate end to the death and destruction in Viet Nam. As a first step toward this goal, we demand the immediate withdrawal of American troops and the end of all U.S. military involvement in Viet Nam.[58]

A detailed meeting agenda from January 30, 1966, suggests that the military background of its members gave V&R a distinct organizational advantage over some of the other groups that would spring up in its wake. On February 5, members traveled to Washington, DC, to "return our discharge papers, medals and campaign ribbons to the President of the United States."[59] About seventy-five veterans showed up in blizzard conditions but found no representative from the White House to hand the items over to.[60]

After their return from Washington, the Veterans & Reservists, which now included Robin Palmer, started holding meetings every Saturday at

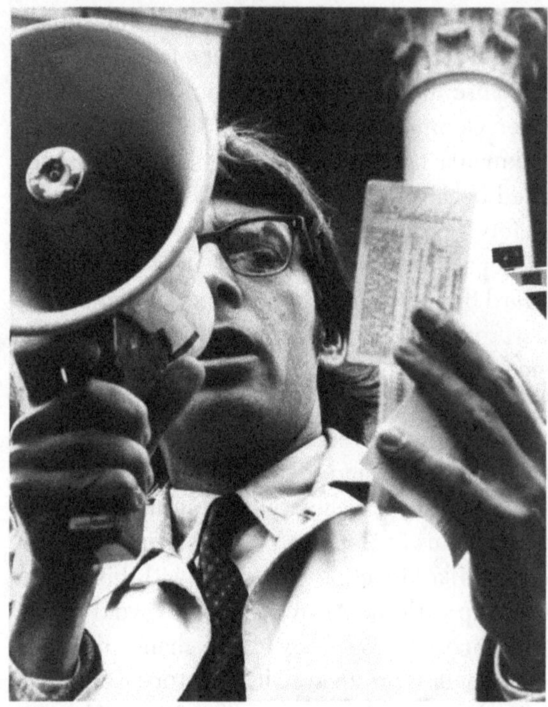

6. Keith Lampe, Foley Square, New York City, 1968. Estate of Louis Salzberg.

1:00 p.m. at 5 Beekman Street, the headquarters of the War Resisters League and several other antiwar groups, followed on an almost weekly basis by some sort of street action. On February 23, for example, they assembled outside the Waldorf Astoria to protest President Johnson being given the Freedom Award; on March 12 they handed out leaflets at Rockefeller Center; and on March 19 they road-tripped back down to Chevy Chase, Maryland, to try to deposit their discharge papers and medals on Vice President Hubert Humphrey's doorstep. Humphrey wasn't home, so for the second time in as many months the protesters returned to New York with their military memorabilia still in hand.

"Twice we have gone to Washington in an effort to return our papers to the White House—and twice we have been ignored," said V&R spokesman Keith Lampe (figure 6) at a press conference later that day to announce the vets' intent to burn their discharge papers on Saturday in Union Square. Lampe, who had served in Korea but never saw combat, was by this time a pacifist, unlike many other members of V&R. Lampe had built up an impressive list of press contacts over the past couple of years, working as a journalist in New York after a stint in press relations for the SNCC in

Atlanta; he would leverage these skills later as a founding member of the Yippies in the run-up to the Democratic National Convention in 1968.[61]

By March 25, 1966, when the veterans group gathered at 5:00 p.m. in Union Square Park, it had fifty active members and a mailing list of about four hundred. They had set up a wooden stage and, after some speechifying by the eighty-one-year-old pacifist preacher A. J. Muste, Mobe leader Dave Dellinger and Afro-Americans Against the War in Vietnam chairman Paul Boutelle, V&R members who had served in either World War II or the Korean War, climbed up to the platform, where they burned their discharge papers in a makeshift stove. One of the antiwar veterans on hand, according to the *New York Times*, was a former freight handler and Bronze Star winner named Frank Kenny; the other veteran name checked by *The Times* was Jack Godoy, who would go on to be very active in a handful of left-wing groups in New York City over the next three years and would ultimately be revealed to be an undercover agent.[62]

If nothing else, the Union Square event was a public relations success, with *ABC News* broadcasting it live.[63] Two weeks later, on Easter Sunday, V&R took part in a march sponsored by the New York Workshop for Nonviolent Action. A dozen or so Veterans & Reservists joined a group of close to 150 marchers, a third of whom had begun their journey five days earlier on foot in Philadelphia. One V&R protester named David Murray was heckled for marching with a reproduction of the Spirit of '76 banner (figure 7)—an American flag with the numerals "76" underneath a crescent of thirteen stars.[64]

While carrying the thirteen-star flag was popular within V&R and elsewhere within the antiwar movement, the persistent efforts of Robin Palmer to fly the Viet Cong flag did little to boost his popularity among the more moderate rank and file. In fact, this obsession of Palmer's led to some

7. Spirit of '76 flag and Viet Cong flag, February 1967, New York City. Walter Teague Collection.

in the group calling him "Flag Head," a nickname he claims was coined by Godoy.[65] Palmer, who would maintain a fairly clean-cut look that belied his radicalism throughout the decade, was fortunate that his boss at International Underwater Contractors, the diving company whose bread and butter was installing cable on the seabed, was a Frenchman named Andre Galerne with a benign view of Robin's radical politics. "Robin," he would say, somewhat mangling George Bernard Shaw's famous quote, "If you're not a Communist at age twenty you have no heart; if you're not a capitalist at age forty you have no brains." Palmer, born in 1930, did not appear to be on track to meet this schedule. Even so, like so many people at this time, Galerne was playing for both teams. While being so easygoing to Robin's face, the diving company boss was providing the FBI with occasional updates about his employee's activities.[66]

Protests in April continued apace: V&R participated in a four-thousand-person demonstration in Times Square organized by the Fifth Avenue Peace Parade on April 16 and a silent vigil at the St. Albans Naval Hospital in Queens on April 23.[67] May's actions included joining the Women's March through midtown, picketing at the Armed Forces Day Parade, and handing out leaflets at both Cooper Union and the Port Authority (figure 8).

8. Paul Krassner, Art Farrier, Myron Shapiro, and Lew Friedman hand out flyers on Sixth Avenue and Eighth Street. Roz Payne Sixties Archive, University of Nebraska-Lincoln, Center for Digital Research in the Humanities, https://rozsixties.unl.edu.

Putting an exclamation point on a busy first six months, twenty or so members of V&R set out on foot on July 3 for Philadelphia from Valley Forge, Pennsylvania, where George Washington and his troops had spent the brutal winter of 1777–78. On July 4, the cohort of antiwar activists—which included Lew Friedman, Jack Godoy, and Robin Palmer—marched to Independence Hall. Upon arrival, they were cheered by seven hundred onlookers before Friedman and Palmer burned their discharge papers. Palmer capped the day off with an "excellent" speech, according to the July 27 V&R newsletter.[68] The definition of patriotism in the United States was expanding.

Chapter 3

Getting Inside

TOWARD THE END of the summer of 1966, worried that his obsession with collecting radical literature might land him in hot water with the FBI at some point, George Demmerle decided it was time to move ahead with the next stage of his plan. On August 9, 1966, just before noon, he dialed the number for the New York office of the FBI and asked to speak to Special Agent Arthur Greene, a name he had been given by a John Birch Society contact. Told that Greene was on vacation, Demmerle was forwarded to Special Agent James F. Reilly and wasted no time in making his pitch. "Demmerle related that he was going to attempt to infiltrate a subversive group and also attempt to raise himself to a policy making position in this group in order to compile subversive information for more than a single purpose," Reilly wrote afterward in an internal memo.[1]

While waiting to hear back from the Feds, Demmerle continued his independent fieldwork. At the end of August, his pursuit of radicals led him to the Free University, a loft at 20 East Fourteenth Street that was becoming one of the central nodes of the Movement, the broad umbrella term for the eclectic mix of civil rights crusaders, antiwar protesters and, later, feminists and gay rights advocates committed to fighting the status quo. Launched in July 1965 by Allen Krebs, a former Adelphi University professor who had been fired for espousing Marxist views and taking an unsanctioned trip to Cuba, and Jim Mellen, who had been let go by Drew University for statements in support of the Viet Cong, the Free University was the nation's first alternative educational institution of the New Left.[2]

As its original course catalog put it, "The Free University of New York has been forged in response to the intellectual bankruptcy and spiritual emptiness of the American educational establishment."[3] In an article about the school's launch, the *New York Times* described the Free University as a "clearing house for the more radical concepts of politics and education."[4]

For $24 a class, anyone could sign up to learn about a wide range of left-leaning topics: "Latin America—the Next Vietnam?" by John Gerassi; "The Ghetto: Law and Social Change" by Freedom Now Party chairman Conrad Lynn; "Marxism and American Decadence," "The Bankrupt Intellectual Establishment," and "Rebellions that Failed," all by Allen Krebs.[5] Other spicier topics included "The Sexual Revolution" and "Hallucinogenic Drugs: Their Uses and Social Implications."[6] The new school attracted interest right off the bat: In its first semester, the school had 30 teachers and 230 registered students.[7] (Popularity did not mean pay, however. Not only were the initial faculty recruits not remunerated for their time, but they were asked to pony up some startup cash as well.)

Edward Grossman, on assignment for *Harper's* in 1966, described a visit:

> It is housed inconspicuously in a loft over a café, and to reach it you must climb two long flights of stairs. "VIETNAM—WE WON'T GO!" declares a homemade poster near the door. "F— COMMUNISM!" urges another. Announcements of antiwar marches, rent strikes, and a breakdown of moneys collected at a beer blast for the Berkeley Free Speech Movement are tacked on the bulletin board. Deft woodcuts from Cuba having anti-Yanqui themes decorate a wall. Cardboard partitions divide the loft in five classrooms, more or less drafty and none too clean.[8]

Shortly after the school's July opening, cofounder Krebs and USCANLF's Walter Teague joined forces to defy House Committee on Un-American Activities (HUAC) efforts to make the two of them, along with nine other antiwar figures, testify. Not only did Teague and Krebs refuse to answer questions at their appointed time but they sued the committee with the help of the American Civil Liberties Union (ACLU) to force them to create a three-judge panel to rule on their contention that HUAC's mandate to investigate un-American "propaganda activities" violated the First Amendment's right of free speech.[9] In the end, the Congressional committee decided not to cite the men for contempt for failing to appear, fearing it might hurt the government's standing in the lawsuit.[10]

9. U.S. Committee to Aid the National Liberation Front of South Vietnam information table, Sixth Avenue and Eighth Street, 1965. Walter Teague Collection.

Speaking truth to power was becoming natural for Teague. "Walter was totally committed to dramatizing the legitimacy and credibility of the Viet Cong," said Palmer, who would often spend his Saturdays with Teague on the corner of Eighth Street and Sixth Avenue selling Viet Cong flags and Vietnamese English-language newspapers (figure 9). "He did every conceivable legal thing that could be done to maintain communications with the Vietnamese, the North Vietnamese and the Viet Cong."[11] Although he bristled at Teague's controlling nature and sometimes know-it-all demeanor, Palmer deeply respected his politics and conviction. Teague's feelings toward Palmer were equally ambivalent: "On the one hand I respected, and was peripherally involved at times with, Robin and his people, but not really because they were not dependable."[12]

Only three months later, in December 1966, the ACLU would again represent Teague (along with his sometime research assistant, the devoted but deluded Charlotte Polin), this time over the confiscation of a shipment of Vietnamese literature addressed to him on the grounds that procuring such literature violated laws designed to stop the flow of currency to enemy nations.[13] Teague and Polin contended that the "burdensome and time-consuming administrative procedures" required by statute and regulations violated the First Amendment.[14] This legal challenge was less successful than the HUAC suit: in August 1967, Judge Harold Tyler Jr. of the U.S. District Court denied Teague and Polin's motion (which the Mobe and the Free School had also joined) with the rationale that the inconvenience the plaintiffs suffered was "outweighed by the national interest in restricting the flow of dollars to North Vietnam and Red China."[15] The loss didn't have a big practical impact though, as the government wasn't able to stop much of the flow of cultural propaganda anyway. "The reason some of our stuff was getting to us was because there were some people in the post office who were sympathetic," Teague later explained. "So instead of giving it into the government box, they were sending it on to us."[16]

The Free University, or the Free School as it was forced to rebrand itself when it failed to meet state-mandated legal and financial standards, stayed open through the summer of 1968, but the seeds of its dissolution were sown a year earlier when Allen Krebs left for London, ostensibly to help launch a similar school there but perhaps also because his marriage to fellow Free School staffer Sharon Krebs had fallen apart. In his absence, Allen had appointed Columbia University dropout Frank Gillette to run the school. All of twenty-four at the time, Gillette had been teaching a class on Marshall McLuhan and, along with Sharon, had recently produced the first issue of the school's magazine *Treason!*[17] (In a sign of the upside-down world of the New Left, Gillette's arrest in April outside General Westmoreland's speech at the Waldorf Astoria if anything *helped* him land the leadership position.[18])

Also on the *Treason!* staff, albeit in a production role, was Robin Palmer who had begun his relationship with Sharon certainly before she was officially divorced and quite likely before she had split with Allen for good. The Free School is also where Palmer first encountered Abbie Hoffman, in a small workshop the future Yippie leader taught to a dozen or so people in preparation for the march on the Pentagon in the fall of 1967. "Yippie wasn't born yet but Abbie was already the high priest of guerrilla theater," recalled Palmer, who himself had already been involved with several demonstrations, both for civil rights and against the war, since taking part in a Congress of Racial Equality (CORE) sit-in at a Howard Johnson's in Greenwich Village in the early 1960s.[19] But Palmer was just getting warmed up.

Hoffman had put himself on the Movement map just a few weeks earlier when he and Jerry Rubin, Jim Fouratt, Stew Albert, Super Joel, and other future Yippies had infiltrated the visitors' balcony at the New York Stock Exchange, not a terribly difficult thing to do at the time with a little creativity, and thrown the epicenter of global capitalism into chaos by flinging a flurry of one-dollar bills down upon the traders, who scurried around like hungry mice after the money. Abbie and Jerry capped the escapade off by burning a $5 bill for the film cameras and making the evening news. (The idea for the whole stunt had come in fact from Fouratt, an antiwar, and later gay rights, activist who had helped organize the Central Park Be-in on Easter of that year.) According to Paul Krassner, publisher of the satirical *Realist* magazine and a Yippies founding member, the press attention in the wake of the August 24 action on Wall Street was an "Aha!" moment for Hoffman and the group that was forming around him: "You don't have to manipulate the media if you can manipulate the events which the media cover," said the curly-haired patron saint of protest.[20]

Located on East Fourteenth Street between Fifth Avenue and University Place, the Free School was on the northern border of a large swath of Downtown Manhattan known then as the Lower East Side. In the early 1960s, the Lower East Side was a true melting pot, a mostly Puerto Rican ghetto dotted with pockets of Jewish and Eastern European immigrants. Abbie Hoffman, who left his wife, children, and job as a pharmaceutical salesman in Worcester, Massachusetts, to move to a shared apartment on Eleventh Street and Avenue C in 1966, described this "cultural fruit salad" in his autobiography.[21] "Ukrainian crones in babushkas waddling out of bakery shops, dashikied blacks with new Afros practicing Islamic chants on stoops spread with pieces of carpet, Puerto Rican kids boogeying to bongo drums, black-clothed Hasidic Jews clutching their breasts and scurrying along the sidewalk, mad artists dangling off fire escapes painting the side of buildings, and vendors dealing grass from hotdog carts," he wrote.[22]

In the mid-1960s a new ingredient was added to this mix. As Osha (née Thomas) Neumann, who dropped out of Yale to become an artist and moved into an East Seventh Street railroad flat in 1965, described in his memoir, "They were mostly white, long-haired, dropouts who . . . set up crash pads in rundown tenements, dragged their mattresses onto the floor, and formed fragile, everchanging communities." Jobless and ambitionless, these kids "spent many hours hanging out on St. Marks Place, panhandling in front of Gem's Spa [*sic*], and getting stoned on the benches of Tompkins Square Park."[23] Their arrival sparked an early version of gentrification-related conflict: "Troubles started when the hippies who came from middle-class backgrounds, subsidized by their parents, were taking some of the living space that the crowded minorities needed," said Captain Joe Fink, who watched the whole dynamic unfold from his perch at the Ninth Precinct on East Fifth Street.[24]

The captain, noted historian Vincent Cannato, was temperamentally well suited to navigate the racial conflict and radical antics that dominated the East Village: "Fink was the type of policeman whom [New York Mayor John] Lindsay had hoped would 'humanize' the department; a Jewish cop who grew up on the Lower East Side and was tolerant of the hippies."[25] Ronald Sukenick, a writer who chronicled the East Village scene at great length in his novels and a memoir, recalled that Fink, who required the cops in his precinct to live in the neighborhood rather than commute in from Long Island or an outer borough, "was generally known as a good guy"—strong praise from the counterculture for a cop.[26] According to Lindsay aide Sid Davidoff, though, Fink's tolerance for the counterculture made him something of an outcast among the NYPD leadership.[27]

Fink had an unconventional but particularly good working relationship with Hoffman, according to Barry Gottehrer, Lindsay's youthful right-hand man, known for forging alliances with a mix of radicals and underworld figures in his effort to keep the city from exploding.[28] "[Hoffman and Fink] had an informal agreement that Abbie could have a good deal of leeway if he didn't put Fink in the position of having to arrest him," Gottehrer told Cannato.[29] "Fink used to call up Anita [Hoffman] to make sure Abbie was okay after his busts," said Susan Carey, a childhood friend of Hoffman's. "He really loved Abbie."[30]

Upon returning from his vacation at the end of the summer of 1966, Special Agent John W. Robinson followed up on the phone call from the Brooklyn machinist with his sights set on becoming an undercover agent. Robinson summarized the September 13 meeting he had with Demmerle at the 200 East Sixty-Ninth Street offices of the FBI in a memo soon after. "Subject advised that he is greatly concerned with the present trend of the US toward Socialism and possibly Communism which is apparent to him because of recent Supreme Court rulings and legislation that is being passed by the US Congress," Robinson wrote. "The subject stated that he is a patriotic American and feels that he cannot sit idly by and let this happen without trying to do something about it."[31]

Clearly aware that this was a job interview of sorts, George did his best to demonstrate that his independent mission already had some legs. In addition to two lectures he had attended at the Free University, George mentioned that he had gone to meetings of the Citizens Committee Against Napalm (CCAN) in Brooklyn. He also claimed to have become acquainted with Walter Teague. "According to the subject, [Teague] has stated to him that he considers himself engaged in guerilla warfare behind the lines by working in the US for the Viet Cong," Robinson recorded in his September 19 report.[32] Decades later, Teague, by then a retired psychotherapist living in the Washington, DC, area, didn't dispute the timeline but bristled at any suggestion that he and Demmerle were close. "From the first time I met Demmerle, I didn't trust him," he said. "His insincerity and working-class crudeness had not been tempered by education." In the beginning at least, Teague didn't feel much more than a bad vibe from George. "Did I know he was an agent? No. Did I suspect it? Yes."[33]

When Demmerle heard from Special Agent Robinson next, the news wasn't great: the Bureau would not work with him in any official capacity at that time. However, George was told, there would be nothing illegal or improper about his submitting tips. In fact, Robinson told him, it could be worth checking out the congressional campaign of a communist candidate in Brooklyn named Hal Levin who, the Feds believed, was being secretly backed by Progressive Labor.

Started in 1962 to reinject revolutionary zeal back into the listless and defanged communist cause in America, the Progressive Labor (PL) movement first gained attention by organizing a student trip to Cuba in 1963. The following year, the group helped stage the first major antiwar march in New York City, an event that spawned a youth-oriented offshoot of PL, as it was commonly referred to in Movement circles, named after the date of the event—the May 2nd Movement (M2M).[34] Members of M2M, according to historian Irwin Unger, "believed in the revolutionary potential of the working class and claimed that capitalist America only held off the day of reckoning by its imperialist exploitation of subject peoples around the world."[35] M2M, which like its parent organization was Maoist in orientation, staged two protests in Times Square later in the summer, both of which turned bloody.

At the beginning the most progressive thing about Progressive Labor was that it moved the communist conversation beyond white members of the working class. "The open, hard militancy of the group, their free acknowledgment that they were communists, their heavy emphasis on organizing 'Afro-American' workers in the ghettos, their bold student trips to Cuba in defiance of the government and their finger-wagging attitude to HUAC upon their return, their imaginative analysis of the war in Vietnam as consistent with an American 'imperialism,'" wrote Kirkpatrick Sale in his definitive book about the student left, *SDS*, "made it noticed, and attractive on the college campuses."[36] Popular in the middle of the decade, that is. Ironically, it would be Progressive Labor's failure to prioritize racism and imperialism over class issues, along with a general culture clash between its clean-cut members and the wilder wing of the student left, that would lead to a fatal schism within SDS at the end of the decade.

Over the fall of 1966 George Demmerle displayed a stamina that would serve him well as he continued his audition for the role of FBI informant—volunteering at the Levin campaign headquarters on Franklin Avenue in Bedford Stuyvesant, attending Marxism study groups organized by Progressive Labor ("I was bored to death," he later said), and watching antiwar films at the Free School, all while continuing to work days as a machinist at the Spartan Dye Company in Brooklyn.[37] On the night of October 27, George confirmed the FBI's suspicions about the link between Hal Levin and Progressive Labor when he went to pick up some campaign literature from the Brooklyn apartment of a Levin worker, "who stated during the course of the conversation that she was a member of the Progressive Labor Party as well as her husband and her father is a member of the Communist Party." The woman also told George that PL had grown disappointed in Levin and was going to stop supporting him.[38]

Soon after, George was invited to attend a meeting at the Progressive Labor Party West Side Club at 225 West 100th Street to help with the campaign of another PL candidate for office named Wendy Nakashima. When he and the other 40 or so volunteers showed up, they were taught how to be poll watchers. "Demmerle stated that he had been advised to make sure that Wendy Nakashima's name was on the machine, make sure that the machine was in working order, and that no irregularities occurred," Robinson's report read.[39] It may not have been the stuff of spy novels, but, from the perspective of the FBI's New York Office, George was showing promise. In a year-end assessment, referring to intelligence obtained about the Levin campaign, his handlers concluded that, "From the above information it can be seen that Demmerle has the initiative and ability to infiltrate a subversive group."[40]

By the fall of 1966 tensions were rising in Morningside Heights, home of Columbia University, around the school's aggressive real estate strategy and tactics. For years the Ivy League institution had been gobbling up buildings and using its lawyers and money to evict long-time, usually low-income and minority, tenants. To neighborhood activists and increasingly to students, this smacked of the same arrogance and imperialism, albeit on a local level, that was on display in many third world countries by the U.S.

government. The scope of Columbia's colonization was quite staggering: Between 1959 and 1968, the school bought more than a hundred buildings and cleared out roughly 60 percent of the 3,700 apartments.[41]

Enter Sam Melville. A few months earlier, unhappily towing the line as a draftsman at the Midtown office of Syska Hennessy—the international engineering firm where he'd worked as a designer since early 1964, after lying about his credentials to get hired—and increasingly alienated from his more traditional wife, Melville had met a twenty-something City College teacher and activist in Riverside Park. Soon after, Sam, who had changed his last name from Grossman in 1964, moved out of his family apartment at 645 West End Avenue and into the woman's West 108th Street apartment. There she proceeded to introduce him to both radical politics and marijuana.[42]

One evening in November 1966, according to *American Time Bomb*, the 2021 book by Sam's son, Joshua Melville, George Demmerle headed up to this very apartment to attend an SDS meeting on the topic of gentrification in the Columbia area. Although the elder Melville was not home from work yet, the apartment was already full of people when, according to Joshua, a thirtysomething man in a grease-stained factory smock appeared and refused to sign the attendance sheet, citing a concern that the meeting might be infiltrated by the Feds. It was George. "His dim, sleepy gaze was the perfect camouflage for the cunning wannabe FBI informant who was hoping to rile the room into subversive acts he could then report," recounted the younger Melville, displaying some of the creative license he employs throughout the book.[43] More than an hour later there was a knock on the door, and in walked a woman in her early thirties and her slightly older mutton-chopped but otherwise clean-cut boyfriend: Sharon Krebs, not yet divorced from Allen Krebs, and her new boyfriend, Robin Palmer.[44]

Richard Robin Palmer was born in New York City on April 7, 1930, less than five months before George Demmerle, in what is now New York Presbyterian Hospital in Washington Heights. The second son of Katherine Van Winkle Palmer and Ephraim Lawrence Palmer, both from families that had been in the United States for several generations, Robin grew up in the middle-class neighborhood of Cayuga Heights, close to the Ithaca campus of Cornell University where his father was a professor of biology. During Robin's childhood, his father's conservative political views dominated the family culture. "He was always bitterly outspoken against President Franklin Roosevelt and blames him for the troubles which beset the world today," Palmer wrote in 1954. While not particularly interested in politics during high school, Robin was aware of the darker side of his father's conservatism, which "extended to an unreasoning and unreasonable prejudice against minority peoples in the United States, especially Jews and Negroes." When Robin was thirteen his older brother died of rheumatic fever, an event that had a profound impact on family dynamics. "[My parents] became so wrapped up in me, so protective of me, and so solicitous of my welfare, that I felt stifled," he wrote. "This over-protective attitude led my father, and my mother to a lesser degree, to exercise a sort of autocratic dominion over my life."[45] Perfect conditions for breeding resentment and rebellion.

Robin was a distracted student at Ithaca High School and did poorly enough that his parents worried that, despite being a "fac brat," he might not be accepted to Cornell. They decided to send him for his senior year to Loomis, a boarding school in Windsor, Connecticut, where, by his own admission, he spent more time playing sports than studying. Still, the plan worked: he was accepted by Cornell and matriculated in the fall of 1949. The Robin Palmer who showed up on the Cornell campus was long on charisma but still unfocused on academics. This began to shift as he took an interest in English literature and, as freshman year progressed, politics. "I found myself reading the newspapers with new interest, and I found myself reading my history books much more avidly," he wrote. "The problem of peace fascinated me, and I toyed with the idea of being a pacifist."[46] He also became a member of the drama club and joined a cooperative living group called Watermargin.

At Watermargin Palmer was surrounded by several politically active students and realized his own lack of knowledge. As he grew more engaged, he "became more acutely aware of civil rights problems," and in 1950 joined the Cornell chapter of the National Association for the Advancement of Colored People (NAACP). His consumption of news sources increased to include not only the *New York Times* but also the *Nation*, the *New Republic*, and the *National Guardian*. The political awakening he was having did little to help his grades though, and early in his second semester, Palmer took a leave of absence through the end of the school year. He found a job working for a local landscaping company, making sure to remain involved with the drama club and Watermargin back on the Cornell campus.[47] Mowing lawns was not long in his future, though. On June 25, 1950, North Korea invaded South Korea and within two weeks, U.S. forces had arrived to support to the badly outmatched South Korean army. Over the next three years, the U.S. Army would draft more than 1.5 million men, on top of the 1.3 million who volunteered.[48] Robin was one of the former.

When Palmer reenrolled at Cornell in the fall of 1950, his schoolwork did not improve much—his grade point average for the first half of the year was just 74 percent. His motivation level could not have been helped by his being called by the army for a preinduction physical in the middle of the semester. According to FBI records, at the December 1 medical screening Robin told the examiner that he would "gladly serve in the medical corps and go anywhere and do anything (other than bear arms) that I am commanded to do by my superiors."[49] Convinced that he would be drafted imminently, Palmer failed most of his classes in the spring and was asked to leave, this time for good. Next stop: Ithaca College, just down the road.

While studying drama at Ithaca and waiting to be called up by the army, Palmer maintained his connection to Watermargin and, through a housemate named Howard Goldfinger, became involved with Students for Peace. In the fall of 1951, Robin also founded the Ithaca College chapter of Crusade for Freedom, an anticommunist organization set up to raise money for Radio Free Europe. He was also associated with the National Student Conference for Academic Freedom, Equality and Peace and the Committee for International Student Cooperation.

Palmer was inducted into the army on September 24, 1952, and ended up doing medical basic training at Camp Pickett in Blackstone, Virginia, followed by airborne training at Fort Benning, Georgia, for almost six months, after which he became a noncommissioned officer. Even in the early weeks of service, Palmer displayed the kind of impish, antiauthoritarian streak that would come to define his later radicalism. While giving the new recruits a lecture on communism and Korea, a sergeant made the outlandish claim that the Communist Chinese would eat the hearts of freshly killed American soldiers. "This statement seemed to me to be somewhat incredible," Palmer recalled, "and so, during the question period, I asked the information and education sergeant, ironically, whether he could tell us what the average number of American hearts consumed by the Chinese during a stated time was." This did not go over well with his superiors.[50]

In 1953 it came to the army's attention that Palmer, while in the service, had been corresponding with a "known Communist"—his friend and fellow student Howard Goldfinger—for at least two years, a discovery that triggered a "subversive type background check" by his superiors. The assessment that followed was not, to say the least, the sort of thing that would earn him a promotion anytime soon. "Palmer has been designated Class B Restrictee on the basis of investigation reflecting report that Palmer expresses himself as a follower of Communist ideologies, is under the influence of two suspected Communists, infers he is a Communist, is on the committee of an organization infiltrated by Communists and associates with a woman he claims is a Communist," wrote the commanding general of Fort McPherson to the Department of the Army in Washington, DC, on May 15, 1954.[51] All of the supposed communist influences cited in the report were acquaintances from college.

Told of the report on July 16, 1954, Palmer had no choice but to take it seriously. In preparation for the Board of Inquiry hearing set for the second week in December on Governor's Island in New York City, he put together a somewhat combative twenty-six-page affidavit in his own defense, which he submitted along with testimonials from family friends, college friends, and fellow soldiers. "I believe that these papers have clearly shown that I am highly individualistic and that I could never bow to the authority of any sort of totalitarian philosophy or totalitarian government," he wrote. "My main concern has been for the rights of individuals and groups of individuals, for their rights to think as they would and to express their opinions as they saw fit."[52] The hearing resulted in a general discharge—not quite as bad as the dishonorable discharge that Demmerle had received a few years earlier but still a stain on his record. Palmer appealed the decision, appearing before the review board on February 10, 1956, and on April 16, after a persistent campaign, was retroactively awarded an honorable discharge.

After his military service Palmer was readmitted to Cornell and finally graduated in the spring of 1958, just weeks after his twenty-eighth birthday, with a BA in English. He stayed in Ithaca for one year of graduate work before bailing on his master's thesis and taking an apartment at 151 West Tenth Street in New York's West Village. Soon after he began a three-year stint as a junior high school English teacher in the city and started dating a jazz singer four years his junior named Arlene Corwin. In 1960 Arlene moved in with him. They were married two years later but divorced within months when Arlene fell in love with another man.[53]

It was in the aftermath of this marriage that Robin picked up a side gig as a porn actor. There is not much concrete information on this career diversion other than a 1968 FBI report noting that he was arrested on January 19, 1965, on charges of "indecent exposure, obscene exhibition and posing for indecent motion pictures."[54] According to his friend and fellow activist Carola Hoffman, Robin's head was so ensconced between the legs of his female costar, who turned out to have been cooperating with the police, that he did not know the cops had raided the set until he got a tap on the shoulder.[55] On April 29, Palmer pleaded guilty to disorderly conduct, resulting in a sixty-day sentence in the workhouse on Hart Island in the Bronx.[56] Palmer's biggest moment as an adult film star came two years later when stills of him in flagrante accompanied an article in the November 1967 issue of *Playboy* about the history of the pornography industry.[57]

Despite his negative experience in the army, the political clashes with his father, and the failure of his marriage, Palmer remained an optimist when it came to the United States of America and its political potential. "In the early 1960s Palmer had been confident, in his words, in the 'perfectibility of man' and in the virtues of the democratic process," wrote New School professor Jeremy Varon, who interviewed Palmer extensively for his 2004 book *Bringing the War Home*.[58] That sense of idealism would not last.

At the SDS meeting on West 108th Street in November 1966, Sharon Krebs had just risen to solicit donations to the Free School when George Demmerle and Robin Palmer launched into a spirited conversation about the group that called itself the Veterans and Reservists to End the War in Vietnam, with George critiquing their stance on the Vietnam War as being "too soft" and Robin responding something to the effect of, "Oh, yeah, man, the V&R is yesterday." The conversation ended with the two of them exchanging phone numbers.[59]

That month, roughly two thousand people took part in the Veterans Day Parade, which commenced on Thirty-Ninth Street and Fifth Avenue and proceeded to Madison Square Park, where Mayor John Lindsay, the patrician liberal Republican elected a year earlier by New Yorkers fed up with the corruption of the union-friendly Wagner administration, took part in a memorial service.[60] In his speech Lindsay tried to balance his own antiwar position with respect for those who had served the country, saying, "Those of us who understand the fight to keep the peace salute these veterans and the memory of their comrades who did not survive."[61]

After the ceremony, members of the Veterans of Foreign Wars marched the six blocks down Park Avenue to Union Square Park to place wreaths at a monument there. Toward evening, V&R held its own ceremony in the park: after a performance by the famed Bread and Puppet Theatre of Greenwich Village, thirteen veterans burned their separation papers in front of a crowd of more than four hundred supporters while a handful of young men from the National Renaissance Party called them "Dirty Commies" and shouted, "Turn around so we can see your yellow streak."[62]

George Demmerle's campaign to root out "Dirty Commies" continued apace as 1966 wound down. He made further inroads with Progressive Labor, which, by this point, had already established a foothold in SDS. In November he was invited to become a member of a front group, soon to be named the Committee for Independent Politics (CIP), that PL planned to use to "destroy the people's faith in private enterprise . . . through the tie-in between the war and high prices."[63] And in the first week of December Demmerle attended a PL meeting at 853 Broadway, which featured a speech on Marxist revisionism by the group's founding chairman, Milton Rosen, in which he argued that people "must learn to hate the ruling class."[64]

The December 13 meeting of CIP, called to elect the new organization's officers, "developed into such a chaotic state that nothing was accomplished," according to George's report to the FBI. This description would become increasingly applicable to Movement meetings in general in the final three years of the decade as the notion of hierarchy fell more and more out of favor. Knowing what we know now about the PL playbook for infiltrating and controlling leftist organizations like CIP, there is a good chance that this incident was orchestrated to create a pretext for a follow-up meeting, this one to be held at a member's residence. "Demmerle stated that this was done in order that the PLP would be able to have officers elected that are either PLP members or sympathetic to the PLP, which would enable them to control the organization."[65]

"Demmerle has made remarkable progress strictly on his own, getting into the PLP which shows that he apparently was very serious in his stated intent," read the memo from the New York office to the FBI director in Washington in December 1966. So serious, the memo went on, that he should be brought onboard in an official capacity, despite the fact that he had been called to testify before a grand jury in the Queens district attorney's case against Minutemen leader Richard Roe, testimony that could publicly reveal his previous relations with the extreme right group.[66] The praise continued: "Demmerle talks very well, appears stable and gives every indication of being determined to infiltrate the PLP and someday 'put them out of business.'" Perhaps anticipating the concerns from the higher ups and reflecting the types of personalities that were drawn to the Movement as it drifted farther and farther left, Special Agent Robinson added, "It is felt that Demmerle's earlier troubles might be beneficial in his being accepted by PLP members, the majority of whom have also shown certain traits of instability themselves."[67]

A January 18, 1967, letter from Washington, however, laid out the director's lingering leeriness: "Before giving any consideration to New York's request, additional investigation should be conducted to resolve the current character, reputation, and stability of Demmerle."[68] Of particular concern were the two years in the late 1950s that he had spent getting treatment at the New York Foundation of Religion and Psychiatry. (Apparently the FBI never learned about Demmerle's more recent stay at the Creedmoor Psychiatric Center in Queens.)[69] Undeterred, the wannabe spy proceeded with his entrepreneurial endeavor. Someone had to bring down the communists and, even if he were still not officially recognized by the FBI, George would stay the course.

Chapter 4

The Revolutionary Contingent

IF MEMBERS OF THE FBI brass in Washington had visited New York City in early 1967, they might have better understood why their Big Apple brethren were beginning to push harder for hiring George Demmerle. Things were starting to get weird. And loud. The weirdest and loudest agitator of them all was Ben Morea (figure 10), an abstract-expressionist painter who dressed only in black and, according to a 2006 *New York Press* article, would "strut around St. Marks Place and Second Avenue, long-haired and bearded like any number of hippies, but instead of adorning himself with flowers and beads, he wore a leather jacket, carried a switch-blade and peddled manifestos full of cryptic poetry and angry agitprop."[1]

Morea grew up in Hell's Kitchen, where he began hanging out with drug dealers, jazz musicians, and street kids as a teenager. Born in 1941 with hepatitis, Morea began using heroin at the age of fourteen and was an addict by seventeen, when he was arrested and sent to jail. "When I was at the prison hospital, I had a therapist that told me that as long as I remained connected to the jazz world, I would remain a heroin addict," Morea said. "So she said, 'Why don't you try painting instead of music?'" After prison, Morea moved to the Lower East Side, where he had a short-lived marriage to an actress who supported them both while Morea pursued his painting.

In 1958, as Robin Palmer was graduating from Cornell, George Demmerle was entering therapy, and Sam Melville was preparing to get married, Ben Morea began hanging around with the avant-garde couple Judith Molina and Julian Beck, founders of the ground- and rule-breaking

10. Ben Morea, January 1968. Estate of Louis Salzberg.

acting troop known as the Living Theatre. "They were staging anti-nuclear protests, saying that the government was conditioning people to the inevitability of war," Morea recalled. "I was very interested and really liked them. They were anarchists, which I was, but without the name. I didn't know the terminology yet."[2]

In 1966 Morea started an art magazine with Ron Hahne and Dan Georgakas called *Black Mask* that very quickly became political. "*Black Mask* attracted a lot of people—like guerilla theater folks, poets, ex-beatniks—who agreed that politics and art were bedfellows," Morea said.[3] The group put out ten issues of the magazine while beginning to experiment with the kind of street theater that the San Francisco–based Diggers were already engaging in and the New York–based Yippies would soon adopt. An early action, for instance, involved shutting down an art lecture in 1966 at NYU's Loeb Center by handing out flyers advertising to the drunks on the Bowery that free food was available there. "We are neither artists nor anti-artists," stated one of the group's manifestos. "We are creative men—revolutionaries. As creative men we are dedicated to building a new society, but we must also destroy the existing travesty. What art will replace the burning bodies and dead minds this society is creating?"[4]

Such language suggests the level of urgency that these Lower East Side artists, like their political counterparts, felt toward the war machine and those running it. Art is rarely more powerful or productive than when made in opposition to something, and this time was no exception. Early 1967 was a fertile period for Morea and his *Black Mask* collaborators. "That first year *Black Mask* seized every possible opportunity of fucking up culture," according to a zine-like pamphlet called *Black Mask & Up Against the Wall Motherfucker: Flower Power Won't Stop Fascist Power*. "They moved in at a moment's notice and improvised as they went along; they heckled, disrupted and generally sabotaged dozens of art congresses, lectures, exhibitions, happenings."[5]

At the end of January, Black Mask collaborated with other artists to organize Angry Arts Week in protest of the Vietnam War; performances and exhibitions culminated in the Collage of Indignation, a giant group mural at NYU's Loeb Center that attracted ten thousand people.[6] "Before that it had been loose, but we really came together as a group around Angry Arts Week," Morea said.[7] On Sunday morning of the same weekend, Morea and twenty others crashed high mass at St. Patrick's Cathedral, marching down the aisle waving posters of mutilated Vietnamese.[8] Moral clarity amid a sea of hypocrisy, as far as the interlopers were concerned.

On February 10, dressed in black robes and head scarves and carrying sticks with large white skulls on their ends, Morea and two dozen others descended upon the financial district handing out a flier that read:

> WALL STREET IS WAR STREET
>
> The traders in stocks and bones shriek for New Frontiers—but the coffins return to the Bronx and Harlem. Bull markets of murder deal in a stock exchange of death. Profits rise to the ticker tape of your dead sons. Poison gas RAINS on Vietnam. You cannot plead "WE DID NOT KNOW." Television brings the flaming villages into the safety of your home. You commit genocide in the name of freedom.
>
> BUT YOU TOO ARE THE VICTIMS!
>
> If unemployment rises, you are given work, murderous work. If education is inferior, you are taught to kill. If the blacks get restless, they are sent to die. This is Wall Street's formula for the great society!

"Nobody was willing to point the finger at Wall Street," Morea explained decades later. "Everybody talked about the war, but nobody talked about the cause of the war, the capitalist foundation of it. So that was my feeling, that we should call out what caused the war, what caused wars in general. We didn't have an animosity towards the Vietnamese, right? I mean, it had to do with control of the world and money and power."[9]

The city was now coming alive with demonstrations. Ten days after Black Mask's occupation of Wall Street, activists used the occasion of Presidents' Day to stage more protests. Veterans and Reservists to End the War in Vietnam put on a particularly colorful "pageant-parade" from Columbus Circle to Herald Square at which three hundred marchers, many of them dressed in Revolutionary War costumes and carrying thirteen-star Spirit of '76 flags, chanted antiwar slogans and held up signs like the one that said "Then and Now: Washington—The President Who Could Not Tell a Lie; Johnson—The President Who Cannot Tell the Truth." That same afternoon, 250 demonstrators took over the upper level of Grand Central Station and chanted "love" for an hour until being dispersed by police.[10]

On the same January 1967 day that he was rejected by the FBI, George Demmerle reported to Special Agent Robinson that he had been appointed to the executive committee of the Committee on Smog and Air Pollution, a subcommittee of the Progressive Labor–backed Committee for Independent Politics, further evidence of the organization's increasing trust in him.[11] The group's main focus was organizing marches in Brooklyn, much like the one in held in Flatbush on January 14, linking the antiwar and environmental causes. A few weeks later, in the wake of George photographing and identifying some thirty protesters at a demonstration against war and pollution outside Macy's on Flatbush Avenue in Brooklyn, the New York office of the FBI made yet another attempt at getting Demmerle approved for the intermediate but still official status of potential security informant (PSI).[12] It was not to be. "In view of the derogatory information developed on Demmerle, it is felt that he presents too great a risk of possible embarrassment to the Bureau," the FBI Director wrote from Washington, DC, on February 23.[13] If George was discouraged, he didn't show it.

The rejection was not for lack of due diligence on the part of the FBI, who had been interviewing many of George's acquaintances. In one case, Jennie and Julius Berkman, his landlords at 1403 Gates Avenue since 1960, described their longtime tenant as "conscientious, hardworking, dependable and devoted to his family."[14] George's boss at the Environmental Equipment Company in the Bushwick neighborhood of Brooklyn denigrated him as a "pseudo-egghead and frustrated artist" but admitted to Feds that he had been a reliable worker who was known for making patriotic statements.[15] Still another interviewee, a longtime neighbor, said she would recommend George and his wife as "persons of good character, reputation and associates," even though George, according to his son, had moved out a few years earlier because his wife's pattern of cheating on him.[16] Still, the FBI overlords were not convinced.[17]

Yet George persevered. When Special Agent Robinson met with him on Tuesday, March 14, 1967, to break the news of his rejection, the aspiring spy promised to stick with his project regardless, declaring that it would be "absolute treason" to quit now. He promised to continue to furnish information to the FBI without recognition or pay and doubled down on his efforts to infiltrate Progressive Labor.[18] Three days later, Demmerle was standing on the corner of Franklin Avenue and Eastern Parkway handing out leaflets for CIP. Saturday he was doing the same thing at an apartment complex on Washington Avenue, and he spent Sunday helping a fellow CIP member create a massive banner for the upcoming National Mobilization Committee to End the War in Vietnam (Mobe) march in Central Park.[19] It was becoming clear that the high school dropout was developing a knack for the spy game, too. His report from a CIP meeting in late March was notable for the number of people he described and the detail with which he described them: height, hair styles, complexions, clothing, weight, teeth, university affiliation, children, choice of automobile. How much longer could his talents go unrecognized?

Born at the Morrisania Hospital in the Bronx on October 14, 1935, to William and Dorothy Grossman, Samuel Joseph Grossman had been living with his two sisters and hard-drinking mother for several years already in a small town outside of Buffalo called Tonawanda when George Demmerle fled the Gould Home for good in December 1945.[20] Like George, Sam's childhood had been marked by divorce, poverty, and neglect. His mother's failure to get him medical care when he got a cinder in his left eye at age six or seven resulted in lifelong discoloration and loss of sight.[21] She also turned to prostitution at times to support Sam and his younger half-sister of unknown patrilineage. Endowed with more charisma and greater physical stature than George, though, Sam possessed a resilience and independence that served him well. In 1951, at age sixteen, he punched one of his mother's boyfriends and then walked out, never to return.[22]

Sam first moved into the YMCA in Buffalo and supported himself by working at the local bowling alley while continuing to go to school. Unbeknownst to Sam, his father, also named Samuel Grossman, had been trying to track him down for a few months when, one day, coming out of a building in downtown Buffalo, Sam saw a man at the bottom of a long flight of stairs. "I don't know how I realized it was him. I'd never seen a picture," he told Jane Alpert soon after meeting her. "But I recognized him as if it was a dream. I think I must have flown to the bottom of those steps."[23]

Sam stayed in Buffalo for his final year of high school—his strengths were math, music, and memorizing poetry—and then, in 1954 at the age of nineteen, moved to the Bronx to live with his father and stepmother. Sam supported himself as a short-order cook while studying guitar and voice at City College.[24] He soon met Ruth Kalmus, a recent graduate of City College and an elementary school teacher. The couple married in 1959, and Sam gave up his dream of being a professional musician to take a more sensible job as a draftsman in an engineering firm, lying about having a college degree to get hired. Never interested in status or material acquisition to begin with, Sam was at odds with his more aspirational wife almost from the start. "I never wanted to have a lot of money and live in a stuffy duplex on Park Avenue," he said." I couldn't believe that anyone else did either." Within a couple of years, while Ruth was pregnant, they split up, reuniting only briefly after the birth of their first and only child, Joshua, in 1962.[25]

As the 1960s wore on, Sam's increasing skepticism of the capitalist society in which he found himself manifested in a developing political conscience. On a cold day in March 1967, wearing only overalls and a T-shirt and now calling himself Sam Melville after his favorite author, he cut across the snowy Columbia campus toward the Mathematics Building, where he had recently begun directing a student singing group. There would be no practice this day, however. Upon arrival, Sam discovered that the rehearsal room had been commandeered by Tom Hayden, now twenty-seven and in his third year of running an economic development program in Newark, for an urgent SDS meeting about a recently unearthed memo authorizing the CIA to recruit on campus that spring. Sam spotted his roommate, the City College professor who had hosted the SDS meeting where Robin and George met, in the audience and sat down with her. When Hayden finished, Mark Rudd, the increasingly militant leader of the Columbia chapter of SDS, stood up to urge everyone to show up at a protest the next day.

As the meeting was breaking up, Sam's roommate spotted Robin Palmer and Sharon Krebs and introduced them to him. The four of them adjourned to a nearby hamburger joint where they discussed the next day's protest. When Sharon warned everyone to be ready to get arrested, Sam bragged that he had been charged by police a few years earlier for refusing to cooperate with an air raid drill at City Hall Park.[26] According to an FBI report, the arrest had happened in 1961 and resulted in a misdemeanor conviction and a $50 fine.[27] Palmer grinned. "Shit, man, tomorrow will make my fifth arrest this year."[28]

"Support the Vietnamese Revolution," read the flyer put out by a group called the Revolutionary Contingent in advance of what was shaping up to be the biggest antiwar demonstration yet: the Spring Mobilization to End the War in Vietnam in Central Park on April 15, 1967. The Revolutionary Contingent was one of several umbrella groups that sprang up in the late 1960s to help pool the efforts of multiple organizations and, sometimes, provide political cover for groups whose existing reputation might hinder their ability to get approval for demonstrations. Made up of members of the most far-left groups in New York—the U.S. Committee to Aid the National Liberation Front of South Vietnam (USCANLF), Veterans and Reservists Against the War in Vietnam (V&R) and Youth Against War and Fascism (YAWF), among others—the participation of the Revolutionary Contingent was a source of worry not only for the police but also for the more moderate leaders of the Mobe. An NYPD report written eight days before the event detailed how the Mobe planned to assemble and organize the various factions of marchers, whose numbers the police expected, quite correctly, to total more than 100,000.

> The committee was particularly concerned about a group of "revolutionary extremists" . . . which in the past has sought to cause incidents by displaying a flag, alleged to be that of the National Liberation Front of Vietnam. Such flags have been banned by the organizing committee, but from all indications, this group plans to display both these flags, and others. . . . Because of their possible danger to the orderly progress of the parade, the committee has designated a separate division for this group and their sympathizers.[29]

With a week to go before the Mobe march, one of the "revolutionary extremists" organizers were worried about—Walter Teague—was drumming up publicity for the event at his regular perch on Sixth Avenue between Waverly and Eighth Streets. With its high foot traffic, this stretch of the Village was a popular place for proselytizers of all stripes to set up tables with literature to engage pedestrians in earnest discussion. And Teague was pretty good at it. "Very charismatic, articulate as hell," is how Brent Sharman, who worked side by side with Teague in the early 1970s, when they were both based out of the offices of the Washington Square Methodist Church, described him. "He was a strong man, a hard worker and exuded energy and discipline." Teague wasn't good at *everything*, though. "Walter couldn't dance for shit," Sharman recalled. When someone pointed that out to him, Teague responded, "Well, I'm not going to dance until the war is over."[30] This evening in particular, Teague was doing more than standing on a soapbox: "Using a portable generator in the trunk of a Ford Convertible for electricity and 3′ by 3′ screen on top of the roof of a gray Saab, Walter Teague showed, spoke about, and narrated 6 reels of [Vietnamese] film, each of which ran about 20 minutes," according to a NYPD surveillance report. "Between films Walter Teague would speak to the passersby denouncing US involvement in Vietnam."[31]

April 15 started gray and drizzly. George Demmerle met up with the mostly Maoist members of the Committee for Independent Politics (CIP) underneath the clocktower at 1 Hanson Place in Downtown Brooklyn around 10:00 a.m. and then boarded an uptown train. Coming up the subway steps half an hour later carrying an eighteen-foot banner he had helped make that read, "U.S. Get Out of Vietnam Now," he was swept along in a sea of people. While majority young and white, the crowd was surprisingly diverse: African Americans; Native Americans toting placards saying "Americans—Do Not Do to the Vietnamese What You Did to Us"; straight-looking older people, some of them wearing clothing and hats identifying them as union members and World War II veterans; Vietnam vets; even priests, nuns, teachers, and doctors.[32]

"Suddenly, hundreds of black people came tearing through the grumbling, chilly marchers [and] the crowds parted like the Red Sea divided for the children of Israel," wrote the well-known lawyer and Black peace and civil rights activist Flo Kennedy in the San Francisco alternative monthly paper *Movement*. "Some of the blacks were singing, not the usual freedom songs, but different chants. 'Hell, no, we won't go,' and 'Down with LBJ' reverberated through Central Park."[33] The group of approximately three thousand Black men, women, and children, organized in large part by the Black United Action Front, had begun its feeder march at 135th Street and Lenox Avenue earlier that morning, according to a NYPD report.[34] As the newsletter of the Harlem-based Coordinating Committee of Black Organizations Against the Draft described it, the protesters of color were expressing their "deep disgust at racist U.S. imperialism's aggression against the heroic people of Vietnam who are in a great armed struggle for their political independence. Their struggle is inseparable from our struggle for Black liberation."[35]

Nearby, a physical monument, albeit not a particularly sturdy one, to the cause of Vietnamese freedom towered over the crowd: Robin Palmer, Walter Teague, and other USCANLF members had constructed a forty-foot-high structure out of cardboard tubes and decorated it with distinctive blue, red, and gold Viet Cong flags (figure 11). Not far away, the thirteen-starred Spirit of '76 flag indicated where the V&R contingent should gather before they and other veterans groups led the entire parade out of the park.[36] As the crowd chanted "Resist! Resist!" the military men—two hundred of them, according to the *New York Times*, though it was tough to keep count—passed around a flaming coffee can that they dropped their draft cards into. At around 2:00 p.m., while protesters were only just beginning to gather in San Francisco's Kezar Stadium, the crowd in the Sheep Meadow, now up to the awesome size of 400,000, began to disperse, with many of them marching to the United Nations, where Martin Luther King Jr. and the Student Nonviolent Coordinating Committee's Stokely Carmichael were scheduled to speak.

Organizers had obtained a permit for a very specific route—down the west side of the park loop, out at Avenue of the Americas, east on Fifty-Ninth Street and down Madison Avenue to Forty-Seventh Street, and then east on Forty-Seventh to the United Nations. The tens of thousands of marchers who stuck to the planned path were greeted by violent overtures from pockets of conservative counterdemonstrators. One group of young right-wingers, which included members of the Nazi-friendly National Renaissance Party, was stationed at Fifty-Ninth Street and Sixth Avenue and met marchers with heckling and their own signs saying things like, "Bomb Hanoi!" and "Dr. Spock Smokes Bananas."[37] On a stretch of Lexington Avenue, right-wingers threw eggs out windows at the lefties below. And when the sea of people reached UN Plaza, they were greeted by more hecklers, some of them from the Peter Fechter Brigade, a right-wing group named after an East German man shot trying to make it over the Berlin Wall,

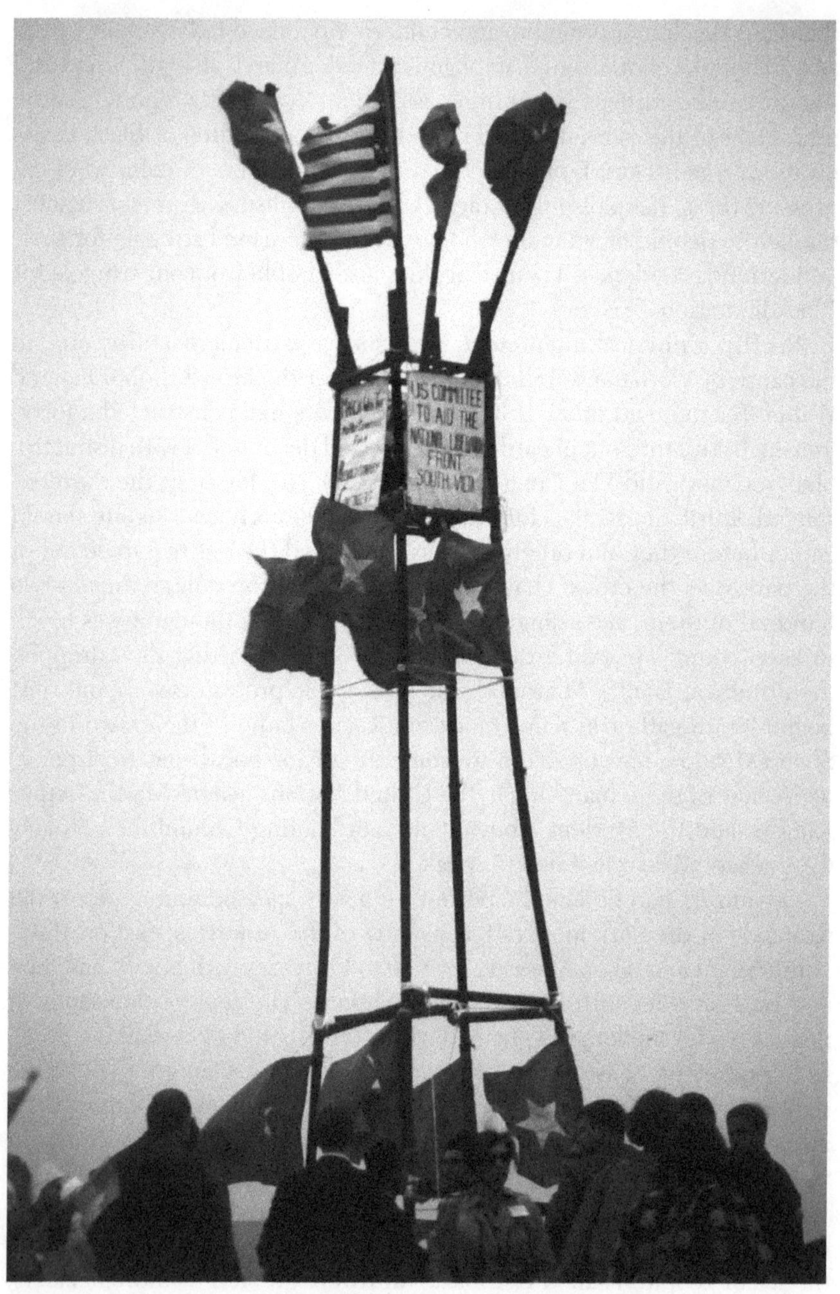

11. Teague's Tower: the Revolutionary Contingent's cardboard tower with Viet Cong flags in Central Park, April 15, 1967. Photograph by Richard Levine, Alamy Stock Photo.

which had received a permit for the "sitting park" at Forty-Second Street and First Avenue. A force of two thousand police officers also awaited.[38] Dag Hammarskjold Plaza was a tinderbox.

Not all the antiwar demonstrators stuck to the prescribed parade path though. According to a postmortem report on the march by the House Committee on Un-American Activities, the recently cobbled together Revolutionary Contingent joined up with the "militant contingent from Harlem" (presumably a subset of the Black United Action Front feeder march) and veered off the approved route.[39] The rebel factions swarmed west to Times Square, where they overturned U.S. Army recruiting signs and tried to break into the recruiting booth; heading east on Forty-Second Street, they clashed with "counter-demonstration fascists" on their way to the United Nations, where they joined the crowd to listen to Martin Luther King Jr. speak.[40]

As Jonathan Eig points out in his 2023 biography, King and his advisors had been wrestling with whether to risk diluting his civil rights message—and angering President Johnson—by speaking out against the war. After seeing a series of graphic photographs in *Ramparts* magazine in January, however, the Nobel Peace Prize–winning preacher decided he could avoid the topic no longer. He made his first public comments at a conference in Los Angeles on February 23 and in March led an antiwar march in Chicago with Dr. Benjamin Spock. He had been planning to make his first major speech on the war at the Mobe march on April 15, but his advisors convinced him instead to do it eleven days earlier at Riverside Church in Morningside Heights because, they argued, it would be an easier environment in which to control his message. In front of three thousand people in the jam-packed church, King condemned the war not only from a racial angle—twice as many Black men as white men were in combat, proportionally—but also from a Christian perspective, emphasizing the shared humanity of Vietnamese villagers.[41]

In the days leading up to the Mobe march, King was pilloried in the mainstream press and even by some leaders in the Black community. Perhaps most important, he had infuriated and permanently alienated President Johnson. But on April 15, King stayed the course, leading tens of thousands of Mobe marchers with Stokely Carmichael, Harry Belafonte, and others from Central Park to the UN before taking the microphone. "I join you in this mobilization because I cannot be a silent onlooker while evil rages," the civil rights giant bellowed. "I am here because I agree with Dante that, 'the hottest places in hell are reserved for those who, in a period of moral crisis, maintain their neutrality.'"[42] This theme would be echoed by the radical left in the coming years as they chased and chastised liberals, even those who had come out against the war and racism, for not taking a strong and unambiguous enough position on either count.

The coming together of Revolutionary Contingent (also "the Contingent") member groups—in response to what founding member Frank Gillette called the Left's "verbal diarrhea and accompanying passivity"—marked an escalation in rhetoric and philosophy that caught the FBI by surprise.[43] Despite its open-door policy toward communists, the coalition was "completely alienated from the 'ceremonial left,'" Gillette told the *National Guardian*, referring to the "holy trinity" of the Communist Party, the Socialist Workers Party, and the Progressive Labor Party.[44]

In addition to "dramatic, radical, peace demonstrations" at home, the Contingent also called upon Americans to join communist guerrillas around the world. "We can no longer talk—we must fight!" Gillette exhorted in the summer 1967 issue of the Free School magazine *Treason!*[45] However, the group rejected the notion that there was any glory or romance in getting arrested. As one of its *Bulletin* publications said that spring, "The organization which carries out the action must take credit in some way, especially after the fact, if it has succeeded, but the participants need not—must not!—be apprehended. Only then will it become a force to be reckoned with."[46]

At the same time, the comparatively cerebral and line-toeing SDS was beginning to arc in a similarly radical direction. "At its sixth annual convention here June 25–30, the nation's largest radical student organization embarked on a collision course with the United States government," wrote Jack A. Smith in the *National Guardian* in July 1967. "The pattern: Left-liberal politics is out, resistance is in."[47] Even Tom Hayden, drafter of SDS's Port Huron Statement five years earlier and still the spiritual figurehead of the group in mid-1967, was coming around to the idea of tearing down the system rather than changing it from within, telling the *National Guardian* three months later, "Urban guerillas are the only realistic alternative at this time to electoral politics or mass armed resistance."[48] For the increasing number of activists on the left who saw themselves involved in a fight for the soul of a corrupt nation, compromise was no longer an option, and there was no turning back.

George Demmerle's entrée to the Revolutionary Contingent would come the night of the Spring Mobe. After the rally concluded at the UN he headed straight uptown to 320 West Eighty-Fifth Street, where the group was holding its first open event, a fundraiser to finance placement of an advertisement in the *National Guardian*. According to journalist Lee Merrick, this was the first time anyone remembers Demmerle appearing at a New Left event, an assertion contradicted by Joshua Melville's account of the SDS meeting in Morningside Heights the previous November. The Movement's lack of organization certainly benefited Demmerle as he popped up in more and more places until it just seemed like he belonged. "Since [the Revolutionary Contingent] was an amalgam of Vets, May Second refugees and various political groups around the Free School of New York, no one knew which of the groups he had come from," Merrick wrote. "Everyone assumed he was from some other group than their own."[49]

On April 25, three days after the Revolutionary Contingent met at the Free School and decided to continue together on a permanent basis and just one day after Frank Gillette was arrested for burning General Westmoreland in effigy on Park Avenue outside the Waldorf Astoria, the New York office of the FBI sought approval for George to travel to Montreal with the radicals for a sit-in at the World's Fair.[50] The response from Washington came the next day: "Authority is denied to send George Demmerle to Canada. . . . While we do accept information he volunteers, it is not felt that we should operate him."[51]

Demmerle did his best to provide the FBI with information on the Revolutionary Contingent in the subsequent weeks—he managed to get his hands on a copy of the first issue of the "The Bulletin of the Revolutionary Contingent" on May 17 in which the group described itself as "taking on the responsibility of arranging for the first step in the process of providing liberation movements in Latin America, Africa and possibly Asia with American volunteers" and warned that "applicants should understand that in addition to the use of their specialized skills, they will also be engaged in combat"—but was limited in his access at first.[52] "Demmerle advised that he has not been able to penetrate the inner circle of the Revolutionary Contingent due to limited Marxist training, which the others are aware of, and he is only trusted up to a point by the inner circle at this time," according to Special Agent Robinson's May 25, 1967, report.[53]

On June 1, six veterans of the Vietnam War, led by a twenty-four-year-old West Point dropout named Jan Barry, launched a new organization called Vietnam Veterans Against the War (VVAW). Having marched a few paces ahead of the existing group Veterans for Peace, which included mostly survivors of World War II and Korea, at the Mobe event, Barry and the half dozen others he met that day felt the need for their own group, despite the Veterans for Peace efforts to keep them under their umbrella. "I felt that we would be losing that direct ability for us to say, 'We've been there—this is the experience," Barry explained two decades later. "I [also] didn't think we'd get very many Vietnam veterans to join something just called 'Veterans for Peace.'"[54] The group grew steadily into a national organization, launching its own newspaper called *1st Casualty* in 1971.[55] That same year the group's membership reached 8,500.[56] Interestingly, the V&R group, whose members included Robin Palmer and Lew Friedman, never had much overlap with VVAW, save for attending a few of the same marches. "We had a broader range in terms of our membership and more of a sense of humor," remembers V&R regular Michael Spector.[57] "We were more radical," said Friedman. "We were more of an activist organization and were not members of the Communist Party."[58]

In May 1967, the same month that two dozen armed Black Panthers from Oakland showed up on the steps of the state capitol in Sacramento to protest a piece of legislation aimed at putting a stop to the Panthers' "police patrols," Stokely Carmichael was replaced as head of the Student Nonviolent Coordinating Committee (SNCC) by twenty-three-year-old H. Rap Brown, former head of the Washington, DC–based Nonviolent Action Group. Despite hope among SNCC's leadership that Brown would dial down the combativeness that had characterized the latter months of Carmichael's chairmanship, Brown, if anything, raised the temperature of the rhetoric. On July 24, 1967, he famously delivered a fiery speech from atop a car in the small town of Cambridge, Maryland, that helped spark a riot. "You'd better get you some guns," he shouted. "The man is moving to kill you and the only thing the honkie respects is force."[59] Brown spent much of his year as head of the organization calling the shots from jail, where he landed several times on charges of everything from inciting to riot to interstate transport of firearms. He went underground in March 1970, where he remained until being captured and sent to the Attica Correctional Facility in upstate New York in October 1971.

The summer of 1967 might have been the Summer of Love in San Francisco, but it certainly did not feel like it elsewhere, especially in urban centers with high concentrations of long disenfranchised Black people. The uprising in Maryland was only one of several race riots that took place in U.S. cities that summer. The worst of these was the Twelfth Street Riot in Detroit, which began shortly after 3:00 a.m. on July 23 following a police raid of an after-hours bar on the city's west side. Arson, looting, and civilian sniping brought thousands of National Guardsmen into the city, resulting in forty-three deaths and more than seven thousand arrests over five days.[60] Coming just two weeks after a multiday conflagration in Newark that resulted in twenty-six deaths and more than seven hundred injuries, the explosion of anger in Detroit was really about years of discrimination and segregation, most specifically in the areas of housing and schools, as well as a declining local economy that had hit the city's minority population disproportionately.[61]

After focusing his civil rights efforts in the South earlier in the decade, Martin Luther King Jr. had helped shine a light on the hypocrisy of race dynamics in the North starting with an essay he wrote for the *Saturday Review* in November 1965 in which he said that the "blindness, obtuseness, and rigidity" of whites in the North "would only be altered by a dynamic movement."[62] His pacifist proscriptions however were now being questioned by more established Black leaders like Brown and Malcolm X as well as by up-and-comers like Huey Newton and Bobby Seale, founders of the nascent Oakland-based Black Panthers. These more militant men saw little choice but to fight an oppressive system with force.

In addition to the headline-grabbing events in Detroit and Newark that summer, 1967 saw race rebellions and riots occur in more than 150 cities, including major centers like Atlanta, Boston, and Chicago. The Kerner Commission, appointed by President Johnson, produced a report about the period of mass unrest: "Virtually every major episode of urban violence in the summer of 1967 was foreshadowed by an accumulation of unresolved grievances by ghetto residents against local authorities (often, but not always, the police). So high was the resultant underlying tension that routine and random events, tolerated or ignored under most circumstances . . . became the triggers of sudden violence."[63] The armed conflict seemed unlikely to end when, in early August 1967, Stokely Carmichael attended the Organization of Latin Solidarity conference in Havana, Cuba, where a resolution was passed calling on "the Negro people of the U.S. to answer the racist violence of the U.S. imperialist government by increasing direct revolutionary action."[64]

New York's Lower East Side was experiencing its own conflagrations and fractures. "The Hippies irritated the ethnic groups in the neighborhood and added to its long-standing heroin problem with major trade in speed and acid," wrote Ronald Sukenick in his book *Down and In: Life in the Underground*. "Racial tensions were escalating, not only between the Hippies and the ethnics, but also the Puerto Ricans and Blacks were getting into turf fights, and the drug scene increased the tempo of muggings and burglaries." Violence was not limited to petty crime either. "The murder ratio went up really bad on Avenue A," recalled Sukenick. "We saw a woman chopped up and died right in front of us. And then the guy across the street who had a sewing machine store, I mean a kid just walks in and hove in his head with a brick."[65] Abbie Hoffman concurred. "It was not all flowers and smiles in the slum," he wrote in his autobiography. "We had our Mansonesque moments: Murders, rapes and sadistic beatings and the papers magnified them as much as possible."[66] Tragically, the victims were often the teenage runaways who, as Sukenick put it, "however street smart, were fundamentally defenseless, and . . . were followed by predators of various kinds just as surely as the wildebeests on the veld are followed by the lions, the jackals and the vultures."[67]

These problems—drugs, violence, predatory older men—were not limited to Alphabet City or the East Village. "Dope addicts freely wandered through the streets, the Bowery bum population had moved [west] over to our section of the Village, and on weekends young mobs shouted and screamed throughout the nights, set off firecrackers, revved up their motorcycles and even attacked and robbed several local residents," said Woody Klein, Mayor Lindsay's press secretary at the time.[68]

In a sign that law enforcement was getting increasingly concerned about the potential for violence on the streets, Demmerle was visited by two U.S. Treasury agents on June 20, according to an FBI memo, based on an anonymous tip that he was in possession of a machine gun. The most likely explanation was that George had been doing some baseless bragging in hopes of beefing up his street cred. Regardless, the agents found nothing and that was the end of the matter.[69]

The spikes in drug use and crime in downtown Manhattan were by no means the only kinds of trouble in the city that summer. Racial tensions roiled other neighborhoods, from East Harlem, where looting and riots followed the police killing of a knife-wielding Puerto Rican assailant in late July, to Bedford Stuyvesant, where, just a few days later, a fiery anti-white speech by a local leader of the Congress for Racial Equality (CORE) resulted in a similar conflagration. A rash of false fire alarms followed by attacks on the firemen who answered the calls also took place across the city that summer.[70] The boiling point had been reached.

Since late 1966 George had been cultivating a nonromantic relationship with a young woman he had met at a Marxism class, an impassioned but unstable supporter of the Vietnamese cause named Charlotte Polin (née Charlotte Saxe). His first real interaction with her had come when she had dashed out of a meeting in tears after being shouted down and mocked for her sincerity and emotionality. According to a 1995 interview in the *Dallas Observer*, Demmerle followed Polin out to make sure she was okay and stunned her by not only giving her money for food and a hotel room but not demanding any sexual favors in return, "like so many other men in the movement who preyed on her vulnerability."[71]

Despite being emotionally and psychologically unstable ("Demmerle advised that [Polin] is psychotic," read a June 1967 FBI report[72]), Polin was better steeped in the culture, history, and politics of Vietnam than almost anyone in the Movement except perhaps Walter Teague, for whom she worked as a researcher for a time. (In April 1967 she had explained to Demmerle that she was the one who received the regular mailings of contraband films and literature from overseas for Teague.[73]) While writing a six-hundred-page tome about Vietnam and teaching a class on Vietnamese culture at the Free School, Polin had established a pen-pal relationship with the president of North Vietnam, Ho Chi Minh.[74] "I highly appreciate these efforts of yours and of the American youth, students and other friends who are valiantly fighting for freedom, justice and for friendship between our two people," he had written her in November 1965. "The U.S. imperialist aggressors will certainly be defeated [and] the Vietnamese people will be victorious. I wish you good health and good success. With affectionate greetings. Uncle Ho."[75]

In the summer of 1967 Polin had an opportunity to repay George for his kindness. It would be hard to imagine a more valuable gift for someone trying to infiltrate the radical left than a personal reference from Ho Chi Minh himself, and that's just what Polin sought to provide. In early June she sent a seven-page letter to the North Vietnamese leadership vouching for Demmerle's commitment to the cause. This letter, which spins George's devotion to the Vietnamese as a dramatic reversal, shows that he had not hidden his conservative roots from Charlotte, an interesting dramatic touch by the high school dropout. "Having been mindlessly pro-American most of his 36 years, it has only been in recent years that George Demmerle discovered the meaning and promise of Socialism and of anti-imperialist struggle," she wrote. "To George, revolution is life, there is nothing more sacred in life, and he is prepared to sacrifice his life in the revolutionary cause to spare future generations from the suffering that the present generation of Vietnamese is undergoing. His every word, every deed, is geared to this goal." In the same letter Charlotte also alluded to the culture of suspicion that existed in the radical scene. "In the Revolutionary Contingent, as in all leftist groups in the United States today, the members do not trust each other," she said. "Paranoia dominates their behavior, and they spend much of their time trying to figure out who the 'rat finks,' the police agents, are."[76]

Within a day of this letter being written on his behalf, Demmerle, no doubt with some measure of pride, provided a copy to the FBI. After all, a year earlier, infiltration on this level had been just the half-baked scheme of a factory worker from Brooklyn; now he was in the mix with Uncle Ho himself. Two weeks later, on June 26, the aspiring spy tipped his handlers off to the fact that the Revolutionary Contingent and the Veterans and Reservists were planning a disruption at the Armed Forces Induction Center on Whitehall Street in Lower Manhattan: one of the group's members had been drafted and was going to try to distribute literature inside the building while others picketed outside.[77] Demmerle also passed along information regarding the planned use of firearms by both the Revolutionary Contingent and USCANLF.

In July Demmerle wrote to Hanoi himself.[78] Ostensibly a letter supporting Charlotte's petition for Vietnamese citizenship, most of George's obsequious verbiage was devoted to touting his own devotion to the cause, but with just enough humility and self-deprecation to be believable—once again, not bad for someone with just a GED. "To play my part towards the destruction of U.S. imperialism—that for me constitutes the meaning of life," George proclaimed. To further evidence his insider credentials, he also provided a play-by-play account of votes and arguments at a recent Revolutionary Contingent meeting, including specific proposals put forth by Polin, and alerted the FBI that Polin and Teague (and probably others) had been using an intermediary in Prague as a mail drop for corresponding with the North Vietnamese government.[79]

The holiday weekend of July 4 presented an opportunity for New York radicals to practice their particular versions of patriotism. On July 2, V&R held a march at Columbus Circle to honor the "Spirit of 76." The flyer for the event drew the same analogy that Walter Teague had been making on street corners for months: "Today, in Vietnam, the descendants of the American revolutionaries are the 'Red Coats,' the foreign mercenaries, trying to maintain an old, despised order, while the rebels are the sandaled peasants—who march and fight under the flag of the National Liberation Front" (figure 12).[80]

On July 10 Demmerle passed along some intelligence—hearsay, more like—that was immediately elevated to the head of the New York office, a sign of the fear of racial uprising seeping into the ranks of law enforcement:

12. Walter Teague (wearing Vietnamese hat) leads the Spirit of '76 march through Times Square, July 4, 1967. Estate of Louis Salzberg.

> At 2:50 PM, this date, George Demmerle . . . advised that he heard from a friend, who heard from another, that there was a negro group who loiters at the intersection of Myrtle and Dekalb Aves., Brooklyn, N.Y., who had tentative plans to engage in a "shoot-out" on the evening of 7/11/67. This "shoot-out" is reportedly to take place at the intersection of Cypress and Myrtle, and there has been some talk that this group is in possession of a machine gun.[81]

On July 15, days after receiving a $50 bonus from the FBI for providing details about the Revolutionary Contingent's plans to hold target practice in Upstate New York, Demmerle drove up to Lake Sebago, near Bear Mountain, to take part in the training. The group had held similar exercises every couple of weeks throughout this summer, at least one of which was attended by Robin Palmer.[82] George, who had experience with guns both from his time in the army and more recently from target practice with the Socialist Workers Party, estimated that a thousand rounds were fired.[83] Reports like these, on the heels of the race riots over the summer, could have left no doubt within the FBI that white radicals were also preparing themselves for armed struggle.

Credible information on protests and firearms were strengthening Demmerle's case within the FBI, and on July 28 the New York Office made yet another request to Washington to approve him as a PSI. "He is in a strategic position as a member of the inner circle of the RC, and he is the only source available to further furnish information concerning the activities of this organization." Given the prevalence of informants among radical groups a year later, the fact that Demmerle was the FBI's only option in mid-1967 is striking. For all that, noting that George had "exhibited a rational sensible attitude," the memo also said that he would need some financial assistance to keep up his frenetic pace. "If Bureau approval is given to utilize Demmerle as a PSI, close supervision and control will be maintained over his activities to prevent any possible embarrassment to the Bureau from his utilization," the memo concluded. This same memo also pointed out that in recent weeks the leadership of Progressive Labor—whose politics, tactics, and demeanor was increasingly at odds with the wilder wing of the New Left—had given George an ultimatum: Pick PL or the Revolutionary Contingent. He opted for the latter.[84]

At the end of July, Cuba Week took place at the World's Fair in Montreal, catnip for New York leftist radicals (figure 13). On July 28 George, who had gotten the green light from the FBI to attend, met up with Robin Palmer and fifteen or so members of the Revolutionary Contingent at the Free School, where they piled into three station wagons and headed north.[85] Upon arriving in Montreal, they handed out antiwar leaflets at the U.S. Pavilion before spending the night on the floor of an apartment at 75 Rue Saint-Cuthbert, just north of Mount Royal Park. George, camera in hand, attended an SDS meeting at the Cuban Pavilion the next afternoon and a party thrown for them by the Cubans that night. On the final day, at a meeting with two Cubans and an interpreter at the Cuban Pavilion, the Contingent declared its position of "total anti-imperialism," and the two groups discussed how to work together in Latin and South America.[86] Upon returning to New York, Demmerle handed over three rolls of film and IDed the entire crew.[87]

George's inclusion in the Canada trip appears to have boosted his standing in the RC, because three weeks later he was invited to be part of a secret three-person committee to plan the formation of a "sabotage ring" to "commit acts of destruction against electrical installations, petroleum

13. George Demmerle in front of the Cuban Pavilion at the 1968 World's Fair in Montreal. Estate of George Demmerle.

and water facilities in the United States during the summer of 1968." This piece of intelligence was deemed serious enough to be forwarded to the director of the FBI by the New York office.[88] In addition to his inclusion in the sabotage committee, George was also asked a few days later to join the security investigation committee; apparently the RC had decided it needed to start vetting potential members so they would not be infiltrated.[89] The irony was as sweet as the opportunity.

In September George was appointed to the RC's arms committee, which seriously entertained the idea of purchasing dozens of .30 caliber semiautomatic rifles to bring to the march on the Pentagon scheduled for October. It was at a meeting in the runup to this march that Demmerle first encountered Abbie Hoffman and Jerry Rubin. "I thought they were a bunch of crackpots," he said twenty-five years later.[90] Fortunately, a lack of funds ultimately made the bulk gun purchase impractical, but not before Demmerle had passed on the worrying news to the increasingly freaked-out Feds.[91] The arms committee decided instead to settle for the arm-waving of a snake dance, a form of crowd resistance developed in Japan, in Washington instead.[92]

At the end of the summer the New York office of the FBI made yet another bid to get approval to bring George on board as a PSI, the first step to becoming a full-fledged informant. "We have no source other than Demmerle to furnish information on the RC at this time," says the memo. "It is potentially volatile and warrants close scrutiny." Washington was finally warming to the idea. "He has impressed New York with his sincerity and dedication to fight the enemies of democracy," the DC team wrote. "His brief association with right-wing organizations reflects this desire, and at the same time his subsequent rejection of them attests to his recognition of their radicalism."[93]

Unable to argue with Demmerle's track record as an amateur, and spooked by their lack of access to the increasingly militant groups on the left, the Washington office gave official approval the next day by checking the top box on its informant designation form: "Authority is granted to designate captioned individual a Bureau-approved PSI and to proceed to develop source as a security informant in accordance with instructions set forth in Section 107 of the Manual of Instructions."[94] Within six weeks, after not only providing tips about plans to blow up utility plants and the Statue of Liberty but also furnishing the keys to the Revolutionary Contingent's storefront office at 41 East First Street, George was promoted by the FBI to Full Security Informant (FSI).[95] His FBI Number: 223 244A.[96] In a October 3 memo, making the case to increase his new charge's pay to $100 a week, Special Agent Robinson summarized the ground Demmerle had covered in the less than two months since becoming a PSI: ten Revolutionary Contingent meetings; seven Demonstration Defense Course classes; two sabotage strategy meetings; five CIP meetings; sixteen PL Marxism study groups; nine oral reports; and twelve written reports. He was ready for his first official mission.[97]

Part II

INFILTRATION

Chapter 5

The Pentagon

OCTOBER 21, 1967. Looking east from the Lincoln Memorial over the reflecting pool, a swarming sea of people—fifty thousand-plus, according to news reports—stretched all the way to the Washington Monument. Black and white photos of the crowd reveal a surprising lack of cartoonish hippies and unkempt youth, with even the most defiant twenty-somethings looking like they are on their way to class if not an office job. But their khakis, sports coats, and cleanly cropped haircuts belied a boiling anger and frustration that had spread from the cafes and street corners of Berkeley, Ann Arbor, and the Lower East Side to much of mainstream America. Veterans, union members, housewives, high school students and clergymen from more than 150 different political groups carried signs saying, "Get the Hell Out of Vietnam," "Wipe Out Poverty Not People," "Hell No, Don't Go!" And while there were plenty of placards touting the cause of civil rights, there were noticeably few Black faces in the crowd, a sign of the growing reluctance of Black leaders to risk diluting their message by joining mass protests against the war.

Newly minted FBI informant George Demmerle could hear the speeches from the likes of novelist and pugilist Norman Mailer, Pulitzer Prize–winning poet Robert Lowell, and the famous pediatrician and antiwar activist Dr. Benjamin Spock ringing through the tinny loudspeakers, even if he couldn't see the orators themselves. Spock reflected the widely held belief of the crowd when he proclaimed, "The enemy, we believe in all sincerity, is Lyndon Johnson, who we elected as a Peace candidate in

1964 and who betrayed us within three months."[1] The speech that Walter Teague and others in the pro-Vietnam camp were most excited for was by the Vietnamese-born Nguyen Van Luy. "Both the National Liberation Front in the South and the defenders in the North stand firmer and more determined than ever to fight this war to a finish, to drive out all foreign troops, and to decide for themselves the future of Vietnam," he said, just moments before the event organizers, controversially, pulled the plug on him.[2]

After the speeches and musical performances by Phil Ochs and the folk trio Peter, Paul and Mary, Fifth Avenue Peace Parade chairman and future Chicago Seven defendant Dave Dellinger sent the crowd off across the river to the Pentagon. "There is always a time when an idea's time has come and we are going to present that idea to the troops and the police!" he shouted.[3] "We were trying to show that we were stepping up the militance," Dellinger recounted in the early 1990s. "I knew what it did to people when they had their first . . . cattle prod or their first club."[4]

About half the crowd made the three-mile march over the Memorial Bridge and across the Potomac River to the Pentagon, where two of the day's organizers, Abbie Hoffman and Jerry Rubin, were scheduled to begin their much-publicized "exorcism" and "levitation" of the military headquarters. Hoffman was still glowing from having duped members of the press and Fifth Precinct a few days earlier into believing that he'd invented a new aphrodisiac he called Lace that, he claimed, would induce anyone sprayed with it into a state of immediate and unstoppable sexual frenzy. Reporters from the City Desk of the local papers seemed convinced enough when they were invited to a demonstration at Abbie's apartment where three men were sprayed with the agent and proceeded to have sex with three of the women in the room in front of everyone.[5]

Leading the charge from the Washington Mall to the Pentagon were members of the U.S. Committee to Aid the National Liberation Front and the Revolutionary Contingent. Carrying a Viet Cong flag at the head of the phalanx, just feet from group's traffic-directing chairman Walter Teague and his special guest Nguyen Van Luy, was George Demmerle. Contingent members had been attending self-defense classes in the weeks leading up to the march and had learned a series of hand signals (open hand = stop; clenched fist = help; waved fist = run, etc.). Most marchers were carrying placards or Viet Cong flags, some wore crash helmets, and others had six-inch broom handles concealed in their clothing; almost all of them sported a yellow band on their wrists (figure 14).[6]

As the mass of marchers neared the Pentagon, Teague's battalion of

14. Walter Teague's back with George Demmerle holding flag immediately to his right, March on the Pentagon, October 21, 1967. Walter Teague Collection.

perhaps three hundred radicals branched off and headed into the woods. Robin Palmer recounted the story from here in a 1994 interview with historian Jeremy Varon:

> We all came up to this plateau-like parking lot area [which] had these stanchions where the rope . . . was maybe three feet high, and there was maybe fifteen feet from stanchion to stanchion. This was what they had as a fence or a barrier. There were marshals and police on the other side saying, "You can peacefully organize, peacefully demonstrate on the other side." But that wasn't what we were coming to the Pentagon for. We were coming to the Pentagon to levitate it or destroy it.
>
> Everyone had been racing to the Pentagon but when they came to this little screen they stopped. But I said, "This is crazy! Why are we stopping here?" And somebody had a big hunting knife and I said, "Goddammit, give me that knife!" I sawed the rope and made it collapse all down the line. And then I took one of the cardboard tubes [we were using as flag poles] . . . and charged up to this marshal who

> was from Michigan and just started pounding him. And of course, the other marshals closed in around me and started pounding on me with their sticks.[7]

For today's reader, the parallels to the imagery of right-wing radicals laying siege to the U.S. Capitol on January 6, 2021, are eerie and unavoidable, but this footage in 1967 would have to wait for the evening news—after all, it would be another thirteen years before the launch of CNN and almost thirty years until Fox News debuted. Lack of cable news notwithstanding, the day's events would generate some of the most memorable images of the Vietnam era. The photograph of Robin Palmer being beaten with nightsticks is on the back cover of the paperback edition of Norman Mailer's famous account of the Pentagon march, *Armies of the Night*. "I was probably the first bust [of the day]," Palmer bragged later.[8] Within minutes though, he had been released back into the crowd. The marshals, who had only sidearms, were quickly reinforced by troops wearing gas masks and carrying bayoneted rifles.[9] Meanwhile, the view from inside the Pentagon, where Secretary of Defense Robert McNamara and other senior officials were holed up, was a worrying sight. "I'd had experiences with mobs all over the world and I didn't like the look or sound of this one bit," said Stanley Resor, secretary of the army at the time. "It was a very impressive thing, thirty-five thousand people right there under your nose."[10]

Tornabene, aka Super Joel, a Bay Area activist and future Yippie, created one of the definitive photo ops of the decade when he was captured placing a flower in the b arrel of a soldier's rifle, a fragment of hippie hopefulness amidst a decidedly unpeaceful—and noisy—backdrop. East Village band The Fugs had arrived earlier in the day with a rented flatbed truck carrying a PA system, a cow, dozens of bags of cornmeal, and flowers.[11] With several competing rituals unfolding around him, Fugs' singer Ed Sanders delivered an impromptu, sexually provocative invocation punctuated with repeated calls of "Out, demons, out!" (In addition to fronting his band and running the Peace Eye Bookstore on East Tenth Street, Sanders published *Fuck You: A Magazine of the Arts*, made films like *Mongolian Clusterfuck*, wrote poetry, rabble-roused for myriad peacenik causes, and advocated for cannabis legalization.) Meanwhile Hoffman was busy pairing up couples to perform public displays of affection of varying degrees to surround the Pentagon in communal love. While traditional Mayan healers sprinkled cornmeal on the ground and Allen Ginsberg recited mantras, hundreds of people formed a circle around the Pentagon and started singing and chanting ancient Aramaic exorcism rites. Whether the Pentagon actually levitated or not was beside the point.

Another group of aggressors, fed up with flowers and protest songs, had even bolder ambitions. Among the gang of two dozen men determined to make it past the ring of military police and inside the heavily fortified building were two who would be at the center of a radical, militant scene in New York over the next two years—Robin Palmer, one arrest already under his belt that day, and Ben Morea, the take-no-shit leader of the Lower East Side anarchist group Black Mask, who navigated life with no apparent concern for his own safety.[12]

At about 6:00 p.m. Morea, Palmer, and a handful of others, including a student radical from Japan, overpowered the small number of guards posted outside a service entrance and charged inside. Those that made it in were confronted by troops, many of whom had spent the weekend camped out in the building's halls, who used the butt end of their bayoneted rifles to bash the insurgents before carrying them out, leaving, as the *New York Times* said, "patches of blood behind."[13] As Morea recalled fifty years later, "They pounded people, bloodied them up. They beat us out."[14]

Shortly thereafter, a police van departed from the Pentagon, one of many that evening full of arrested protesters and bound for Occoquan Workhouse (a.k.a. Lorton Prison). One passenger was Ray Mungo, editor at the time of the Boston University student newspaper, who later described the roster inside the prison, a veritable Who's Who of the Movement:

> Inside the cell again, Dave Dellinger is cool and cheerful as he sips his coffee; Noam Chomsky is neat and academic, worried about getting back to M.I T. for a Monday morning symposium; the poet Tuli Kupferberg is wonderful just to look at; Norman Mailer is unusually quiet and struts from one end of the cell to the other, his hands in his pockets; Walter Teague of the Committee to Aid the NLF has drawn up a statement accusing the Mobilization Committee of disorganization and duplicity, which some sign while others bitterly argue that the opinion, intended for publication in the National Guardian, will be exploited by the capitalist press.[15]

A total of 682 people—including Robin Palmer (twice) and Dr. Benjamin Spock—ended up being arrested, and forty-seven people were injured. By 7:00 a.m. Sunday, only two hundred protestors remained.[16] Abbie and Anita Hoffman hopped a ride back to New York with Robin and Sharon Krebs in Palmer's Ford Falcon. It was an important few hours for Palmer. "We became friends, and I really began to get a glimmer about what was going on with this so-called cultural revolution that was really happening on my blind side," Palmer said of the drive.[17]

After the Pentagon, the Revolutionary Contingent unraveled quickly. When one member stole $200 from its bank account, leaving the organization with just $38, infighting and paranoia became rampant. On October 31, less than eight months since inception, a motion was put forward and a vote held that formalized what was already obvious: the group was done.[18] Seven of the members, including George Demmerle, tried to continue on their own, but ultimately nothing came of it.[19]

Not that the members of the RC were going into retirement. Far from it. On the night of November 14, a group of three thousand antiwar activists, along with another thousand policemen, showed up at the Hilton Hotel, where Secretary of State Dean Rusk was scheduled to speak. Demonstrators hurled stones, bottles, and eggs at law enforcement; Black Mask members pelted tuxedoed guests with bags of cow's blood they had procured from a local butcher shop.[20] All the while, passers-by shouted at the protesters: "You're a bunch of Communists—take a bath!" yelled one older man. A couple of hundred more demonstrators broke off and ran through Times Square, trapping theatergoers and diners inside and stopping traffic.[21] Police ended up arresting forty-six people on charges of resisting arrest, inciting to riot, and harassment.[22] Walter Teague was elated, calling it "the largest, most disruptive and successful demonstration in this city so far."[23]

"Stop the Draft Week" kicked off on Monday, December 4, with a major demonstration in front of the Whitehall Induction Center in Lower Manhattan. The first day was fairly calm, with the first arrests not coming until the early morning hours of December 5, when 264 protesters, including Allen Ginsberg and Dr. Spock, were booked for attempting to barricade the front doors of the building. Mayor Lindsay's aides, Barry Gottehrer and Sid Davidoff, had worked out the logistics with organizers down to where and how people would be arrested, so this first round of arrests was relatively smooth, just another day at the office for both sides. Tensions escalated as the week went on, however, and by Wednesday there were upward of five thousand police officers present.[24]

On December 8, the final day of the Stop the Draft Week protests in New York City, after a large-scale draft card burning ceremony in front of Whitehall (figure 15), Robin Palmer, carrying the NLF flag alongside Walter Teague, led the USCANLF faction into the sea of people. The crowd, many of whom were outfitted in "defense-wear" and practicing "mobile street tactics," was crawling with right-wing rabble-rousers and

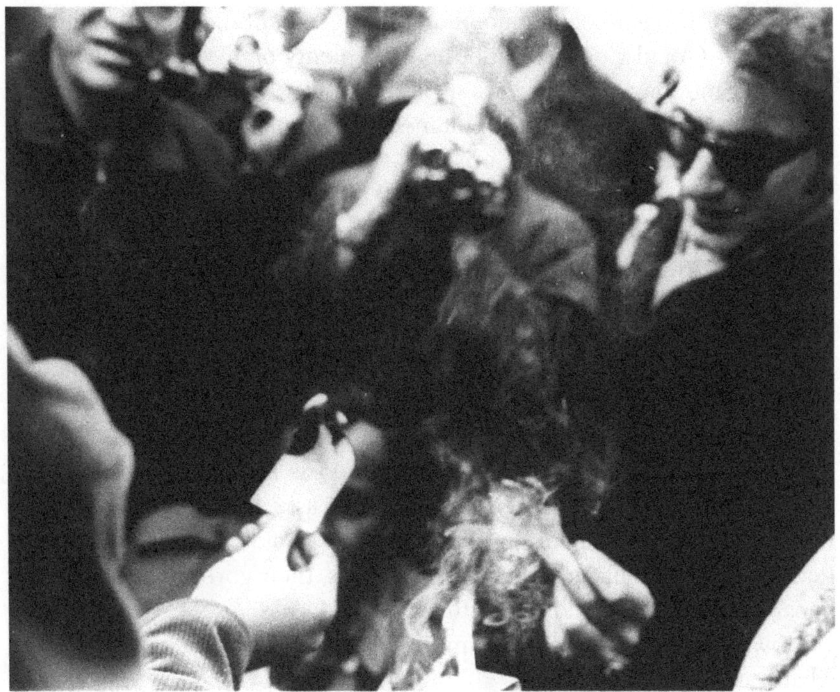

15. Draft card burning, Foley Square, November 1967. Estate of Louis Salzberg.

plainclothes police officers too. Not only was the crowd younger and rowdier than earlier in the week, but "the police were restive and angry, and were less concerned with the niceties of civil liberties," according to Gottehrer.[25] After the plainclothes officers in the crowd made several unsuccessful attempts to take the Viet Cong flag away from Palmer, the mounted police came for him. Reaching Teague first, the police beat and detained him; when they finally got their hands on Robin they smashed him in the head and the groin. Ultimately Teague was charged with assaulting a policeman with a knife, inciting a riot, and possession of a dangerous weapon and was let out on $1,000 bail. Another member of USCANLF, Mike Gimbel, was arrested a few days later when he went to pick up his backpack from the police station and was arrested for drugs the cops had planted in it.[26] The week of antidraft demonstrations ended later that day with police laying into a rowdy crowd of protesters around Union Square; the ensuing melee resulted in 140 arrests.[27]

On December 19, three weeks after Eugene McCarthy, the antiwar senator from Minnesota, announced that he would challenge President

Johnson for the Democratic nomination, Movement members turned out in force at Grand Central Station. So did plenty of TV cameras. Holiday shoppers and tourists were gawking at the swarm of long-haired, unkempt youths when "suddenly, and simultaneously, from all entrances to the station, came people carrying Christmas shopping bags," according to one news account. "The bags were opened, and doves (they looked like pigeons) fluttered into the air. There was a cheer, a muffled cry 'Peace,' and the demonstration was over."[28]

Only three people were arrested this time out at Grand Central, one-tenth the number that were taken away by police from the scene of "The Great Christmas Mill-in" four days later at Saks Fifth Avenue. Designed to jam the gears of capitalism at their annual peak, the demonstration featured not only hippies clogging the aisles while shouting "Merry Christmas" and "Peace in Vietnam" but also someone dressed as LBJ in a wheelchair and a suspiciously political Santa Claus who, when asked how he would explain what was going on to a curious kid in the store, said, "I'd want to tell him that while his parents are buying toys at Saks, their government is buying napalm at Dow to kill kids in Vietnam."[29]

It was a theatrical end to a tumultuous year, but nothing compared to what was to come.

Chapter 6

Yippies and Motherfuckers

ON THE AFTERNOON of New Year's Eve, Abbie Hoffman and Anita Hoffman (figure 16) had a few friends over to their ground-floor apartment on St. Marks Place: Nancy Kurshan and Paul Krassner, as well as the two cofounders of the *East Village Other* newspaper, Allan Katzman and Walter Browart. As the joints were passed around, the group began brainstorming about staging some kind of protest at the Democratic National Convention, which was slated to take place in Chicago at the end of August. Everyone was excited about the idea, but first things first: to pull off a large-scale event like this, they would need a name for their group.

"I tried Youth International Festival. YIF. Sounds like KIF. Kids International Festival? No, too contrived," explained Paul Krassner in his autobiography *Confessions of a Raving, Unconfined Nut.* "What could make YIP? Now that would be ideal because then the word Yippie could be derived organically from YIP," reasoned the former Merry Prankster. "'Yippie' was a traditional shout of spontaneous joy. We could be the Yippies! And then working backward, it hit me. Youth International Party! Of course!" Krassner, who would go on to function as "a kind of minister of wit and propaganda" for the group raised his hand and made a vee sign.[1] "See, it's really a 'Y' sign," he said.[2]

Jerry Rubin (figure 17), who had cofounded the Vietnam Day Committee in Berkeley in 1965 and would lead the Yippies along with Hoffman, later described the group as a "middle point" between the New Left, which was "very unsatisfying because . . . it did not relate to music; it didn't

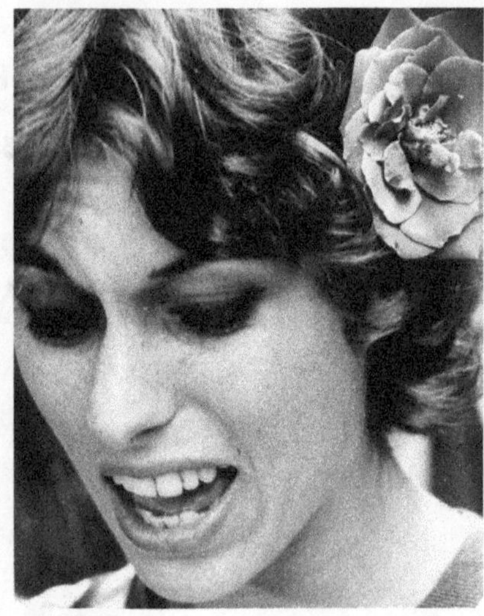

16a–b. Abbie Hoffman and Anita Hoffman. Estate of Louis Salzberg.

relate to style of life; it didn't relate to the way people looked" and the hippie movement, which "had separated itself from the action and passion of everyday existence."[3] Historian David Farber described their thinking: "Yippies believed they could make a revolution by simulating a revolution that looked like fun. The simulation would play to the mass media and through the mass media it would be made available to apolitical youth."[4]

Following a kickoff meeting on January 11 at the home of Mellon banking heiress Peggy Hitchcock, the Yippies went public on January 16 with the first press release announcing their intention to put on a massive "Festival of Life" in Chicago alongside the Democratic National Convention in August.[5] According to an article Hoffman wrote later in Paul Krassner's *Realist* magazine, the Yippies had four foundational objectives:

1. The blending of pot and politics into a political grass leaves movement—a cross-fertilization of the hippie and New Left philosophy.
2. A connecting link that would tie as much of the underground together as was willing into some gigantic national get-together.
3. The development of a model for an alternative society.
4. The need to make some statement, especially in revolutionary action-theater terms, about LBJ, the Democratic Party, electoral politics, and the state of the nation.[6]

17. Jerry Rubin. Estate of Louis Salzberg.

While the Diggers and Black Mask had pioneered radical street theater as a means of protest, Hoffman and the Yippies made it a full-time profession. Although video footage of Hoffman dressed in his American flag shirt speaking his mile-a-minute Yippie patois can feel ridiculous in retrospect (and his bipolar disorder–related suicide in 1989 suggests that he was likely plagued by mental illness for much of his life), there is no denying that he possessed a brilliant marketing mind. "No need to build a stage, it was all around us," he wrote in his autobiography. "We would hurl ourselves across the canvas of society like streaks of splattered paint. Highly visual images would become news, and rumormongers would rush to spread the excited word."[7] He was also a rhetorical genius. "Abbie is the best extemporaneous speaker I've ever heard," wrote Canadian journalist David Lewis Stein. "His style is borscht-belt comedian, a small-time hustler spitting wisecracks and aphorisms out of the corner of his mouth. But underlying the laughter is a perceptive political analysis and a shrewd grasp of the realities in the outside world."[8]

As the Yippies were preparing to introduce set themselves loose on the world, Morea and the Black Mask contingent were about to execute one of their most theatrical zaps. It was January 8, a Monday, as Morea and his merry band of anarchists approached the intersection of Second Avenue and East Tenth Street. Set against the clear blue winter sky, the steeple of the 170-year-old St. Mark's Church towered over neighboring townhouses and tenements. At six feet three inches, Allen Van Newkirk cut an imposing figure in his black trench coat as he approached the Georgian brick building set back from the street by a small plaza. "He looked like the perfect anarchist," recalled Morea.[9] The "pistol-packing, motorcycle-riding early Detroit advocate of surrealist and Dadaist ideas" had relocated for a time to the Lower East Side and fallen in with Morea and the members of "the Family," as the expanded group of Black Maskers was now referring to themselves. On this day, Van Newkirk, Morea, and a small cadre that included poet and future NPR contributor Andrei Codrescu took their seats in the pews in advance of a poetry reading by Columbia professor Kenneth Koch.[10] The well-mannered aesthete made the perfect target for Black Mask. According to Morea, "Koch was a symbol to us of this totally bourgeois, dandy world."[11]

A few minutes into the reading, Van Newkirk pulled out what looked like a gun and strode down the aisle shouting "Death to bourgeois poets!" before reaching the podium and yelling "Koch!" as he fired off a round of blanks.[12] As the natty professor fainted from shock—or went along with the joke, depending on whose memory you trust—leaflets rained down from the church balcony with photos of poet Amir Baraka and the slogan "Poetry is Revolution." Baraka, the well-known Black writer and friend of Morea's who had changed his name from LeRoi Jones after the assassination of Malcolm X, had been arrested on gun charges during the Newark riots in July when police pulled over the green Volkswagen station wagon that he and two other men were driving along South Orange Avenue. The thirty-three-year-old graduate of Columbia University's writing program, who was known not only for his poetry but also for his antiwhite rhetoric, had been charged with possessing two loaded .32 caliber pistols. The language of the "former darling of New York's literati,"[13] so called after winning an Obie in 1964 for his off-Broadway play *The Dutchman*, had grown increasingly extreme as the sixties wore on, and at the time of his arrest was on record as having called for Harlem to be an independent, Black-run state and encouraging Blacks to "smash [the] jelly white faces" of their oppressors.[14] It was a sign of Morea's unparalleled credibility among Black militants that Baraka would even associate with him by this point.

Little less than a week later, on Monday, February 5, Demmerle's quarterly report card from the FBI came out. There was no doubt he'd been hitting all his marks. In the previous three months he had gone to six meetings of the Revolutionary Contingent as well as four meetings with six former RC members after the group disbanded; he had attended four Marxism study groups and one trade union class, both organized by Progressive Labor; and, in addition to joining the Pentagon march in Washington, DC in October with the RC, he'd gone upstate with former RC members in January for target practice. George had submitted information about eighty individuals who had previously not been on the FBI's radar. In all, he had generated thirty-two written reports and seven oral reports, a rate of more than three a week. Of particular note, the now-official undercover agent also had submitted "an unusual pamphlet he obtained at the Free School of NY, which gave instructions to Negro rioters on how to make Molotov cocktails and how to kill police [and] included instructions for Negro snipers."[15] The booklet was J. Edgar Hoover's worst nightmare, but also a dream gift, since it provided cover for Hoover's continued campaign against Black radicals, a campaign that showed no signs of abating.

On February 6, twenty Black students were arrested when they sought to enter a bowling alley in Orangeburg, South Carolina. Soon six hundred more students arrived outside the building to protest the arrests, a turnout that sparked a violent reaction from the 150 policemen on the scene. Girls were hit with clubs, and twenty students had to be treated at the infirmary.[16]

The next day at noon Ben Morea headed down to the United States Courthouse in Foley Square. Among the sixty-plus demonstrators there with him was Walter Teague. The Youth Against War and Fascism–sponsored event protested the jailing of two antiwar activists, the group's own leader, Key Martin, and an activist named Maryann Weissman, on charges of trespassing on government property in their attempt to attend the court martial hearings of GI Andrew Stapp at Fort Sill, Oklahoma, the previous June. Stapp had been brought up on his own set of antiwar charges, including trying to unionize enlisted men in the American Servicemen's Union. Martin and Weissman briefly addressed attendees who held up signs saying things like "Unionize the Army, Bring the G.I.s home now" and "Stop Union Busting in the Army" before entering the courthouse to surrender themselves for six-month sentences.[17]

The front page of the *New York Times* the following day trumpeted the biggest topic in city at that moment: "Mayor Gives Garbage Men 7 A.M. Deadline to Return." Sanitation employees had already been working without a contract for eight months when, on the morning of February 2, seven thousand members of Teamsters Local 831 showed up in City Hall Park to protest the mayor's refusal to give them a $12-a-week raise.

After just twenty-four hours the city's poorer neighborhoods, which lacked buildings with incinerators as well as the financial means to hire private contractors like wealthier neighborhoods and business districts were doing, were already feeling the effects of the walkout. "A tour of the Lower East Side yesterday showed that the contents of not one can had been collected and much of the day's refuse was strewn in the streets," reported the *Daily News* on February 3.[18]

From the stench and clutter was born one of the better political pranks of the era. On the night of February 10, in reaction to the growing mountains of garbage on the Lower East Side, Morea and twenty or so Black Mask members shlepped bags of garbage uptown and deposited them on the steps of Lincoln Center. (Hoffman claims in his biography that he took part in this event too.) The action ended up being a pivot point for Morea and his crew. "We put out a leaflet explaining why we were doing this, but those of us involved realized that we weren't really Black Mask anymore and so we didn't want that name on it," explained Morea three decades later. "There was a poem by LeRoi Jones with the line 'Up Against the Wall, Motherfucker' in it and I suggested we put that on there. Somehow it stuck and from then on everyone referred to us as that."[19]

The name was apt. "Ben Morea's Up-Against-The-Wall-Motherfuckers gang was probably the most anarchistic local group of all," wrote Abbie Hoffman. "The Motherfuckers lived like gutter rats and supported themselves any way they could. They dressed in black and brown and snarled a lot. They presented themselves as the middle-class nightmare."[20] Nevertheless, the Motherfuckers were not as ideologically divorced from some of the more mainstream groups of the New Left as one might expect. "At the center of SDS's and SNCC's politics was the desire to eliminate asymmetries in decision-making power and to inculcate initiative in ordinary people—goals that all anarchists endorsed," according to historian Andrew Cornell.[21]

The Motherfuckers were not just "violent gutter rats," though. On the contrary, they were conversant in the most important writers and political philosophers of the time and, even today, Morea sprinkles his conversation with references to all sorts of authors, isms, and movements. "Their theoretical inspiration was a hybrid of European anarchism and the Marxism of the Frankfurt School, whose best known exponent was Herbert Marcuse," according to activist and historian Todd Gitlin.[22] Herbert Marcuse, pushing seventy at the time, was perhaps the biggest intellectual influence (save for household names like Mao and Marx) on the group of radical showmen that emerged in the Movement in late 1960s. A critic of both capitalism and communism, or at least the Soviet version, Marcuse provided theoretical inspiration and cover for a generation of radicals who rejected the bourgeois emptiness they had grown up in. His 1964 book *One-Dimensional Man* was a withering critique of repressive forms of government that also saw hope for redemption for those who could break out of the rigid economic mold that society expected.

In an essay called "Repressive Tolerance," Marcuse warned people not to be taken in by the state's allowance of certain nonthreatening forms of dissent.[23] For Hoffman, who had studied under Marcuse at Brandeis University, this essay was not only a call to arms but also a roadmap. "It wasn't enough to leaflet on street corners when three networks maintained a nonstop thought barrage directed at millions," he wrote in his autobiography. "The implication of Marcuse was clear: to publicize radical ideas, you needed prime-time access. No one would volunteer the space. It would have to be stolen."[24] Morea was also influenced by Marcuse. In his autobiography Hoffman remembered standing in the audience with Morea for a speech the German-accented polemicist gave at the Fillmore East:

> "De only proper response to dis von-dimensional machine of destruction can be total and complete rrrrrefusal!" cried the philosopher, standing on the Fillmore stage. The joint went crazy. Ben Motherfucker, leader of the Lower East Side's most nefarious street gang, spat on the floor, raised his fist, and exclaimed, "Dat cat's duh only fuckin' brain worth listnin' to in de cuntree!"[25]

The Motherfuckers could be politically savvy when it suited them too. The day following Marcuse's speech at the Fillmore, the Motherfuckers were approved as the Lower East Side chapter of SDS, which gave them the ability to attend (and sabotage) SDS meetings anywhere in the country; it also marked the first time a nonstudent chapter had been granted a charter. "We joined Students for a Democratic Society not to argue ideology but to disrupt and chastise suitably impressed students for their lack of daring," said Morea. "We saw that all these traditional left groups and Maoists like Progressive Labor were trying to take it over [and] we thought it was important for other kinds of people, like us, to get involved and show the students that there were many choices, many ways they could go."[26]

The headquarters for the Motherfuckers was a storefront at 341 East Tenth Street, where the group operated a non-profit called the East Side Services Organization (ESSO). "We had free clothes, doctors and lawyers on retainers, a mimeograph, information for people who wanted to dodge the draft and get fake ID, information on crash pads, etc.," Morea explained later. "We did free food a couple nights a week. We got some papers from a church saying we were a non-profit and that allowed us to get day-old or incorrectly marked stuff at the food outlets for free."[27] Before opening their storefront the Motherfuckers used the basement kitchen of the St. Mark's Church to serve their free meals, just as the Black Panthers would when they began running their free breakfasts for children the following year.[28]

Although the Yippies would open a similar storefront a block away at 264 East Tenth Street a few months later and the Black Panthers' breakfast program would start in 1969, in early 1968 the Motherfuckers were by far the biggest operators of these community services on the Lower East Side. Despite their creativity in sourcing free food, the Motherfuckers still needed money to keep the program running. In addition to small individual benefactors like Paul Krassner, the meal program was supported in large part by Abbie Hoffman. "Abbie was getting money from the Mobe and the city but he wasn't doing a lot so he contributed a lot of it to us," recalled Morea, referencing a down-low deal Abbie had cut with the mayor's office to be expediter/envoy between City Hall and the freaks on the Lower East Side, a role that came with a sizeable slush fund.[29] "He was way into the media and I was anti-media but I respected him and he respected me," said Morea of Hoffman. "We were really, really good friends."[30]

The first few weeks following the founding of the Yippies in January 1968 were busy ones. "Over the winter . . . Yippies threw soot at Con Edison executives and plastic bags of 'blood' at Dean Rusk," wrote David Lewis Stein. "They gave out free food in Tompkins Square Park and ran from Washington Square to Times Square, darting in and out of stores shouting, 'The war is over! The war is over!'"[31] To build awareness and momentum for the gathering in Chicago, the Yippies, working out of an office at 32 Union Square at first, began holding regular meetings—Saturday afternoons at the Free School mostly—and planning a few events for the lead-up to the convention. During this early period the Yippies' steering committee—a group of five men and one woman—worked nonstop on organizing and promotion. In addition to Hoffman and Rubin, Ed Sanders, Paul Krassner, Nancy Kurshan, and Keith Lampe devoted themselves full-time to the cause. Sanders focused on lining up the musical guests and other star power for Chicago, while Lampe quit his writing and teaching to work full-time on press relations and promotion.[32] Other early diehards included Jim Fouratt, who had organized the Central Park Be-In, and Tuli Kupferberg, Lower East Side poet and Sanders's bandmate in The Fugs. Like any successful media campaign, the Yippies also had good branding in the form of their logo, which was designed by Judy Lampe, wife of Keith Lampe, and drew inspiration from Japanese lithography.[33]

On the afternoon of March 16, George Demmerle, who had moved from Brooklyn to a walkup at 58 East First Street a few weeks earlier, attended one of these early Yippie meetings at the Free School with about a hundred other people (figure 18). The subject was a major zap scheduled for the following Friday. "Current plans call for the Yip-In at Grand Central to be peaceful," Demmerle reported back to the FBI. "However, if entrance is denied to the group other plans will be made at that time." Participants were encouraged to meet at the Free School at 10:00 p.m. to put on their costumes.[34]

This internal meeting about the Grand Central action was followed the next day by the group's first press conference at which they announced the six-day "Festival of Life" at the Democratic National Convention (or "National Death Convention," as Hoffman had rebranded it). At the Hotel Americana (now the Sheraton on Seventh Avenue and Fifty-Second Street), folk singer Judy Collins performed, and poet Allen Ginsberg described the Yippies' Chicago plans as "a gathering together of younger people aware of the planetary fate that we are sitting in the middle of." Ginsberg wrapped up his portion of the program with a ten-minute Hare Krishna chant for the television cameras.[35]

Nine blocks south of the Americana, the Hotel Diplomat was a fundraising focal point for Black causes the following day. In the afternoon, more than 250 people attended a "Protest and Memorial of Orangeburg Student Massacre," raising $1,090 from the sale of literature and donations (including two checks "from the girls of Smith College") for the college kids' defense. That evening, approximately forty-five members of the Movement gathered in the West Forty-Third Street penthouse of the hotel for a benefit to raise money for H. Rap Brown's legal fund. The SNCC head, long targeted by the FBI, had been arrested on gun possession charges a few months earlier. "At the reception there was lots of singing of songs and reading of poetry," read George's report. "The atmosphere was very militant."[36]

18. Yip-in Poster, March 22, 1968.

Barring a few fundraisers for civil rights activists and some joint press statements, there was surprisingly little overlap and regular in-person connection between the whites of the New Left and the members of the Black Power movement, at least in New York. One exception to this rule was Morea. "[Morea] was closer I think to the Black Panthers than I was," said Osha Neumann. "But to the black community at large, [the Motherfuckers] didn't have any particular connection with them."[37] Morea got one noteworthy nod from the Panthers, according to James Carr's prison memoir *Bad*:

> All this militaristic Leninism was never seriously thought through as is shown by the way Bobby Seale, probably in a casual, off-the-cuff way, wanted to appoint Ben Morea, of the anarcho-situationist (often splendid, but as often a sacrificially militant, confused and contradictory group) Up Against The Wall Motherfucker, to some kind of position in the BPP—a position Morea laughingly turned down. Seale was probably jesting anyway, because, for certain, he'd never have got such a proposal through the Central Committee![38]

"The Black guys didn't trust the white guys, and rightfully so," Morea said, especially given the high levels of infiltration in the New Left. "They trusted me because I wasn't following them, I was an ally doing my own thing in parallel." Seale did ask Morea to be his vice presidential running mate on the Peace & Freedom party ticket in 1968, but Morea turned down that offer too. "I said, 'Are you crazy, man? I'm an anarchist!'"[39] As a result, Jerry Rubin received the nomination.

The leaflet distributed in the days leading up to the March 22, 1968, Yip-In at Grand Central Station made the event sound deceptively playful and benign. "It's a spring mating service celebrating the equinox, a back-scratching party, a roller-skating rink, a theater . . . with you as performer and audience," the handwritten text read. "Get acquainted with other Yippies now, for other Yiptivities and Chicago Y.I.P. Festival this summer. Bring: Flowers, Beads, Music, Radios, Pillows, Eats, Love and Peace. Meet later on at Sheep Meadow to Yip Up the Sun."[40]

Thirty or so Yippies met at the Free School at 10:00 p.m. as planned to put on their outfits before joining a couple thousand more people in the main hall of the train station at midnight.[41] One of those who showed up in the full regalia that he would become famous for—shiny purple cape and centurion's helmet with an orange plume—was George Demmerle, who had not started calling himself Prince Crazie yet but was looking the part. "The first time I ever saw him at a big demonstration was at Grand Central," remembers Lew Friedman. "He was in his Prince Crazie outfit."[42] Going forward, Demmerle's over-the-top duds, inspired in no small part by Hoffman and Rubin, would draw plenty of attention, but on this night he blended right in with the hippie Halloween vibes. "They poured into the vast main concourse of Manhattan's Grand Central Station 3,000 strong, wearing their customary capes, gowns, feathers and beads," reported *Time*.[43]

The festive atmosphere did not last long. According to an article in the *New York Free Press*, the first half hour of the protest went swimmingly. It was a "gay carnival" with "balloons and clowns, speed freaks and the painted lady, the Wild Man from Borneo." Chants of "Hell no, we won't go" and "Draft cops" rang through the air. At 12:30 a.m., a cherry bomb went off and lines of people snake-danced through the great hall.[44] When members of the Motherfuckers, who had spent the previous evening throwing eggs at cops outside the Ninth Precinct house on East Fifth Street to protest the growing number of raids on East Village "crash houses," climbed up on a giant clock and pulled the hands off, proclaiming "Time is meaningless," the police batons began to fly.[45]

> With no warning and for no apparent reason, about 50 tactical patrolmen charged in from an adjacent waiting room and began cracking skulls. Unable to clear the terminal the first time, they repeated the tactic over and over again. Yippees [*sic*] and commuters alike were bowled over. People were pressed up against the marble walls and beaten. A number of Yippies were thrown through plate-glass doors.[46]

Morea himself wasn't there and doesn't remember why: "Maybe I was high on LSD or something." The Motherfuckers were, after all, enthusiastic users of both acid and marijuana; it was only the "death drugs"—speed and heroin—that they were opposed to. Drugs, in the Motherfuckers' worldview, played an important role: "Their purpose was to reprogram the compulsiveness of this culture so that people could replace work with living," said Morea.[47]

Sid Davidoff, one of the mayor's assistants for community affairs, tried to intervene in the melee, telling police that he would "negotiate with the leadership, [but] Abbie at one point was no place to be found." By 3:00 a.m. many of the demonstrators had already begun to walk up to Central Park. There were still a thousand people in Grand Central Station, but Abbie was not one of them—he had had to go Bellevue Hospital after getting clubbed from behind by a policeman.[48] In fact, so many demonstrators were beaten up by the police that on March 28, Allen Levine of the New York Civil Liberties Union, who had been quoted in the papers calling the event "the most extraordinary display of unprovoked police brutality I've seen outside of Mississippi," hosted a meeting at the Judson Memorial Church on Washington Square South to organize and catalog all the cases of abuse.[49] According to Ed Sanders, the Grand Central massacre, while a galvanizing initiation to some of the greener recruits in the crowd, was nonetheless "the beginning of the death of Yippie."[50]

Despite the injuries and bad press from the takeover of Grand Central Station, the Yippies stayed the course: The following week, three hundred of them, along with members of the Motherfuckers and a group called the Transformation, met up at the Museum of Modern Art to protest the Dada and Surrealism gala scheduled for that night. Eighteen months earlier, Black Mask members had first picketed and shut down MOMA on their own because the museum "had pushed art as a commercial enterprise rather than a spiritual, aesthetic exercise," according to Morea.[51] Though well attended, the second protest was calmer than the helmeted members of the Tactical Police Force had feared. Demonstrators dressed in quilts and robes heckled gala attendees for patronizing the "Mausoleum of Modern Art." The two most famous artists who made it to the black-tie dinner on the museum's seventh floor, Marcel Duchamp and Salvador Dali, told the *New York Times* they approved of the protesters' antics.[52]

In the wake of the Grand Central melee and a *Daily News* article predicting a turnout of three thousand protesters at MOMA, the police had decided to play it safe and shut down the entire block of West Fifty-Third Street between Fifth Avenue and Avenue of the Americas. Despite the smaller number of demonstrators that ultimately turned up, it is probably a good thing they did. "About 20 people from the Transformation performed a ritual dance of exorcism in beautiful costumes bearing aloft Halloween-like totems," wrote Allan Katzman in the alternative weekly *East Village Other*. "The Black Mask stood across the street yelling at everyone and anyone who went into the museum."[53] The pièce de resistance of the night came when Ralph Ortiz and Jon Hendricks released two chickens inside the exhibit. They (the chickens, not the protesters) immediately defecated all over the floor.[54] The MOMA zap became a big win for Hoffman and company when Salvador Dali was quoted in *Newsweek* two weeks later calling the political practical-jokers "the Dadaists of today."[55]

The busy month of March came to an end for the Yippies at an organizing meeting of about 140 people on March 30 at the Free School to discuss two upcoming actions: the Yip-Out planned for Easter Sunday in Central

Park and a separate march in Washington Square Park with several other groups, including Walter Teague's U.S. Committee to Aid the National Liberation Front of South Vietnam, on April 27. At the same meeting the Yippies reported having about $4,000 in their treasury, which was quite a lot of dough compared to the hand-to-mouth existence of most of these groups.[56] The Yippies had been having trouble getting Mayor Lindsay's office to grant permits for the Yip-Out, but after Hoffman and a couple dozen others descended on City Hall the mayor's right-hand man, Sid Davidoff, made it happen. In striking contrast to what was to occur four months later in Chicago, the Central Park festivities went off without any conflict between protesters and police.[57]

By the end of March, however, the Yippie leaders were secretly starting to worry that their Festival of Life might not happen after all. Ironically, a handful of recent *positive* political developments—Democratic presidential candidate Eugene McCarthy's surprising primary victory in the New Hampshire primary, President Johnson's unexpected announcement that he would not run again, and Bobby Kennedy's March 16 entrance into the race—called into question the need and strategic rationale for an event designed to question the Democratic Party status quo. "As a byproduct of Bobby Kennedy entering the race, the enthusiasm of Yippie leaders became replaced by doubt, and there was serious talk about calling off Chicago," wrote Paul Krassner.[58] "The people who could have been expected to take to the streets during the Democratic convention suddenly believed they had a stake in the old politics," echoed David Lewis Stein.[59] After all, why tear down the system if there was still hope of changing it?

That flicker of hope was extinguished by the crack of a bullet a few days later. On April 4, just after 6:00 p.m., Martin Luther King Jr. was shot on the balcony of the Lorraine Hotel in Memphis, Tennessee. Alongside deep grief, the assassination unleashed anger and rage, with riots and looting breaking out in major cities around the country. In New York alone two men were killed, dozens of fires were set, and hundreds of stores were looted. King's assassination, along with the subsequent killing in June of Robert Kennedy and unlawful raid of Jerry Rubin's apartment, turned the tide. The Festival of Life was back in business.

Chapter 7

Riots of Spring

IN NEW YORK CITY, just about everything comes back to real estate, especially when you are, like Grayson Kirk in the 1950s and 1960s, the head of a prestigious university consumed with growth and locked in an amenities arms race with your Ivy League rivals. "Kirk's main functions as president [of Columbia University] since 1953 have been keeping his Establishment government and corporation ties flowing smoothly and raising additional capital with which to buy more and more real estate," wrote the editors of *Ramparts* magazine in June of 1968. "Kirk's mentality has clearly been that Columbia can do what it damn well wants—as long as he pleases the trustees. This includes running roughshod through Harlem with a shovel."[1]

Perhaps nothing symbolized Columbia's overreach more than the gymnasium Kirk was obsessed with building in Morningside Park. Having spent the better part of the decade pulling strings to get city approval for the new structure, the school erected a twelve-foot-high chain-link fence in February 1968 in anticipation of finally breaking ground. Even though the parkland in question was "virtually useless to everyone," according to historian Irwin Unger, pulling off a land grab of public space through backroom negotiations with the city—"the big steal," as the angry protest flyers called it—smacked of arrogance and, even worse, racism to the surrounding largely brown and Black population, which had been subjected to decades of condescension and paternalism by the university.[2] The 1955 prospectus of Morningside Heights, Inc., the nonprofit real estate development vehicle controlled by Columbia and Barnard, included this likely unintended pun that spoke volumes: "With wisdom at our disposal we are better able to inform our neighbors and co-workers as to the best means of improving their lot."[3]

By 1968 the gym was no longer just a local issue. Mayor Lindsay's new parks commissioner, Thomas Hoving, thirty-seven years old and a liberal idealist, had been very publicly trying to overturn the ninety-nine-year lease for the 2.1-acre site that the preceding Wagner administration had leased the school for a mere $3,000 a year.[4] Of a patrician background and bent, Hoving had already done a stint as head curator at the Cloisters when Lindsay appointed him to his new job as head of parks.[5]

Hoving was far from the only person from outside the immediate Columbia community to oppose the project in advance of the groundbreaking in the spring of 1968. For example, H. Rap Brown, the radicalized chairman of the Student Nonviolent Coordinating Committee, gave a fiery speech in Harlem in December 1967 in which he railed against the planned project. "If they build the first story, blow it up. If they sneak back at night and build three stories, burn it down. And if they get nine stories built, it's yours. Take it over, and maybe we'll let them in on weekends."[6]

Adding further insult to injury, the school had tried to stem the backlash against the new gym by allowing public access to the basement through a separate door on a lower level in the park rather than using the main entrance. There was some logic to this—many locals would be approaching through the park and would have had to climb an extra set of stairs to reach the main entrance—but the optics could not have been worse. In total, the "community" space was to represent just an eighth of the total square footage.[7] After the fence went up in Morningside Park, there was a demonstration at which a dozen people were arrested; two other protests quickly followed.[8]

Columbia's real estate avarice was just one of the sins that the university was under fire for at the time. Two years earlier, members of the Columbia chapter of SDS had organized a two-hundred-person protest of Columbia's policy to allow the CIA to recruit on campus and achieved a significant victory the following year when school administrators agreed to stop releasing class rankings to the draft board.[9] Mounting frustration about the university's relationship with the military-industrial complex (including, among other things, defense contractors on the school's board and a research relationship with the Institute for Defense Analyses) came to a theatrical head on a chilly March day in 1968. The newly elected head of the Columbia chapter of SDS, Mark Rudd, just back from a month-long trip to Cuba, where he "fell in love with the idea of socialism and the 'heroic guerilla,' Che Guevara," had gone down to the Lower East Side for a brainstorming session with Morea and the Motherfuckers about how to deal with an upcoming campus recruitment effort.[10] Rudd described how the resulting plan played out in his 2009 autobiography.

> Colonel [Paul] Akst, stuffed into his uniform, pudgy red cheeks shining beneath his proud cap, stood up at the podium of Earl Hall, the campus religious center, to deliver his patriotic message. I was sitting right in front of him, holding a big white bakery box on my lap, too excited to be scared. Just as he was beginning his talk, a commotion broke out in the back of the hall. The several hundred people who had packed the enormous domed room turned to see what was going on. A fife-and-drum corps, dressed in mock-Revolutionary War uniforms and armed with toy guns, was playing a ragged rendition of "Yankee Doodle." Turning back to the front, as if with one head, the crowd let out an enormous collective gasp: The distinguished colonel's face was plastered from cap to chin with lemon meringue pie![11]

Rudd, it turns out, wasn't the one who threw the pie. That was done by a long-haired hippie from Berkeley named Lincoln Pain, who managed to escape with Rudd out a side door without being detained. "Everyone on campus thought this was the best thing SDS had ever done (though we disavowed any part in it and said it was the NY Knickerboppers who had done the job)," Rudd wrote a year later. The administration seemed to buy this story too; in a telegram to Akst, Columbia vice president David Truman wrote, "we have reason to believe that those responsible were not from Columbia."[12] "Only two groups on campus did not dig what became known as the pie incident," Rudd wrote. "The first was the administration of Columbia University. Second was the old leadership of Columbia SDS, which disapproved because the action was terroristic and apolitical and would jeopardize our base on campus."[13]

Rudd had been growing increasingly enamored of the Motherfuckers and their downtown, devil-may-care attitude since witnessing them disrupt the SDS national conference earlier in the year with chants of "That's bullshit and you know it." Morea acknowledged as much decades later, saying of the most radical student leaders, "They were all influenced by us in terms of our demeanor and activism." How did Morea feel about Rudd himself? "I liked him as a person," he said. "He was trying to move out of the student nexus and so I was supportive."[14] The Motherfuckers' influence could be found literally in Rudd's open letter to President Kirk that followed on April 22. "You call for order and respect for authority; we call for justice, freedom, and socialism," Rudd wrote. "I'll use the words of LeRoi Jones, whom I'm sure you don't like a whole lot: 'Up against the wall, motherfucker, this is a stick-up.'"[15]

On April 23 student and community frustration came to a head once again. The Student Afro Society (SAS) and SDS had called for a joint demonstration at the sundial in the middle of campus on at noon. Prevented from entering Low Library, the group proceeded to the gymnasium site and, shortly before 1:00 p.m., tore down the fence. "This one symbolic act opened the floodgates of anger and strength and resolve against the racism and pro-war policies of the university," Rudd said later.[16]

Returning to campus, demonstrators entered Hamilton Hall and took Dean Coleman hostage in his office. University officials agreed to meet with students but with conditions. "We will discuss anything," Provost David Truman told them, "But we will not act under coercion." Truman also said that there would be no amnesty for students who had violated the school rule against indoor demonstration. This issue of amnesty would become the biggest stumbling block to a settlement that might have avoided the violence and strife that followed. As the afternoon went on, more students joined the sit-in at Hamilton Hall, and the takeover extended to the upper floors. With protesters sitting on the ledge above him, Rudd riled up the crowd through a megaphone (figure 19).

Among those joining the students inside the building were Robin Palmer and Sam Melville, who had seen each other recently at an SDS meeting about CIA recruitment efforts on campus and had rendezvoused on 110th Street a few minutes earlier.[17] The two men made their way through the crowd surrounding the administrative building and proceeded to scale the ivy-covered facade (figure 20), their youthful frames helping them blend in with the students.[18]

Everything about the invasion of Hamilton Hall from rhetoric to facial expressions looked serious from the outside, though some students swept up in the rebellion were more ambivalent than they might have let on. James Simon Kunen, who chronicled his experience as a student inside Hamilton Hall in a book called *The Strawberry Statement*, was riddled with internal debate. "I do not know many people who are here, and I have doubts about why they are here," he wrote of that first afternoon. "It's possible that I'm here to be cool or to meet . . . girls or . . . to be arrested. Of course, the possibility exists that I am here to precipitate some change at the University." Kunen's inner monologue wanders to such quotidian concerns as whether to skip crew practice, a first for him, to remain with

19. Mark Rudd with crowd in front of Hamilton Hall, Columbia University, April 1968. Estate of Louis Salzberg.

his fellow occupiers. He ultimately decided, however, not to let his fellow oarsmen down.[19]

Chants of "Up against the wall, motherfucker!" could be heard again the next day from Rudd and other white members of SDS as they marched in the early morning hours through the rain from Hamilton Hall, which they had vacated at the request of the Student Afro Society ("the black people ought to be able to do their thing," Rudd conceded), to Low Library, where they proceeded to use a bench to batter in the front door. Overnight, students took over the architecture building known as Avery Hall and the graduate school classrooms of Fayerweather Hall. While there are no FBI reports to back it up, Joshua Melville, in his book about his father, places Demmerle at Columbia during those days, enthusiastically chanting "Tear it down, Motherfuckers!" along with the others.[20]

Pat Swinton, the daughter of communist parents from Washington, DC, and at twenty-six a veteran of the Movement, worked a couple of blocks

20. Robin Palmer scaling Hamilton Hall, Columbia University, April 1968. Estate of Louis Salzberg.

away for the anti-imperialism think tank North American Congress on Latin America (NACLA), and she was among those who broke into Low Library. "We were the ones who put ladders up, climbed into the president's office and grabbed the files which showed that the university was all tied in with big banking interests and big real estate interests and that there was this corporate-military interlocking of people who ran things," she said in a television interview in 2020.[21]

Swinton gave the documents to the *Rat Subterranean News (Rat)*, a biweekly East Village paper launched in March of that year, which published excerpts from them in its May 3 issue, and NACLA subsequently compiled all the stolen files in a booklet called *Who Rules Columbia*. "The documents liberated from Grayson Kirk's office clearly substantiate our theories," according to the introduction. "They are in fact the proto-textbook which negates everything the students were being taught here at Columbia; the courses were irrelevant or themselves a form of pacification; what they taught was abstract, misleading, calculated to conceal the roles for which students were being trained."[22]

The students might not have gotten into Kirk's office at all if Walter Teague had not shown up from downtown. "They were looking for a way to get evidence of how the administrators were corrupt in doing all this shit," he recalled. "They had taken the building, but the office was secured with a strong wooden door with a big lock and just little glass panels." A bunch of the male students were trying to bash their way in, and they were not getting far. "They had a wooden stand with a big square foot that they were using like a battering ram; they didn't understand basic stuff," said Teague, who was arrested outside soon after on the pretext that the antenna of his transistor radio was a weapon. "So, I said, that's not going to work. Instead, take the thing, put the corner into the glass, then it'll break." That's what they did. The glass broke, and the students reached in and opened the door.[23] Other than the broken doors and a dent in Kirk's wine collection, the all-white Ivy Leaguers were restrained as far as occupying forces go. "The temptation to loot is tremendous, middle-class morality notwithstanding, but there is no looting," wrote Kunen.[24]

Robin Palmer's involvement in the occupation of Low Library was freighted with meaning for him. On his way to scale the facade of the building, he spat in the face of one of the faculty members who had tried to impede his progress. This was not only a symbolically loaded interaction for the son of two academics who had grown up in the Cornell community with nothing but respect for professors, but also a scales-from-the-eyes epiphany (a "quintessential moment of alienation," he called it) about the war movement and the U.S. system in general. "I had always held in the highest esteem all the elements that make up a university [especially] the faculty [that] was the heart and soul of the university," he said. "And here I saw these professors forming a hand-holding line to prevent students from joining the occupation . . . knocking themselves out to starve us out; they were choking this manifestation of objection to the war."[25]

On the third day of the occupation, Kunen, the musing rower, returned to Low to find a debate underway about whether to try to push cops off the ledge of the building. "A guy in a red crash helmet begins to say that maybe we won't fight because we're not as manly as the blacks, but it is well-known that he is loony as hell and he is shouted down in a rare violation of the democratic process," wrote Kunen.[26] The red-helmeted loon in question? Robin Palmer.

Sometime after midnight on April 26 Tom Hayden and John "J. J." Jacobs—one of the heads, with Rudd, of the Action Faction within the Columbia chapter of SDS—led a group of hand-picked supporters, including Palmer and Kunen, out of Kirk's office window and past the skeleton crew of security guards.[27] Picking up another twenty or so demonstrators from Fayerweather Hall, the group marched toward the next and final takeover target, the Mathematics Building. "We were the nucleus of the Mathematics commune," claimed Palmer.[28] According to a report by the New York Civil Liberties Union called *Police on Campus*, "They immediately piled furniture at the single front entrance and tied the doors shut with ropes and hoses." By 3:00 a.m. the building was theirs.[29]

The Mathematics Building at Columbia sits on the site where George Washington's troops launched an offensive against the British in September 1776; the McKim, Mead & White design is also where the most violent confrontation of the entire Columbia conflict took place. The last building to be commandeered ("Liberated Zone 5," proclaimed the banner on the facade), the Mathematics Building attracted the most seasoned and militant radicals, many of them older and unaffiliated with the university—including Hayden, Morea, Hoffman, Palmer, and Melville. "They called us and they said, 'We have four buildings, there's a fifth one if you're interested,'" Morea said many years later, recalling a contingent of about thirty outsiders, mostly Motherfuckers and Yippies, heeding the battle call.[30] "We saw our role as organizing the defense of the building—the defense when the police came and attacked, and also the defense against the right-wing and conservative students . . . who were preventing us from . . . getting resupplied from the outside," said Osha Neumann, Morea's de facto lieutenant in the Motherfuckers."[31] A contemporaneous report in *Ramparts* put the total number of people inside the Math Building at about sixty people, not a mathematician among them.[32]

Over the next four days the building resembled a Lower East Side crash pad more than a citadel of learning. "Lecture halls became communal living spaces strewn with piles of clothing, remnants of meals, backpacks, and bedding," remembered Neumann. "Blackboards that had been covered with equations now sprouted slogans—*Up Against the Wall* prominent among them—and drafts for manifestos [and] wood partitions between toilet stalls were torn down to build barricades."[33] The barricades consisted not only of the stall partitions but also, according to Morea, desks and other furniture. "We had it all booby trapped," he says. "If the cops came up the stairs, they were done."[34]

Abbie Hoffman described the scene vividly:

> In Mathematics Hall we, the denizens of the Lower East Side, held the fort. The Motherfuckers, Jim Fouratt, Anita—the whole gang was there, all battle-wise veterans by the spring of '68. Our colors were anarchist black or yippie pink and purple. . . . I came and went through secret passageways we had discovered . . . we taped the windows to keep them from shattering, and along with the food that was smuggled in came Vaseline and plastic bags—protection against mace. . . . Bodies sprawled all over; rock music blared. We talked endlessly of issues and strategies, fought boredom, fought fear, got hung up on how decisions were to be made, worked out evacuation routes, laughed, made love, smoked dope, sang, argued, and waited.[35]

None of the occupiers had firearms, according to Morea, but he and his crew did have knives, axes, and clubs, not to mention refashioned pieces of furniture.[36] Neumann recalled one particularly notable conversation about guns, though. Valerie Solanas, whom Morea had met on St. Marks Place and sometimes let crash at his apartment, showed up at Columbia and at some point during the occupation climbed through a window of the Math building to ask him a very specific question: What would happen if she shot someone? Morea said it would depend.[37] Two months later, angry at Andy Warhol's lack of interest in producing a play she'd written called *Up Your Ass*, she shot the prince of pop art as he was talking on the phone at the Factory.

After days of negotiations and tense confrontations outside Hamilton Hall, where various factions including police, faculty, and counterdemonstrating students had gathered, the police stormed the building at 2:00 a.m. on Tuesday, April 30. They soon cleared Low, Fayerweather, and Avery as well. That left the Mathematics Building.

"When they reached Math, it took the cops forty-five minutes to dismantle that barricade and get through the front door," remembered Motherfucker Johnny Sundstrom. "We were singing [and] chanting our demands," recalled another Math occupier, Tom Hurwitz. "Yet this was a strangely calm moment, as cops went about being moving-men, extracting the furniture, once a barricade, and passing it out, chair by desk by file cabinet." When the cops finally broke through, many of the students and outside revolutionaries were seated on the staircase, arms over their heads.

"As they marched past us, everyone was slugged on the back of the head by a plainclothes cop with a small club," said Sundstrom. "Some of them were using handcuffs as brass knuckles."[38]

On the upper floors, where the most militant occupiers had hunkered down for the final siege, things deteriorated quickly. "The police . . . were angry," said one participant. "I stood up when they entered and stated that I am coming. I was then hit on the head and, while on the floor, kicked and hit out of the room." Another protester recounted this same moment: "After smashing down the door, a group of 10–12 uniformed TPF [Tactical Police Force] police entered the room. As they jumped and climbed over furniture toward us one of them [yelled], 'Let's get these motherfuckers.'" By dawn 174 people from inside and outside the Mathematics Building had been arrested. The physical damage was not as extensive as one might think from the descriptions of what it was like inside during the occupation; in fact, the lion's share of the destruction appears to have been caused by the police raid, not the student occupation.[39] Nonetheless, by the morning of April 30, all five buildings had been cleared.

Tensions at Columbia flared again at the end of the school year. Once again the flashpoint was real estate. On May 14, the government unleashed COINTELPRO, its nationwide initiative aimed at surveilling and disrupting radical groups, on the New Left.[40] On the same day, the Community Action Committee (CAC)—a group formed earlier in the year to advocate for tenants' rights in the vicinity of Columbia—held a sit-in and demonstration at 618 West 114th Street, a twenty-five-foot-wide, five-story tenement that the university had purchased in 1965 (figure 21).[41]

After three years of eviction efforts, the four remaining tenants complained of "sickeningly unsanitary conditions and fire hazards" as well as a lack of heat in half the building.[42] The fifty CAC members who occupied the building in the afternoon were joined by a couple of hundred supporters who stayed on the sidewalk until, at the order of the university, police cleared the building at 4:00 a.m. In all 117 people, 56 of them students, were arrested for trespassing on university property, among them CAC head John Cohen and a scraggly-haired, disaffected man in his mid-thirties named Sam Melville, who reportedly was asleep in one of the upstairs apartments when the cops grabbed him. "In the holding cell [Sam] and John shared that night—the first of several—they formed a bond to destroy the establishment by any means necessary," Joshua Melville wrote.[43] They were arraigned and fingerprinted the next day and, according to the younger Melville, the FBI started files on both men.

21. Protester with Community Action Committee poster, Columbia University, April 1968. Estate of Louis Salzberg.

A few days later George Demmerle headed out to Brooklyn at the invitation of the Black Panthers. His destination: Fulton Street Park in Bedford Stuyvesant for a ceremony to declare May 19, Malcolm X's birthday, a "National Day for Black Unity" in honor of the slain civil rights hero. One of the only white faces in the crowd, Demmerle looked on as Bobby Seale of the Black Panthers, Sonny Carlson of Brooklyn CORE and others spoke about the importance of the Blacks arming themselves and organizing into groups of two or three to "kill whites, housen—gers and Uncle Toms." Poet Amir Baraka, of *Up Against the Wall, Motherfucker!*

fame, also performed a reading. Panthers kept all reporters and police out of the park, and after the speeches the crowd marched to Kingsbridge Housing Project and declared they were renaming it the Malcolm X Housing Project.[44]

Two days after the Malcolm X demonstrations in Brooklyn, Sam Melville narrowly escaped being arrested for a second time in as many weeks at Columbia. According to Jane Alpert's telling, Sam had hauled two large garbage cans up to the roof of Low Library on May 21 and was preparing to throw them down onto the swarm of cops below when two of them grabbed him from behind. The police took Sam to an office downstairs and tied him to a chair with a telephone cord. Next, Alpert said, the cops hit him with their clubs until they heard an alarm ring down the hall and departed. Sam wriggled his way out of bondage and escaped.[45]

On the evening of May 22, Ben Morea headed uptown to the Columbia campus, where less than a month earlier he had holed up in the Mathematics Building. At a 6:00 p.m. rally on West 116th Street and Amsterdam Avenue, with Walter Teague and Tuli Kupferberg looking on, Morea joined Mark Rudd and fellow Columbia SDS chapter leader Ted Gold in condemning the university administration and calling on students to keep fighting on. "Morea urged the students to organize around force and violence," according to a police report, explaining that "the struggle at Columbia must lead to a revolutionary struggle."[46]

In all, more than seven hundred people were arrested at Columbia between April 23 and May 22, when there was a final occupation of Hamilton Hall. Among them were Robin Palmer for criminal trespass, criminal mischief, and resisting arrest; Walter Teague for inciting a riot and possession of a dangerous weapon; and Sam Melville for his part in the sit-in at West 114th Street. In addition, 120 charges of police brutality were filed against police. Rudd later said that the Student Afro Society was the key to the success, such as it was, of the Columbia rebellion. "Without the action of the SAS students holding Hamilton Hall for seven days [in April], the other four buildings would not have been occupied, the Harlem community would not have been mobilized to defend us, and the strike that followed the police bust never would have materialized."[47]

Melville must have been feeling energized by his first taste of the revolution, because the same month as his arrest at Columbia, he quit his job designing plumbing and HVAC systems at Syska Hennessy to protest the firm's involvement with a construction project in South Africa. Instead, he began teaching a class on air-conditioning installation at the Voorhees Technical Institute at 450 West Forty-First Street. Having left his wife,

Ruth, their son Joshua, and their roomy Upper West Side apartment three years earlier, Sam was now free of all the bourgeois trappings that had long felt antithetical to his worldview.

For George Demmerle, opportunity knocked louder than ever. Recognizing the FBI's growing fear of the Black Power movement in the wake of the Columbia sit-ins, he pitched his handlers on a scheme. Since his arrest the previous October in the death of an Oakland police officer, Black Panther cofounder Huey Newton had become a cause célèbre on the left. With Newton's trial set to begin in California in June, George convinced the FBI not only to let him throw a "Free Huey!" fundraiser but also to funnel contributions through some other undercovers to make himself look like more of a macher. The plan worked. George raised $4,000 for the Newton defense and raised his stature in the New York scene. What's more, the apparent success of the event caught the attention of Abbie Hoffman and elevated George's standing within the Yippies.[48] On that note, another scheme he was working on at this time—spiking the food at a Tactical Police Force dinner with LSD—would certainly have caught Abbie's attention had it happened.[49] In all events, by late May George was referring to himself—in FBI reports, at least—as being a member of the Yippie steering committee.[50]

All along, George Demmerle, whether as participant or observer, kept his eyes open for intelligence he could feed to his FBI handlers. That spring, amidst all the turmoil on campus and in the streets, several of the radical groups—USCANLF, YAWF, V&R, and others—joined to form an umbrella group called Co-Aim, short for Coalition for an Anti-Imperialist Movement. "Co-Aim is an alliance of organizations and individuals who agree on the need to take militant action to expose and fight the government's policy of aggression abroad and growing fascist repression at home," read a flyer produced by the group under Walter Teague's aegis in the summer of 1968.[51]

The group's first joint effort on April 27, a feeder march before the larger Parade Committee rally in Central Park, fizzled when "hundreds of plainclothes and uniformed police used brutal assault and made over 100 arrests" in Washington Square Park; one of those arrested was Walter Teague himself (figure 22).[52] Co-Aim members had been vocal about their disagreement with the Parade Committee's decision to give Mayor Lindsay—a "banker-politician whose loyalty to the war-making establishment is underscored by the fact that he will also speak at the pro-war 'Loyalty Day' parade on the same day"—a speaking spot and planned to disrupt the proceedings in Central Park.[53] Their plan was to "call upon

22. Walter Teague arrest, Washington Square Park, April 27, 1968. Walter Teague Collection.

people to leave the Lindsay and come join us in support of the Columbia students in the liberated buildings."[54]

Carola Hoffman, the teenage runaway who'd been taken under the wing of Palmer and some of the older Yippies, pinpoints this day as when she really joined the Movement. "When the cops came in swinging, I guess you could say that's when I became radicalized," she reflected. Later in the day the nineteen-year-old Hoffman found herself up on the same stage in Central Park with the Coretta King and Dave Dellinger at the main event. In the spur of the moment, she even stepped up to the mic in front and told the crowd of more than eighty thousand what had just happened in Washington Square. "I was nervous as all hell," she recalled, "but after that I got really active."[55]

Not to be discouraged, Co-Aim planned a do-over for May 18. This time Teague and his compadres were well prepared. The night before, Dave Hughey, the twenty-one-year-old son of a Southern Baptist minister and sometime boyfriend of Pat Swinton, broke open the heavy door to the Washington Square Arch. Unobserved, Hughey made his way to the top, two banners and a CB radio in hand, and settled in for the night. He bided his time until the next afternoon, when hundreds of demonstrators congregated around the fountain in the park. Following Teague's instructions, the protesters began to circle the fountain like a school of fish. Teague described the scene half a century later:

> This was my idea: Start in the center of Washington Square and march in a circle. No beginning, no end. So [the cops] wouldn't know where to attack and they wouldn't know where the circle was going. To keep their attention, there was Dave Hughey in the monument. When I radioed him, his job was to throw a big NLF flag over one side and a big sign over the other that said, *The Streets Belong to the People*. The cops started banging on the metal door, but they couldn't get in. At that point, we broke the circle and went through the Lower East Side. And for an hour or two, the police couldn't catch us. We had bicycle spotters, young people from high school who volunteered with CB radios to watch if the cops were coming.[56]

Leading the police on a "hare and hounds chase," according to the *New York Times*, the marchers, Viet Cong flags held aloft, snaked through the East Village and coalesced for a final parade up Third Avenue that ended at Union Square Park (figure 23). Key Martin, head of YAWF, gave a speech before the crowd disbanded, all with no arrests or violence. "I think the police deserve congratulations," the executive director of the New York

23. Anti-imperialism march, East 4th Street at Bowery, May 18, 1968. Photograph by Bev Grant/Getty.

Civil Liberties Union said afterward. "I've had no reports of misconduct."[57] The lack of conflict with law enforcement was significant. "This time we'd marched in the street with no interference from cops, so it was seen as a bit of a victory," recalled Carola Hoffman.[58]

Throughout the spring and summer, the Veterans & Reservists continued to conduct their own demonstrations too. On April 14 they sponsored a march of eighty men from Columbus Circle to Union Square. Walking four abreast and carrying signs that read "Reservists Resistance" and "National Guard Not Going," the participants—most of whom were in their twenties, the *New York Times* observed—encountered some prowar hecklers along the way. At Broadway and Forty-Sixth Street, one hostile onlooker shouted out, "I spent four years in the Army, buddy, four years!" to which one marcher replied, "Three years here, baby," and another, "Six years, baby, six years."[59]

Two months later, another V&R-sponsored demonstration took place outside the Warner Theatre on Broadway between Forty-Seventh and Forty-Eighth Streets, where the John Wayne movie *The Green Berets* was premiering on June 19. About 150 picketers, including Palmer and Myron Shapiro, showed up, toting signs saying things like, "Up Against the Wall, John Wayne," and "Green Berets—Saga of the Fascist Terror" and waving their trademark Spirit of '76 and Viet Cong flags.[60] The *New York Times* film critic disliked the film as much as the antiwar protesters: "The 'Green Berets' is . . . unspeakable, stupid . . . rotten and false. It is vile and insane. An outrage . . . sick. The right-wing extremist's ideal of what we ought to be."[61] It was low-hanging fruit, too easy almost, for the radicals who usually preferred to call out liberal leaders for their moderation.

By the middle of 1968 there was increasing worry among radicals about infiltration. On June 21, nineteen days after Valerie Solanas shot Andy Warhol and seventeen days after Bobby Kennedy was assassinated, George Demmerle faced the closest thing to an interrogation he had ever experienced. The Progressive Labor Party members, humorless and dogmatic to the end, were still trying to figure out what to make of this high school dropout who was so eager to join their ranks. On this early summer day, George was summoned to an apartment in Brooklyn and from there invited by his two interviewers for a stroll through the Botanic Garden. "The whole background of George was gone over from childhood on," according to an FBI memo. On the walk George expressed some frustration that he had never had much chance to apply what he had learned in the study groups. After all, one of the teachers had given him good marks, saying he was "very enthusiastic and eager to learn and probably was the most vocal and read more than anyone else in the group." George's interviewers told him that they did not think his current job had much potential in terms of advancing the communist cause and decided to punt on his candidacy. "It would be best if both had a chance to look each other over," he was told.[62]

Undeterred, Demmerle kept playing the informer, veering sometimes into the role of entrapper. One day around this time, Walter Teague was at the USCANLF loft in Chelsea when he heard a knock on the metal door. Looking through the peephole he saw George and, against his better judgment, agreed to let him in. Demmerle proudly presented Teague with a spiked metal object, a crow's foot or caltrop, designed to puncture tires and wound the feet of horses. Being a welder by trade, Demmerle said, he could produce a bunch of these things that they could use to topple mounted police. He also tried to interest Teague in some giant fireworks—"small bombs, big enough to blow something up," according to Teague—that he claimed to have a line on. At that point Teague told him, "Look, I don't want any part of what you're about; it makes no sense what you are doing." As Teague later explained, "He was just trying to get me to go, 'Oh yeah, let's get a lot of those and fuck up the police.' But my goal was never to fuck up the police. Police had guns! They had the law on their side!"[63] Teague's failure to bite aside, though, the FBI thought George was doing a great job, and in June it gave him a raise from $100 to $125 a week. In the margin of the FBI memo proposing the raise, one senior FBI official wrote "fully justified."[64]

Chapter 8

Summertime Blues

UNDER LYNDON JOHNSON, liberalism had come to stand for the federal government's use of the country's postwar bounty to address long-standing inequalities—both racial and economic—throughout society. Shouldn't every card-carrying member of the left be able to get behind this idea? Well, yes, and for a while, until the war reared its ugly face, Johnson was quite popular among young, college-educated people. Take Robin Palmer, for example: "I was in my car on Eighth Avenue and 42nd Street when Johnson gave his speech in Congress calling for the passage of the '64 Civil Rights Bill," he said. "At the high point of the speech he said, 'And we shall overcome!' and I stopped the car and got out and did a big cheer for Lyndon Johnson."[1] Palmer couldn't contain himself. "You fucking LBJ, you great motherfucker. I'm proud to be an American."[2]

By 1968, however, liberalism no longer stood for food vouchers, work programs, and desegregated schools, as far as the New Left was concerned. Instead, it represented not only political moderation and cooptation but also the preservation of the kind of old-boy power structure that needed to be upended. Most important of all, it connoted an insufficiently militant opposition to the war. "Liberals who didn't work the live-long-day to end the war were worse than hawks—they were hypocrites," said Carola Hoffman.[3] This way of looking at the world echoed something Martin Luther King had said more than five years earlier: "I have almost reached the regrettable conclusion that the Negro's greatest stumbling block is not the White Citizens Council or the Ku Klux Klanner but the white moderate who is more devoted to order than to justice."[4] A similar analogy was frequently drawn to the "Good Germans" of the 1930s, without whose tacit acquiescence the Nazis likely would not have been able to seize power and commit genocide.

While George Demmerle had not succeeded in tempting Walter Teague with his offer to provide him with "fireworks," his FBI report card in June told a tale of almost superhuman spy stamina. Since mid-February, while still holding down a full-time job, Demmerle had attended twenty-seven Movement meetings, written up forty-three reports, and given his handlers fifty-five new names of those traveling in radical circles. These numbers were significant not only because they reflected his diligence but because they hinted at the chain reaction of protest groups, militant organizations, activist subsets, political zealots, mischief makers, student coalitions, and hippie dropouts that were molting, mutating, and multiplying on what felt like a daily basis. While in our current day of scalable social media the idea of a few dozen people chanting anti-imperialist slogans can seem almost quaint, in the later years of the 1960s, many people truly believed with an optimism powered by anger that a small group—that is, their small group—could catalyze massive change. That self-assurance and sense of destiny, however, could also lead to peripheral blindness that could prove fatal.

More than eight hundred people attended the SDS National Convention that was held in East Lansing, Michigan, on June 9–15, 1968, and accounts of the week provide a good snapshot of the influential student organization in the weeks leading up to the Democratic National Convention. The central and growing conflict, already on display at Columbia and other campuses earlier in the year, lay between an old-line Progressive Labor caucus, very much in the minority in terms of numbers, still clinging to its working class–centric view of the world, and the existing leadership of SDS, the so-called National Office, which had embraced the New Left position that true change was more likely to come from the coalition of teachers, social workers, and technocrats, an alliance that a group of SDS leaders referred to as the "new working class" in their 1967 "*Port Authority Statement*."[5] At one point more than half the convention delegates in the hall stood up and, with clenched fists raised, chanted "PL Out!"[6]

The Motherfuckers, still officially the Lower East Side chapter of SDS, contributed to the chaos and were arguably the biggest thorn in Progressive Labor's side. Wrote Ann Gordon in *SF Express*:

> It is funny to watch the Motherfuckers play with PL: they have a sense of fun about their politics which is lifesaving at conventions

> and they literally tease PL—a group never accused of having a sense of humor. [The Motherfuckers'] free-wheeling "life-style"—appearance, likes, dress, language, and again humor—are suited to their philosophy and their base in the East Village. The Progressive Labor Party takes its role as a revolutionary party very seriously, looks very straight, is interested in organizing the working people of the country.[7]

According to a report in the Progressive Labor newsletter in October, the Motherfuckers "interrupted debate and shouted down any speaker with whom they disagreed, particularly when the speaker was a member of PLP. Their behavior at the Convention disrupted constructive political debate, intimidated people new to SDS, and gave the meeting at times the aura of a fascist gathering."[8] At one point the Motherfuckers staged an elaborate marriage ceremony between one member dressed up as a worker and one as a student. This was upstaged soon after by the theatrics of Motherfucker Osha Neumann. "I seized the microphone during an interminable debate between non-ideological new lefties and the Maoist Progressive Labor Party faction," he wrote in his memoir. "Dropping my pants, with my penis flapping in the wind, I condemned intellectual masturbation."[9] Not taking any aspect of their membership in SDS seriously, the Motherfuckers' chapter report was a poem about Molotov cocktails. Their one attempt at adhering to procedural convention—a proposal for "The Destructuring of SDS"—was voted down by a large margin.[10]

In addition to the significant political and tactical differences between the approaches of PL and the SDS leadership, there was another reason for all the anti-PL sentiment: By this point, it was clear that PL was engaged in an all-out power grab of SDS. "Unable to organize a mass base on its own," wrote sociologist Harold Jacobs, "PL eventually decided to take control of SDS or, if that proved impossible, to prevent SDS from functioning effectively." In one way, though, PL did have a leg up on the rest of SDS, says Jacobs. "When PL fought for its politics it had the advantage of disciplined organization and greater facility with Marxist terminology over its loosely organized and ideologically heterogenous SDS counterparts."[11]

Perhaps the most notable thing about a convention characterized by chaos and a total lack of decorum was that nothing was accomplished. No bills were passed, no rifts repaired. "The SDS convention hall represented at times a circus," wrote Gordon in *Connections*. "Members laden with assorted literature wandered in and out of the room, lined up at microphones to take part in mass 'discussions,' lobbied in corners, jumped on the stage to sit behind the chairman rather than in front, slept on the uncomfortable chairs, and sometimes listened."[12]

The month leading up to the Democratic National Convention was a busy one for Movement members, even those not planning to attend the Festival of Life in Chicago. In July Co-Aim—the umbrella organization spearheaded by Teague and including groups like Workers World Party, USCANLF, Veterans and Reservists, and YAWF—held the Action Conference at the Hotel Diplomat at 108 West Forty-Third Street. The flyer for the event neatly summarized the growing extremism: "The repressive war currently being waged against the people of Vietnam and Black America is not in the interests of the vast majority of the American people who have the right to stop it by whatever means necessary."[13]

George Demmerle, along with about fifty others, attended a Co-Aim meeting to plan an upcoming demonstration outside the Waldorf Astoria designed to test a recent New York State Supreme Court ruling on the right to public protest. It is not known for sure whether Palmer was at this gathering but, if he wasn't, perhaps it was because he was out celebrating the fact that the charges against him in connection with his involvement in the Columbia occupation had been dropped that day.[14]

A few weeks later, on July 23, Henry Kissinger, at this point serving as foreign policy advisor on Nelson Rockefeller's stealth campaign for the Republican presidential nomination in addition to his ongoing professorial duties at Harvard, squared off against Vice President Hubert Humphrey in an auditorium at Columbia University. The establishment aura was shattered when Sharon Krebs and YAWF leader Key Martin ripped their clothes off and hoisted a pig's head in the air. The stunned audience watched as the pair marched to the front of the room and deposited the bloody head, now on a silver platter, in front of Kissinger.[15] The two rabble-rousers were quickly arrested for "inciting to riot and disorderly conduct," and bail was set at $1,000. It was the first documented instance of this porcine provocation, one that would become the signature stroke for Krebs and some of her crazier companions over the next year.

The rally outside the fundraising dinner at the Waldorf-Astoria for Hubert Humphrey that same evening attracted about a thousand people, many of them members of the groups under the Co-Aim umbrella. A wooden speaking stand had been erected on the west side of Forty-Eighth Street and Park Avenue, flanked by a Viet Cong flag on one side and a thirteen-star American flag on the other. Palmer was the emcee that night.[16] "This is the flag I am proud of," he told the crowd, placing his hand on the Viet Cong flag. "This flag, or rather its counterpart, the 50-star flag, is the flag I am ashamed of."[17] Far more shocking was what Palmer said when he introduced Rubin, who had recently been injured in a police raid of his apartment. "Jerry Rubin is someone that we care more for his hairline-fractured coccyx than all the shattered bones in Robert Kennedy's head."[18] Radical words even in these tumultuous times.

After waving signs ("Keep America Hump-free"), chanting ("GI's die, politicians lie") and scuffling with the police in front of the hotel, several hundred of the demonstrators embarked on a march through Midtown Manhattan. Palmer and Krebs were two of thirty-six people arrested for protesting outside the Waldorf. Most of those arrested ended up being charged with misdemeanors but Sharon was hit with the much more serious charge of incitement to riot.[19]

The scene in Greenwich Village continued to be a lawless, filthy mess, as a *New York Times* article, "Derelicts and Hippies Are Making Washington Square a Nightmare Area," attested. "Each night a youthful mob, clamorous and raunchy, foregathers under the arch. Holy Trinity Chapel . . . had defecation in their confessionals and one case of attempted rape. The derelicts were so menacing that . . . Village shopkeepers said panhandlers and rowdies were scaring away customers."[20] Amid this lawlessness, the FBI circulated a tip sheet to Demmerle to help get his creative juices flowing. Suggestions for stirring up unrest within the Movement included "taking advantage of personal conflicts between New Left leaders" as well as creating the impression "that certain New Left leaders are informants" and "drawing up anonymous letters regarding individuals in the New Left" and sending them out to parents, neighbors, university officials, and politicians.[21]

Meanwhile, in Brooklyn, center of gravity for the Black Panthers in New York City, tensions were rising between cops and the Black revolutionaries. Physical altercations ensued when police tried to break up an unpermitted rally of about fifty people outside the Nostrand Avenue headquarters of the Black Panthers on the afternoon of August 1. When law enforcement attempted to stop twenty-year-old Gordon Cooke from using a bullhorn to address the crowd, the police claimed, he shouted profanities and assaulted them before fleeing on foot. Cooke and a seventeen-year-old named Darrell Baines were busted for harassment and resisting arrest, though New York City Panther minister of defense, eighteen-year-old Jordan Ford, denied Cooke's involvement in the physical altercation.[22]

Two other incidents involving the Black Panthers made the *New York Times* in the next month as well, an indication, according the Panthers' attorney Gerald Lefcourt, that "a general roundup of the Panthers is on the move now."[23] On August 21 three Panthers—George Correa, Daryl Baines, and John Martinez—were arrested for assault when cops arrived on the scene of a trash fire in front of 780 Nostrand Avenue to provide cover to the firefighters who were being pelted with bottles and rocks. At the hearing at the Brooklyn Criminal Court building on Schermerhorn Street two weeks later, two dozen local SDS members, including Mark Rudd, demonstrated on the sidewalk before joining a small group of Black Panthers in the sixth-floor courtroom. During the proceedings, dozens of off-duty cops who had been unable to fit into the courtroom attacked a group of several Panthers, sporting black berets and necklaces of machine-gun shells, in the hallway. The intimidation tactics did not end there. Brooklyn Panther boss David Brothers was kicked numerous times, a young Panther named Thomas McCreary had his head bashed, and a *New York Times* reporter was kicked in the shins.[24] Brothers subsequently filed a formal complaint with the Police Civilian Complaint Review Board. Ten days later "Captain Ford" and four other Panthers were arrested in Brooklyn for involvement in two separate incidents—a demonstration in front of the Seventy-Third Precinct in the Brownsville neighborhood and, farther afield, a fire in Baltimore.[25]

As the Democratic National Convention approached, Demmerle and Palmer were seeing a lot of each other, not only at Yippies meetings (and the filming session for the Yippies movie) but also at the regular Veterans & Reservists meetings. On Monday, July 29, for example, both men showed up at 5 Beekman Street to plan the group's participation in the upcoming Co-Aim march from Herald Square to Times Square. At this same meeting, the group discussed the possibility of a V&R contingent going to the DNC.[26] Over the next few days, a final decision was made for them to travel together to Chicago, even though the Chicago Yippies, who knew firsthand what Mayor Richard Daley was capable of, had been telegraphing their own grave doubts. "If you're coming to Chicago, be sure to wear some armor in your hair," warned *Chicago Seed* editor Abe Peck in an August 5 article distributed by the Liberation News Service.[27]

On August 9 the New York office of the FBI put in a request to the Washington, DC, office for approval for Demmerle to travel to Chicago with one of three groups—V&R, Co-Aim, or the Yippies. "The source has approached Abbie Hoffman, Yip leader, with the idea that someone should act as liaison between the various groups in Chicago, and he expressed his willingness to them to act as such if Hoffman so desired," according to the written request. "Hoffman was receptive to the source's idea but did not commit himself to the source."[28] Not included in the travel request was the fact that Abbie had asked Demmerle and Palmer to serve in his security detail, an overly official-sounding term for what the role actually called for.[29]

At the August 12 meeting of V&R—which was chaired by Demmerle, a sign of his acquired credibility and stature, and attended by fifteen people—the timeline and logistics for Chicago were set. They would leave at 6:00 p.m. on August 24 by car; members were instructed to bring helmets, gas masks, canteens, and medical supplies but leave anything illegal behind. Demmerle's travel approval came through on August 15. "While he may more logically fit with the Veterans & Reservists Against the War in Vietnam, he may also be able to put a foot in two groups and maintain liaison with the Yippies while in Chicago," the memo from the DC office stated. "Since the latter is such an unpredictable, volatile and unconventional group, it is felt coverage of this group should be as thorough as possible." And: "Consistent with the informant's security, therefore, he must make every effort to excuse himself from meetings or other situations in time to afford the Chicago office as much advance notice as possible."[30] What was not written down in any memos was George's other set of marching orders from his government minders: to provoke as much mayhem as possible in order to make the radicals look as bad as possible.[31]

On Saturday afternoon, August 24, a handful of V&R members, including Demmerle and Palmer, piled into a Volkswagen and a rented station wagon and departed New York for Chicago. After losing a few hours to engine trouble, the two-car convoy arrived at 10:00 the next morning in Evanston, north of the city, where one of the member's army buddies had arranged a place for them to stay.[32]

Ben Morea never made it that far. He had set out for the convention with a girlfriend in her blue Volkswagen, stopping periodically to check in with organizers by phone. He kept hearing a worrying message: authorities were stopping blue Volkswagens on their way into the city, looking specifically for him. After hearing this for the third time, Morea gave up. "They had roadblocks, they had my picture, they had guns. So, I didn't go to Chicago."[33] Instead, Morea just kept driving all the way to California, switching and ditching rental cars along the way to stay one step ahead of the law.[34]

The Morea manhunt was just one in a long line of signs that Chicago was not rolling out the welcome mat for the radicals. Mayor Daley's thwarting of both Mobe and Yippie leaders' efforts to obtain permits to march in the city's streets legally and congregate and sleep in its parks spoke even louder than the steady stream of tough talk he pumped out over the airwaves and in the newspapers. "The Mayor knew his political territory was being threatened and challenged by forces that claimed national and symbolic, rather than municipal and civil, jurisdiction," wrote historian David Farber. And like so much undergirding the motives of the existing power structure, race played a big role. "More than anything else," according to Farber, "Daley feared that these 'outside agitators' would ignite and, maybe worse, organize Chicago's powerless blacks who were learning that they lived in the most segregated city in the North."[35]

In the weeks leading up to the convention, Hoffman did try to engage with the Blackstone Rangers and other Black groups in Chicago to encourage their participation, but they had been listening to Daley and decided that it was not worth their while to throw their lot in with the white radicals. Back in January and February the Mobe's Rennie Davis and Dave Dellinger had also tried to cultivate Black interest and involvement in the DNC demonstrations, to no avail. "It was not that black leadership was indifferent to the war," wrote David Farber. "It was just that they believed that they had more important issues to organize around."[36]

Another diehard Movement member who did not make it to Chicago was Charlotte Polin. After her earlier exchange of letters with her "Uncle Ho," she had flown on July 4, via London, to Hanoi to finally meet the North Vietnamese leader.[37] She would remain in the country, as a guest of the Committee for Cultural Relations with Foreign Countries, until November 8.[38] Polin's drive to commune with the Vietnamese had become truly self-destructive, causing her to combine prostitution with her part-time job at Chock Full o' Nuts coffee shop to raise funds, according to Demmerle's June 5, 1968, report to the FBI. The same report also notes that Polin had said she wanted to destroy Mount Sinai hospital before she left because they had told her she was crazy.[39] Walter Teague also was not in Chicago; he had gone to Japan at the end of July at the invitation of the largest peace group in the country.[40]

When they arrived in Chicago, George and Robin found they had missed the initial Yippie festivities—the nomination of a live pig, christened Pigasus, as their candidate for president. The pig had been obtained by a group of Yippies that included a bearded, martial-arts-practicing poet named Wolfe Lowenthal, a Black hippie named Vince (last name unknown), the popular folk singer Phil Ochs, Yippie co-leader Jerry Rubin's consiglieri Stew Albert, and Albert's girlfriend, known to all by the name Eldridge Cleaver had given her, Judy Gumbo. The day before, the group had driven to a farm outside the city where Ochs gave the farmer $20 in return for an oversized pig which they squeezed into the back of their station wagon and transported back to the city.[41]

The next morning, the unlikely crew of livestock herders, along with Rubin, pushed and tugged the 150-pound swine out of the head shop on North Wells Avenue where they had stashed him for the night and back into the car. When they arrived at the Civic Center the plaza was full of press—as well as cops. "[Pigasus] was born in Montana, studied law by candlelight [and] is affiliated with the Roman Catholic and Protestant churches in addition to being a Jew," stumped Joel Tornabene aka Super Joel, famed for placing flowers in rifle barrels at the Pentagon levitation and now one of the Yippie core team, his own baby slung papoose-style over his back.[42] Rubin was only a few lines into his campaign speech on behalf of Pigasus—"We stand for a garbage platform . . ."—when he was shut down by cops. Everyone involved in procuring the pig was arrested for disorderly conduct. According to the apocryphal account in Judy Gumbo's memoir, Jerry and Stew were sitting in their jail cell a short time later when a pot-bellied cop lumbered over to them. "Boys, I have some bad news for you," he said, managing not to crack a smile. "The pig squealed."[43]

Noticeably absent from the Pigasus campaign launch was Abbie Hoffman, the result of a falling out he and Rubin had had the previous day about the optimal size and aspect of the pig they should procure.[44] While their disagreement over whether to go with Abbie's smaller, cute pig or Jerry's bigger, ugly pig almost brought them to blows, the truth is that a larger stylistic clash had been building for some time. "Jerry wants to show the clenched fist and I want to show the clenched fist and the smile," Hoffman explained later that week. "He wants the gun; I want the gun and the flower."[45] Perhaps, or maybe the Yippies organization just wasn't big enough for the two gigantic egos. "If I ask myself today what triggered Abbie and Jerry's big pig fight, the answer is obvious—who . . . could claim to swing a bigger dick," wrote Gumbo a half century later.[46]

Waking up on Sunday morning, the Veterans & Reservists from New York, including George Demmerle and Robin Palmer, still had four very long days and nights in front of them. Late Sunday afternoon the V&R crew went into Chicago to scope out the scene at Lincoln Park. With just a year or so of Tai Chi study under his belt, Wolfe Lowenthal—"the captain of field maneuvers for the Yippie Karate Corps, his body bulging with muscles," as Ed Sanders described him in his fictionalized account—was instructing lines of demonstrators in the Japanese art of snake dancing, a technique used by protesters to break through walls of cops, while nearby a couple were heeding Hoffman's call for making love in public.[47] Lowenthal might have looked the part of a revolutionary bad-ass, but he always had his doubts. "My image as the anti-war movement 'super-warrior' was mostly illusion, smoke, and mirrors," Wolfe wrote later, "but in the land of the powerless, warriors were desperately sought."[48] The crowd that had gathered to listen to rock music that day was, at no more than two thousand people, disappointingly thin but not totally lacking in theatricality. Historian David Caute described the scene:

> When the band stopped, Humphrey Dumpty was introduced in the shape of a painted egg with legs, striding through the crowd as "the next president of the United States." Other Yippie clowns followed: a hideous Miss America; a symbolic representation of Mayor Daley's political machine; and a Green Beret done in "some sort of wax vomit pop art," as Norman Mailer noted, strolling through the park.[49]

It was at the concert on Sunday afternoon that the first serious police violence occurred. Ed Sanders had managed to get the sound system started by drawing electricity from a nearby refreshment stand, but the program had barely begun when the angry concessionaire pulled the plug. Waiting for Super Joel to arrive with a flatbed truck and some generators, Hoffman fumed while the crowd and the cops grew restless. As the flatbed finally rolled into sight, a bunch of kids jumped on board. The police refused to let the truck be used as a stage and arrested Super Joel.[50] The cops then swept into the crowd, taking swings at demonstrators along the way. Daley's troops seemed to know exactly who the Yippie leaders were because in a matter of minutes they had tracked down and destroyed a couple dozen walkie-talkies, the Yippies' only means of real-time communication. At some point amid the chaos the music started up. Minutes later, the police cracked Stew Albert's skull open with a baton while a green helicopter hummed overhead and the Detroit band MC5 hammered their way through their set from atop the truck.[51]

As it grew dark, the situation became even more confused. Hundreds of cops roamed through Lincoln Park, stomping out small bonfires. Tom Hayden and Wolfe Lowenthal, growing tired of the plainclothes policemen who had been assigned to them for the week, were caught letting the air out of the tires of their tails' car, though because of the swarm of protesters present the pair was not actually placed under arrest that night.[52] As the 11:00 p.m. curfew set by Daley approached, the police surrounding the park broadcast warnings over their loudspeakers to vacate. As the crowds spilled out of the park, some in a snake dance, the situation became even messier. Gumbo, who was still in the park with her recently bandaged boyfriend as well as Jerry Rubin and his girlfriend Nancy Kurshan, one of the founders of the feminist group WITCH (Women's International Terrorist Conspiracy), recorded what happened next:

> I heard a shout. I turned. Behind me, on a hill, a grey-white cloud billowed a few feet off the ground while in front of the cloud an army advanced. They looked to me like robots marching in lockstep, illuminated by globules of white light like landing lights on an alien spacecraft. . . . The spectral line advanced. Screams punctuated the gloom. I opened my mouth to breathe, only to inhale gas so toxic I might as well have snorted Drano. Tears burned a channel down my face; my eyes shut of their own accord. . . . I grabbed Stew's hand and ran down a slope and toward a tree. . . . Under it, famous poet Allen Ginsberg sat prophet-like in lotus position chanting *Oh-m-m-m-m-m* as if to remind the planet that even in the midst of chaos all life is interconnected.[53]

Out on the streets, the city was combusting: trash cans aflame, traffic snarled, shouts of "Motherfucking pigs!" and "Oink-oink!" greeting the paddy wagons full of gun-toting reinforcements. "This is fantastic," exclaimed Rubin. "And it's only Sunday night!"[54] As demonstrators and members of the press were boxed into a parking lot adjacent to the park and attacked by police, a group of several hundred took off through the streets toward the Loop chanting "Ho-Ho-Ho Chi Minh!"[55]

Early Monday afternoon the V&R cadre headed back into the city from Evanston. They stopped by the offices of the *Chicago Seed*, whose editor,

Abe Peck, despite his sense of foreboding about the event, had been working closely with the Yippies for months, and then the Mobe office, where they discussed the rally scheduled for later in the day in Grant Park.[56] Next the New Yorkers headed to Lincoln Park in hopes of being made marshals for the demonstration. Donning helmets and gas masks, the Veterans & Reservists posed for photos with their banner. Nearby shouting was heard: *Tom Hayden's been arrested!* It was true. The SDS figurehead had been sitting quietly in the grass with Wolfe Lowenthal when a police wagon rolled up behind them and put Hayden under arrest for the tire sabotage caper the night before. Fearing for Hayden's safety if left alone with the cops, Lowenthal told them to arrest him too. A crowd of demonstrators followed the two martyrs to the station.[57]

The Yippies and other radicals were only able to take to the streets in Chicago because of the blessing of the Blackstone Rangers, by far the biggest and most powerful Black gang in the city. Despite its members having received strict instructions to make sure they were out of town during the DNC to have airtight alibis in case the protests became violent, the Rangers told an intermediary, Jerome Washington, a Chicagoan and according to Paul Krassner the "first black Yippie leader," that the white radicals were welcome. "We never could have come if they hadn't okayed it," Washington told Krassner. "They really owned those streets."[58]

From the police station, Demmerle, Palmer, and the others proceeded to Grant Park in time to join the rush of bodies up the hill to the statue of John Logan on horseback. Robin, in his green Levi's, went charging ahead with the NLF flag and joined several others in scaling the statue. Sitting on the tail of the horse, he handed his flag up to another protester at the top. Soon the cops arrived, and all the demonstrators fled except for one young kid who had to be forcibly removed from atop the statue. The Veterans & Reservists then went to get a bite to eat and check in at a Yippie crash pad known as "the Theater."[59]

Later that day, back in Lincoln Park, the V&R crew were carrying their banner at the front of a march when they were jumped by several policemen (figure 24). One of the team was tackled, held down, and sprayed in the face with mace. The play-by-play for the next few minutes is heavily redacted in available FBI documents but is rife with action verbs: *screamed, forced, questioned, clubbed, stripped,* and *drew (his gun)*.[60] Most of the Veterans & Reservists scattered and then met at the car to drive back to Evanston, missing some of the worst looting and violence that took place in the early morning hours.[61] Two of them, selected for their clean-cut

24. Veterans & Reservists members in Chicago, with George Demmerle on left, August 1968. Estate of George Demmerle.

looks, had to drive back to the Eighteenth Precinct to bail out one of their brothers in arms who had stuck around and been arrested. The three of them finally made it back to Evanston at about 4:00 a.m.[62]

On the morning of Tuesday, August 27, clouds of tear gas still hung over Lincoln Park. After lunch the V&R members staying in Evanston drove to the park, where Abbie Hoffman had appeared sporting a judo jacket and sipping a codeine concoction for his sore throat. His hourlong monologue to a small crowd that followed was partially broadcast on the New York counterculture radio station WBAI: "Our thing's for TV. Fucking Mobes, they want to get on *Meet the Press*. We don't want to get on that. What's that shit? We want *Ed Sullivan*, the *Johnny Carson Show*, we want the shit where people are looking and digging it."[63]

In the early evening, Bobby Seale addressed the crowd of two thousand people. "Get your shotguns, get your .357 Magnums and get your .45s and everything else you can get," the Black Panther leader exhorted the crowd, while local Panther head Fred Hampton looked on. "If the pigs treat us unjustly tonight, we'll have to barbecue some of that pork."[64] From the park the Veterans & Reservists joined a group of people, including some Black Panthers, marching to support striking bus drivers at a garage to the north. On the way they skirmished with a cluster of right-wingers who tried to grab their NLF flags before bailing on the expedition to the garage when it became clear it was a police trap.

Although city officials had denied Mobe and Yippie organizers permits to march and to sleep in the park, they had allowed them to use the Coliseum, an old sports arena, for a rally on Tuesday night. "Up against the wall, motherfuckers!" shouted that evening's emcee, Ed Sanders, before bringing on Dave Dellinger, then a hoarse Allen Ginsberg, and finally the folksinger Phil Ochs, who led a sing-along of "I Declare the War is Over" while draft cards were burned on the arena's oval floor and Viet Cong flags were unfurled from the balcony.[65]

After dinner, Robin, George, and the other V&R members returned to Lincoln Park, where a few hundred clergymen and other "respectable citizens" had come to support the protesters' right to remain in the park. The men of the cloth, sporting black armbands and singing pacifist hymns, encouraged demonstrators to gather around the twelve-foot-high cross they had brought with them.[66] Around midnight, the ministers carried the cross closer to where the police were assembled and many in the crowd, Palmer and Demmerle included, followed. The police announced that they were giving people five minutes to disperse. The crowd remained behind the cross until Palmer broke the stalemate by marching with his NLF flag into the no-man's land between the protesters and the police. Three plainclothes officers emerged from the sea of people, grabbed the flag, and took off for the safety of the police line, but not before Palmer hit one of them and fetched another flag, which he attached to the branch of a tree.[67]

Then came the police offensive. According to testimony by Allen Ginsberg, who was watching from a nearby knoll, "there was a burst of smoke and tear gas around the cross, and the cross was enveloped with tear gas, and the people who were carrying the cross were enveloped with tear gas which began slowly drifting over the crowd."[68] *Village Voice* writer Steve Lerner also witnessed the scene. "Huge tear gas canisters came crashing through the branches, snapping them, and bursting in the center of the gathering," he wrote. "Gas was everywhere. People were running, screaming, tearing, through the trees."[69] The clergymen dropped the cross and fled with almost everyone else. Ginsberg and fellow writers William S. Burroughs and Jean Genet were seen holding hands and running for the front doors of the Lincoln Hotel.[70]

Not everyone dispersed, however. Robin Palmer, with George Demmerle never far behind, led the crowd of 150 to 200 people through the street. Demonstrators began throwing rocks, breaking windows, and setting trash cans on fire.[71] At one point Palmer saw a police car and shouted, "There goes a pig, let's get him!" Demmerle egged Palmer on. "I remember going out trashing with George," Robin said. "We took a big chunk of concrete and put it in the back window of a Cadillac."[72] They did this to another half dozen police cars as well as some storefront windows.[73] By this point, the group of rioters was down to about fifty people. The Veterans & Reservists took their plain shirts off to reveal bright shirts underneath; they also switched helmets with each other to make it harder for the cops to identify them. Most of them made it back to the apartment in Evanston by 3:30 am. Not Robin Palmer, though: he was arrested and ended up in jail with Jerry Rubin.[74] Battlefield statistics on the night: a hundred protesters arrested, seven policemen injured, and sixty demonstrators requiring medical care.[75]

The next morning, Wednesday, August 28, the V&R squad drove into Chicago, parking two blocks from Grant Park. Hoffman had been arrested that morning for public lewdness, having written "Fuck" in magic marker on his forehead before entering a diner. In Grant Park the afternoon started calmly enough, with demonstrators lazing in the grass and police handing out flyers asking for cooperation. A Vietnam vet spoke from the grandstand, and Phil Ochs sang "I Ain't A-Marching Anymore." But then, just as former SDS head Carl Oglesby began to speak, a teenager who had climbed a nearby flagpole to lower the American flag was clubbed by cops. When a group of Yippies who had gathered around the flagpole hoisted some sort of rebel flag (reports differ on whether it was a red T-shirt or a Viet Cong flag), the police rushed in. Tear gas and billy clubs from the cops overlapped with shouts of "Kill the pigs!" Demonstrators lobbed rocks and bottles through the air. In the chaos Mobe manager Rennie Davis, who had raced over to organize a line of marshals to buffer protesters from the police and the National Guard, was clubbed in the head. Hayden, enraged, took the microphone and in an uncharacteristic loss of self-control screamed, "Let us make sure that if blood is going to flow let it flow all over this city." Dave Dellinger, sensing a point of no return, tried to talk the crowd down. "Get back! Get back!" he shouted and, amazingly, both the cops and the crowd pulled back. That did not stop the police from arresting Davis, however, along with Wolfe Lowenthal and several others.[76]

Demmerle, who had been feeling sick all day, was sent to scout the area south of Grant Park and returned to report that he had seen the National Guard with gas masks on, a sign of things to come.[77] The scene inside Grant Park was getting increasingly frenzied, as it became clear that the crowd was penned in on all sides; demonstrators could see the trucks of soldiers rumbling by and word was that all the bridges were sealed off. It became clear that a mass march to the amphitheater was never going to happen.

Somehow, amidst the mayhem, a new destination was set: the Hilton Hotel, just on the other side of Michigan Avenue. Keith Lampe, Ed Sanders, and journalist David Lewis Stein followed the crowd as it neared the footbridge, now blocked, and on past the statue of Abraham Lincoln, parallel to Van Buren Street.[78] Ahead, the Jackson Street bridge was open and the crowd—Hayden, Albert, and Gumbo among them—poured out onto Michigan Avenue.[79] Demmerle and some of the Veterans & Reservists had also made it to the lawn across from the Hilton, headquarters for the campaigns and delegates, and set up their banner along with some VC flags.[80] "It was dark or late dusk by this time," recalled Linda Morse, a Mobe staffer who had worked closely with Dave Dellinger to try to secure permits from Daley's office and was with him at this moment. "There were really brilliant lights shing on the crowd and people were chanting, 'The whole world is watching, the whole world is watching. Flash your light, flash your lights.'"[81] The crowd was up to several thousand people now. "Hell no, we won't go!" they screamed. "Dump the Hump! Fuck the Pigs!"[82]

Demmerle (figure 25) and some other V&R men slipped into a side door of the Hilton.[83] "Demonstrators, reporters, McCarthy workers, doctors, all began to stagger into the Hilton lobby, blood streaming from face and head wounds," wrote the *Village Voice*'s Jack Newfield.[84] The cops were now in the lobby of the hotel where they, famously, proceeded to the fifteenth floor and roughed up a suite of McCarthy campaign workers. Demmerle fled the hotel and reconnected with other members of his group. They walked around a bit but were spent. After grabbing a bite to eat, most of the group returned to Evanston.[85] Again, no Robin Palmer, though. He spent the night rampaging through the streets, inciting the crowd, and throwing more rocks and bottles. Shortly before 1:00 a.m. he was observed near the corner of LaSalle and Clark Streets shouting obscenities, continuing to throw objects, and ultimately being arrested for the second time in as many nights.[86]

Much of America, though stunned by what had happened in Chicago, was largely unsympathetic to the protesters; a University of Michigan survey taken two months later found that only 19 percent of respondents agreed with the statement that "too much force" had been used by Chicago

25. George Demmerle in front of the Chicago Hilton, August 1968. Estate of George Demmerle.

police.[87] The conflagration that historian Lewis Feuer called the "culminating achievement of hallucinogenic politics," however, in the words of Stew Albert was "a revolutionary wet dream" because it signaled to the most militant members of the New Left that this was war.[88] With Hubert Humphrey, Johnson's enabling aide-de-camp, now the official nominee of the Democratic Party and their worst fears about the police state confirmed, the leftist radicals had their work cut out before November 5.

Chapter 9

Let's Go Crazie

The radicalization and resolve that many Movement members felt as they returned to New York City from the Democratic National Convention indicated a growing polarization in the country—a polarization that, much like today's political climate, left little room for moderation or middle ground. "The Movement emerged committed to an impossible revolution; the Right emerged armed for power and a more possible counter-revolution; liberals barely emerged at all," wrote Todd Gitlin, who witnessed the bloodbath firsthand as a young activist.[1] Even twenty-six-year-old Linda Morse, an organizer for the distinctly unradical Fifth Avenue Peace Parade Committee since 1965, embraced violence for the first time. "Prior to the Democratic Convention I had believed that the United States system had to be changed, but the way to bring about that change was through nonviolent means, through nonviolent action, and through political organizing," she said in her testimony at the Chicago Seven trial.[2] All that changed when Daley denied protesters their constitutional right to march and the police unloaded on the largely defenseless crowd. "I think at that point I gave up on pacifism," she said. In the weeks after the convention, Morse began learning karate and how to shoot a gun.[3]

The violence in Chicago also proved to be a powerful marketing tool among the young, with SDS adding a hundred or so new campus chapters that fall alone. At the same time, some of the more moderate members of the Movement—the traditional antiwar types active in the Mobe, for example—were turned off. Chicago "scared the shit out of an awful lot of people," recalls Doug Dowd, an economics professor who was briefly Eldridge Cleaver's running mate on the Peace and Freedom Party platform that year.[4]

The fever pitch also brought formerly alienated camps closer together, and on the Lower East Side the chasm between the hippies and the political radicals narrowed. "While only last year militants looked down on the hippie and Yippie communities as undisciplined and hedonistic, since Chicago the two factions seem to have come together: the hip community is looking more militant and the militants are looking more hip," wrote Steve Lerner in the *Village Voice* in late November 1968. "They have learned from Chicago that they are more powerful together than apart."[5]

Gitlin described this marriage of convenience in more colorful language:

> The interface between "hippies" and "politicals" melted into a new creature: the hairy, anarchic, activist, implacable, creatively desperate "street person" whose life conditions admit no chance of reform solutions, who says with his actions: "Your schools, your offices, your shops, your army have vomited me up, and now your cops come to mop me up, but you can't take from me the only place you have left me, the place where I live and breathe my being, the base from which I launch my assault on your barbarism; I *will fight*.[6]

Even Ben Morea, the gnarliest Motherfucker of them all, and his fellow East Village anarchists realized their value systems now overlapped most closely with the hippies. "While they were utterly disgusted by everything about Flower Power, they recognized that, out of the whole white opposition, the dropouts were the group potentially closest to them," according to an anonymous pamphlet about the Motherfuckers. "[They] completely agreed with their basic conviction that work was to be avoided at any costs, that the American dream was so much crap and that life should be devoted exclusively to experiment with the perimeters of lived experience."[7] Perhaps more than anyone, Abbie Hoffman recognized the potential in this melding: "More and more people on the New Left started to do drugs, and more and more hippies started to go to demonstrations," said Paul Krassner. "Abbie saw that people who could be organized to go to a smoke-in could be organized to go to an antiwar rally."[8]

The events in Chicago were also the death knell of Democratic nominee Hubert Humphrey's bid to become the next president of the United States. Already despised by so many of the young members of the party for his reluctance over the summer to embrace an antiwar position, Humphrey's words in the wake of the violence in Chicago hardly endeared him to the radical wing of the party, to the extent they even considered themselves as being in the party. "I think we ought to quit pretending that Mayor Daley did anything wrong," the candidate told CBS reporter Roger Mudd. "The obscenity, the profanity, the filth that was uttered night after night . . . was an insult to every woman, every mother, every daughter, indeed, every human being. . . . You'd put anybody in jail for that kind of talk."[9]

Despite Humphrey's later attempts to walk back such comments with qualifications that Daley had "overreacted" to the protesters, the damage was done. Not even President Johnson's announcement of a halt to the bombing in North Vietnam and the commencement of peace talks during the last week of the campaign could save his vice president, who ended up losing the popular vote by less than one percentage point but getting trounced in the electoral college. The DNC debacle, historian Milton Viorst wrote, was the nail in the coffin of the Democratic Party's chance for victory: "The Democrats revealed at Chicago they were so deeply riven that they could not manage their own affairs, much less the nation's."[10] Looking back twelve years later, Abbie Hoffman agreed: "What happened in the streets had destroyed any chances the Democrats might have had of holding onto the Presidency."[11] Robin Palmer represented the far left's feelings when he said, "With the nomination of Hubert Humphrey, we, in a sense, gave up on democracy. Democracy was proving to be bankrupt."[12]

If Chicago was a knife to the throat of the Democrats, it was also a challenge to the student movement's previously democratic disposition. "By the fall of 1968, SDS was racked by an inner divisiveness which not only prevented important political work at the national level from getting done, but soon sapped the entire organization of its vitality," according to the editor of one of the early books on the Weather Underground, Harold Jacobs.[13] Many of its original leaders were gone and the organization was rife with factionalism. Of all the factions, Progressive Labor was the biggest thorn in the side of SDS leadership and the biggest clash in terms of both style and substance. "PL peoples a Tolkien middle-earth of Marxist-Leninist hobbits and orcs and speaks in a runic tongue intelligible only to such creatures," wrote journalist Andrew Kopkind. "The real world begins where PL ends."[14]

For Robin Palmer and many other members of the Movement in New York, Chicago would alter their trajectories and put them on course for violent collision the following year. "When Hubert Humphrey was [nominated] we became convinced that the system wasn't working and we were going to have to do something outside of the Democratic process to aid the Vietnamese," Palmer said twenty-five years later.[15] "Chicago was when I decided to become what I thought was a communist because this was Pig America. The citadel of democracy was now behaving like Nazi Germany. In those days I thought communism was good. I oversimplified it. An enemy of your enemy is your friend." Wolfe Lowenthal, who would later stand trial as one of the Chicago Seven, became similarly radicalized. "[After Chicago] I and so many other people started going in the direction of the ultra-Left and the violence. We were, in a sense, indulging how hurt we'd been by Chicago."[16]

Chicago was also a major turning point for George Demmerle, who had gone from trying to incite others to commit violence back in New York to running side by side with Robin Palmer through the streets, breaking car windows, and tangling directly with the police. "The government was committing more crimes than the people were. They were framing people, planting drugs on antiwar activists, breaking and entering," George reflected decades later. "The police declared war on the people [and] I said, 'This is not my government.'"[17] He noted this inflection point in a series of 2002 interviews with researchers at the University of North Texas. "After the Democratic Convention, I struck back and I struck back hard. I did everything I could to undermine the government."[18]

In Chicago Demmerle had already begun to display real camaraderie and concern for his fellow protesters. "He protected us many times," Veterans & Reservists member Lew Friedman recalled.[19] Was George truly looking out for his protester pals or just trying to build his radical bona fides? Both, probably. George would later claim that after Chicago he began to water down his intelligence reports, just enough to stay on the FBI payroll but not enough to damage the people in the Movement whom he considered friends by this point. In particular, he desperately wanted to avoid being called to testify against Palmer in the Chicago case. "I knew if I quit the Bureau, I would definitely be used as a witness," he said. "So, I figured I'd stay on, minimize my reports, make them as vague as I could."[20] He added in a separate interview, "I tried to protect as much as I could without the government saying, 'He is not worth a shit. Let's get rid of him.'"[21]

At a V&R meeting in the wake of the Democratic National Convention, George even ratted out a bunch of other undercover agents. What pig would do that? "I had their names, phone numbers, where they lived, the whole nine yards and I gave it to the press." With hindsight, George appeared to have at least some sense of the psychological dichotomy required of him. "I guess I had an element of schizophrenia, dual personality, alter ego, or whatever. But whatever I was doing I was that person. You know, it is like when a good actor becomes that person he is portraying."[22]

It is impossible to know exactly, more than fifty years later, what a person, especially an undercover informant living a double life, was thinking and feeling. If witnessing the violence in Chicago led to a broadening of worldview or even an epiphany for George, he would have been but one of many moved further left by the brutal or fascistic behavior by the state. Ken Wachsberger, who worked as a media coordinator for the Yippies in the early 1970s, called it becoming an accidental revolutionary. "I think a lot of our generation were accidental revolutionaries," he said. "We went to a legal rally and got the shit beat out of us."[23]

The cursive lettering on the awning of 504 West 112th Street could be seen from the steps of the grand Cathedral of St. John the Divine on Amsterdam Avenue: St. Marc Arms. The stately name and facade of the seven-story prewar building, however, belied its current station as a rooming house full of older, mostly minority, residents. In 1968, the St. Marc Arms along with eight other buildings on the block had been targeted for demolition by developers who wanted to put up a fourteen-story nursing home in their place. Vacate orders had been given and more than half the units in the buildings had been cleared out by the time the Community Action Committee (which had played such an important role drawing attention to Columbia University's aggressive real estate tactics in the months leading up to the campus uprising earlier in the year) and the 111th–112th Street Amsterdam Avenue Tenants Association held a demonstration in front of the building on September 25.

About a hundred people, mostly students, were gathered outside on the sidewalk and a policeman was posted at the door when a shaggily handsome man, tall and dressed in jeans and a work shirt, walked down the block with a stack of newspapers under his arm. Although there to protest as a member of the Community Action Committee—the group's leader, John Cohen, had become a close friend and mentor since they'd been arrested together at the sit-in in May—Sam Melville, less than a month shy of his thirty-third birthday, was also looking to sell some copies of the *National Guardian*, the left-wing paper where he had been working in the circulation department since quitting his job as a teacher at the trade school in the spring. Jane Alpert, twenty-one, was pleased when the spectacled stranger sat down next to her and introduced himself. "He caught my attention with his energetic stride when he was still halfway down the street," she wrote.[24]

More put together and affluent looking than the crowd of students and older Puerto Rican activists, Alpert projected a certain poise and purposefulness despite being young enough to still be in college. Jane described her physical appearance in her autobiography, *Growing Up Underground*: "An inch or two shorter than average; a sturdy, not glamorous, figure; dark brown hair which wouldn't grow long; pale skin; a broad Jewish peasant's nose; wide-set hazel eyes." Having graduated from Swarthmore a year earlier, the former classics major had been working at Cambridge University Press as an editorial assistant and, more recently, had begun taking graduate classes in classics at Columbia. Seated on a stoop, the two discussed communes and Sam's idea of buying property in upstate New York before walking down the block to get coffee. As they were parting, Jane gave Sam a check for a year's subscription, making sure to write her phone number on it first.[25]

Within a week of meeting they had slept together, and Jane had given Sam the keys to her apartment. For the next few weeks they spent every night together at her studio on 106th Street and Riverside Drive. "The combination of sexual love and radical ideology was more than irresistible," Jane wrote twelve years later in her autobiography. "It consumed me." Jane also saw a flash of Sam's budding revolutionary spirit. "This country's about to go through a revolution," he told her one night early on. "I expect it to happen before the decade is over. And I intend to be part of it."[26]

Wanting to carry on the tradition of irreverent street theater, but worried that the Movement's figureheads had lost some of their anarchic spirit in the wake of the Democratic National Convention, a group of a couple dozen activists drawn from the ranks of the Yippies and the recently defunct Free School began to loosely coalesce on the Lower East Side in the Fall of 1968. Their raison d'être was to call out mealy-mouthed members of the Liberal establishment who remained long on lip service but short on action when it came to the war.

Leading the charge of this amorphous and yet-unnamed cohort were

Robin Palmer and his live-in girlfriend, Sharon Krebs. Never far from the action was George Demmerle. "Abbie was out there promoting himself, so they started this new group," says Lew Friedman who knew Demmerle and Palmer from V&R meetings and had been with them in Chicago. In the early months the group's meetings were very informal: the get-togethers were organized by word of mouth and took place at someone's apartment, no one "chaired" the meeting, and they did not spend much time talking about political positions. And there were usually drugs. "So, there you were, high with your 'affinity group' in an East Village lair, bouncing ideas off each other," remembers Carola Hoffman, who had been working as a waitress at the popular nightclub Max's Kansas City while taking part in numerous actions with groups like the Yippies, USCANLF, and V&R. "Robin might suggest the basic action, but we all built on top of it in creative collaboration—like free jazz improvisation where one person lays down a riff and other players expand on it."[27]

Before the internet, one of the easiest and cheapest ways to promote a cause was with a can of spray paint, an activity that many radicals took to with zeal. At the time, the mailboxes that dotted street corners all over the city were painted red and blue, which meant that a strategically placed yellow star could instantly transform an item of U.S. government property into a pro-Vietnam piece of propaganda (figure 26).[28] In early November George was one of two dozen downtowners participating in a late-night stenciling blitz. Days earlier the crew had received a handout, a primer of sorts, that included such advice as "Always pretend to be mailing something" and "Everybody have a story for the pigs in advance." The tenth and final pointer reminded team members to "say twenty-five (25) 'Hail-Ho's'

26. Mailbox with Viet Cong star. Roz Payne Sixties Archive, University of Nebraska-Lincoln, Center for Digital Research in the Humanities, https://rozsixties.unl.edu.

sometime just before the job," a reference to the North Vietnamese leader Ho Chi Minh.[29] Indeed, run-ins with the police were not unusual on these missions. "When the pigs caught up to us, Crazy George and me laid flat on the sidewalk," Palmer told Sam Melville's son Joshua many years later. "It took ten blue meanies to scoop us into the paddy wagon. We yelled, 'Sieg Heil!'"[30] George and Robin were not the only ones to take up a spray can in rebellion. After being arrested during the Columbia protests in the spring, Melville himself had taken to tagging buildings around the Lower East Side with the words "George Metesky Was Here," a reference to the former disgruntled Con Ed employee who earned the moniker "Mad Bomber" for the dozens of explosions he set off around the city in the 1940s and 1950s.

The first notable post-DNC action by New York radicals came on September 10, when Co-Aim, YAWF, V&R, and USCANLF members joined in a Peace & Freedom Party-sponsored protest outside the Chrysler Building, where they believed the State of California had offices. The rally, in support of Black Liberation in general and recently convicted Huey Newton in particular, was attended by about two hundred demonstrators, including Robin Palmer, Carola Hoffman, Walter Teague, and the cowboy hat–wearing leftist lawyer Florynce ("Flo") Kennedy (figure 27).[31]

Born in Kansas City in 1916, Kennedy was a groundbreaking activist and lawyer who had already been writing, advocating, and lecturing for two decades by the time Movement people got hip to her. The daughter of a Pullman porter, Kennedy grew up with her parents and four sisters in a mostly white neighborhood of Kansas City during the depression before moving to Harlem in 1942. While working a series of low-level jobs, she put herself through Columbia's School of General Studies, graduating with a degree in pre-law in 1949. When she applied to Columbia Law School, however, she was rejected; only after meeting with the dean and threatening to sue the school did she become the first Black woman to matriculate. She graduated in 1951 and within three years had opened her own practice focusing mostly on matrimonial and criminal work.

Flo Kennedy was not just a breaker of ceilings but also a first-class wit who loved nothing more than lampooning the traditions and hypocrisies of the society she lived in, starting with an essay she published in 1946 called "The Case Against Marriage." In her autobiography she summarized her argument by asking, "Why should you lock yourself in the bathroom just because you have to go three times a day?" (The headline of a section of the same book arguing for the legalization of prostitution reads, "Nobody Ever Died from a Blow Job.") Flo was raised to think for herself and not

27. Flo Kennedy, shown at the Columbia University protests, April–May 1968. Estate of Louis Salzberg.

take any guff from anyone, especially those in positions of authority. "We were taught very early in the game that we didn't have to respect the teachers, and if they threatened to hit us we could just act as if they weren't anybody we had to pay any attention to," she wrote.[32]

The first major piece of street theater put on by the Yippies in the wake of the DNC took place at Pier 23 on the Hudson River on a warm Saturday at the end of September (figure 28). It featured a familiar face from the first day of the convention, Pigasus (or "J. Pigasus Pig," as he was referred to in a NYPD report). George Demmerle had been given the role of lead antagonist in the propaganda production. Unshaven and dressed in a black trench coat, he arrived early and pretended to be reading the *Daily News* as a crowd of a hundred or so people—including Abbie Hoffman, Sharon Krebs, Roz Payne, and Carola Hoffman—arrived carrying placards that said things like "Pig for President" and "Dump the Hump, Free the Pig."[33] They were all being observed, it would turn out, by a member of NYPD's Bureau of Special Services, John Finnegan.

Shortly after noon Lew Friedman, sporting the dark suit, white shirt,

28. Pig for President flyer. Estate of George Demmerle.

and sunglasses of a Secret Service agent, pulled up in his blue Volkswagen Beetle with the presidential nominee in the back. Wolfe Lowenthal, his left arm in a cast from getting cracked at the convention, and Robin Palmer carried the pig out to the pier, escorted by two men also dressed up as Secret Service operatives, Jack Godoy and Myron Kopchynsky, both of whom were revealed later to have been undercover agents (figure 29).[34] As the nomination ceremony began on the Gansevoort Street pier, George started getting into a noisy argument with the crowd around him and then pulled out a bowling ball with a fake fuse. In an act of patriotic valor, five fake Secret Service men tossed the would-be assassin in the Hudson River.

A grinning Demmerle was pulled out of the water and "arrested" by Godoy and Palmer, who was also in FBI attire and sporting wrap-around sunglasses (figure 30). (The Movement men playing Secret Service roles referred to themselves as the Pig Intelligence Guard, or P.I.G.)[35] George climbed into a car while the crowd of 150 marched through Washington Square Park to Tompkins Square Park for a "pignic" and a press conference (figure 31). Marching through the cobblestoned streets of Greenwich Village, demonstrators held signs saying, "Free Hubie," "Pig Power," and "Which is the real Hump?" The unredacted NYPD report provides an unusually clear look at who was there. In addition to the people described above, the list of thirty or so names included Jerry Chodek, Ramona Di Suvero, Maury Englander, Art Farrier, Paul Krassner, Keith Lampe, Myron Shapiro, and Walter Teague.[36]

At the presser, Abbie Hoffman, dressed in his American flag shirt, and Paul Krassner answered questions about the Pigasus campaign platform before Walter Teague, his patience for pig pageantry worn thin, urged the crowd to head up to the governor's office at Fifty-Fifth Street and Fifth Avenue to protest the recent arrest of Eldridge Cleaver. Some seventy-five people headed to the Astor Place subway station for the ride uptown. The pig was dropped off by car at the Noah's Ark pet store on Greenwich Street.[37]

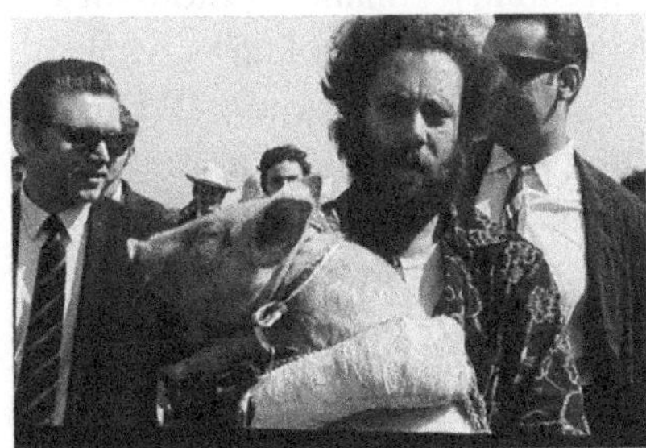

29. Wolfe Lowenthal with pig. Roz Payne Sixties Archive, University of Nebraska-Lincoln, Center for Digital Research in the Humanities, https://rozsixties.unl.edu.

30. George Demmerle after being plucked from the Hudson River. Roz Payne Sixties Archive, University of Nebraska-Lincoln, Center for Digital Research in the Humanities, https://rozsixties.unl.edu.

31. March through the Meatpacking District, with undercover agent Jack Godoy holding pig. Roz Payne Sixties Archive, University of Nebraska-Lincoln, Center for Digital Research in the Humanities, https://rozsixties.unl.edu.

The scene on the pier was another credibility-enhancing moment for Demmerle. As Jerry Rubin wrote later (and anyone who knows what the Hudson River was like fifty years ago would have to agree), "What policeman would be so devoted to do a thing like that? That was one of the freakiest guerilla theater acts ever." Rubin continued. "You got to be a little mentally unbalanced to live so many different lives. You got to be a little crazy," he concluded. "And it is these people who the government counts on for its information and convictions against us."[38] Fair point, especially when you consider that the undercover agents were incentivized financially to report—or manufacture—as much sensational intelligence as they could.

An *International Times* reporter visiting from London that fall described the Lower East Side as "a ghetto of mixed Puerto Rican, Afro & Hippie-population, an area where there have been several uprisings. The Motherfuckers are under constant threat of arrest and being wiped out."[39] Below 14th Street, it felt like things were ready to explode. The first week of October, tensions flared when the Workshop for Tactical Street Action, a group headed by Carola Hoffman to counter the increasing presence and perceived overreach of the Tactical Police Force on St. Marks Place, gathered on Second Avenue for a "Let the People Speak" meeting. Passing out leaflets, the demonstrators were met by a force of over two dozen policemen. "It was a real riot, with cops being knocked down, fires being set, etc.," said Carola (figure 32).[40] Eight people, including her, were arrested for resisting arrest and arson.[41]

The Workshop continued to try to "Liberate St. Marx" that fall,

32. Carola Hoffman at the Workshop for Tactical Street Action, St. Marks Place and Second Avenue, October 1968. Estate of Louis Salzberg.

organizing more efforts to push back against the "Pig Army that occupies our community." The effort was not without its humorous moments. Osha Neumann, arguably the number two man in the Motherfuckers, once walked up and down the block soliciting donations to the group's free store in a toilet bowl, a spectacle that attracted the attention of a beat cop. Onlookers chanted "Free the toilet! Free the toilet!" as Neumann was forced to put the porcelain throne in a trash can, where the cop proceeded to smash it to bits with his nightstick and arrest him for littering.[42]

One month out from election day the Black Panthers took the unusual step of joining forces with the Yippies to express disdain for the candidates and the system that enabled them. Under a page-wide headline in the *Berkeley Barb*, "YIPANTHER PACT," ran Eldridge Cleaver's essay alongside a companion piece penned by Hoffman, Rubin, and Albert. Both pieces echoed Dave Dellinger's comment from the spring that the war had to be won on the streets, not at the ballot box.[43] "The Republican Party and the Democratic Party have told black people to kiss the ass of the elephant and the donkey . . . the only recourse is to join in a second Boston Tea Party," wrote Cleaver. "There's nothing left for us to do but break up this crap game, to pick our money up off the wood and demand a brand-new pair of dice." The Yippies called for more zany acts of street resistance. "Don't vote in a jackass-elephant-cracker circus," they said. "We are the revolution. Nobody goes to work. Nobody goes to school. Nobody votes."[44]

Protests continued to meld the political with the absurd. On October 19, according to FBI files, several V&R members showed up at Trinity Church on Thirty-Fifth Street for a speech by Senate hopeful Paul O'Dwyer, a sixty-seven-year-old lawyer and New York City Council member who had first made his name in the 1940s opposing U.S. involvement in World War II and then in the 1950s defending people accused of Communist activities. This day, O'Dwyer was holding a campaign rally in his effort to unseat Republican Senator Jacob Javits. "During O'Dwyer's speech [Palmer] jumped out of his seat and started shouting at O'Dwyer calling him a liar, pig, hypocrite, and offering him a Viet Cong flag," noted the report. Another protester marched a Viet Cong flag to the front of the room. As a third person started to read aloud from a pamphlet, others threw flyers into the crowd. And then, from the back of the church, Robin and Sharon, nude but for the Viet Cong flags draped over their shoulders, paraded toward the front of the church. They were stopped about a third of the way up the aisle and, after a small scuffle, returned to the back of the church to fetch their clothes and retreat to the lobby. Another radical made a brief speech from the back of the church before they left.[45] Miraculously, no arrests were made.

In another instance, two dozen members of USCANLF and V&R showed up at P.S. 41 on the evening of October 21, where three hundred people were gathered for a political panel discussion titled "Which Way to Peace." On the stage that night again was O'Dwyer, a representative from Senator Jacob Javits's campaign, City Council member (and future mayor) Ed Koch, and State Senator Whitney Seymour. "These men are liars . . . they clothe themselves in liberal bedtime stories to put America to sleep," read a leaflet distributed by a group called the National Liberation Front of South New York that night. Of all the men on stage, O'Dwyer, the former city council and mayoral candidate, seemed to have attracted the ire of the most radical and theatrical segment of the downtown left.

The troupe—which this night included Walter Teague and Robin Palmer—was pulling out all the stops:

> Rising from various places in the audience, the hecklers unveiled a Vietcong flag, placed a pig's head on a platter at the foot of the speaker's platform and ran through the aisles of the school auditorium, shouting and singing. They shouted, "fascist pig" at Mr. O'Dwyer, and chanted "Long live Mao," and "Long live the National Liberation Front," referring to the political arm of the Vietcong. The audience of well-dressed people appeared momentarily stunned.[46]

An NYPD memo later confirmed that the person who'd placed the pig's head in front of O'Dwyer had been Sharon Krebs and that Carola Hoffman had been the one brandishing the Viet Cong flag; the same report named Palmer and Teague as the two men who led the chanting. (Also, in the crowd that night were three undercover agents: Jack Godoy, Myron Kopchynsky, and George Demmerle.) There were a dozen policemen on hand but O'Dwyer waved them off, and even allowed Teague on stage for a brief exchange of words. The evening ended with no arrests.[47]

With four days left until the presidential election, there was still reason for hope among Hubert Humphrey's campaign staffers as they prepared for Halloween night festivities at the Manhattan Center on West Thirty-Fourth Street. They had managed to find 2,800 people willing to give up their trick-or-treating plans to sit in an auditorium and listen to three hours of speeches. In the past two weeks the Democratic candidate had narrowed Nixon's lead from eight percentage points to one, leaving third-party challenger George Wallace in the dust.[48] The headliners that evening were liberal economist and elder statesman John Kenneth Galbraith and, hot off three starring roles in Hollywood that year, Shelley Winters.[49] Known best for her appearances in such hits as *Lolita*, *A Place in the Sun*, and *Phone Call from a Stranger*, the forty-eight-year-old actress had no way of knowing how off-script the evening would go.

While organizers were finalizing the run-of-show at the venue, another group was further downtown making its own plans for the evening. As the late autumn sun set over the Hudson River on that last day of October, George met up with Robin and Sharon at their West Village apartment. Indicative of the short-sighted militancy of the left, Humphrey remained in the crosshairs that night and not the Republican challenger Richard Nixon, who was holding a campaign rally of his own across the street at Madison Square Garden. "I'll tell you the truth," Stew Albert said later. "We didn't care between Hubert Humphrey and Nixon."[50] As Jeff Shero, editor of downtown alternative newspaper *Rat* and a former SDS organizer, put it a few months later, "A new logic emerged: if the destruction of Vietnam couldn't be halted by choosing between Nixon or Humphrey, or by staging the largest peace marches in history, the hour had arrived when the machine itself must be shut down."[51]

It was almost 11:00 p.m. by the time Winters welcomed Galbraith to the microphone. He had just begun his remarks when there was a commotion at the rear of the auditorium. As Galbraith tried to keep speaking, Sharon Krebs (figure 33), dressed in nothing but a pair of tennis sneakers, waltzed toward the stage. As she passed Robin's row, he made his way to the aisle and shed his trench coat. An older woman jumped up and started hitting Palmer with an umbrella, which compelled Teague to leap to his feet and, in his booming voice, shout, "Some of you are more upset by nakedness than you are by napalm!" In Teague's telling, a group of nuns in the audience, won over by his logic, began applauding.[52]

Palmer and Krebs were followed by another dozen or so protesters carrying VC flags and chanting the familiar refrain of "Ho-Ho-Ho Chi Minh." Another audience member grabbed Sharon and threw a coat over her, causing her to trip. "At this moment [Palmer] ran down the center aisle, completely nude, and picked up the platter and pig's head," according to the FBI report. "He proceeded to the speakers' platform and placed the pig's head on the speakers' stand" (figure 34). After presenting the pig's head to Galbraith, Robin paraded triumphantly around the stage, doffing his Uncle Sam hat to the crowd. Quick to the draw, Winters doused the nude provocateur with a pitcher of water and chased him off the stage. As the stunned audience looked on, Palmer then led several policemen on a ten-minute chase through the crowd until he was finally caught; he and Krebs were detained for almost half an hour but were not arrested.[53] They exited through a side door, unable to contain their glee.

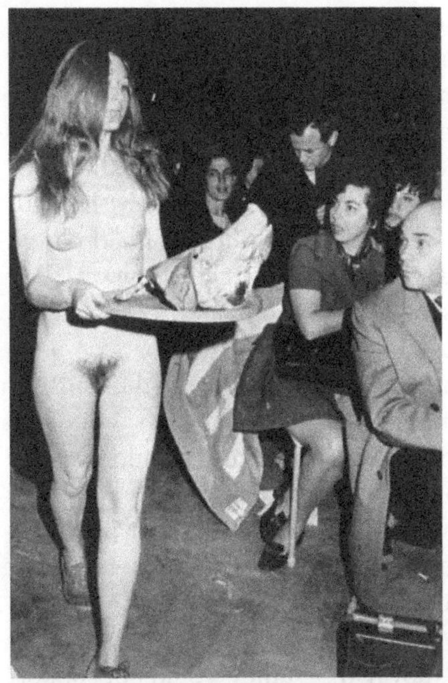

33. Sharon Krebs with pig's head, Manhattan Center, October 31, 1968. Estate of Louis Salzberg.

34. Robin Palmer with pig's head, Carola Hoffman with flag on stage, Manhattan Center, October 31, 1968. Estate of Louis Salzberg.

When the protesters had been chased out of the room, Winters took the microphone and compared the demonstrators to Hitler's storm troopers. "Nothing in my experience has prepared me for this political striptease," Winters said to the remaining stragglers. "When I see this, I see how the trouble in Chicago started." Galbraith, on the other hand, was not surprised to be the target of the left's opprobrium; he was aware how his decision to back Humphrey toward the end of the campaign had played on campuses and in coffeehouses. He was a bit distracted anyway. "My thought as I struggled on with my speech," he wrote later, "was that the man looked infinitely more indecent than the woman."[54]

For the Humphrey staffer standing in the wings, this was the end. "At that moment, as the campaign event turned into a shambles," the aide wrote two decades later, "I felt strongly that Humphrey would lose the election and that it would be a long time before the Democratic party would have the coherence and strength to govern again."[55] The night was etched in Palmer's memory too, not only because of his naked theatrics but also because of what the liberal politicians on stage symbolized. "This was a panoply of hypocrisy as far as we were concerned. All these people were totally unmasked that night because they had said they would not support Humphrey because his hands were dripping with blood from Vietnam, from his support of Johnson's policies in Vietnam," he said years later. "That's what this whole gathering was about, to show the country, to show the Democratic Party, to show the Republican Party that . . . it was more important to be a good Democrat that it was to be a good human being."[56]

The presidential election cycle ended for New York's radicals on the afternoon of November 5 in Union Square Park. By about 2:30, there were five hundred or so protesters—almost all high school and college students, according to a police report—gathered at the north end of the park. Jeff Jones, leader at that point of the New York Regional Chapter of SDS and a future Weatherman, was the master of ceremonies. Per a NYPD memo, after a speech from Steve Halliwell of Columbia SDS, performances by the countercultural theater troupe Sixth Street Players, and the burning of a flag with Richard Nixon's likeness on it, "Richard Robin Palmer, a member of the Veterans and Reservists to End the War in Vietnam, and one of the leaders of the Coalition for an Anti-Imperialist Coalition, who has three times in the recent past stripped along with his female partner, Sharon Krebs, in front of Liberal Party assemblages without official complaint, donned a pig mask and spoke as the officially endorsed candidate of the new left and Yippy [*sic*] movements."[57]

While Robin, George, and Sharon and other radicals were targeting national figures, local politics in the East Village had been getting increasingly complicated. Ground zero was the Fillmore East, San Francisco promoter Bill Graham's new venue on Second Avenue and Sixth Street. Since opening in March the former Yiddish theater had quickly become the place to play for any rock band worth its countercultural salt. Starting with Big Brother and the Holding Company on opening night, the spring and summer saw the likes of the Doors, the Who, Jimi Hendrix, Jefferson Airplane, and the Grateful Dead take the Fillmore stage.

By the fall, however, the venue's success was becoming its undoing. Local activists, led by Motherfucker Ben Morea, had been pressuring Graham to share the wealth they assumed he was accumulating with the community. "As we saw it," remembered Osha Neumann, "he was making big bucks off our culture and it was time for a little payback."[58] These feelings had been brewing for a few weeks already: at one meeting earlier that fall at the Common Grounds coffee shop on East Sixth Street, a plan had been hatched for George Demmerle to purchase eight quarts of chloroform, which activists would disperse at a paid concert at the Fillmore. This plan was abandoned when Graham agreed to "donate" $1,000 a month to the Motherfuckers for community projects, a type of arrangement perhaps more common a few blocks south in Little Italy.

In early October Morea, still spoiling for a fight, paid Graham a visit in his office. When the Motherfucker leader demanded that the promoter hand over the theater to the community one night a week, Graham said, "Over my dead body!" Morea responded: "That could be arranged." At this point Graham opened his desk, reached in, and took out three silver bullets. "The Hells Angels gave me these because they wanted me to do something, which I didn't do," Graham said. Morea grinned and responded, "Uh-huh. The only difference is their bullets are on your desk and our bullets . . ." he trailed off, letting Graham fill in the blanks.[59]

As a result, tensions were running high on the night of October 22, the occasion of a benefit for the Living Theatre troupe. After the first skit of the night was booed off the stage, WBAI radio host Bob Fass brought out Abbie Hoffman, who rapped about his experiences in jail. Two more speakers succeeded in driving many onlookers into the lobby to watch the Sixth Street Players. For the remaining audience, next up was the main event, the Living Theatre's performance of *Paradise Now*. "The actors stripped down to jockstraps and bikinis in the middle of the crowded stage and people climbed up curtains, speakers, scaffolds and ropes," reported the Liberation News Service.[60] Many in the crowd joined the actors in a state of disrobe.

As the performance concluded, the actors began chanting from the stage, "Open the Doors, Bring in the People, Occupy the Theatre," before a voice, a Motherfucker who'd commandeered the PA system, boomed from the speakers: "This theatre is returned to the community!" A shower of leaflets fluttered down from the balcony.

> Tonight the people return this theater to themselves. Originally our demands were modest, one night a week free for the people of the FREE community. Bill Graham (who within the archaic legal frames was technically in control of the theater) refused our demands. Now we take what is ours anyway. The theater now belongs to the people.[61]

From the stage, Morea (figure 35) and Neumann went on about Graham and how he was making a killing off the community and refusing to give anything back. The public address system was cut. No shrinking violet and not one to be pushed around, Graham charged out onto the stage and became embroiled in a shouting match with Morea. "Graham lectured on the facts of his owning the Fillmore and on how he disliked the do-nothing scum of the Lower East Side (in general) and asked his questions," reported the *East Village Other* in its next issue. "Motherfucker representative gave no answer, stunning silence prevailed, and then burst out with: Shoot-bomb-kill! And Graham told him to get the hell out of his place."[62]

Amidst all the shouting, a mimeograph machine had been wheeled down the aisle and as the debate continued reports were printed and sent out to the crowd outside. "FROM THE LIBERATED ZONE FREE PRESS BULLETIN: We have been in the free zone for only a short time—already are experiencing the real problems of freedom—Should we stay until we get exactly what we want or leave and come back next Wednesday . . ." By three in the morning Graham had had enough. "The only way you're going to take this theater is by killing me," he said. "I wish you wouldn't, but you can't take the theater and have me be a part of the operation." After another hour of negotiation, the microphones were turned back on and Julian Beck, one of the Living Theatre cofounders, announced that an agreement had been reached. The theater was theirs one night a week, provided that a list of performers was submitted to Graham ahead of time.

35. Ben Morea at the Fillmore East, October 22, 1968. Photograph by Bev Grant/Getty.

A final communiqué was sent to the crowd outside: "Bill Graham, hippy entrepreneur, who has made money from our music, but claims the right to his property for himself may tonight have been a little bit liberated. Or he may not. Next Wednesday will tell."[63]

Next Wednesday did not go well. Nor did the following few Wednesdays. "They messed up the floor and peed on the walls and put their feet on the chairs and brought in cooking utensils, so it became like an overnight shelter for the homeless," Graham wrote in his autobiography.[64] After just a few weeks of community nights marked by flagrant drug use, public urination, and vandalism, the Fire Department threatened to shut down the venue. Graham had his excuse, and that was the end of the community nights. It was not the end of conflict at the Fillmore East, however.

On the other side of the world, Charlotte Polin was spinning out of control. A three-month stay in North Vietnam came to an end on November 8, and when she arrived back in New York five days later the tales she told must have shocked even George's FBI handlers when he passed them along two weeks later:

> While enroute there she was hospitalized with dysentery in Cambodia. She had sex with her interpreter. She said that she threatened to kill herself about 20 times and received psychotherapy in Hanoi. . . . She said that they destroyed over 100 pages of her writings. But nevertheless, she managed to smuggle out 48 pages of carbon copies. She was only allowed outside of Hanoi once. . . . She said that she was told that if she ever wanted to come back to Hanoi she must first prove herself by doing more work with the peace movement in this country. She said it was told to her as an order.[65]

This was not the first time that Polin had been kicked out of a communist country for her obsessive, bipolar behavior. According to Walter Teague, for whom Polin worked as a researcher, years earlier she had become consumed with the Soviet Union and some of its leaders and found a way to sneak into the country. Once there she started hounding the leadership, which presumably did not know what to make of this American teenage girl. They sent her home only for her to find a way back in. "She was very emotional in her politics," Teague said. One need only make it to the third paragraph of a 1967 letter to the Hanoi government to see his point. "Because I love the DRV [Democratic Republic of Vietnam] beyond everything, I want to serve its needs to the best of my ability," she wrote. "When Hanoi was bombed, I was too overwhelmed by grief, anxiety and sorrow to function."[66]

Still living on the Upper West Side, Jane Alpert was getting a crash course in New Left politics from her new boyfriend Sam Melville. "As Sam and I became closer to each other, I became drawn into the world of radical politics which I had admired from the outside for so many years and to which

I'd never quite managed to gain entry on my own," she later wrote. "I read the *Guardian* and the counterculture papers *Rat* and *East Village Other*, went to CAC meetings every week, and abandoned any lingering interest in electoral politics, learning to focus instead on grass-roots protests—riots on the Lower East Side, campus take-overs in Ithaca, New York, and Lawrence, Kansas, barricades in Paris, guerrilla war in Latin America."[67] By November, Jane would have dropped out of graduate school at Columbia and, to the even greater horror of her bourgeois parents, moved into an apartment with Sam, his former City College girlfriend, and her new boyfriend on East Eleventh Street between Avenues B and C in the East Village, a far cry from where she was raised in Forest Hills, Queens. Avenue C was even a far cry from many of the countercultural centers of gravity—Gem Spa, the Fillmore East, Common Grounds coffee shop, and the offices of the alternative newspapers—which were clustered closer to St. Marks Place, Union Square, and the subway. In fact, the blocks east of Avenue B, the eastern border of Tompkins Square Park, would largely elude the forces of gentrification for at least another three decades.

Alphabet City in general at this time was no joke: decrepit tenements, garbage everywhere, burned-out car carcasses, junkies and winos galore, violence thick in the air. "Like the dedicated leftist intellectuals of an earlier era who went to work in factories for the sake of their politics, I regarded life on the Lower East Side as an exercise to toughen me up for the revolution," Jane wrote.[68] Even though very few locals had any money and the city was in poor fiscal health, finding an apartment in the Village was the same difficult task it remains today. Ronald Sukenick, a writer who lived downtown for most of his adult life, recalled a ruse that a friend of his, a writer named Lynn Gingrass, resorted to in her search for a rental. The *Village Voice* classifieds section was the only place to look for apartment listings, but just lining up on Wednesday morning to seize a copy of the weekly wasn't enough to ensure finding a decent apartment because there would be a whole crowd of others trying to do the same. "People came in pairs, one waiting in line, the other at the near pay phone," recalled Charles Merrill in a letter to the editor of the *New York Times*.[69] Gingrass's solution? "One of us got in the line . . . and the other person systematically went to every phone booth in the Square, and removed a little gizmo under the mouthpiece," she said. "People would run to the phone booth while ripping the classifieds open . . . they were screaming into the phones and nothing was happening." As Gingrass casually strode into one of the booths with the paper under her arm, put the gizmo back in the mouthpiece, and started calling the listing numbers, they "just stared in disbelief." The scheme paid off too: Gingrass ended up with two floors of a brownstone on Leroy Street for $90 a month.[70] Susan Sherman, a poet and feminist, did not have to resort to such underhanded tactics to land her rambling East Sixth Street apartment in 1968. "I was working three days a week at the *Village Voice* classifieds, so I got the listing before it came out in the paper," she said in a 2023 interview. "I mean, I knew the brokers because I was typing up the ad!"[71]

Over Thanksgiving weekend, just days after the FBI had upgraded Robin Palmer's status in their files to "Key Activist," a bunch of Movement members traveled north from New York to Montreal for the Hemispheric Conference to End the War in Vietnam, where the stars of the show were a delegation of Viet Cong representatives. In addition to Teague, who piled into a Volkswagen sedan with Tom Wodetzki, USCANLF office manager Karen Altkin, and as many VC flags as they could fit, Melville and Alpert made the trip so that Sam could sell issues of the *Guardian* to the 1,300 attendees taking part in workshops with uneconomical names like "The National and International Task of the United States Antiwar Forces Fighting Against Neo-Colonialism and Imperialism" and "The Continuing Struggles of Black, Brown, Red and Yellow Peoples for Survival and the Assisting Roles of the White World in that Struggle." Jane must have been the one at the wheel on their trip, since on Wednesday of that same week Sam had been involved in a fatal car accident in the Hell's Kitchen neighborhood and had had his license suspended.[72]

Before the conference even began, tensions between the "liberal and manipulative organizers" (as they were referred to in *New Left Notes*) and the radicals were on full display. A contingent of Black Panthers expressed their frustration that the organizers had not provided them with enough funding to bring Bobby Seale, who had been advertised as a speaker ahead of time, and his full security detail from California. "By evening, violent disagreements arose, and a flurry of fighting, pushing and shoving, briefly disrupted the proceedings," reported the *New York Times*. In the end, the Canadian hosts ended up coming up with the money, and Seale arrived the next day.[73] Echoing the ongoing battle for the soul of SDS, the radicals were continually bumping up against "the rigidity of old CP [Communist Party] types who were more interested in generalized speeches about struggle than the details of the work that makes struggle happen," according to *New Left Notes*.[74]

Both Teague and Wodetzki recalled the conference being a bit of a snooze—very formal, lots of Vietnamese speakers, the only splashes of color the flags that Wodetzki and Altkin dutifully held aloft at either end of the stage (figure 36). A former SDSer from Southern Illinois University who had taken part in drugstore counter sit-ins in the South earlier in the decade, Wodetzki had other things on his plate anyway. Recently relocated from Plattsburgh, New York, where he had taught at an experimental school for three years, Wodetzki had been so inspired by his brief brush with the Free School before it collapsed in the summer of 1968, a victim of an unsustainable business model and the geographic scattering of its founders (not to mention the split of Allen and Sharon Krebs), that he set out to salvage it. "It was such a cool thing with such a great range of courses [so I] asked them if I could have the mailing list," he said. And so the Alternate U. was born, a few hundred feet west on Fourteenth Street from where the Free School had been. "I was never a sectarian; I was for the open part of the Free School thing," said Wodetzki. The space opened in early 1969, and in addition to the wide variety of classes on a range of political and cultural topics it served as a meeting space for lots of groups, from the nascent women's liberation and gay rights movements to the Yippies and the Black Panthers.[75]

Shortly after returning from the Montreal conference, Jane came home from the office to the East Village apartment she shared with Sam and another couple to find a stranger sitting at the kitchen table with Sam. "This is Pat Swinton," he said, gesturing at the tall woman with dirty-blond hair sporting a sleeveless pink mohair sweater. Jane was stunned. "Many women on the Lower East Side cultivated that careless, sexy look, but few managed it with such ease," she later wrote.[76] Having grown up in Washington, DC, and watched the lives of her parents and many of their friends

36. Hemispheric Conference, Montreal, Thanksgiving weekend, 1968. Walter Teague Collection.

be ruined by the anticommunist purges of the late 1940s and early 1950s, Pat Swinton had leftist blood running through her veins. Upon graduation from college in 1962 she had moved to the newly independent country of Tanganyika (now Tanzania) in East Africa, where she lived and worked as a teacher in the then capital, Dar es Salaam. "It was the adventure of a lifetime," she reflected years later. "I was around history-making revolutionaries." Swinton stayed for five years, marrying a psychologist named Spencer Swinton and having a daughter named Jennifer, before divorcing and returning to New York in 1967. "The antiwar movement was really heating up. There was no way I was going to walk away from that."[77]

Arriving back in New York in early 1967, Swinton landed an apartment at 235 East Fourth Street and found work first as a researcher for the *Guardian* and later as advertising manager for *Rat*. During this time she became very involved with another group, the North American Congress of Latin America (NACLA), which was dedicated to exposing the "imperialistic exploitation" of Latin American countries by U.S. corporations. It was while she was employed at NACLA that she made off with a pile of documents from the office of the president of Columbia University during the campus uprising and handed them over to *Rat* for publication. While firmly against the war in Vietnam, NACLA was most focused on changing the discussion from "What can we do to help develop the countries of Latin America?" to "What can we do to stop the U.S. government agencies and private companies from hindering the independent development of Latin America?" This meant not only tracking and publicizing the allocation of U.S. foreign aid and the presence of any U.S. covert forces but also actively supporting and promoting the national liberation movements of individual countries in the region.[78]

On the evening of December 5, Jane and Sam (and almost certainly Pat) attended the twentieth anniversary party for the *Guardian*, where Melville had worked for several months. Speakers at the event included Bernadine Dohrn, Herbert Marcuse, and H. Rap Brown.[79] According to Jane, "the evening was a fiasco," ruined largely by the rantings of Brown, who was upset that the *Guardian* had put Eldridge Cleaver on the cover of its most recent issue. Brown, who'd resigned as chairman of SNCC in June, stormed off the stage, followed by Carl Oglesby and Dohrn, who, according to Jane Alpert, "cut an astonishingly glamorous figure in a velvet minidress and whose walk-off in support of Rap Brown was dramatic, unexpected, and a harbinger of splits to come."[80]

At the reception afterward, Melville spoke briefly with Brown, who remembered him from Columbia, according to Joshua Melville, and even offered his Eleventh Street apartment as a Black Panther safe house. A few weeks later Brown inspected the place and decided it did not work as a safe house but asked if he could instead store weapons there. Alpert was freaked out, but Dave Hughey, who worked at the *Guardian* with Melville and was Swinton's lover, was all for it, as was Sharon Krebs, who grabbed the cigar Sam was smoking and, blowing a smoke ring, told Brown, "We're in."[81] Ultimately, Jane put her foot down, and it didn't happen.

John David Hughey III had dropped out of Duke University in 1966 and moved to New York City. The son of the Rev. John Hughey, a high-ranking member of the Baptist Church, he had spent his childhood with his parents and four siblings in Switzerland before moving to Richmond, Virginia, where he finished high school at the top of his class. Hughey was widely respected within the Movement for his even-temperedness and friendly, if somewhat reserved, demeanor. "Davey was very quiet and very efficient and we all liked him enormously," said his editor at the *Guardian* newspaper, where he worked in late 1968 and the first half of 1969, overlapping with Melville for a few months.[82] Teague described him as a "very quiet and serious guy, a good volunteer."[83] Carola Hoffman, who was Dave's downstairs neighbor in a walk-up on Avenue C and 6th Street for a spell, concurred: "Dave kept his own counsel; he could keep his mouth shut."[84]

As the end of 1968 approached, the Motherfuckers were still burning at Bill Graham's cancellation of community nights at the Fillmore East when it was announced that the MC5, the Detroit proto-punk band best known for its newly recorded song "Kick Out the Jams" and due to appear on the cover of *Rolling Stone* days later, would play a free show at the East Village venue on the day after Christmas. Elektra Records, which had recently signed the group and was footing the bill for the show, gave away most of the 2,300 tickets over the radio and let Graham keep a few hundred to hand out himself. The Motherfuckers called the label and threatened to burn down the Fillmore if the tickets were not given to them. They were incensed that Graham, who was afraid that the concert would get out of hand and be shut down by the cops, had been holding back the tickets. Graham had good reason to worry. Two weeks earlier, one of the Motherfuckers had jumped on stage at an MC5 show in Boston and exhorted the crowd to "burn this place down and take to the streets."[85]

As David Peel, a twenty-six-year-old from Brooklyn who had released a song earlier in the year called "Up Against the Wall" (leaving out the Motherfucker from the title), opened the show, there were still hundreds of empty seats and hundreds of frustrated people on the sidewalk in front of the venue. After chants of "Open the Doors!" from the audience inside, Graham agreed to let in a few hundred more people, leaving scores of increasingly rowdy music fans still stranded on the street. "Meanwhile, as all this is going down out front, the band is on-stage trying to do our big NYC debut show," remembered MC5 guitarist Wayne Kramer. "The stage wings were crowded with Motherfuckers waiting for us to give the word to burn the place down."[86]

By now the crowd was in a frenzy, and Graham went to the door himself to address the crowd outside. "I can't tell my staff to fight you, because that's not why they're hired," Graham shouted. "But I'm gonna stand in front of the building and if you try to come in, I'm gonna try to stop you." A Puerto Rican kid from the neighborhood, loosely affiliated with the Motherfuckers, whipped Graham in the face with a chain, and his broken nose spurted blood.[87] Graham responded by launching into a tirade about how he had survived the Nazis as a child, and if they wanted to burn down the building then they would have to take him down first. It worked. The crowd went silent and retreated.[88]

Inside, however, the Motherfuckers were still looking for a fight. As the MC5 rushed to finish their set the crowd went on a rampage, trashing instruments, slashing the curtains, and badly injuring an audience member and an usher. Band members made a run for the two limos outside as the angry mob shouted "Bastards! Pigs! Phonies! Sell-outs!" It was a fitting end to a tumultuous year, during which the Motherfuckers' over-the-top antics and hooliganism had been losing them friends in the Movement. Shortly after the MC5 incident, the *East Village Other* posted an account that laid blame for the violence squarely at their feet and called Morea and his cohorts "creeps, brain-farts, shit-mouthed fascist assholes [and] stoned primitive shits."[89]

It wasn't just the alternative press that was getting turned off by the Motherfuckers' violent tendencies. Even some of the group's own members were having second thoughts. "I had watched Bill [Graham] get hit with the chain and felt a door open between our violent rhetoric and reality," said Osha Neumann. "I did not want to walk through it. The vulnerability of the flesh of my opponent gave me no pleasure."[90]

In the final days of the year the FBI circulated an internal memo, effectively congratulating itself for taking a chance on the machinist from

Brooklyn. There could be no doubt: Demmerle had been a good bet. He had provided a written report on average more than once a week and attended almost thirty meetings. There were also the classes, the informal gatherings, and the many protests. He had been eyewitness to the flourishing of one activist group after another and had tried to help his handlers sift through the doctrinal splits and alliances.[91] Little did they know that the disillusionment Demmerle had experienced at the DNC had resulted in his diluting his intelligence reports all fall. More trouble would follow.

Part III

IGNITION

Chapter 10

Sixty-Nine

A WEEK AFTER the underdog New York Jets edged out the Baltimore Colts in Superbowl III and two weeks after Robin Palmer and Sharon Krebs appeared nude on the cover of the *Rat* ringing in 1969 with, well, a sixty-nine, thousands of protesters traveled to Washington, DC, for Richard Nixon's inauguration. The counter-inaugural, as the radicals branded their sideshow, turned into a weekend-long event, with its own parade, tent, and ball. Even Pigasus, the Yippies' porcine presidential candidate, was scheduled to have one last hurrah—an in-hog-uration (figure 37)!

The weeks leading up to the event had been a scramble, with Mobe leaders Dave Dellinger and Rennie Davis camped out in Washington working around the clock to hammer out a deal with government officials to avoid the kind of conflagration that happened in Chicago. "I felt that if we could get them enough freedom to speak out that we would limit the violence a great deal," Philip Hirschkop, a local civil rights lawyer serving as chief counsel for the Mobe, said. "We believed that if we did have an ordinary outlet for speech, it would not seek the extraordinary outlet it might otherwise seek."[1]

Amazingly, given the distrust sown by Daley and his shock troops in Chicago, Mobe and District leaders were able to reach an agreement on both a permitted parade route for a counter-inaugural march (figure 38) and erection of a large tent on a triangular section of lawn bounded by Fifteenth Street, Maine Avenue, and Independence Avenue, across the street from what is now the National Holocaust Museum. A few other factors

37. Yippie flyer, January 18–20, 1969.

gave organizers and law enforcement alike hope that things would proceed peacefully. Not only was it exam time at some colleges (not to mention an inhospitable time of year for an outdoor gathering), but the DC police, who already had a good track record of managing heavy demonstrations with a light touch, had received many hours of special training leading up to the Inauguration. "Don't let those [radicals] get under your skin," they were told. By the time contractors were assembling the giant striped

38. Inside the counter-inaugural tent, Walter Teague at right, January 18–20, 1969. Walter Teague Collection.

tent on the Mobe's patch of lawn, both sides were feeling optimistic. "The cooperative nature of the permit negotiations made it clear that a 'blood-bath' was not expected," according to a task force report that was published in the aftermath of the long weekend. "This spirit of cooperation, nurtured during the negotiations, came to play a significant role in the drama which was about to unfold."[2]

Pigasus arrived on Thursday, before the Mobe tent was up. Some ceremonial silliness involving the pig at the Sylvan Theater near the Washington Monument was overseen by Super Joel Yippie.[3] According to the *Washington Spark*, a "small guerrilla theater group," which included members of the Women's International Terrorist Conspiracy from Hell (WITCH), led the small crowd in a special version of "You're a Grand Old Flag"—"You're a grand old pig, you're a high-flying pig . . . you're an emblem of the land we love."[4] The scene devolved into slapstick when the pig escaped and led a motley crew of police officers, reporters, and photographers on a chase across the mall.[5]

Shortly before 10:00 a.m. on Saturday morning, January 18, two station wagons full of Veterans & Reservists—Demmerle, Krebs, and Palmer among them—departed Washington Square Park for Washington, DC. Upon arriving in DC that afternoon, they hooked up with some local contacts who were providing housing for New Yorkers. That evening three hundred protesters showed up outside a Young Republicans event at the Washington Hilton to watch a group wearing white rubber Nixon masks mutilate and burn a rubber doll while shouting "Kill for Peace."[6] While this was going on, Palmer was picking up Jerry Rubin at the airport.[7] Palmer appears to have served as an occasional bodyguard, or errand boy at least, for Rubin at various points going back to the Democratic National Convention.[8] In fact, Robin claimed not only to have helped protect Rubin when they were in a Chicago jail together but also to have possibly even saved his life in Greenwich Village when Tom Forçade, who ran the United Press Syndicate at the time and would go on to found *High Times*, attacked Rubin on West Fourth Street. "[Forçade] hated Jerry, I never knew why," said Robin, "but I got ahold of him and wrestled him to the ground."[9]

At around 10:00 on Sunday morning the V&R contingent assembled at the massive green and white Mobe tent, where they were scheduled to join Rubin and Abbie Hoffman in a "Pigasus for President" skit later that day. By noon more than five thousand demonstrators had gathered, most trying to fit underneath the tent to avoid the rain that was in the process of turning the ground into a muddy mess more suitable for the pig than thousands of protesters. As the speeches began, it quickly became clear that the crowd was in no mood to stand around hearing the same-old, same-old. "As the early afternoon wore on, a feeling of restlessness engulfed many, and cries of 'to the streets' began competing with the speakers for attention," noted the task force report.[10]

Such was the backdrop when Marilyn Webb, one of two token women speakers, was introduced by Mobe leader Dave Dellinger. Webb, only twenty-six but with several years of activism already under belt, had never addressed a crowd of this size before. She was only seconds into what she later described as "the mildest [feminist] speech you can imagine" when the catcalls from the audience began. "Take her off the stage and fuck her!" shouted one man. "Take it off!" yelled another.[11] None of the men, even Movement leaders and supposed grownups in the room like Dellinger, did a thing to stop the harassment, a sign of how little progress had been made to date by the feminist movement.

It was yet another missed opportunity for men in the Movement to put their money where their mouth was. While women's brains and skills had been appreciated and incorporated on an organizational level in SDS and other groups, women were still second-class citizens when it came to leadership. "Men sought them out, recruited them, took them seriously, honored their intelligence—then subtly demoted them to girlfriends, wives, note-takers, coffeemakers," wrote Todd Gitlin. "The fantasy of equality on the barricades shattered against the reality of the coffeepot and the mimeograph machine."[12] Stokely Carmichael's famous 1964 quip that "the only position for women in SNCC was prone" helped set the tone, too.

So it was that on this wet afternoon in early 1969—six years since the publication of *The Feminine Mystique*, two years since women's consciousness-raising groups had begun popping up in cities around the country, and less than six months before Stonewall—another woman had to be the one to stand up to the men in the crowd. As Webb, visibly shaken, finished her speech, the second woman on the program, Shulamith Firestone, a painter and cofounder of the group New York Radical Women, took the microphone.[13] "Let's start talking about where you live, baby, and wonder whether capitalism and all those systems of exploitation might not just begin there at home," she shouted over the boos and catcalls. "Because we women often have to wonder if you mean what you say about revolution or whether you just want more power for yourselves."[14]

Afterward a group of women who had witnessed the evening's appalling events, many of whom had begun the weekend with different ideas about feminism's relationship to the broader Movement, gathered at Webb's apartment. Where there had been much handwringing before about the wisdom and viability of diluting and splintering the New Left and SDS, there was now clarity. "Everyone in that room came to the conclusion that there had to be a separate movement," said Webb, who a year later would go on to start the feminist paper *Off Our Backs*. Less than two weeks after the inauguration debacle, Firestone took to the pages of the *Guardian* to make the position of radical feminists clear: "We have more important things to do than to try to get you to come around. You will come around when you have to, because you need us more than we need you. . . . The message being: Fuck off, left. You can examine your navel by yourself from now on. We're starting our own movement."[15] To be fair, not all Movement women were on board with this message. That very night Webb received a call from an SDS member she believes was Cathy Wilkerson, later of the Weathermen, who told her that if she or anyone "ever gives a speech like that again, we're going to beat the shit out of you wherever you are." The threat was noteworthy given how Webb and her fellow Washington feminists were *much* less radical than Firestone and many of the New Yorkers she ran with.[16]

After Firestone stormed off the stage, a group of New York City radicals tried to take the microphone but were rebuffed. Bored and frustrated, they left the tent and drifted out to the parade route well in advance of the start time that Mobe organizers had agreed upon with the city; enough of the demonstrators in the tent assumed this was the official start to the march that, within a few minutes, the unsanctioned group of marchers had grown to almost a thousand people. Confronted by police, some in this vanguard tried to turn back; others continued on, ultimately ending up back at the Washington Monument where they formed a large circle and danced around the five-hundred-foot stone obelisk.[17]

Shortly after this miscue, the official counter-inaugural parade got off to a smooth start. Other than a skirmish with a group of Nazis, the marchers processed peacefully down Pennsylvania Avenue, playing kazoos, singing, and carrying banners with phrases such as "Defeat Imperialism Everywhere" and "Victory to the Vietcong." However, near the end of the march, around Third Street and Independence Avenue, police attacked a group of demonstrators they thought were going to march on the Capitol, eliciting a volley of sticks and bottles; ultimately, parade organizers got between the two groups and deescalated the situation. The march ended up in front of the Department of Health, Education, and Welfare, where tensions flared when a couple of young men made a "half-hearted attempt" to lower the American flag flying on a pole outside the building. After much shouting and scuffling, the decision of what to do about the flag was put to a crowd vote, which ended up in a landslide decision not to set the flag at half-mast; in the wake of the vote, and given that it was past 5:00 p.m., Dellinger and Davis agreed with officials that the safest thing to do was to take the flag down completely for the night.[18]

Mob mentality set in as evening fell. As protesters were on their way back to the Mobe tent for the counter-inaugural ball, they passed tuxedoed guests arriving at the Museum of History and Technology for a reception in honor of Vice President–elect Spiro Agnew. The event and location had been flagged ahead of time by SDS as a demonstration target,[19] and soon five thousand onlookers had converged. The police, significantly outmanned with a team of just sixty, began using officers on horseback to push back the crowd. While most of the crowd remained passive, a couple of dozen radicals were intent on creating trouble. They threw firecrackers at the police horses and hurled manure at the cops along with epithets like "fascist pig" and "imperialist." A few sticks and rocks were lobbed at arriving guests, and when a firecracker almost hit one of them, the police escalated their use of force. "One policeman began swinging his club at the demonstrators as his horse pushed into the crowd," according to the task force report. "Another lost control of his horse, which thrashed about wildly into the crowd. . . . People were crying that they or their friends were being trampled by horses or beaten by police. Several rocks and sticks were thrown at the police." The entire scene was over and cleared in under two hours and resulted in fewer than ten arrests and even fewer real injuries, but the hope for a violence-free weekend had been quashed by the actions of a tiny minority of militants.[20]

The party that night in the Mobe tent included performances by The Fugs and other rock bands as well as a light show and plenty of out-in-the-open weed smoking. It also included a skit in which George Demmerle, in his cape and plumed helmet, climbed a scaffold and fired a blank starter pistol at another actor—most likely Robin Palmer—who was sporting a pig's mask.[21] Sam Melville, who had just quit his job at the *Guardian* and had reluctantly accompanied Jane Alpert to Washington, bumped into Robin that evening, and the two of them discussed their growing sense of desperation and rising stakes. "We have to bring the war home. Make it real here, not 12,000 miles away," Melville said. "Yeah," Robin nodded. "We can't let America become Nazi Germany."[22] On their way out Jane and Sam also bumped into Dave Hughey, who had come down to the nation's capital without his on-again-off-again girlfriend and fellow radical Pat Swinton.[23]

Inauguration Day itself was cold and gray. The night before, leaders of various New York City–based groups had confronted Mobe brass about their disappointment with how tame the counter-inaugural parade had been and demanded to have their own demonstration alongside the actual inaugural parade. The wary Mobe organizers, trying to walk a fine line, agreed to reach out to city officials and, first thing in the morning, secured verbal approval for a feeder march from Franklin Park to the official parade route. The police presence was sizeable, given intelligence they had received that this particular group would be outfitted in the tactical gear of the era—helmets, gas masks, and, for the men, athletic cups—and participants would be armed with sticks and clubs.[24]

The freezing wind whipped out of the northeast and the skies threatened to open as two hundred demonstrators gathered in Franklin Park. The group was made up mostly of New York radicals, members of SDS, Co-Aim, and Progressive Labor, according to the task force report, and likely included familiar names like Palmer, Demmerle, and Teague. But the members of the Yippies and U.S. Committee to Aid the National Liberation Front who formed the core of the Co-Aim umbrella group were also joined by a sizeable contingent of SDSers from the Midwest. Aware that they lacked a physical permit, the demonstrators, led by Teague (a stickler for precision and preparation), were careful at first to stay on the sidewalk and wait at crosswalks, and the first portion of the march proceeded without incident. The first sign of trouble came on Fourteenth Street as the procession neared Pennsylvania Avenue. A spectator, presumably a Nixon fan, jumped out of the crowd and went after one of the Viet Cong flags at the head of the procession. When the police broke up the ensuing scuffle, they arrested not only the instigator but also four of the lead marchers, including Teague.[25]

After finishing his inaugural address replete with references to world peace, racial justice, and generational unity, Nixon climbed into his limousine shortly after 2:00 p.m. His head and torso poking up out of the sunroof, the newly minted leader of the free world waved at the onlookers who lined either side of Pennsylvania Avenue. Most of the protesters were peaceful, focusing on signage, chants, and props to express their political opinions. "One group carried coffins filled with manikin body parts splattered with red paint; a few girls carried dead baby dolls," according to an article in *Campus*. "The Yippies confused everyone with their chant of "Higher pay for Cops!"[26] As the motorcade reached the intersection of Twelfth Street and Pennsylvania Avenue, a group of protesters (which, according to the task force report, included Mark Rudd) threw a barrage of rocks, sticks, and some small homemade explosives at the presidential limousine.

At Fourteenth Street, across from what is now the White House Visitor Center, a steel cable was all that separated the Franklin Park posse from the stream of cars and pedestrians in the official procession. The cops were nervous. "The group [from Franklin Park] had congregated at the widest spot along Pennsylvania Avenue," the task force report noted. "Police at the curb could not see or control the dozens of demonstrators who stood many feet back from the curb. They also feared that the Presidential Motorcade would be forced to slow down as it reached this intersection as earlier parade contingents made the turn at 15th Street."[27]

The police had good reason to be afraid. Some protesters had climbed trees and were waving Viet Cong flags, while others were yelling obscenities and burning the miniature American flags that a Boy Scout troop had been handing out.[28] But, as a second account in *Campus* noted, law enforcement was ready: "Regular police forces were reinforced by riot police, who were reinforced with National Guard troops linked arm in arm, who were reinforced by armed Airborne troops."[29] With the presidential motorcade still a few minutes out, unarmed U.S. Army Airborne troops from Fort Bragg arrived and locked arms with police. Two hundred National Guardsmen, in full gear and toting rifles, arrived from their former position at the Capitol. As a police captain ventured into the crowd to stomp out a pile of burning flags, a young protester hit him on the head from behind. The captain retreated but continued to be targeted and taunted by the crowd, many of whom were in tactical gear. The protesters now began swaying against the steel cable that separated them from the parade route. When city officials called in to the mayor's office that a riot was breaking out, Police Lieutenant William Burchette arrived to take control of the scene. The captain was pulled back from the fray and a policy decision was made not to let any more officers enter the crowd; instead, they lined up in the street, three feet away from the steel cable, and stood there passively with their batons held across their chests. Burchette walked slowly up and down the line behind his men, talking slowly to them. A calm came over not only the officers but also the radicals on the other side of the dividing line.[30]

Then Nixon's car rolled past. "Two-four-six-eight, organize to smash the state!" the crowd chanted, shaking placards saying, "Stop the War Against Black America" and "Nixon is the one—the #1 War Criminal" and launching an aerial attack of smoke bombs, stones, bottles.[31] Carola Hoffman, who that fall had organized "tactical workshops" on the streets of the East Village to prepare for just this kind of situation, was ready. "[Carola] was ecstatic," wrote Canadian journalist David Lewis Stein, who was embedded with the twenty-one-year-old New Jersey native and her eighteen-year-old roommate, Vincent Tsao, for the weekend. "She jumped up and down, waving her arms like a mad puppet."[32]

After the motorcade had passed, the crowd of radicals surged into the streets. "It was as though we had suddenly been unleashed," wrote Stein. "The crowds charged up the middle of the road, tying up traffic."[33] Policemen clubbed a demonstrator in the head, and he collapsed by the side of the road, gushing blood. Demonstrators pelted cops with more rocks and bottles. "Mayday! Mayday!" the call went out over police radios.[34] Carola Hoffman became separated from Stein and Tsao. When a protester broke a police car window with a rock, one of the cops leaped out and grabbed the first person he could. "He got [Carola] in a hammerlock and beat her on the helmet with his club," reported Stein later in his first-person account of the weekend *Living the Revolution*. "Another squad car pulled up, but Carola swung her behind around and slammed the door on the cops. The button had popped open on her jeans, and they were sliding down," Stein continued, "but she still managed to clamber over the back of the squad car and make it to the safety of the crowds."[35]

Meanwhile Stein and Tsao had heard that people were regrouping at Lafayette Park, and they made it there with only a minor incident—"a couple of small clunks" on Stein's helmet. There were dozens of cops waiting at the park, and when a group of Lower East Siders branched off, Tsao and Stein decided they were done for the day; the two bought hot dogs and headed back to the house where they were staying.[36]

However, the day was not over for everyone. Just as he had done in Chicago, Robin Palmer kept at it long after his mates packed it in. As helicopters circled the sky, Robin and a pack of several hundred young protesters continued to run through the streets of downtown Washington. "Traffic was snarled for several hours as Yippies led the police on a free-wheeling rampage through downtown streets, smashing store windows and showering the police under torrents of rocks and sticks," reported one student newspaper.[37] Palmer and eighty others were arrested for "engaging in throwing rocks at police cars, bank windows, and other business establishments during street disorders in connection with counter-inauguration activities." Palmer also "reportedly hit a policeman from behind and ran away," according to an FBI account.[38] In addition to a handful of banks being vandalized, the plate glass windows of the National Geographic Society and the National Association of Home Builders were smashed, and the national headquarters of the Daughters of the American Revolution, site of a preinaugural concert attended by Nixon, was painted with the message "Viva N.L.F."[39] Between the bad weather and rioting, however, one thing fell through the cracks: Pigasus was never in-hog-urated.

Home from Washington, the loose-knit bunch of downtown shit-disturbers who had begun pranking liberal politicians with pig's-head platters in the fall began to, if not formalize, coalesce at least. It is difficult to put a finger on an exact date when the Crazies, as they began to call themselves, formed. The term "crazies" (lowercase c) was often used to refer generically to "a small, hard core of the country's disaffected youth," as the *New York Times* put it in its coverage of Nixon's inauguration. Two months later, *Newsweek* defined crazies as "more radical than the radicals" and said, "they believe in direct action—whether it's disrupting classes, throwing stink bombs or kicking in doors."[40]

Many of the participants in the new group had been causing trouble together for months before they put a name on it, whether with the Yippies, Veterans & Reservists, U.S. Committee to Aid the National Liberation Front, or one of the umbrella organizations like the Revolutionary Contingent, Co-Aim, or the Free School, which made it harder to draw lines around the new clique or even determine which group had called any given meeting. The disruptions of both Paul O'Dwyer events in October 1968 as well as Robin and Sharon's disrobing at the Humphrey rally at the Manhattan Center on Halloween night "were Crazie events before Crazie was 'officially' Crazie," according to Carola Hoffman, herself one of the core Crazies.[41]

Demmerle's report to the FBI written the week before the counter-inaugural mentions the plans of V&R and the Yippies—not the Crazies—to put on the Pigasus skit.[42] His FBI "report card" on December 3 listed a half dozen political groups he had interacted with in the second half of 1968 and did not make any mention of the Crazies, though it is possible this omission could have reflected his tendency after the Democratic National Convention to omit incriminating information from his reports.[43] Still, a good guess, based on all available information, is that the Crazies formed sometime around Valentine's Day of 1969. The first mention of the Crazies in George's calendar is Wednesday, February 5: "Crazies Borned Yippie dies," reads the grammatically challenged entry (figure 39). A second entry on February 9 lists meetings of V&R, WITCH, and the Crazies. The Crazies met again the following Wednesday, February 12, and took part in an action at the Women's Detention Center on February 14, the same day that the cover of *Rat* declared "The Crazies Is Coming!" and that hundreds of New Yorkers received a surprise present in the mail.

In the lead-up to Valentine's Day, Abbie Hoffman had summoned Demmerle to his apartment to help with a top-secret project—the mailing of marijuana cigarettes to thousands of New Yorkers, including doctors, school principals, and clerics. Even Mayor Lindsay was sent one. Each white envelope contained a yellow piece of embroidered paper that said "Happy Valentine's Day. This cigarette contains no harmful cancer-causing ingredients. It is made from 100 percent pure marijuana."[44] The stunt, Abbie claimed, was funded by Jimi Hendrix.[45] Perhaps more interestingly, in his report to the FBI, Demmerle named the person he believes provided the weed—"a Mexican who . . . brought a load of marijuana into

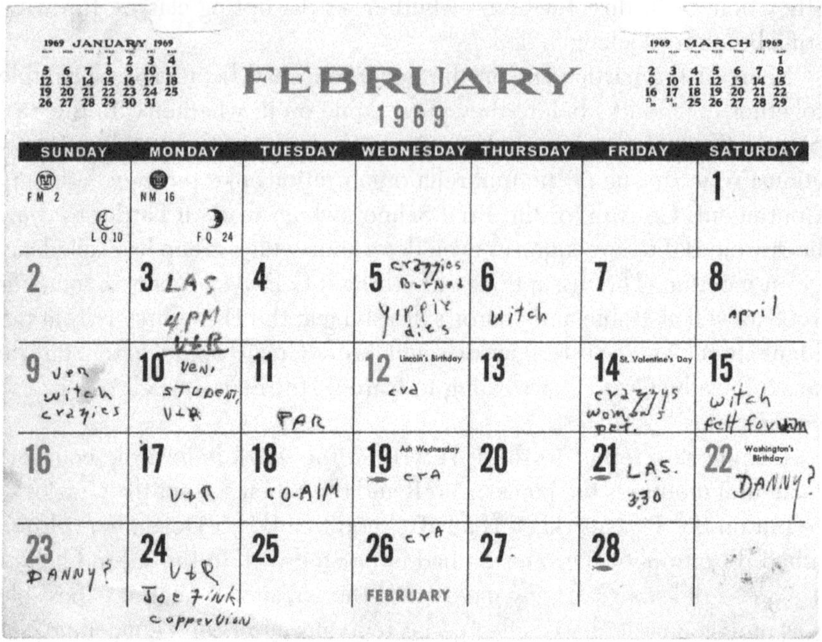

39. George Demmerle's personal calendar, February 1969. Estate of George Demmerle.

the United States by hiding it in the tires of a car he drove across the border"—as well as the address where the smuggler was staying. This is one of the only times in hundreds of pages of FBI files where George so explicitly ratted on someone. He also noted that he believed that one of the people involved in the caper was a teacher who had his school-age children type up the envelopes.[46] Like so much at this time, it was hard to separate fantasy from the merely far-fetched.

An FBI report with the heading "Meeting of 'Crazies'" that George submitted about a meeting on February 16 leaves no doubt that by this date the Crazies were official:

> There is no Chairman. The only officer is that of Treasurer, held by GEORGE DEMMERLE. The concept being, no members and no leaders, only a focal point in which people meet and plan actions. The group was formed because [Abbie Hoffman] and others in YIPPIE seemed to be more concerned with making money from YIPPIE than doing YIPPIE things.[47]

In a separate internal memorandum the FBI summarized Demmerle's reports to them about the nascent group, writing that "the Crazies feel that revolution in the United States cannot be brought about along organized, disciplined Marxist-Leninist lines, and the youth in the country must be radicalized and used to disrupt, make trouble and demoralize others."[48] A final proof point that a new group was on the scene was contained in an army "counter-intelligence spot report" sent by teletype at 5:50 p.m. on February 27. "A group known as the 'Crazies' composed of persons in the Youth International Party and another group called 'Up Against the Wall' plan to announce their formal 'birth' by engaging in the following activities on 1 March 1969," began the report. "The Crazies plan to enter Bellevue Hospital . . . with toy guns and steal one of the patients. . . . [They] plan to travel to the Staten Island ferry and . . . threaten the boat's captain by demanding that he take them to Cuba."[49]

The overall sequence of events is supported by an article by *Rat* contributor Lee Merrick, who also noted the symbolic role that George adopted in addition to his position as treasurer. "After the Inhoguration, when the Crazies formed themselves, [Demmerle] created his Prince Crazy image, and he became a familiar sight on 8th Street and 6th Avenue, strutting in his lavender jeweled Nehru shirt and dayglo pink helmet with two feather dusters on top like a Roman guard."[50] This is the image of Demmerle that Jerry Rubin remembered. "George was the craziest cat around. If you wanted anything flippy done, call George," Rubin wrote in his autobiography. "He lived on the streets and worked with the people. He never took off his Yippie button. When the Crazies were born, in an attempt to get an identity distinct from Yippie, George nicknamed himself 'Prince Crazy, Son of Yippie.'"[51]

Asked later about how he came up with his persona, George said, "I just imitated Abbie Hoffman and Jerry Rubin. They made fools out of the kids, and I did the same thing." George's "Crazies outfit" varied but was usually some combination of a purple cape and/or Nehru jacket topped off with a plumed centurion's helmet or, for street action, a white crash helmet. To some people he came off as a goofy uncle, harmless and vaguely amusing, an image further bolstered by his penchant for avoiding detection by dressing up as an old man, as he did for an event on February 24 at Cooper Union (figure 40); his tendency to help street kids, runaways, and other needy people—once he'd determined they had no intelligence value and posed no threat to his own position in the Movement—also helped cultivate this fatherly aura. "Whether prancing in the streets in his make-up

40. George Demmerle in his "old man" disguise, Cooper Union, February 24, 1969. Estate of Louis Salzberg.

or spouting wild schemes at meetings," wrote Jay Levin in the *New York Post*, "he was accepted as the Fool of the movement, a slightly frantic, slightly silly 'old man.'"[52] Paul Krassner had a slightly more charitable take: "He seemed older than the rest of us but there was a certain sweetness about him."[53]

To others in the Movement, he was a bleeding-edge radical with the semantics to back it up. "Wherever the talk went far and fierce about the need for bombs and burnings, there Prince Crazy stood out for his 'revolutionary boldness,'" according to a profile in *Dissent*. "No one could outdo him in his verbal readiness to smite the Establishment with fire and sword."[54] And to still others he was a fake, whether he was a pig or not. "Demmerle was either crazy or he was an agent," said Walter Teague.[55]

Speaking of crazy, Jane Alpert began to have her doubts about Sam Melville's mental health after they returned from the inauguration. "When he wasn't absorbed by his health regimen, [Sam] was talking to the leaders and groupies he met in movement storefronts," she wrote. "A conversation with Abbie Hoffman preoccupied him for days. 'That guy's really crazy,' he would say, and meant it as high praise." Sam started taking LSD with greater frequency just as he and Jane began spending more and more time with Pat Swinton, so much time, in fact, that Jane, who was still working at Cambridge University Press, became increasingly nervous as her month-long business trip to Europe loomed. "I always liked talking to [Pat]—she was honest and funny, and her conversation traveled more easily between the political and personal than anyone else's—but I was apprehensive about what her visits would be like when I was in England and Sam was left to entertain her alone."[56]

While George Demmerle may have been the most visual manifestation of the Crazies, the real leaders were Robin Palmer and Sharon Krebs. As Carola Hoffman described it, in the aftermath of the Democratic National Convention, "an affinity group of 30 or 40 people grew up around Robin and Sharon."[57] As for the origin of the name, it may go back as far as the same night that the Yippies were created. In his book *Down and In*, the writer Ronald Sukenick relays Don Katzman's claim that the Crazies name was pitched at the December 31, 1967, meeting between him, Abbie Hoffman and the two cofounders of the *East Village Other* newspaper, Allen Katzman and Walter Browart, before opting for the less literal, more playful, moniker of the Yippies. "Rubin and Abbie Hoffman came up with the idea of the Crazies," says Katzman. "I said, 'If you wanted to have a reason for the cops to take a good shot at you, call yourself the Crazies. You got a perfect reason for them to take out their guns and shoot you.'"[58]

A flyer that began "Bellevue is Sane—The Crazies are not" (and was signed, with adolescent humor, by none other than Jack Meoff) called for the faithful to assemble at First Avenue and East Twenty-Ninth Street at 1:30 on Saturday, March 1, to "liberate our brother back into insanity." The army intelligence report from two days earlier had been right: The piece of political theater involved busting out their Crazie brother, in this case played by Vincent Tsao, from the notorious mental hospital. From there, the plan called for catching the 3:00 Staten Island ferry (figure 41), where "as Crazies we will smoke dope—paint images—bring balloons—make love—play kazoos—fuck and be Crazie."[59]

The star of that day's show, Vincent Tsao (figure 42), was the youngest Crazie of them all. The son of a Chinese man who had never learned to speak English and a mother of Afro and Latino descent, Vincent was a regular at Movement marches and Yippie and Crazie disruptions throughout 1968 and 1969, usually dressed in his go-to outfit of a Sergeant Pepper military jacket and Converse high-tops (though on this day he was sporting a straitjacket). "He was a really smart guy, but someone who didn't fit into school," recalls Carola Hoffman. "He went to the Yip-in at Grand Central expecting a big party . . . and it turned into a big cop bust. That was where he got really radicalized."[60]

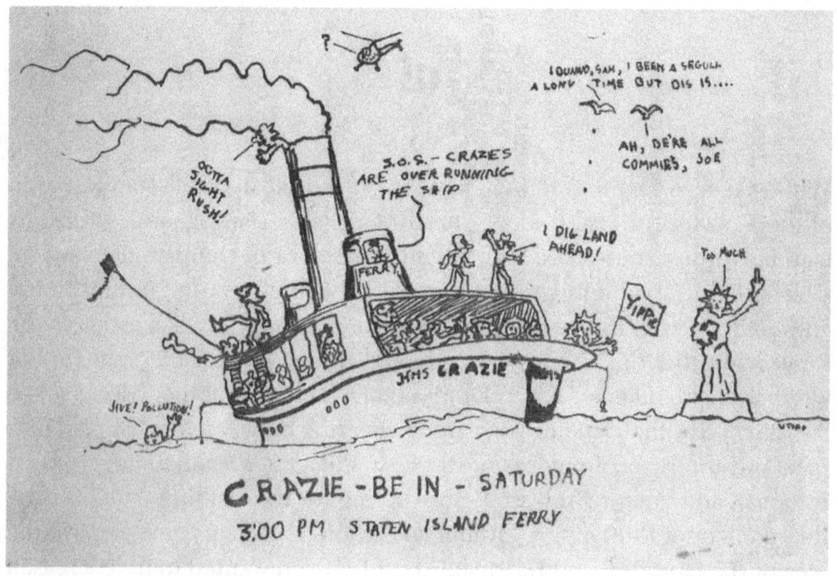

41. Staten Island Ferry Crazie Be-In poster, March 1, 1969, by Vincent Tsao. Estate of Louis Salzberg.

42. Vincent Tsao held aloft as George Demmerle, far right, looks on, outside Bellevue Hospital, March 1, 1969. Estate of Louis Salzberg.

"I'd thought maybe I'd see a couple of cops moving on some guy who was like making too much noise," Tsao told journalist David Lewis Stein. "I never thought I'd see a whole wedge of cops running down a tunnel into a crowd. I was running around saying, 'You can't do this! This is America!'" Stein, who spent a long weekend in January 1969 with Tsao and Carola at Nixon's inauguration, said of Vincent, "He was only eighteen, but he seemed much older and more mature."[61] He was also resourceful. "[Vincent] slept on floors, ate filched turkeys from Lion, slipped by the Fillmore bouncers for the nth time, lived off Mickey's tolerable steam table hors d'oeuvres," Eric Darton, who was roommates with Vincent, wrote in the lingua franca of the time. "[He] was the world the adman wanted to buy a

43. Crazies sticker.

coke for and it was [Vincent] who dreamed up the agitprop dayglo blood orange oval Crazie button logo, letter shaping a black AK-47" (figure 43).[62]

On the evening of March 5, the watchdog group Fund for Education in World Order (later called the Fund for Peace) hosted the First National Convocation on "The Challenge of Building Peace" at the Hilton Hotel on Sixth Avenue between Fifty-Third Street and Fifty-Fourth Street. In the morning and afternoon sessions, attendees listened to panel discussions on such topics as "Is America Becoming a Militaristic Society?" and "Can We Build an Effective Constituency for Peace?"[63] Among the two thousand people gathered in the grand ballroom at lunchtime to hear New York Senator Jacob K. Javits and Senate Foreign Relations Committee Chair J. W. Fulbright speak were several (the *New York Times* said a "half dozen") Crazies, including Palmer, Krebs, Demmerle, (Carola) Hoffman, and Wodetzki, who now had stature in the radical scene as the proprietor of the Alternate U.[64]

Newsman Chet Huntley opened the luncheon with optimistic remarks about the prospect of peace before introducing Senator Fulbright. Moments into the senator's remarks, however, there was a commotion. Stage left, three red-jacketed waiters mounted the dais and put napkin-covered plates in front of Senators Javits, Fulbright, and McGovern and then ceremoniously removed the napkins to reveal raw pig's heads (figure 44). Meanwhile, Carola Hoffman danced across the stage, unfurling a NLF flag. After five rounds of chanting "Ho, Ho, Ho Chi Minh, NLF is Going to Win" by the Crazies, Palmer took the microphone: "I want to introduce to you Mr. William Racist Fulbright Pig. There you are, sir. Now I want

44. Crazie Tom Wodetzki serves Senator George McGovern a pig's head, New York Hilton, March 5, 1969. Estate of Louis Salzberg.

you to remember only one thing. Remember only that 'Sirhan Lives.'"[65] The reference was to Sirhan Sirhan, the Palestinian man then on trial for the assassination of Robert Kennedy the previous summer. The balcony erupted as NLF flags were unfurled over the rail and leaflets fluttered down on the crowd. As chants of "Ho-Ho-Ho Chi Minh" resumed, the waiters returned to their seats and took off their red jackets.[66] Notably, when asked by a *New York Times* reporter, Palmer identified himself as a member of the Veterans & Reservists.[67] On the other hand, the *Ann Arbor Argus* ran a story in which it reported, "On being questioned about their organizational affiliation, demonstrators proudly said they were Crazies." That was maybe not so surprising, given that the writer of that piece was Carola Hoffman.[68]

"We were expecting something of a demonstration today," said cochairman Stewart Rawlings Mott with good humor. "We would have been disappointed if we hadn't had it." Fulbright also tried to be a good sport. "You never come to New York if you don't get interesting meetings," said the man who, as head of the Senate Foreign Relations Committee, had been the first mainstream politician to express skepticism about Vietnam, initially through a series of Senate hearings on the war in 1966.[69] "I suppose that's one reason we just can't get along without New York because it adds spice and interest to our life." From the audience, Palmer shouted, "You're a racist, Fulbright!"—a reference, perhaps, to Fulbright's support for the Declaration of Constitutional Principles, the 1956 manifesto opposing racial integration in public spaces. Fulbright was interrupted again, to the crowd's mounting frustration. Mott then offered the protesters the microphone for one minute to say their piece. One of the Crazies, described by the *New York Times* only as a "long haired man with a drooping mustache," stepped up. "This country is riding roughshod, economically suppressing people in South America in Asia and in Africa," he said. "Until we stop the power elite of this country from doing that, we will not have peace and there are people—and they are my brothers and they are here—we're going to pull it down around your heads!"[70]

At this point, according to Carola Hoffman's account in the *Ann Arbor Argus*, a policeman placed Palmer under arrest. As Robin was led from the dining room, the remaining Crazies followed, chanting "Sirhan lives" over and over. At the Eighteenth Precinct Palmer was booked and charged with disorderly conduct; he represented himself in court and was released on his own recognizance, making it back in time for a 5:00 p.m. picket line in front of the Hilton.[71] Throughout the entire event, though, Fulbright was able to keep it light. "There is nothing I could possibly say that would be nearly as eloquent about the difficulties of achieving peace as you've seen here today," he told the crowd. McGovern was less amused. "We diminish our chance for peace and degrade our society when we do not do each other the honor of hearing."[72]

Two days later, the Crazies' target was a symposium at the Society for Ethical Culture on Sixty-Fourth Street and Central Park West titled "The Crisis in Democracy: A Search for Sanity." The pews of the Upper West Side landmark were filled for an all-star liberal lineup that included United Federation of Teachers leader Jules Kolodny, NYU philosophy professor and recovering Marxist Sidney Hook, former Sarah Lawrence president and free speech advocate Harold Taylor, and SUNY sociology professor and outspoken war critic Edgar Friedenberg. Kolodny was at the podium when the phalanx of Crazies entered the vaulted, semicircular chamber. Led by Robin Palmer, wearing an Uncle Sam hat and carrying a flag with a swastika on it and accompanied by Sharon Krebs dressed like Little Orphan Annie and carrying a napkin-draped pigs-head platter, the group moved up the central aisle through the crowd of three hundred as Kolodny continued to speak. One of approaching protesters carried a placard reading "The Search for Sanity." Whispered chants emanated from the audience: "The Crazies are coming; the Crazies are coming." Kolodny forged on. "These groups use anti-intellectualism . . . they don't want to read the same books or take the same courses their dads did . . . this whole thing is an attack on our value system. The liberal system is being attacked!"[73]

Arriving at the front of the room, Robin and Sharon stepped onto the low dais. "We're here to make a special presentation," shouted Robin. With that, Sharon put down the platter at Kolodny's place at the table and removed the napkin, revealing a pig's head with an apple in its mouth. Other Crazies leapt on stage, one of them placing a sign saying "Racist Pig" at Kolodny's place. Another Crazie tried to drape a VC flag over the old man's shoulders.[74] Stage right stood George Demmerle, plumed helmet on his head, Crazies flag in hand (figure 45).

Kolodny's crime? In the fall of 1968 the United Federation of Teachers had called a two-month strike of the entire New York City school system in response to the purging more than eighty white, mostly Jewish teachers

45. Crazies at the Society for Ethical Culture, March 7, 1969. George Demmerle with Crazies flag, Danny Schneider with Yippie flag. Estate of Louis Salzberg.

from its schools by the recently empowered community-controlled school board in the predominantly Black neighborhood of Brownsville. To the radical left, any action that sought to constrain the self-determination of Black people was worthy of condemnation. More, siding with the rights of the Black community over those of workers was yet another sign of how little the vanguard cared about the traditional Marxist framework. In the radical paradigm, civil rights trumped working-class dogma any day of the week.

Now, chanting "Ho-Ho-Ho Chi Minh, the NLF is going to win," the Crazies headed toward the door at the back of the auditorium.[75] As the stunned audience looked on, the panelists tried to process what had happened. Kolodny was indignant, pointing out that the UFT had supported every progressive social reform since FDR. Hook, the most law-and-order voice on the stage, joined Kolodny in condemning the Crazies, while Friedenberg and Taylor were largely sympathetic. Taylor called it a "relatively harmless piece of guerrilla theater" and Friedenberg pointed out that "99 per cent of our violence is produced by the legitimate forces of this country, the police and the Army."[76]

Around the time of the Crazies' antics at the Hilton Hotel and Ethical Culture, Wodetzki, Palmer, and Demmerle had an escapade that nearly turned disastrous. "The cities were going up in flames, so we thought we better learn how to make and use Molotov cocktails," Wodetzki recalled. They gathered the necessary materials—wine bottles, cans of gas, soap, and, for fuses, tampons—and drove up to Westchester in search of outdoor space to conduct their chemistry experiment. They had just parked in a deserted area and were about to begin building their homemade bombs when a police car rolled up and an officer climbed out. "What're you guys doing here?" he asked. "Oh, we're scouting for a film location, officer," they responded. "Hmmm, let's see what you guys got in your trunk." One of the Crazies popped the trunk and the cop just stood there looking at the stuff, mystified. Finally, unable to make sense of the assortment of items, he shrugged and left. Spooked, the aspiring bomb makers jumped into their car and headed back to the city.[77]

All the while, tensions were mounting among the various factions in New York's radical scene. At a meeting on March 10 some of the Veterans & Reservists and Crazies hatched plans to stage a coup at the next day's Co-Aim meeting; the two groups wanted to get rid of Co-Aim's co-chairmen to reduce the influence of YAWF. "Lollypops, cookies, candy, musical instruments and other props will be brought to meeting," warned an FBI report. "Grand entrance by Prince Crazie, Son of Yippie is to be met with standing ovation. George Demmerle is playing the role."[78] At the actual Co-Aim meeting, after hash brownies had been handed out, Robin and Sharon marched in carrying the Yippies and Crazies flags, followed by George in his Prince Crazie outfit. As a confederate announced the arrival of "Prince Crazie, son of Yippie," supporters in the crowd cheered and applauded. The meeting ended on a more constructive note, with attendees deciding to make a concerted effort to bring more groups—"SDS chapters, high school students, possible Black groups . . . Yippie-type people"—under Co-Aim's umbrella.[79]

When Jane Alpert's flight from England touched down at JFK on March 15 and she exited through customs, Sam Melville was waiting for her. "He looked subtly different. His mustache was a bit shaggier, his hair thinner and longer," she wrote. "And there was something else changed—the shadows of his jawline, the play of light in his eyes." This could have been due to the regimen of weightlifting, health food, and LSD that he'd been on since the beginning of the year or his father's death in February. In the taxi home, the conversation was stilted. Jane was still crushed by the news, received via airmail, that Sam and Pat had slept together in her absence. Back at the apartment Sam packed his pipe with marijuana and handed it to Jane, who was still fighting off tears. He had yet to tell her his biggest news.[80]

"Have you ever heard of the FLQ?" he asked, referring to Front de Libération du Québec, the left-wing separatist group that had set off dozens of bombs in recent months. Jane said she had. Two of the three central figures in the group's February bombing of the Montreal Stock Exchange, Jean-Pierre Charette, twenty-two, and Alain Allard, twenty-six, had escaped from Canada and were hiding in New York City, he told her. Sam went on to say that while Jane had been away he had not only become their caretaker, running daily to the post office and newsstand, buying them clothes and groceries, but had let them stay in the Eleventh Street apartment with him. Jane was stunned. But when Sam asked for her help in creating fake identities to enable the fugitives to get out of the country, she overcame her misgivings and agreed to help. Those were not the only hang-ups she overcame: in the coming days, Jane took LSD with Sam and Pat, and the three of them went to bed together.[81]

March 22, a Saturday, was a particularly busy day for the Crazies. After attending a morning rally for the Black Panthers with Abbie Hoffman, Jerry Rubin, and Dave Dellinger in Foley Square, the Crazies headed up to Riverside Church on the Upper West Side, where William Fitts Ryan, a former Assistant District Attorney and a Democratic Congressman representing the Upper West Side since 1961, was holding his Ninth Annual Conference on World Problems and American Powers. Sponsored by several local Democratic and Liberal clubs, speakers included former Supreme Court Justice, Secretary of Labor and U.S. Ambassador Arthur Goldberg, former Democratic Senator from Oregon Wayne Morse, and Ryan himself. All staunchly antiwar, the three men made up just the kind of liberal lineup the Crazies loved to lampoon.

Ryan had just introduced Goldberg when choral music came blasting out of a speaker from somewhere in the audience, followed by this message spoken, the idea was, by "God," who, apparently, was a Black woman:

> Arthur Goldberg, Wayne Morse, William Fitts Ryan!!! Do you hear me? This is God speakin'. God!! You know, the landlord here. What are you doin' in my house? I don't remember askin' you in here. In fact, I've been watchin' you real close for a long time and, frankly, I don't like what I've been seein'.[82]

"God" spoke for another minute or so before Janis Joplin's howling voice brought the recorded message to an end. Then all hell broke loose: fifty people from the audience of eight hundred stood up and began shouting epithets and invective at the panel (figure 46). "From all over the room disrupters, erupters and destroyers of many revolutionary persuasions pointed accusing fingers and hurled verbal abuse of every variety at all the speakers," reported *Rat*.[83] Their interjections ranged from the merely baiting ("Lady, how much did you pay for that necklace?") to the more topical ("You're soft on napalm, and you're responsible, too, for the dead GIs!").[84]

After a few attempts to reach the stage, the stars of the Crazie show were able to deliver their signature coup de grace, placing a raw pig's head in front of Goldberg while supporting actors waltzed and whirled their red-blue-and-yellow Viet Cong flags around them. The Crazies showed remarkable resolve that afternoon, keeping up the circus-like atmosphere for more than half an hour while Wayne Morse held his ground at the microphone in a defiant filibuster. To bring the event back to order, the Crazies

46. Robin Palmer (in crowd) and Arthur Goldberg (at podium) exchange words, Riverside Church, March 22, 1969. Estate of Louis Salzberg.

were offered six minutes of time at the microphone in return for agreeing to be quiet afterward, wishful thinking on the part of the organizers. When Goldberg tried to continue, the Crazies carried on until, finally, Ryan took the microphone and declared the event over.[85] Palmer later described this afternoon as "one of the best Yippie zaps we ever pulled."[86]

That evening Demmerle and Palmer helped lead a demonstration that was titularly sponsored by the Alternate U. (but "planned and organized by the Crazies," according to the police report). The marchers assembled outside the *New York Times* building at 229 West Forty-Third Street around 8:00 p.m. to protest "yellow journalism" and "racist hiring practices" at the paper of record. The plan had been to block the paper's delivery trucks, but the strong police presence meant that the protesters were limited to milling about with their signs that read "N.Y. Times is Press Agent for the Pigs" and "Capitalism Is Behind the Times."[87] From there the protesters were to march to Grand Central Station to celebrate the one-year anniversary of the Yippie Be-In by laying a wreath at the information booth.

At about 9:45 p.m., after meeting inside a neighboring restaurant called the Hectori Cafeteria, Robin Palmer, carrying a Yippie flag, and George Demmerle, carrying a Crazies flag, led dozens of protesters east on Forty-Third Street toward Times Square. Among the marchers were fellow Crazies Carola Hoffman, Sharon Krebs, Vincent Tsao, and Eric Darton as well as other bold-faced Movement names like Walter Teague and Flo Kennedy. At Sixth Avenue the procession cut down to Forty-Second Street and began heading east again toward Grand Central Station. When a police captain stopped the marchers and said they would be arrested if they did not lower their flags, the demonstrators complied. However, as they neared Fifth Avenue, Demmerle and Palmer, along with Tsao, were ambushed by Tactical Police Force officers (figure 47), pushed into a doorway, and handcuffed. They were searched and placed under arrest for disorderly conduct and parading without a permit. Although Palmer and Demmerle were waylaid, most protesters made it to Grand Central but upon arrival were denied entry by "a couple of busloads" of cops. Square-looking commuters were the only ones permitted access—no freaks allowed.[88]

While Robin and George were taken to the Fourth Precinct for the night, some of those who had not been arrested or dissuaded by the large police presence at Grand Central marched north on Park Avenue toward Central Park, passing a posse of policemen on motor scooters and horses. "Free the animals!" they shouted. Arriving at the park, they shouted, "This is Pigs Meadow!" At 11:15 p.m., the hundred or so remaining protesters headed toward the southeastern exit from the park, whistling the marching song from *Bridge on the River Kwai*. Leaving the park, some of the Crazies climbed into the Pulitzer Fountain, across the street from the Plaza Hotel, depositing a wreath in the arms of a nude cement statue and chanting "Law and Order!" The crowd marched from there down to Bryant Park, where more cops blocked the entrance and dispersed the crowd with the help of their billy clubs.[89] It was all over by a few minutes after midnight.[90]

In the morning, Demmerle and Palmer were taken from their holding cell to 100 Centre Street for arraignment. While waiting to see a judge the two Crazies were joined coincidentally by their pal and fellow Yippie Abbie Hoffman, who had been arrested, he claimed, when cops had planted drugs and guns in an apartment he used as an office.[91] All three men ended up being represented that day by an ACLU staffer named Arthur Turco (figure 48), a white lawyer who had defended numerous Black Panthers and would go on to try to organize a group of white militants to support and report to the Panthers.[92] "Like many radicals, Turco saw the Panthers as setting the standard to which all rads should aspire," Carola Hoffman,

47. George Demmerle as Prince Crazie arrested for parading without a permit from the New York Times Building to Grand Central, March 22, 1969. Estate of Louis Salzberg.

who dated Turco briefly around this time, said. "Art was into being mucho macho, and the Panthers appealed to him on that level as well."

In the audience at the arraignment were Sharon Krebs, Carola Hoffman, Flo Kennedy, and Jerry Rubin.[93] George, Robin, and Abbie, who were standing behind Turco as he was interviewed by reporters in the press room, all ended up with their faces on the local television news that night. In the following days George assured the FBI that he would try to avoid getting arrested in the future but that he needed to continue to be active in

48. Art Turco, lawyer to leftists and the Black Panthers. Estate of Louis Salzberg.

demonstrations if he was to "obtain any place of leadership in the YIP and Crazies movements and gain the respect and confidence of the individuals involved."

After Demmerle's court appearance on March 31, at which his case was postponed, Turco cryptically mentioned that he wanted to meet with him to discuss an "organization of militants on the West Coast,"[94] an obvious reference to the Black Panthers. Turco, who had been providing legal representation to the Panthers in New York for months, was preparing to put together a paramilitary organization of white radicals to support the Panthers and wanted Demmerle and Palmer to join.

The Crazies made the national news on March 24 when a *Newsweek* article highlighted a zap a week earlier at Harvard in which five Crazies—at least that's what the magazine called them, suggesting that the term "Crazies" had started to take on broader usage in popular culture—had interrupted a sociology class called "Personality and the Social System." As Professor Alex Inkeles tried to speak, a Columbia Teachers College dropout named King Collins who had been a part of the Columbia occupation a year earlier stood up and challenged him to explain what a university was. Each time Inkeles tried to answer, Collins and his four cohorts would hoot and holler. This lasted ten minutes until the police showed up and arrested the five men, none of whom were Harvard students.

By the spring of 1969, there were enough people attending meetings that the Crazies began to congregate at the Alternate U., the successor space to the Free School started by Tom Wodetzki in the wake of the latter's demise. Out of a rented office at 69 West Fourteenth Street, Wodetzki, who was also the founder of *Times Change Press*, hosted classes on "Revolutionary Poetry" and "Anarcho-Communism" as well as more practical topics like graphic design and Spanish.[95]

A joint Crazies/Co-Aim meeting at the Alternate U. on March 28 shows the extent to which undercover agents had infiltrated the scene by early 1969. "If you couldn't find [the meeting], just look for the cops," wrote Paul Krassner in an article title "The Crazies Are Coming." After two men, clearly outsiders, strolled through the meeting room during setup, the two Crazies working the door slammed it shut. "Do you have a search warrant?" they shouted. "I just want to know what's going on in there," responded one of the cops. "We don't care about you Crazies—we knew about you even before you organized." The Crazies may have been partially responsible for the intrusion. A recent article in the *Village Voice* had quoted one of them saying, "We have everything completely open to everyone because . . . we figure if the police want to infiltrate, they will, no matter what."[96]

The following day, March 29, several Crazies began their afternoon by joining what had become a weekly protest outside the Women's House of Detention on Lower Sixth Avenue, handing out leaflets with a statement from the "Vets of the Woman's House of Detention—Crazies Branch" that some passers-by might have taken offense to: "The Woman's House of Detention is an ungreased rectal thermometer, a harsh and itchy uniform, a pair of backless paper slippers and bull dyke matrons with hands like hams . . . It is the slam of cell doors, the hopeless feeling of being caged . . . it is being called an animal; it is being lonely and scared; it is the destruction of women as human beings. The Woman's House of Detention in turn must be destroyed."[97] The Crazies brought with them a guillotine which they used to conduct a mock beheading of likenesses of J. Edgar Hoover and Robert Kennedy in pigs' masks, just another example of the radical left putting liberals in the same moral basket as law-and-order, war-supporting conservatives.[98]

From the House of Detention, the Crazies headed crosstown, through the stately stretch of prewar apartment buildings on Lower Fifth Avenue known as the Gold Coast, to St. Mark's Church on East Tenth Street and Second Avenue for a panel discussion. According to *Cavalier*, a Crazie sat down at the piano and played background music and when one of the speakers said, "the Crazies represent the Liberal conscience of the nation," the Crazies booed him. Shouting "Liberalism is bad!" they shot off water pistols and threw paper airplanes.[99]

As March stretched into April and their efforts to obtain false identities for the Canadian fugitives faltered, Alpert and Melville decided to travel to Montreal to seek help. Upon arrival, Melville met alone with an FLQ contact at a cafe and was told that the documents would take a week to prepare.[100] Later that day, the couple attended an antiwar demonstration at McGill University, a move that prompted the Royal Canadian Mounted Police to make an allegedly routine visit to their hotel room the next morning. After checking the Americans' identification, the policemen left, and the couple returned to New York.[101]

A week later, having received no word from the contact in Montreal, Sam returned, this time alone. Denied entry at the border, he hitchhiked to another crossing some fifty miles away in Blackpool, Quebec. Refused entry again, Sam caused "such a disturbance that Canadian immigration held him, provided him a hearing, and officially deported him," according to an FBI report.[102] He was told he would not be allowed into the country again without written clearance from the Canadian government. "The story frightened me," Jane wrote later. "And a persistent doubt lingered that Sam had somehow fucked up and that as a result, we were no longer quite safe."[103]

■■■

On April 2 twenty-one Black Panthers were arrested in a predawn raid and charged with planting bombs at the Forty-Fourth Precinct in the Bronx, the Twenty-Fourth Precinct in Manhattan, and the offices of the Queens Board of Education in January. Furthermore, authorities charged that the accused had left behind a long-range rifle at the Queens location with which to shoot at cops as they ran out of the adjacent precinct. The arrests shocked and galvanized the left, Black and white alike, and led to numerous rallies and protests over the coming weeks and months.

The day after the arrests anyone worth his or her salt in the New York-based Movement assembled in front of the Criminal Courts Building at 100 Centre Street. In addition to many Black Panthers and activists, the crowd included white leaders like SDS's Mark Rudd and David Gilbert (who, twelve years later, would receive a life sentence for his involvement in a deadly Brinks robbery), YAWF head Key Martin, USCANLF's Walter Teague, Mike Gimbel, and Karen Altkin, Alternate U.'s Tom Wodetzki, and, from the Crazies, Robin Palmer, Vincent Tsao, and Carola Hoffman. (Presumably George Demmerle was there too, but no documentation exists to prove it.) From 11:30 to 1:00 the crowd waved signs saying, "Pigs Out of the Ghetto" and "Free the Black Political Prisoners," while SDS leaders "addressed the group using a liberal assortment of profanity, condemning the indictments and arrests as a racist plot by D. A. Hogan and the establishment in an effort to break up the Black Panthers."[104]

On April 5 tens of thousands of people, including Robin Palmer and several Crazies (figure 49), marched through the early spring rain from Bryant Park to Central Park in the annual Mobe Peace Parade. Chants of "Bring the Troops Home" and "Free Speech for G.I.s" rang through the air as right-wing and neo-Nazi counterdemonstrators heckled marchers and hoisted racist and anti-Semitic signs in the air. At the front of the march, alongside the actor Ossie Davis, was one of the Crazies' favorite punching bags, Paul O'Dwyer, still smarting from his unsuccessful Senate bid in the fall.[105]

The Yippies' Be-In at the Sheep Meadow in Central Park on Sunday did not turn out to be all peace and love either. "About 500 hippies and 3,500 hippies-for-a-day staged a kite-flying, guitar-strumming 'love-in, be-in' on the Sheep Meadow in Central Park yesterday, but the frolic was marred by scattered violence," the *New York Times* reported. Three civilians were arrested for punching policemen in pursuit of a fourth man who had thrown rocks at them; two other attendees were arrested for smoking marijuana. Another man stripped naked and threw himself into one of the several bonfires that littered the grassy expanse, and a couple disrobed to engage

49. Robin Palmer holding Nixon poster, Peace Parade, April 5, 1969. Estate of Louis Salzberg.

in a "spiritual wedding."[106] Members of polite society, looking down on the scene from their Fifth Avenue co-ops, must have thought the world had gone mad.

On April 11 a group of Crazies joined the Panther 21 rally in front of the Criminal Courts Building (figure 50). Robin Palmer was one of four Crazies carrying pig's heads on cardboard poles with the names of J. Edgar Hoover, Richard Nixon, Attorney General John Mitchell, and New York DA Frank Hogan affixed to them. Palmer also went after a counterprotester who was waving an American flag but came away the worse for it, his face "badly beaten."[107]

As the weather warmed, FBI chief J. Edgar Hoover and his henchmen turned up the heat on the Black Panthers. The indictment of the Panther 21 was followed by the arrest in May of eight Panthers in New Haven. In June, the same month that Deputy Chairman Fred Hampton famously said, "You can jail a revolutionary, but you can't jail a revolution," a wave of Panther arrests took place in other cities—eight members were charged in Chicago, one each in Washington, DC, and Salt Lake City, two in Denver,

50. Black Panthers in front of Criminal Courts Building, New York City, spring 1969. Estate of Louis Salzberg.

and fifteen in Indianapolis. The FBI's offensive was capped off by a raid on the group's Sacramento headquarters.[108]

Around this time the Crazies staged an action in which "a screaming band of long-haired, outlandishly costumed youths attacked the Bronx Botanical Gardens," according to *Rat*. "While civilians gaped, the band quickly blew up several American Beauty rosebushes, in what was later said to be a diversionary raid. Meanwhile, another squad kidnapped two hundred and ten lily-white lilies from their normally well-guarded hothouse. . . . It is alleged that kidnappers have offered to exchange the lilies for the twenty-one Panthers now being held."[109]

At a meeting on the evening of April 15 Robin, Sharon, and others went back to the drawing board. Hubert Humphrey, no doubt still smarting from his defeat in the November's general election for president, was coming to town to receive an award from the League for Industrial Democracy four days later. In preparation for the five-hundred-person luncheon in the main ballroom of the Commodore Hotel, the Crazies forged a few dozen tickets and printed a bunch of leaflets in the shape of paper airplanes that said, "Bomb Attack, Open Here" on the outside and, on the inside, "Bang, if this were an American bomb, you'd be dead." And, of course, two pig's heads were also procured.[110]

The Crazies never had a chance to launch their paper airplanes or present Humphrey with a pig's head, though. When eight of them showed up at the hotel next to Grand Central at approximately 1:00 p.m. on April 19 and attempted to enter the luncheon, the ticket-taker noticed the inferior paper quality of the forgeries and summoned the police. All eight—including Darton, Tsao, and Demmerle, as well as the other spies in the house of crazy, Louis Salzberg and Myron Kopchynsky—were taken to the Fifty-First Precinct and charged with theft of services and possession of forged instruments.[111] That was the extent of the arrests that day, as others who had also been planning to use counterfeit tickets bailed out.

George's account of an April 16 meeting provided a good snapshot of the Crazies organization, such as it was, at this moment in time. "The Crazies are now made up of about 30 activists, 20 of whom are persons affiliated with the Veterans and Reservists to End the War in Vietnam," the FBI report read. "Ten other individuals are not affiliated with any particular organizations." The group's mailing address as of this date was an apartment at 246 East 13th Street. As for their finances, "The Crazies treasury as of April 16, 1969, was zero."[112]

George Demmerle, now in peak Prince Crazie form, threw a benefit for the Black Panthers at the Alternate U. on April 20, and, two days later he and Robin attended a meeting at 40 East Third Street to discuss Art Turco's efforts to form a paramilitary group of white militants to support the Black Panthers.[113] Turco, just twenty-eight years old at the time, suggested to the twenty or so invitees that this organization would be called the Allied Panthers or possibly the People's Army.[114] Regardless of the name, Turco's goal was clear—to be the most militant cadre of white leftists ever. The defense attorney told his recruits that they would have to rob a store at gunpoint to get into the group and, once accepted, would "be expected to carry out any order given."[115] This was extreme talk, even given the company, but it reflected the rising level of urgency that many Movement members felt as their efforts to push back against the war had yet to yield measurable results. In fact, as Turco was trying to organize his militant contingent, U.S. troop levels in Vietnam were peaking at 543,400.[116]

Turco, it would turn out, was not just blowing hot air. In February 1970 he was arrested in an early morning raid of a Washington Heights apartment in the wake of the firebombing of a New York judge; police found two rifles and a stash of marijuana and barbiturates.[117] Two months after that, he was arrested along with eleven Black Panthers in the July 1969 torture and killing in Baltimore of Eugene Leroy Anderson, a Black man suspected of being a police informant.[118] After a mistrial in 1971 Turco pled guilty to the lesser charge of assault and was released on five years' probation.[119]

Potential recruits for Turco's white paramilitary group met up on April 29 and learned that the young lawyer would pick four of them to attend a meeting with the Panther brass three days later. Soon after, Turco held another meeting at which Demmerle found out that none of the four people invited to join the group, including Palmer, was ready to commit "to the degree asked of them," since they felt that Turco was pushing them too fast. The meeting with the Panthers never ended up happening.[120] Nor did the group ever really get off the ground. "It turned out that no one except George wanted to join," said Lew Friedman, who was a public school teacher by this point. "I was so relieved."[121]

Amidst Turco's recruitment efforts, the Crazies' frenetic pace continued. Their target on April 24 was the Young Republican Club at NYU, which had invited Nguyen Tan, a representative of the South Vietnam Mission to the United Nations, to speak at a meeting. At the appointed hour, approximately fifteen Crazies gathered in Washington Square Park and then stormed Vanderbilt Hall, the neo-Georgian brick building that houses the heart of NYU's law school. According to Robin Palmer's FBI files, "the demonstrators shouted obscenities, displayed Viet Cong and Chinese Communist flags, and dispersed after Tan concluded his speech."[122] All in a day's work.

Meanwhile, Sam Melville and Jane Alpert's efforts to aid the Canadian fugitives were getting nowhere. With no progress on the fake I.D. front, the two FLQ leaders and their Lower East Side conspirators were feeling desperate. By late April, the Canadians concluded they had only one possible way out: to hijack a plane to Cuba. When Sam broke the news to Jane, her initial reaction was one of incredulity and fear, especially when she heard what would be involved. "They're going to need a gun, preferably two," Sam told her. "A guy named Robin Palmer . . . and his old lady Sharon Krebs are active in the Yippies. They're supposed to be very cool and have a lot of connections. I'm going to see them tonight." More terrified at the prospect of being left out than of what could happen if the Canadians' caper went awry, Jane replied, "I'll help you any way I can."[123]

As Jane threw herself into researching best practices for hijacking, Sam received a tutorial from the Canadians in the ABCs of terrorism—forming a contingent, building a bomb, living underground, etc. On May 1, with Alpert already having picked the optimal flight scheduled for three days later, Melville walked into their apartment with a gun, a six-shooter no bigger than the palm of a hand that, according to Jane's account, he had procured from Robin Palmer.[124] A later interview with Palmer, however, indicated that the gun had come from Krebs, who in turn had been given it by a friend and former lover, a Black economics professor with the first name of Lester.[125]

On Monday, May 4, a few days after an LSD-fueled foursome with Swinton and Hughey, Melville and Alpert trailed the two fugitives to the airport and watched them—one armed with the gun and the other with a seven-inch hunting knife strapped to his leg—board the half-empty flight.[126] Sam and Jane rushed back to their apartment, where they remained glued to the radio until the news hit a short time later. "National Airlines flight number 91 has been diverted from Miami to Cuba, where it has now landed. The plane carried 75 passengers. It changed course about 40 miles from Miami, with no word to ground control. This is the twenty-fourth hijacking since January 1, 1969." Melville was ecstatic. The rush would prove addictive.

On May 11 Prince Crazie returned from a two-day trip to upstate New York with the Allied Panthers, or whatever Art Turco was calling the handful of white radicals who hadn't dropped out of his paramilitary group yet, and three days later joined Palmer, Krebs, and the rest of the Crazies at P.S. 41 on West Eleventh Street in Greenwich Village, where Norman Mailer, one of five men competing in the Democratic primary for mayor, was scheduled to give a speech entitled "Dr. Strangelove in the Seats of Power: City, State, and Nation."[127] The famously pugnacious author had teamed up with columnist Jimmy Breslin for a campaign whose platform included bringing the troops home, decentralizing control of the schools, and making the city the fifty-first state. Their most succinct slogan was "No More Bullshit."

As Mailer attempted to address the thousand-person crowd crammed into the three hundred-seat auditorium, the Crazies—dressed up in a variety of outfits including Santa Claus, a priest and a policeman—went to work, unfurling VC flags, tossing frisbees, flying paper airplanes, and tussling with audience members, all while chanting the familiar refrains of

"Ho-Ho-Ho Chi Minh, the NLF is gonna win" and "Free the Panthers" (figure 51).[128] Mailer was uncharacteristically nonplussed. "If you don't get that North Vietnam Flag out of here in five minutes, I'm leaving," he said, before allowing Palmer to come up on the stage.[129] This was a mistake. Once there, the Crazies' front man unrolled a poster of Ho Chi Minh and proclaimed him the mayoral candidate of the Crazies, the Yippies, and SDS. Mailer, visibly drunk, returned to form and challenged Robin to a boxing match and exhorted the crowd to toss the whistle-blowing Crazies out. "Mailer, his feet planted squarely apart in boxing mode, was for once outmatched," recalled Tom Robbins in the *Village Voice* in 2007. "He tried to shout past his hecklers, denouncing them as CIA agents, but it was hopeless."[130] Exasperated, Mailer and Breslin stormed out, shouting obscenities at the audience.[131] According to an FBI report, Palmer "was involved in fist fights that occurred while trying to prevent the disruption."[132] The FBI report said that the evening was "considered the most successful of any disruption by the Crazies even though it did not go as planned . . . George

51. Carola Hoffman with flag above Danny Schneider, Marty Lewis, Donna Malone, and Vincent Tsao at Norman Mailer rally, P.S. 41, May 14, 1969. Estate of Louis Salzberg.

Demmerle had the people laughing by yelling from the back at [the] Crazies. The key to success was due to the overcrowding conditions."[133] Mailer did another campaign event soon after at the Alternate U. that didn't go much better. With members of the Black Panthers and the Young Lords in the audience, Mailer kicked things off by saying, "I bet you all think I'm full of shit." The room clapped and roared in response but once he began his stump speech, he was booed for the rest of the night.[134]

More than forty people showed up to the Crazies meeting at the Alternate U. on West Fourteenth Street on May 23—a big turnout for a group that prided itself on a lack of organization. The topic of the evening was the formation of a Crazies chapter of SDS. After all, the Motherfuckers had formed their own chapter in early 1968 and used it as a platform to create all sorts of unrest at the national and regional meetings. Having determined that they met the requirement of having five national members already in SDS, the Crazies seemed poised to follow in the Motherfuckers' footsteps.[135]

Journalist Thomas Brooks touched on the relationship between two of Downtown's most rambunctious groups—the Crazies and the Motherfuckers—and SDS in the *New York Times* three weeks later:

> Both see themselves as wandering troubadours, clowns, poets and pioneers of the revolution—as part of the "international werewolf conspiracy"—but, tied as they are to the drug culture, their chief link to the organized New Left appears to be constant police harassment. There is, I am told, a "lot of overlap" in the membership between the Crazies and the Mothers. As to the Crazies' exact relationship to S.D.S., it is perhaps best put by a New York S.D.S.-er who told me: "It's hard to say. I don't think they pay dues, but they do come around." The Mothers actually are a chapter, while the Crazies are an irruption. Both, it seems to me, share a cult of violence, valuing disruption for disruption's sake, even within S.D.S. meetings, and accent a destructive strain now evident on the hippie-cum-acid-head sector of the New Left."[136]

The fact that the Crazies were so closely linked with the Motherfuckers in the mind of a *New York Times* reporter suggests that they had done a good job of following the Abbie Hoffman media manipulation playbook. After all, to the extent he remembers them at all, Motherfucker-in-Chief Ben Morea considered the Crazies to be something of a joke. "To me, they were a fiction: They had no idea what they were doing," he explained. "They had no presence in the community, they did nothing." Moreover,

Morea suspected at least some of them of being connected with law enforcement. "Their whole thing was a set up—the government needed them," he said. "I can't give you any written proof but that's always what I felt."[137] Years after the fact, Robin Palmer claimed that he and Sharon Krebs had conceived of the Crazies as a ruse to throw law enforcement off the scent of the more serious endeavors they would embark upon with Melville and his co-conspirators. "We were using Crazie as a cover, we were saying we're into taking off our clothes [and that] we wouldn't dream of doing a bombing."[138] This claim doesn't really hold water given that the Crazies formed several months before any serious discussions of bombings.

On May 26, Memorial Day, about 150 downtown radicals, including members of the Crazies and Yippies, headed up to Columbus Circle, where a "Youth Fair" was being held at the New York Coliseum. Tommy James and the Shondells (of "Crimson and Clover" fame) were scheduled to play. It wasn't exactly the Crazies' scene, but the cops had been out in force in Tompkins Square Park, and a field trip uptown had seemed like a good idea. "We were in an up mood—a fighting mood," Carola Hoffman wrote a few weeks later. "Pigs tried to put us in pens. Fuck them. . . . We're in the streets and they belong to us." The cops succeeded in separating the radicals, but they reconvened a few blocks down Broadway. At Fiftieth Street, however, a member of the NYPD's Red Squad jumped out of an unmarked car and went after four of the rabblerousers. Sprinting back uptown, the radicals were met by policemen coming down from the Coliseum. Trapped! Carola and another Crazie were grabbed, cuffed, and thrown in the back of a police car before being taken down to the station. "Hate for the pigs is healthy," wrote Hoffman, "but hate in the back room of the precinct house can eat you alive."[139]

At the end of May the New York office of the FBI recommended that George's compensation be increased to $125 a month. As his pay was going up, however, the Lower East Side was melting down. "East Eleventh Street teemed with pushers, knife fights, acid rock blasting from transistor radios, card sharks, tactical police maneuvers, sirens, outbursts of arson, gunfire," wrote Jane Alpert. St. Marks Place wasn't much better: "Formerly the refuge of flower children, it was now the battleground of speed freaks and junkies."[140]

It was against this backdrop of urban dystopia that Melville, Alpert, Swinton, and Hughey spent more and more time together, discussing the need for revolution and assuring each other that it was within reach. "Now that I was not one, not two, but four people, I took it for granted that we would make some extraordinary difference to the movement,"

Jane reflected. Below the surface of this growing sense of grandeur and self-importance, however, was her lingering fear about Sam's instability—mood swings, capriciousness, temper. It was also more and more evident that, while his devotion to fighting the forces of racism and war was unquestionable, Sam could be sloppy. Case in point: When the pair decided to create their own false identities, Sam had some of the paperwork sent to Swinton's address, despite Jane's explicit instructions not to leave any possible trail. But Melville was a man on a mission, one that now included altering his physical look so as not to attract attention. At one point in late May, without warning, Melville shaved his mustache, cut his hair, and started dressing in suits. "We can't afford to look like hippies anymore," he said. "The revolution ain't tomorrow. It's now." A few days after that, Sam casually mentioned that he was thinking of blowing up WBAI, the radio station most associated with the Movement and the downtown scene, "because they're liberal assholes." Jane told him he was crazy and walked out of the apartment, leaving an enraged Melville behind. She went straight to Swinton's and told her that she wanted to move out of the apartment on Eleventh Street that she shared with Sam.[141]

Crazie magazine launched in June 1969 (figure 52a–d). The editor-in-chief of the DIY project, to the extent that there was one, was Eric Darton, who would go on to become a respected novelist and historian in his own right. The rest of the magazine staff was composed of Darton's three roommates in the studio apartment they had sublet from Palmer at 151 West Tenth Street, the "Crazie Commune": Carola Hoffman, Vincent Tsao, and Marty Lewis.[142] By this time Robin Palmer had moved into an apartment with Sharon Krebs at 90 Bedford Street, the building made famous in the 1990s as the setting of the television show *Friends*. The first issue of the magazine laid out the group's goals: "We want equality, justice, jobs, freedom, an end to racism, corruption and terror. We seriously advocate the overthrow of all politicians, current and would-be. . . . Anyone who campaigns for office seriously should be laughed at or shot." Elsewhere on the list titled "What We Want—What We Believe" was legalized marijuana, their own press, and free meeting places on the Lower East Side.

In the space of three months the four Crazies would manage to publish four issues, typically twelve pages in length, an extraordinary level of

52. Crazie Magazine, issues 1–4, June–August 1969. Estate of George Demmerle.

productivity given all the protesting and "zaps" they were also engaged with. The final issue came out in August and featured a cover photo of a Black woman and a white woman each holding up rifles that are crossed in solidarity. In addition to the many cartoons and sketches that dot the pages, articles covered a range of topics, including the rise of the gay rights movement in the Village, the difficulty of obtaining a gun in New York City, and the upcoming Days of Rage protests in Chicago set to coincide with the start of the Chicago 7 trial. Near the back of the final issue of *Crazie* was perhaps the only full-frontal nude masthead in publishing history (figure 53), with all four undressed editorial staffers holding AK-47's. The back page, designed to be torn out and put up as a poster, exhorted readers

53. Crazie Magazine masthead: Marty Lewis, Eric Darton, Carola Hoffman, and Vincent Tsao. Estate of Louis Salzberg.

to, "Take up arms and enlist in the American people's Liberation Army to join the ranks of the international revolutionary struggle!"[143]

Beyond the magazine launch, June was a big month in Crazieland. At the weekly Thursday night meetings at the Alternate U., the assembled discussed a plan to turn St. Marks Place into a public mall, run a Crazie candidate for mayor, and, at Abbie Hoffman's urging, picket a Billy Graham event at Madison Square Garden. Throughout this period Robin Palmer and George Demmerle could frequently be found hawking Black Panther merchandise from a table on Eighth Street and Sixth Avenue. Their contact with the group was not limited to street vending, either. On the afternoon of June 15 the pair attended a Black Panther rally in Mount Morris Park in the Bronx, where two Black men approached them to ask for help getting a gun, according to George.[144] There is nothing to suggest anything came of this. Given the vagueness of his report and his desire to maintain his relevance with the FBI, George could have been making it up. We will never know.

At the final Crazies meeting of the month, Robin and George were elected to a six-person "Steering Committee," an implicit admission that even a nonhierarchical group needed some amount of organization. George also reported good news for the Crazie bank account, which was up to a whopping $77.99.[145] If the Crazies were going fund George's run for mayor on the Crazie ticket in the fall, as they discussed doing on the night of June 25 ("Go Crazie in 69" and "Put a Crazie in Crazie Mansion"), they would need a little more money than that.[146]

While the Crazies had been skewering the liberal establishment in New York City, the New Left had been experiencing growing pains of its own nationally. Nowhere was this more evident than in the ranks of SDS. From the moment the group's four-day national convention began in in Chicago on June 18, 1969, it was clear the student movement was in chaos. "From the beginning, there was a 'High Noon' quality to the convention week, a promise of shoot-it-out on the Coliseum floor: If not with guns, then at least with low-caliber word-bullets and ideological grenades," reported Andrew Kopkind in *Hard Times*.[147] "After the first five minutes of the convention, chairman Tim McCarthy found himself pounding on the table with a rock to restore order," wrote Jack Smith in the *Ann Arbor*

Argus.[148] From there, factionalism and extremism dominated, with many of the more obscure internecine squabbles occurring above the heads, figuratively, of most attendees. "That's the moment when things began to fall apart," Mark Rudd wrote almost fifty years later. "We were so sure of the lessons of Columbia—that militancy would lead to victory—that we completely forgot about organizing, the hard work of education, gaining people's trust, building relationships, forming alliances and 'building the base.'"[149]

The roots of this fracture can be traced as far back as the SDS national convention of 1965, when the group agreed to remove its prior ban on the membership of communists and communist groups. This created an opening for the Progressive Labor (PL) faction not only to get its footing in SDS but also to come mighty close to taking it over. Beyond their square looks and single-minded obsession with the working class, PL partisans had committed two central sins by mid-1969, according to the increasingly revolutionary leadership of SDS. One was that its members failed to support the struggle of the Black Panthers and the Black student movement; the other was that they frequently critiqued the National Liberation Front for fighting to create a new democratic state rather than a socialist or communist one. According to a statement by SDS leadership, increasingly drunk on its own home brew of drugs and dogma, this was evidence that PL was "objectively racist, anticommunist and reactionary" and had to go.[150]

Tensions over PL had been brewing for a couple of years already when Mark Rudd and ten others had been tasked by the national committee in April with drafting an anti-PL document to be presented at the June convention. The first draft of what would become known as the "Weatherman Statement" was further refined at an SDS meeting in Detroit in May at which the PL contingent was not included.[151] No fan of the Weathermen or Progressive Labor, activist and historian Todd Gitlin called the result a "clotted and interminable manifesto . . . which raised obscurity and thickheadedness to new heights."[152] Bryan Burrough describes the sixteen-thousand-word document as a "nearly impenetrable blizzard of Marxist jargon," attributable, at least in part, to the fact that it was written by J. J. Jacobs, "chewing amphetamines like gum."[153] History may give Jacobs a pass for his drug-fueled verbosity, however, given the succinctness and virality of two phrases he coined—"Serve the People Shit" (a twist on the earlier SDS slogan of "Serve the People") which he came up with at the June 1968 national convention and, a year later, "Bring the War Home," four syllables that summarized the Weatherman ethos perfectly and defined the next phase in the left's antiwar strategy.

When Progressive Labor was finally voted out by an overwhelming majority, it was no great surprise. Yet the expulsion of PL did not mean that SDS was necessarily rid of factionalism. Two remaining groups, having put aside their differences temporarily for the elimination of their mutual enemy, were now at greater odds in its absence: the Weathermen, focused on the liberation of the Vietnamese and other oppressed peoples abroad and Black people at home, and a second iteration of the Revolutionary Youth Movement (or RYM II), whose Maoist members still clung to the concept that the working class remained central to long-term revolution but, unlike PL, conceded the near-term relevance of the fight against racism and imperialism as a precondition for unifying the proletariat.[154]

By the end of the long weekend in Chicago, however, there was little doubt which of the two had the power and momentum. The three newly elected secretaries of SDS—Mark Rudd, Bill Ayers, and Jeff Jones—and other high-profile leaders like Bernadine Dohrn and J. J. Jacobs were all members of Weatherman. Possessed with a missionary zeal of their own, the increasingly militant Weathermen were not going to moderate their plan of action on account of some outdated intellectual hardliners, even if, as Todd Gitlin points out, it meant "dismantling the largest organization of the New Left, indeed, the largest American organization anywhere on the Left in fifty years."[155] As it would turn out, the Weatherman's destructive nature would extend much further than its host body.

Chapter 11

Point of No Return

"HOT RATS WHILE you wait," proclaimed the sign on the facade of 201 East Fourteenth Street, a playful appropriation of the lettering leftover from the instant photo shop that had once occupied the ground floor of the *Rat Subterranean News* (*Rat*) office building. The bimonthly alternative paper had debuted on March 22, 1968, exactly two weeks after the Big Brother and the Holding Company played the opening show at the Fillmore East, and quickly made a name for itself in the Movement by publishing excerpts of the papers that had been stolen from the office of Columbia University's president during the occupation of Hamilton Hall a few weeks later. The office at the top of the stairs wasn't much to speak of—four desks, two telephones, one typewriter, and several filing cabinets; stacks of newspapers piled on the linoleum floor; paint-chipped walls covered with posters of Eldridge Cleaver, Che Guevara, Huey Newton, and other radicals—but under editor Jeff Shero, the paper had carved out a place for itself on the left.

The office's shabby simplicity did not bother Jane Alpert one bit. In fact, the disheveled, fly-by-night vibe was just the change she was looking for after quitting her editorial job at the well-appointed midtown offices of Cambridge University Press in May. A week after helping the pair of Canadian terrorists hijack a plane to Cuba, Jane had arrived at the *Rat* offices to pitch Shero on a story, a how-to guide to hijacking a plane. "Write it up," Shero told her, "And I'll read it."[1] When Shero agreed to publish the piece, Jane was so excited she forgot to mention one important thing—that he should leave out her byline.

By this point Jane and Sam had patched things up and taken a sublet in Pat Swinton's building at 254 East Fourth Street. A few days after the couple moved into their new fifth floor apartment, Robin Palmer and Sharon Krebs came over for a meeting on the rooftop to discuss a plan for "bringing the war home" for real. Swinton and her on-again-off-again lover and roommate Dave Hughey were there, as were Robin's fellow unindicted coconspirator from Chicago, Wolfe Lowenthal, and Sam's buddy from the Community Action Committee, John Cohen.

As the de facto leader, Sam noted that his FLQ mentors had told him that the ideal size of a bombing cell was twenty people and asked for suggestions of possible people to bring into the fold. In response, Robin suggested bringing in some Crazies, and one in particular: George Demmerle. Sam was open to the idea, but Wolfe objected strongly, going so far as to accuse George of being an agent. Hughey, who was known for choosing his words carefully, chimed in, "I don't know if George is a Fed, but he's certainly a kook." And that was that, for the time being at least: no new members. "We don't need the Weathermen, the Motherfuckers, the Yippies or the Crazies," sneered Melville.[2]

According to Alpert's account, Palmer objected to Lowenthal's characterization of Demmerle. After all, Robin had gotten into all sorts of mischief (and legal trouble) with George over the past couple of years; even before all of the Crazies' actions in recent months, the two of them had painted the VC flag on dozens of mailboxes, gone to rifle practice together, and rampaged through the streets of Chicago. They'd both marched on the Pentagon as part of the Revolutionary Contingent, too. Robin had been one of the Yippies to haul George out of the Hudson River following his mock assassination attempt on Pigasus. Years later, however, Palmer rejected the idea that he had full-throatedly endorsed George: "I did not recruit George Demmerle and would not have recruited George Demmerle."[3]

Shortly after midnight on July 7, three men in blue jeans and red bandanas, one brandishing a gun, burst through the front door of the Explo Industries warehouse at 590 Zarega Avenue in the Bronx. After easily subduing the elderly nightwatchman, they made off with three crates with the words "Danger—Explosives" stamped on the outside, each containing sixty-five sticks of dynamite; from an adjacent warehouse the three men grabbed two boxes containing fifty blasting caps apiece.[4] Jane was in her apartment waiting with Sharon an hour later when the trio, no longer sporting bandanas, burst in and triumphantly revealed their haul. All three—Sam, Robin, and Wolfe—were adrenalized, but Sam was particularly ebullient. When the others had gone home and the 150 red sticks of dynamite had been stored in the refrigerator, he and Jane had their first good sex in weeks.[5]

Displaying an early indication of what would prove to be his fatal flaw, Melville was unable to keep his mouth shut about their big score in the coming days. After getting his partners in crime to promise to keep their heist a secret, he blabbed to three people: Pat Swinton, Dave Hughey, and John Cohen. Sam was not the only one with loose lips. Sharon had spilled the beans to her friend Lester, (the alleged source of the gun that made its way into the hands of the FLQ hijackers), who in turn told his twenty-one-year-old fiancée. Despite being in on the secret, Swinton and Hughey were excluded from the first official meeting of the Melville Collective, as it would come to be called, at Sam and Jane's apartment on the night of Saturday, July 12. The seven people in the room that night were Melville, Alpert, Palmer, Krebs, and Lowenthal, as well as Lester and his fiancée. Three decisions were made at the meeting: Jane's proposal to include Swinton and Hughey in the group was shot down; Robin's suggestion that they get the Black Panthers' approval before doing the first bombing was reluctantly approved, but only because three of those assembled happened to be headed out to a Panthers-hosted conference in California the next weekend; and everyone agreed that they needed a new place to store the explosives and authorized Sam to find a stash house. Two days later, he rented a top-floor apartment at 67 East Second Street for $30 a month under the alias of David McCurdy.[6] Dave Hughey was given the extra set of keys.

By the summer of 1969, it had been almost three years since the founding of the Black Panthers and a little over two years since they had so powerfully presented themselves, with black leather jackets, berets, and shotguns, on the steps of the state capitol in Sacramento. Since then they had grown from a local group patrolling the streets of Oakland to a national organization with offices in most major cities from Los Angeles to Chicago and New York and a ten-point manifesto. During this time, J. Edgar Hoover went to extraordinary lengths to undermine and discredit the organization; Todd Gitlin counts thirty-one FBI raids on their offices in 1968 and 1969.[7] Several of its leaders, including Bobby Hutton, Fred Hampton, and Mark Clark, were murdered. Yet the Panthers remained unshakeable heroes to the New Left in general and to the more extreme vanguard in particular, with most important decisions being filtered through the lens of "What would the Panthers think?" As Robin Palmer put it, "We were inspired to be more radical, more militant, and more violent because of

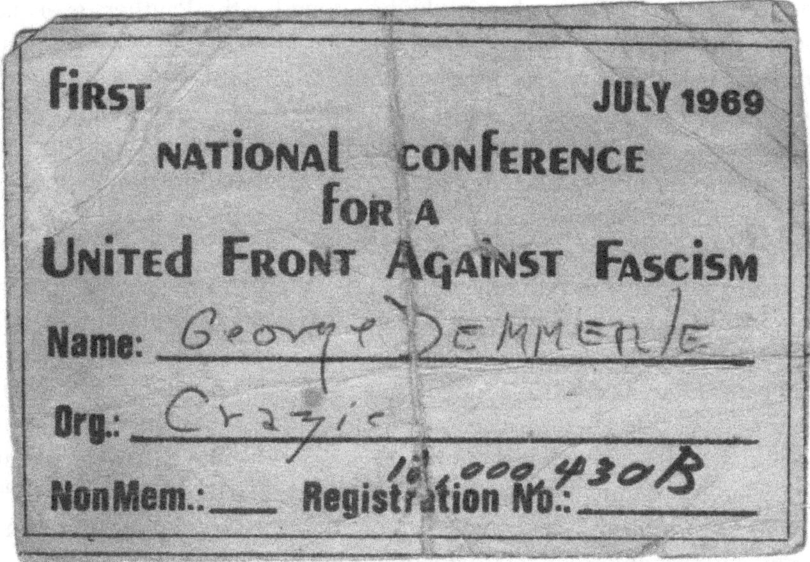

FIRST JULY 1969
NATIONAL CONFERENCE
FOR A
UNITED FRONT AGAINST FASCISM
Name: George Demmerle
Org.: Crazie
NonMem.: ___ Registration No.: 10,000 430B

54. George Demmerle's registration card for the United Front Against Fascism conference, Oakland, California, July 1969. Estate of George Demmerle.

the Panthers. When people asked us what we were doing, we would say, 'We're taking orders from the Panthers.' That's how dedicated we were."[8]

At 9:30 on the morning of July 17, the day after the Apollo 11 launch from Cape Kennedy, George and three other Crazies boarded United Flight 21 from JFK to San Francisco to attend the Anti-Fascism Conference being staged by the Black Panthers in Oakland. After some housing mixups and missed connections, they checked into the Herald Hotel in the Tenderloin. The next morning, they stopped by the Panther headquarters, where they bumped into Movement lawyer and Panther acolyte Arthur ("Art") Turco, and from there went to register for the conference at Saint Augustine Church (figure 54).[9]

The roughly twenty-five Crazies who had made it out to the convention met up before going into the Oakland Auditorium. Demmerle had a plan for them all to make a grand entrance, but only Palmer and Krebs showed any enthusiasm. Fifteen minutes before the opening ceremony the three of them paraded into the arena, George in front wearing his Prince Crazie cape and helmet and carrying the Crazie flag, followed by Robin and Sharon carrying NLF flags. They walked down the center aisle where Prince Crazie, in front of a crowd of 3,500, was ceremoniously seated in the front row, a nod not only to his involvement in Turco's paramilitary group but also to the fundraising he had done for the Panthers over the previous eighteen months. While George was granted this VIP treatment for Bobby Seale's opening speech, Robin and Sharon were sent back to the cheap seats.[10] It was the one show of deference George would receive all weekend. According to an FBI internal memo, "All attempts by the Crazies during the ensuing conference to get near the Black Panthers was rejected by the Panthers as they apparently did not want any association with the Crazies."[11]

Robin and Sharon had flown out with Jane with the specific goal of gaining the Black Panthers' blessing for the Melville Collective's impending bombing campaign. While the trio was bored by most of the speeches and panels they had to sit through, they were exhilarated by the mission they were on. As Jane recalled, "At moments I caught [Sharon's] eye or [Robin's] and felt that we shared a magical secret: the dynamite. What white radical at this conference would not have envied us if they knew?"[12]

The next morning the Crazies attended a "Workers versus Fascism" event, and that afternoon they witnessed a "minor clash" between SDS and Progressive Labor members in Bobby Hutton Memorial Park, the result of SDS's having prodded the Panthers to eject the PL crew from the auditorium the night before.[13] Before returning to the Oakland Auditorium for the evening events, the Crazies went to see Costa-Gavras's film *Z* at nearby Merritt College. And after the last session of the day, George, Robin, and Sharon ended up at the same dinner party with Jane and some other *Rat* staffers. "I had always considered [George] fatuous, but in San Francisco I saw his serious side," Jane wrote in her memoir. "He earnestly tried to convince me to help him drop chemicals in manholes in New York's financial district in order to blow out the supply of electricity to major Wall Street corporations." She added: "Under his silly helmet, his face looked like worn-out rubber."[14] Unbeknownst to Jane, George had told Robin that he thought Jane might be an informant.[15]

Progressive Labor's weekend only got worse. On the morning of July 20, the day of the moon landing, a brawl broke out between the Panthers and PL that sent a half dozen of the outmatched Maoists to the hospital.[16] Progressive Labor had earned the Panthers' antipathy at the SDS convention the previous December by pushing through a proposal that condemned all nationalism, including Black nationalism; in PL's view, Black people would find liberation only through the rise of the working class.[17] That afternoon, the Crazies joined SDS members with clubs and pipes to prevent another fifty or so PL true believers from breaking up an SDS meeting being held in a church. According to an FBI report, Robin "acted as a member of a defense committee protecting a caucus of members of SDS."[18]

Back at the Oakland Auditorium that evening, the PL faction had regrouped and looked like it was going to try another attack on SDS but backed off. While the conference itself ended up being something of a "letdown," according to Alpert, the Melville Collective did achieve its primary objective of getting the green light from the Black Panthers.[19] Robin, Jane, and Sharon returned to New York, exhilarated about the "magical secret" they shared and what the coming weeks and months might bring.[20] Sam and Pat also had a secret. While the others had been in Oakland, they'd set off a small bomb in the dumpster of a grenade factory in New Jersey as a test run for bigger things to come.[21]

Chapter 12

Bombs Away

FROM 1931 UNTIL it was demolished in 1974, the twelve-story Women's House of Detention towered over the intersection of Greenwich and Sixth Avenues and the neighboring Jefferson Market building. The facility was shuttered in 1971 after numerous claims of abuse and mistreatment, but in the summer of 1969 the Art Deco building was not only still open but had also become a focal point of the protest movement in the wake of the Stonewall riots. In fact, the protests outside the prison in June and July marked some of the first times that the gay rights movement and the New Left worked closely together. Issue 4 of *Crazie* magazine described the scene in front of the detention center on one of these occasions. "The pigs' expressions as we all dance and chant is pure repulsion," the article said. "Hippies are bad enough, niggers are worse, but the combination of niggers, hippies, and faggots! What's the world coming to when a nice wasp honkie pig has to face such a mixture of degenerates? It might just be revolution."[1]

On July 26, while the Crazies were demonstrating in front of the prison, Melville announced to Alpert that he was done waiting around for "the Masturbators," as he had taken to calling his foot-dragging fellow Collective members; the time for action had come. It was the sixteenth anniversary of Castro's raid on the Cuban army barracks that set off the Cuban Revolution, a day worth celebrating in leftist circles—and a reminder that sitting through another torturous meeting was a waste of time. Melville and Alpert decided to move ahead without telling anyone in the Collective.

Instead they invited the person they liked and trusted the most, their mutual lover, Pat Swinton.[2]

That evening, as the women watched, Sam assembled two bombs and put each in a separate pocketbook. Then the three of them biked down to Pier 3 at the southern tip of Manhattan, where there was a warehouse with the company name United Fruit emblazoned on the exterior. In her capacity as a researcher at the leftist think tank North American Congress on Latin America (NACLA), Pat was intimately familiar with the myriad imperialist sins of United Fruit; in fact, with business interests all over Latin America, the corporation was a household name among the left at this point, particularly for its complicity in the CIA's overthrow of the democratically elected Guatemalan president in 1954 and its alleged support of anti-Castro forces in 1960. The company had even been name-checked in Phil Ochs's 1965 hit "I Ain't Marching Anymore."

At Pier 3 there was no sign of a night watchman, and the only sound was the traffic rumbling by on the West Side Highway. With the two women standing guard, Sam snuck around to the waterside of the warehouse and left the two bombs against a metal door. The three fledgling terrorists, hopes high, headed back to East Fourth Street to listen for the news on the radio. By the next day, though, with no mention of the bombs on the radio or in any of the newspapers, a deflated Sam phoned in a tip from a pay phone to *WBAI*: "The United Fruit Company warehouse was blasted by a bomb at midnight, in celebration of Cuban Independence Day," he said. "If you have any doubts, you can verify this information with the police."[3]

That evening, WBAI finally ran a short piece that contained dispiriting news for the bombers: not only had the damage been limited, but the warehouse was no longer occupied by United Fruit. Melville was crushed. He had used up forty sticks of dynamite, roughly a quarter of their stock, on the rogue mission. The others in the group were furious at being left out of the plan: "That's why we called him Ahab," Palmer said later, "because he was not a collective animal." But they agreed that Jane could write up a short piece about the bombing for *Rat*, where she had been working full-time since penning her hijacking article a month earlier.[4]

The article, posing as a syndicated story from the Liberation News Service, appeared in the August 12 edition of *Rat*:

> NEW YORK (LNS)—A pier on the Hudson River owned by the United Fruit Company was blasted by a bomb on midnight of Cuban Independence Day, July 26th. Police said the bomb was either

dynamite or a plastic explosive and that they were investigating "motives and method."

An anonymous caller verified that the explosion, which blew a hole in the guard-patrolled pier and tore up a shipping crate and part of a door, injuring no one, was in "celebration of Cuban Independence Day."

This was at least the second act of apparent political sabotage in the New York/New Jersey area in a month. Earlier in July, a military grenade arsenal in New Jersey burst into flames as a result of either deliberate arson or a planted bomb. The arsenal was used to store a variety of demolition equipment for use by the U.S. Army.[5]

Roughly a mile away, at NYPD's Centre Street headquarters, the top detective for Manhattan South, Albert Seedman didn't know what to make of the bombing. "Its most valuable cargo was peat moss, and who would bomb a pier for that?" he thought to himself. It was certainly not immediately apparent why anyone would want to attack the pier's current tenant, a tugboat operator. "Further up the river, of course, there were piers worth plundering," he mused, "but this one?" Not being among *Rat*'s readership, Seedman did not make the connection to United Front immediately. The police investigation over the next few weeks failed to shed further light onto the situation either. Any clues from the bomb itself had fallen into the river and there were no witnesses. Moreover, the police weren't even able to narrow the window of time between it being set and detonated. Besides, there wasn't much pressure on Seedman to crack the case; no one was hurt, and the incident, according to the detective, "barely made the papers."[6]

July 28 was another jam-packed day for the Crazies. First up for Palmer was the initial gathering of the New York Committee to Combat Fascism held at YAWF headquarters, where the Crazie was made leader of the Political Prisoners subcommittee. Meanwhile, after attending the weekly meeting of the Veterans & Reservists, George reported to the Feds that "there is still the problem of what Vets. and Res. are all about; the group is still trying to find itself."[7] Also on July 28, the Crazies Steering Committee met to discuss plans for the group's involvement in the Woodstock music festival taking place in August in upstate New York. On and on it went: weekly ad hoc Crazies meetings on top of other group gatherings, protests, planning sessions, and fundraising.

Still basking in his moment of glory at the fascism conference, Demmerle continued his efforts to keep up appearances with the Panthers. On the morning of August 5 he was the only white person at the Panther 21 rally at 100 Centre Street. Afterward he stopped by the Fifth Avenue Peace Parade demonstration at City Hall before rejoining the Panthers in the afternoon in front of the Federal Courthouse in Foley Square.[8] In the evening George headed to East Sixth Street for a meeting of the Movement City Coordinating Committee, the group responsible for the showcase of political organizations at Woodstock. It was decided that the Crazies, along with another East Village group called Beast, would handle security at Movement City. Being a committed spy was hard work.

Conflict between the radical and more conventional wings of the New Left continued to plague efforts to form a unified front against the war and for civil rights. On August 9, 1969, just a week before Woodstock, the Fifth Avenue Peace Parade Committee—the same group that had organized the demonstration four years earlier that had been George Demmerle's introduction to the radical left—hosted the Nagasaki Day Parade to End the War in Vietnam. The march, which was attended by roughly three thousand people, was scheduled to begin in Times Square at 1:00 p.m. and conclude with music and speeches at the Central Park bandshell. As usual, the buttoned-down leaders of the Mobe were worried about the radicals messing with their carefully laid and city-approved plans, and with good reason. Upon arriving in Times Square, the Crazies, including Demmerle and Palmer, along with Walter Teague and others from the U.S. Committee to Aid the National Liberation Front of South Vietnam (USCANLF), jumped out to the front of the parade right away, VC flags flying and a pig's head on a stick. "The Parade Committee marshals were not ready to begin yet but the young people decided they would not wait and they headed into the street which made the organizers furious," Teague recalled in 2022, a few months before his death. "We [USCANLF] didn't have anything to do at that point so we decided to march with them."[9]

Teague's memory was substantiated by a police report from the time:

> When the head of the walk reached 48th St. and 7th Ave., a contingent of about 200–300 leftist radicals comprised of the "Crazies" and Youth Against War and Fascism among others, broke ranks and ran through the middle of the street north on 7th Ave, and into the park. This group carried numerous Vietcong flags, pigs' heads on poles, and the customary black and orange and black and red banners of the Y.A.W.F.[10]

Arriving in Central Park, the rogue battalion claimed the bandshell for themselves. "We took it over and put up banners—antiwar and other stuff—things that the Parade Committee didn't want to show," said Teague. "I had a good megaphone and I set it up as a microphone and invited anyone, one at a time, to come up and make a statement." This went on for a while until the parade organizers and the thousands of rule-following foot soldiers arrived. The radicals attacked the parade leaders with their cardboard flagpoles, and parade organizers responded by trying to toss some radicals off the stage. Teague finally agreed to remove his megaphone but said the banners, which included Viet Cong flags, were staying.[11] This was a big deal, since the Parade Committee had taken great pains over the years to avoid being visually associated with the controversial symbols.[12]

The Parade Committee set up its own sound system, but it was no match for the Crazies and their unruly cohorts, with any attempts at addressing the crowd by march organizers drowned out by chants of "The Stage belongs to the People," "Fascist Pig!" and "Get the C.P. [Communist Party] off the stage!" or by Teague's intermittent blasting of Viet Cong marching songs. Even Allen Ginsberg could not out-Om the Crazies, though he vowed, "I intend to sing Hare Krishna until Teague moves his body off this stage!"[13] At the center of it all was Prince Crazie (figure 55), decked out in a bright pink satin Cossack shirt and an orange day-glow helmet.

"Get the pigs off the stage," audience members shouted. "You're all agents!" This sentiment was shared by a reporter named Claudia Dreifus,

55. Crazies and other radicals keep the stage from Mobe organizers, Central Park Bandshell, August 9, 1969. Estate of Louis Salzberg.

who approached the stage and asked George, "Isn't there a right-wing rally somewhere where Crazie efforts might prove more productive?" He shrugged. "We Crazies have been trying to get up here for years, but the Fifth Avenue Peace Parade Committee is dominated by the CP [Communist Party], and they won't let any other view get a forum," he replied. "Also, we think the Parade Committee should be more militant, so we're going to force them to be so," he added. "The movement shouldn't be holding peace rallies. We should be out in the streets!" Dreifus responded, quite astutely in retrospect, "Are you trying to split the movement by doing this?" George shook his head. "Oh no, I don't think we're splitting the movement, we're helping it," he responded. "See, we go around making enemies, so that the Parade Committee looks good in comparison and can more easily gain support. Besides, we're not into organizing."[14]

Dreifus, clearly unimpressed, walked away. She was approached by a nurse who was on site with the Medical Committee for Human Rights. "What a jackass," the nurse said. "You can say that again," replied Dreifus, adding, "Bunch of fascists if you ask me." The nurse raised her eyebrows. "Funny you should say that," she said, "because I was working that medical tent maybe an hour ago and I saw three of those guys exchanging papers with a couple of other un-hip fellows. Coulda sworn I saw some kind of badge as well."[15] By this point, it was hard to trust anything anyone said.

The Nagasaki Day shenanigans ended up generating a flood of negative press, and about Teague in particular—maybe the worst of his career as an organizer. The *Guardian* referred to Teague as "a well-known agent," and *New York* ran a photo of him speaking to a cop with no context for why he might have been doing so.[16] In addition, Dreifus wrote a lengthy article in the *East Village Other* that accused many of the troublemakers, including Prince Crazie, of being in cahoots with the police. In retaliation, the alt weekly's office hallway was plastered with Crazies stickers, and Dreifus's mailbox filled up with notes saying, "Prince George Crazie was here. He wants to talk with you." She ignored the messages.[17]

Emphatically dismissing the collaboration charges, Teague joined Palmer, Krebs, and a few others of the "Ultras," as they sometimes referred to themselves, in offering something of a mea culpa three weeks later in a press release:

> Those of us who participated in the occupation of the stage are agreed in retrospect that we could have done the job better. We were not organized and none of us had thought through the political aims

> and effects of such an action. There was absolutely no pre-planning and many of the people involved had never seen one another before. The action can best be described as a spontaneous eruption.[18]

Started in the Lincoln Park neighborhood of Chicago in 1960 as a Puerto Rican street gang, the Young Lords, had rebranded themselves as a political and human rights group in the wake of the 1968 Democratic National Convention. Under the leadership of José "Cha Cha" Jiménez, who'd spent time in jail with Fred Hampton, the Lords modeled themselves on the Black Panthers. "We see and we recognize the Black Panther Party as a vanguard party, a vanguard revolutionary party," he said. "And we feel that as revolutionaries, we should follow the vanguard."[19] In addition to starting a newspaper like the Black Panthers had, the Young Lords structured their organization similarly, with ministers of information, education, and defense as well as a central committee with field marshals.[20] The Panthers had a ten-point program; the Young Lords had a thirteen-point program. In mid-1969 the Chicago branch of the Panthers, which had been started by Hampton and Bobby Rush in November 1968, announced the creation of a local "Rainbow Coalition" with the Young Lords and the Young Patriots, the white working-class group that had begun in Chicago in 1968 and whose New York chapter Prince Crazie was asked to join in the summer of 1969. The coalition was cohesive enough that it even sent representatives to the SDS National Convention in May 1969.[21]

During the summer of 1969, a New York chapter of the Young Lords was formed. As in Chicago, the Lords allied themselves with the Panthers to address housing conditions, police brutality, healthcare for the poor, food insecurity, and education in New York City.[22] The walls of their East Harlem headquarters at 1678 Madison Avenue between 111th and 112th streets were covered with posters of the Black Panthers, Che Guevara, Ho Chi Minh, and the Puerto Rican independence movement leader Pedro Albizu Campos.[23] Over the next couple of years, local chapters would open in Boston, Bridgeport, New Haven, Philadelphia, and Newark.[24]

The group's minister of information was Juan Gonzalez, a former Columbia student who had been a member of SDS and a strong advocate of community residents in the campus uprising a year earlier. Gonzalez had grown up in the housing projects of Cypress Hills, Brooklyn, and attended one of the largest public high schools in the city, where, thanks to the persistent mentoring of one teacher, he became editor of the school paper his senior year.[25]

As New York boiled in the heat of the 1969 summer, the mountains of garbage festering on the streets of its poorest neighborhoods became a symbol of class and racial inequality that the Young Lords seized upon, much as the Motherfuckers had done a year and a half earlier on the Lower East Side. After approaching the Department of Sanitation to lend them brooms to clean the streets of East Harlem and being rebuffed, the Young Lords stole the brooms and organized a community cleaning day. With the help of hundreds of people from the neighborhood, the Lords erected a five-foot high mountain of garbage that entirely blocked the six lanes of upper Third Avenue before group members emptied cans of gasoline onto the refuse pile and set it on fire.[26] They repeated this over several days in August, a campaign that became known as the Garbage Offensive.[27]

While garbage burned in Spanish Harlem, planning for Woodstock was proceeding apace further downtown. Showman and opportunist that he was, Abbie Hoffman had been unable to resist injecting himself into the middle of the increasingly hectic negotiations between organizers and government officials leading up to August 15 start date for the event. Claiming to be concerned that the concert would come off as too commercial and thereby damage the credibility of the counterculture, Abbie demanded that the organizers give him $10,000, build information booths for Movement City, and allow him to leaflet the crowd during the event. In return, Abbie said, he would help keep the peace and handle other issues like attendees having bad LSD trips. According to an FBI report, Hoffman threatened "break up the show" if his offer to help wasn't accepted. The organizers capitulated.[28]

On August 14 Prince Crazie loaded up a car with thousands of buttons and hundreds of Viet Cong flags—bought with $500 that Paul Krassner had secured for the Crazies out of the $10,000 Abbie had received from festival organizers—and set out for the concert site in Bethel, New York, with three other Crazies.[29] While George was on the road, Jane Alpert was finalizing her plans to drive up the next day with Robin and Sharon, as well as Pat Swinton and Dave Hughey, when Sam—whom Jane had busted in bed with a friend of hers a few days earlier—came slinking home and said he wanted to come with them.[30] So the next morning all six of them, plus Pat's young daughter and Robin and Sharon's two dogs, crammed into Robin's station wagon and headed north.[31]

Tom Wodetzki and his crew from Alternate U. had spent the days leading up to Woodstock organizing the area of the grounds called Movement City. "At that time, you could go down to the Garment District and get this 30-inch-wide material to make banners," he told me. "And we hung up eight or 10 of them for different organizations like Gay Liberation,

Women's Liberation, the Alternate U. and the Crazies."[32] Walter Teague, not surprisingly, put a lot of work into the USCANLF booth, as did George with the Crazies booth. In the middle of it all was a printing press purchased by Abbie Hoffman with the money he'd squeezed the concert promoters for.

Conceived of as a hub for the exchange of information and Movement literature, the cluster of information booths ended up being too far from the action (figure 56). "Movement City turned out to be a flop," according to the *Movement for a Democratic Society* newsletter. "In the context of

56. Movement City, Woodstock. Estate of Louis Salzberg.

the gigantic happening, the rain, mud, lack of water and food—the idea of people walking through the woods to some booths to look at literature was absurd."[33] Wodetzki echoed this assessment: "It was so crowded, so rainy and muddy that what we had pictured—a smaller event with people perusing—just didn't happen. It was just chaotic and vast."[34]

Despite failing to attract the attention of the general audience, Movement City was an organizational locus for the radicals. As darkness fell on the first rainy night, one SDS member called everyone in Movement City together and proposed that they raid one of the stands selling sleeping bags, tents, and other camping supplies. About twenty of them, including George, agreed and, like modern-day Robin Hoods, they soon returned with a couple dozen sleeping bags and a few tents. Meanwhile, with Robin's car ensnared in a now legendary traffic jam, Sam and Jane decided to tackle the last leg of the trip to the festival on foot through the rain. "The torrent continued nonstop," recalled Abbie Hoffman in his autobiography. "People ran for cover under trees, makeshift lean-tos, or just huddled together in human piles. Meadows and hills were transformed into mudslides as the first-night arrivals sloshed through the fields looking for lost friends and belongings."[35] Exhausted and waterlogged, Jane and Sam arrived at the festival grounds after midnight. As Sam, a claustrophobe, wandered the grounds all night, Jane crawled into a crowded tent and tried to sleep for a few hours.

The following day, August 16, emboldened by their success the night before, the same group of larcenous lefties set out for the main concession area. When the concessionaires refused to hand over their supply of boxed lunches, they climbed over and started handing meals out to the crowd. They did the same thing at a sandwich counter, a hot dog stand, and then an ice cream booth, where one worker pulled out a gun and the other a knife. (So much for peace and love.) The drug dealers who were set up in a wooded area between Movement City and the main stage they left alone.

When George wasn't on one of these raids, he was dressed in his Prince Crazie outfit and manning the printing press or the Crazies booth in Movement City (figure 57). It was there on Saturday that George encountered a curious and chatty Sam Melville. Sam offered to watch the booth so George could catch some of the concert, but George said no. "I refused because I didn't know who he was," George said. "I thought he was going to rip off all the SDS buttons."[36] His refusal read like dedication to Sam, who was impressed with George's fortitude. After several hours talking with Prince Crazie, Sam was tracked down by Jane, who had found them a ride back to the city that night. What Jane did not know at that point

57. George Demmerle in front of printing press, Movement City, Woodstock. Estate of Louis Salzberg.

was that the two men had spent much of the time talking about a shared interest—bombings—and trying to impress each other with their radical bona fides. Hoping to continue the discussion, Melville offered Demmerle a ride back to the city, but he declined, citing his responsibility to man the booth. As they wandered off, Sam said to Jane, "That George, he really is crazy."[37] Crazy like a fox, it would turn out..

Chapter 13

On the Case

THE CONSTRUCTION OF the fifty-one-story black tower at 140 Broadway, the Skidmore, Owings & Merrill-designed home of Marine Midland Grace Trust, had been completed only two years earlier when Sam Melville, just back from Woodstock, wandered in off the street, took the elevator to the eighth floor, and deposited a small bag in a hallway closet. Perhaps attracted by the red Noguchi cube sculpture out front, Melville had picked his target on the spur of the moment, but given his background as a designer of plumbing and HVAC systems, he apparently believed he had enough knowledge of a building's structural vulnerabilities to improvise. When Jane Alpert returned home from work that evening and learned that Sam had no idea whether there would be people in the building, she rushed to a pay phone to place an anonymous warning call. "I had often suspected [Sam] was crazy," Jane wrote in her memoir, "but I wasn't prepared to hear that a bomb he had placed in a randomly selected office building was going to explode in the next two hours."[1] She reached a security guard at the bank's Hanover Square location who did not take the call seriously, and when the bomb went off at 10:45 p.m. there were seventeen women at work on the eighth floor processing trust records and another fifty on the floor below.[2] The explosion tore an eight-foot-wide hole into the ten-foot-thick floor and shattered twenty-nine of the forty-two windows overlooking Liberty Street. Nineteen out of the 150 or so people in the building, all from the recordkeeping department, were injured, as was one patrolman who was nearby and cut his foot on a piece of glass when he ran into the building shortly after the explosions.[3]

NYPD Deputy Inspector Albert Seedman arrived at the site at midnight. "With all that plaster dust hanging in the light, wreckage three feet deep, the elevator doors blasted apart, and that gaping crater on the eighth floor," he observed, "I felt like I was back in wartime." Over the next week, as Seedman's team conducted a number of interviews, the bomb squad came up with one important clue: the mainspring from a Westclox "Baby Ben" alarm clock that was estimated to have been connected to somewhere between twenty and twenty-five sticks of dynamite.[4] Seedman hazarded a guess to reporters that the bomb most likely had been set off by "someone with deep psychological problems—a disgruntled employee or former employee, or an outsider bearing a grudge against the Marine Midland Grace Trust Company," the eighth largest bank in the city and eighteenth largest in the country at the time.[5] There was no reason to think that the building had been picked on a whim by someone with no connection to the company that occupied it, although Seedman did say later that he had a hunch the explosion was linked in some way to the bombing at the pier a month earlier.[6] And profit motive was quickly ruled out: "There was not a dollar to be made by blowing up [the corporate trust records] department," said the company's comptroller, Robert Decker. "There was no money there; just women working at bookkeeping machines." As for the extensive damage, Decker said, "It was a miracle nobody was killed."[7]

Jane was not the only Collective member to be spooked by Sam's impulsive behavior. Wolfe Lowenthal had become filled with doubt about the overall effort. "It wasn't fun anymore," he wrote later. "I had become a terrorist. Instead of 'relaxation,' my life turned into a desperate conspiracy. My new playthings were guns and dynamite." The day after the Marine Midland bombing, Wolfe, who had not had any direct involvement with either the United Fruit or Marine Midland bombings, quit the group. He was a nervous wreck, racked with guilt and increasingly in conflict with the spiritual path he wanted to be on. "I awoke each night chilled, soaked in a pool of sweat," he reflected twenty-five years later. "I felt guilty to be alive . . . and terrified of the knock at the door in the middle of the night."[8]

While the Melville Collective was now down to six people, Deputy Inspector Seedman had just succeeded in getting the resources to create a twelve-man task force to work on the bombing case. Heading up the team was Pete Perotta. "If I needed someone to draw an absolutely straight line down the center of a highway, I'd pick Pete Perotta," Seedman said. While Perotta and his men were chasing down leads on the Marine Midland case, Seedman started following the trail of the dynamite, which led him back to the Explo warehouse in the Bronx. Still, he was getting no traction. Like the United Fruit bombing, the robbery did not make sense: "Since they had done the research to discover Explo, they must have also learned that outside the city they'd have no trouble purchasing what they needed. Those three fifty-pound boxes plus the blasting caps would sell at retail for less than $200. Who would risk going to jail for a miserable two hundred bucks?"[9]

Despite being shocked at Sam's carelessness, Jane could not pass up the opportunity to leverage the public relations impact of the bombing. Jane wrote up a press release the next day:

> **THIS RELEASE IS FOR THE UNDERGROUND MEDIA ONLY—THERE WILL BE NO COMMUNICATION WITH THE PIG MEDIA**
> *The explosive device set off at the Marine Midland Grace Trust Company on the night of August 20th was an act of political sabotage. Considerable damage was done to the security files and building structure of the W.R. Grace Company, which extensively controls agricultural and chemical holdings throughout Latin America. There was no intent to hurt anyone. The attack was directed only at property. This was the third of such acts, beginning with the explosion of a grenade arsenal in New Jersey on July 15 and the blowing up of a United Fruit pier on July 26, commemorating the Cuban Revolution.*

Based on the NACLA research files that Pat was able to access, Jane also wrote a five-paragraph commentary that ran alongside the release in the Rat that was quite detailed and sophisticated—suspiciously so.

> *U.S. Business spends an enormous portion of its time raping the Third World. . . . If you lived in Latin America, you wouldn't leave out . . . the empire of Peter Grace (which includes, as the banking division, Marine Midland Grace Trust). . . . Grace owns land, shipping facilities, chemical plants, economies, and people. . . . Grace is just the name on another office building. But for Latin Americans, Grace—W. R. Grace, Marine Midland Grace—is an enemy, an owner. That, apparently, is why the Marine Midland Bank was bombed.*

When Perotta walked into Seedman's office on August 29 and put a copy of *Rat*, opened to page 3, in front of him, Seedman smelled, well, a rat. "This stuff struck me as more than commentary," said Seedman. "It had an insider's point of view, as if the writer was telling why he did something, not why someone else did. The last sentence explaining *why* apparently Marine Midland Bank was bombed, rang particularly hollow." Perotta shot over to *Rat*'s East Fourteenth Street offices and, upon asking who was in charge, was directed to Jane's desk. He asked her for the original letter and envelope that the Marine Midland press release had arrived in. "Oh that, I remember typing that up," she shrugged. "All that stuff gets thrown out as soon as it's used." Asked about all the details in the accompanying commentary, Jane told him that the mailing had included a fact sheet that she lifted everything from practically verbatim. Perotta bought several back issues and left.[10]

Back on Centre Street, Perotta started combing through old *Rat* issues. When he came across the article about the United Fruit bombing, he brought it straight to Seedman. There were two red flags. For one, as the *New York Post* pointed out a few weeks later, the *Rat* article "contained details of the bombings, never made public, that could be known only to the perpetrators."[11] The second was that the NYPD had not released details about what the bomb had been made of ("either dynamite or a plastic explosive," the article had said), nor had it made any public comment to the effect that it was investigating the "motives and methods" of the perpetrator. "Somewhere among *Rat's* many contributors," Seedman wrote later, "I felt we would find our bomber." Perotta put the *Rat* office under surveillance, and undercover cops in the neighborhood were told to keep their ears open.[12]

After Woodstock, George and the rest of Crazies appeared to lose some steam. According to comments he made after the fact, George had spent much of the past year increasingly conflicted over his informer role as he grew more at home with his radical friends and more skeptical of a government he had once trusted implicitly. Whether he fully appreciated the irony of the situation—finally finding his métier and his sense of community at the same time and the inherent tension between the two—he certainly understood the pickle he was in. He claimed much later that he did not know how to extract himself from his informant role without risking the loss of community and sense of purpose that being Prince Crazie brought him. "I wanted out as an FBI informant in the worst way, but I was trapped," he said.[13]

We now know that Robin and Sharon's heads were elsewhere by this point. Even though they had yet to play a direct role in a bombing, they were attending meetings with the Melville Collective and presumably were less focused on the adolescent antics of the Crazies. What's more, the Chicago Seven trial, at which Palmer was an unindicted coconspirator, and the accompanying Days of Rage protests that the Weathermen were planning for October in Chicago were dominating Movement mindshare. The September 4 Crazies meeting attracted an all-time low of four people, including "a kid smoking catnip." When Demmerle tried to gin up interest with several members, they said they were not interested in coming to any more meetings. In his report to the FBI, he theorized that "the lack of projects and activities has created a general lack of interest by members of the Crazies."[14]

On the afternoon of September 12 George attended a press conference that Abbie Hoffman was throwing to generate publicity for the upcoming trial in Chicago. *Join the Conspiracy* exhorted the bumper stickers made to stir up support. According to Hoffman, the defendants were out of money and considering having to represent themselves. At the press conference, Abbie asked George to organize a demonstration at Foley Square on September 24, the trial's scheduled start date. That same evening, the complications and contradictions that continued to plague the left were on display when NYU's Transcendental Meditation club threw a party at a bar on Waverly Place that was attended by members of the Crazies, the Gay Liberation Front, and Women's International Terrorist Conspiracy from Hell (WITCH). Everything was fine until one of the TM members jumped on the stage, launched into an antigay tirade, and called out a drug dealer in the audience. "People then started to leave, threatening reprisals," according to the FBI report.[15]

On the afternoon of September 18 the remaining six Collective members—Robin and Sharon, Lester and his fiancée, and Sam and Jane (Pat and Dave were still not officially part of the gang)—gathered in the East Second Street apartment as their leader assembled a bomb, the Baby Ben clock this time wired to fifteen sticks of dynamite. When he was done, Sam placed his handiwork in a stolen purse, and Jane, all business in a white A-line dress and gloves, walked out of the apartment with it.[16] Taking the bus down to Foley Square, she entered the recently completed forty-one-story Federal Building at 26 Federal Plaza that housed some sixty Federal agencies and roughly six thousand workers. Taking the elevator to the fortieth floor, where she thought the U.S. Army office was, Jane left the bomb in an electrical closet.[17]

That evening, as President Nixon gave a televised address to the United Nations, George chaired a joint meeting of Crazies and Yippies at 339 Lafayette Street, the three-story War Resisters League building that by this time was serving as the headquarters for numerous antiwar groups, to plan for a festival in Battery Park City to coincide with the upcoming conspiracy trial in Chicago, just as Abbie had asked. The remaining Crazies, still with a little gas in the tank, also agreed to crash a conference on Vietnam featuring George McGovern and John Kenneth Galbraith scheduled to be held two days later at NYU's Bronx campus, now the site of Bronx Community College. Later that night the Melville Collective reconvened on the roof of Lester's building, watching the downtown skyline for signs that Jane's mission had succeeded. Shortly before 2:00 a.m., the lights of the Federal Building went out.

The *New York Times* described the damage the next day:

> The North end of the 40th floor was covered with debris. A six-foot-square hole had been ripped in a wall opposite the shaftway that contained circuit breakers, electric panels, ducts and utility wires. File cabinets and furniture had been smashed by flying pieces of concrete. A 25-by-40-foot section of the ceiling had been ripped out and the floor of the 41st floor was damaged. Ceiling tiles fell onto the floor, desks and files of the Selective Service offices that are on the 39th floor.[18]

No one was hurt, but the fact that this attack occurred on federal property triggered an important development: the involvement of the FBI. While the NYPD bomb squad sifted through the wreckage over the next several days, New York FBI Bureau Chief John Malone reached out to Seedman to tell him they had a well-placed informant who "might develop leads to the bombers"—but no more info than that. This is the one known reference that could provide possible corroboration to Joshua Melville's theory that Demmerle knew about the Collective as early as July.[19]

The next morning, apparently by coincidence, two FBI agents knocked on the door of Melville and Alpert's old apartment on East Eleventh Street looking for the former inhabitants. Their old roommates pleaded ignorance with the Feds but immediately called Melville after they left to give him a heads-up.

First thing the following morning, September 20, the Collective dropped letters in the mail to several press outlets, one of which appeared in the Sunday *New York Times*. "As Richard Nixon was talking 'peace' at the U.N. on Thursday, September 18 and his masters of war were relentlessly dealing out death and destruction throughout the world, a time bomb was placed in the Federal Building," the missive began. The letter went on to express solidarity with revolutionaries around the world and with "the black and brown communities in this country who are fighting to rid the world of American domination and exploitation."[20]

Despite the waning enthusiasm of its members for meetings, the Crazies still had a few more shenanigans up their sleeves. The day of the *New York Times* piece, "fifteen persons identified by the police as members of the radical 'Crazies'" showed up at the Morris Heights campus overlooking the Harlem River and Upper Manhattan for the NYU conference on Vietnam. "Waving Vietcong flags and shouting antiwar slogans, the protesters rushed onto the stage of the Gould Students Center at 1:50 pm and placed a pig's head at the feet of the two men, who were waiting to speak," reported the *New York Times*. "The disrupters were restrained by security guards and arrested by policemen summoned from off campus." All fifteen Crazies—fourteen men and one woman—were arrested on charges of criminal trespass, unlawful assembly, and disorderly conduct.[21] FBI records confirm that Robin Palmer was one of those present and arrested.[22]

Throughout the summer and fall of 1969, although Palmer and Krebs were spending time with both the Crazies and the Melville Collective, there was little overlap between the two groups. "Jane, David, Pat, and Sam never took part in any of the guerrilla theater events," said Robin decades later. In fact, Palmer and Krebs rarely appeared in public with any of the Melville gang. "Maybe a couple of times we went to a movie with Jane and Sam, but we would really be very, very careful about that," said Robin.[23]

On September 24 the police showed up with a search warrant at the *Rat* offices looking for the original Marine Midland press release. Although the cops failed to find the document they were looking for, when they asked who had opened the mail that day, one of the editors gave them Jane's name. Their search also turned up a copy of the original United Fruit story, which Jane had told them had come from the Liberation News Service (LNS). When the agents brought it back to Centre Street, Seedman was suspicious. "The *LNS* attribution seemed typed in as an afterthought, off center below the headline," Seedman said, "while the copy itself appeared to have been composed and edited directly on the same single page." While Seedman did not think the piece of paper would hold up as evidence, his gut told him that it had not been an arms-length piece of journalism. It had been written, he sensed, by the bomber.[24]

Also on September 24, Melville left the city to attend a two-week guerrilla training camp in South Dakota with H. Rap Brown, the militant former head of SNCC and short-lived minister of justice for the Black Panthers. He stopped in three midwestern cities along the way. Not coincidentally, on the evening of September 25, a time bomb, a Baby Ben clock connected to twenty-four red sticks of dynamite, was found before its scheduled detonation time of 2:30 am the next morning at the Chicago Civic Center. This discovery was followed in the early morning hours by explosions in the second-floor stairwell of the Federal Building in Milwaukee and at the ROTC building at the University of Wisconsin in Madison.[25] While Sam was crisscrossing the Midwest, Jane went to consult with a Movement lawyer who had represented Robin and Sharon several times in the past, Hank di Suvero, about the FBI's recent visit to their old apartment. Di Suvero reached out to the FBI on their behalf and reported back that the Feds wanted to ask Sam and Jane questions about "a matter involving a foreign government" and that they did not believe they were directly involved. Di Suvero declined the FBI's request on his clients' behalf.[26]

George Demmerle's efforts at ingratiating himself with the Black Panthers over the preceding eighteen months—hosting fundraisers, selling merchandise, and, of course, attending protests—had been paying off. In addition to his high-profile entrance at the Anti-Fascism conference in Oakland, George continued to be one of a handful of white radicals in New York with direct access to the Black Panthers. His reputation was burnished even more in the fall of 1969, when he handed over a copy of the Yippies' mailing list to them.[27] Although the Allied Panthers organization had collapsed in August ("The few individuals who were involved in the possible establishment of this group are breaking their ties with [Turco] because he is using drugs frequently and is mentally unstable," explained an FBI report), Turco managed to keep the flame alive by starting the New York chapter of the Young Patriots, the Chicago-based organization whose white leader, William "Preacherman" Fesperman, was known to sport Black Panther pins and Confederate flags.[28] "Fesperman was a fiery orator with a magnetic charisma and the integrity to back it up," according to historians Amy Sonnie and James Tracy.[29] The Young Patriots had recently formed a "Rainbow Coalition" with the Chicago chapters of the Black Panthers and two of the city's major street gangs, the Young Lords, made up of mostly Puerto Ricans, and the Blackstone Rangers, the same group whose blessings the Yippies had needed to secure before the Democratic National Convention.[30]

The New York chapter of the Young Patriots launched in September 1969 and reports from their early meetings suggest the crew of two dozen or so took their involvement quite seriously. "The level of commitment is higher than any other group I've been in contact with," George reported after a September 22 meeting. "They are not into playing games or sitting around talking revolution."[31] While the core mission of the New York Patriots was to try to canvas poor neighborhoods "to find concentrations of welfare and poor working class people that are predominantly white," they had more militant ambitions as well. At the September 29 meeting, one female member was told that she "would have to get used to the idea of working with someone who had killed a pig" and George was asked to travel to Washington, DC, to scope out a bridge that the group wanted to blow up to block an expressway being built through the middle of a Black neighborhood.[32]

At an October 1 meeting of the Young Patriots, leadership positions were announced. "George Demmerle, Defense Captain, has complete charge of New York chapters," according to an FBI report. "All information and directives go through him."[33] The rhetoric at Patriots meetings was growing more extreme, mirroring the arc of the Weatherman contingent within SDS. Minutes of their October 3 meeting were particularly alarming: While one member "was sniffing up a green powdered narcotic," another went on a monologue about how the group had to be ready to bomb hotels and department stores and then gave a demonstration of how to kill someone with a knife. A third person said that, "When we get our office, we will have to blow away any pigs who tried to force their way in." Such extreme talk was alienating potential members, and by the beginning of October the group's numbers had dropped from twenty-five to eleven.[34]

The site of numerous protests up to this point, the Whitehall Induction Center in Lower Manhattan was where draft-age men were required to appear to be, in the words of Arlo Guthrie, "injected, inspected, detected, infected, neglected, and selected." If a young man was unlucky enough to have his number come up, it is also where he reported for duty. On October 7, Dave Hughey, who had learned from Sam Melville how to construct a bomb, walked into the eight-story red brick and sandstone building at 39 Whitehall Street, past the security guards, and up to the fifth floor, where he left a satchel in the restroom.

Hughey was not the first person you would have suspected of being a bomber. "Dave was a quiet, serious guy," Walter Teague said. "I did not know that he'd decided to get involved with Sam Melville but if I had I would've cautioned him."[35] In her autobiography Jane Alpert described Dave (though she referred to him with the alias Nate) as having a dual personality. "For weeks on end he would be remote, distracted, almost impossible to engage in conversation," she wrote. "Without warning the solemnity would vanish and the funny, playful [Dave] would emerge." In the days and weeks leading up to October 7, Jane noted, he had been all business. A day later though, his mission accomplished, happy Hughey was back.[36] If Hughey was as bi-polar as their description makes him sound, he would not have been alone among fellow extremists of the period.

Seedman was uptown having a drink shortly before midnight when he heard the news of an explosion at the Selective Service building and rushed down to the scene. The bombing, which made the front page of the next day's *New York Times*, had "devastated" the fifth floor, according to the fire chief. More than forty windows had been blown out, in addition to exterior bricks and numerous interior wall partitions. Though there had been half a dozen people on the second floor when the bomb went off at 11:25 p.m., no one had been injured and none of the draft records were destroyed.[37] There was, according to the FBI, $90,000 of damage.[38] At some point between midnight and 5:00 a.m. a communiqué, written by Hughey alone, was sent out special delivery to four news outlets: 1010 WINS radio, the Associated Press, the *Daily News*, and UPI.[39] It was briefer than the others: "Tonight we bombed the Whitehall Induction Center. This action was in support of the NLF, legalized marijuana, love, Cuba, legalized abortion, and all the American revolutionaries and GIs who are winning the war against the Pentagon. Nixon, surrender now!"[40]

The day before Dave Hughey set off the bomb at Whitehall, a group of Weathermen blew up a statue in Haymarket Square honoring a Chicago police officer, setting the tone for the overhyped and underattended Days of Rage protests being promoted under the slogan "Bring the War Home." The president of the Chicago Police Sergeants Association called the bombing "an obvious declaration of war between the police and SDS and other anarchist groups."[41] Given the increasing stridency, exclusivity and cultlike litmus tests the Weathermen had been foisting upon its followers (monogamy, worldly possessions, and college were all forbidden), not to mention the organizational shambles they had left SDS in, it is perhaps no great surprise in retrospect that only a few hundred brave and/or deluded souls showed up in Lincoln Park on October 8, dressed in the familiar garb of street warfare—sporting helmets and goggles, and carrying placards and sticks. Not only was SDS in disarray at this point, but the leaders of both the Mobe and the Black Panthers had also come out publicly against the Days of Rage, noting not only the futility but the counterproductivity of courting direct combat with law enforcement.[42] It is not hard to see why so many people whose hearts remained firmly on the left decided to stay home, especially with Mayor Daley telegraphing his plans to use the same heavy-handed tactics he had employed a year earlier at the DNC. "[Weatherman] challenges the validity of an intellectual left, which functions as a comfortable culture of opposition," wrote Andrew Kopkind, who attended the protests in Chicago. "Instead it asks that radicals become revolutionaries, completely collectivize their lives, and struggle to death if necessary."[43]

The four-day event started with a bang at 10:30 on Wednesday night. Milton Viorst described what happened as that evening's speeches in Lincoln Park wrapped up:

> Racing through the streets, oblivious to traffic, the Weathermen broke up into assault groups as they reached the business section. There they took out clubs and chains and smashed the windows of shops and parked cars. When the police vans finally caught up, cops spilled out and engaged the rebels in nasty battles at a dozen intersections. Before long a thousand uniformed men and hundreds of plainclothesmen were roaming the streets in search of demonstrators. Less fastidious than in 1968, they fired their revolvers when they chose, and even struck some bodies with cars. Within in an hour, the rampage had been brought under control. Six Weathermen had been hit with buckshot, and sixty-eight were arrested.[44]

The next three days were full of similar scenes. There was no question that the protests were extremely violent and destructive: somewhere between two hundred and three hundred people were arrested, and more than a million dollars in property was damaged. Still, whether the action was a success lay very much in the eye of the beholder. In the December 1969 issue of *Leviathan*, Weatherman member Shin'ya Ono argued that it was a military victory. "Fifty-seven pigs were hospitalized, including a few who almost got killed, while we ourselves suffered many fewer physical casualties." Moreover, she said, they were successful in establishing the "existence of a pro-black pro-VC white fighting force."[45]

Not everyone agreed with this spin. "It was, in all, a humiliating defeat for Weatherman—all the group's top leaders were arrested and now faced criminal charges, typically assault and incitement to riot," wrote

Bryan Burrough. But even Burrough concedes that the rioting did achieve something: "It marked Weatherman as the leading player on the 'heavy edge' of the New Left, the furthest left, the wildest, the craziest, the most committed."[46] Regardless, SDS itself would never recover from the violent rupture that the Weathermen sowed. "Nominally there was still an SDS," wrote Mark Rudd, who was still national secretary despite his power waning. The organization still had an office, a bank account, and a printing press, but admitted Rudd, "in reality the Days of Rage had killed SDS." In his memoir, Rudd even calls the destruction of SDS "probably the single greatest mistake in my life."[47] Historian Van Gosse found a silver lining to the collapse of the student group: "The real effect of this organizational disaster was to free up thousands of experienced young organizers just as they were getting ready to graduate," he wrote. "These ex-SDSers were a major component of the New Communist Movement of the early 1970s, joining with thousands of young people of color coming from revolutionary nationalist organizations like the La Raza Unida Party, the Congress of African Peoples, the League of Revolutionary Black Workers, the Young Lords Party, and the African Liberation Support Committee."[48]

Back in New York, in the aftermath of the Whitehall explosion, NYPD investigators sifting through the rubble discovered the remains of another Baby Ben clock, but despite having a dozen men on the case, their surveillance efforts in the East Village were leading nowhere. "It was the most exasperating case of my life, and the most ominous," Seedman said. "We were always afraid that next time we'd find a bunch of dead people in the wreckage." Seedman did get one small lead that week, though, when the FBI sent over a clipping from an underground paper in Montreal called *Le Petit Journal*. According to the article, two Canadians who had taken part in the Montreal terrorist bombings earlier in the year had fled to the United States and were hiding out in the East Village; the article also referred to a dynamite heist in the Bronx.[49] At about the same time, the Royal Canadian Mounted Police contacted the FBI to ask them to put an American they suspected of being involved in some way with the Montreal bombers under surveillance. His name? Samuel Joseph Melville.[50] Neither the Canadians nor the FBI, however, seem to have brought the NYPD into the loop.

Melville returned from his tour of the Midwest—Milwaukee, Minneapolis, and Chicago—and H. Rap Brown's guerilla training camp in South Dakota on the evening of October 9. Only then did Jane learn that Sam had set bombs in all three cities.[51] Jane had been keeping a secret of her own though: while Sam was away she had gone to bed with Robin Palmer, according to Joshua Melville.[52] In his 1994 interviews with Jeremy Varon,

Robin confirmed that he and Jane had slept together without pinpointing the date.

As if Sam's news was not enough to put Jane on edge, there were other signs that the law was starting to close in. The morning after his return, on his way back from the grocery store, Sam bumped into two FBI agents standing outside the door of his and Jane's East Fourth Street apartment. "We're looking for Sam Melville," one of them said. "Does he live here?" Playing it cool, Melville responded, "I think he used to . . . but he moved out some time ago." What about Jane Alpert? "Yes," Sam said, "I was just going to visit her." And when asked who he was, Melville inadvertently left a small breadcrumb. "David McCurdy," he said, dropping the same fake name he'd used to rent the "bomb factory" at 67 East Second Street.[53]

It turns out that the FBI had also attempted to interview Robin Palmer the day before, although there is no indication that they thought he was involved in the bombings. An FBI memo suggests that they only wanted to pick his brain about the Days of Rage, which had just begun and which Palmer had not attended.[54] Prince Crazie, however, *had* gone to Chicago, but the intelligence he provided to the FBI, possibly on purpose, was of limited value and incriminated no one.[55]

Three days later, on October 12, Robin and George set out on the seventy-mile trip to Fort Dix, New Jersey, site of the massive U.S. Army base between New York and Philadelphia. By this point, the Crazies were almost done as an organization; Demmerle, the group's treasurer, reported that by mid-October their bank had been drained by all the bail postings, though they still had $400 worth of buttons and flags in inventory.[56] For most of 1969 the stockades at Fort Dix had been full of soldiers who had expressed their opposition to the war with either protest or desertion. Hunger strikes earlier in the year over poor conditions in the stockade had given way to a full-scale riot in the ninety-degree early summer heat over, among other things, racist treatment of Black and Puerto Rican GIs.[57] That first Wednesday in June a couple hundred soldiers had set mattresses on fire and hurled furniture at the windows; thirty-eight of them were charged in connection with the uprising.[58] On October 12, to show support for the antiwar soldiers, thousands of people, many of them from groups like SDS, Black Panthers, and the Crazies, showed up in New Jersey to march in support of the Fort Dix 38 (figure 58).

Sensing the walls closing in, the usually unflappable Melville boarded a plane to Albuquerque the next day.[59] By late October, while Seedman and Perotta were spinning their wheels, the attention of most members of the antiwar movement was focused on the upcoming Mobe demonstration

58. Protesters at Fort Dix, New Jersey, October 12, 1969. Estate of Louis Salzberg.

planned for Washington, DC, on November 15. The same tensions that were on display at the Nagasaki Day rally—shit-disturbing radicals versus the frumpy old guard—remained just as strong. On October 29 a new radical umbrella group announced itself: The Co-Conspiracy, complete with a black-and-red logo of a baseball bat colliding with a time bomb. According to the *New York Post* the new organization "consists of the New Left All-Stars—everyone from the Yippies, the Crazies, Weatherman and the Young Lords to the Women's Liberation Front to the Veterans and Reservists to End the War in Vietnam." While the consortium included a variety of views on the war, "all the participants are to the left of the liberal and moderate leaders of this month's Moratorium demonstrations."[60]

Despite scaring off some potential members with talk of killing cops and blowing up bridges, Turco was getting more traction with the Young Patriots than he had with the Allied Panthers. On November 1, well over a hundred people—including a number of Black Panthers and Young Lords—showed up at the Young Patriots fundraiser, a chili dinner thrown by the Rainbow Coalition at the Alternate U. on West Fourteenth Street.[61]

In addition to donations, which were encouraged to be sent to the Patriots in care of the Black Panthers uptown office, the event generated a half dozen new members for the group. Moreover, George Demmerle, who had earned the title of defense captain for the group, was told that one of the Panthers would send his name "out to the coast so that there could be a link-up between the east and west coast."[62] This fundraiser may have been the peak moment in the short existence of the Young Patriots in New York though. The national group was hobbled in February 1970 when police arrested Fesperman, Turco, and ten others in a late-night raid in connection with the bombing of a New York judge; the charges were later dropped but the reputational damage was done.[63]

As for the Weathermen, they became even more doctrinaire and isolated in the wake of the Days of Rage. "This short period in 1969, from mid-October to the end of December, was the most notorious Weatherman period—more group sex, LSD acid tests, orgiastic rock music, violent street actions, and constant criticism, self-criticism sessions," recalled Rudd. "We were by now a classic cult, true believers surrounded by a hostile world that we rejected and rejected us in return."[64]

Not everyone could handle the intensity—or make the cut. One such person was a young woman named Barbara, who was expelled from the Weathermen in the fall of 1969 and ended up moving into the East First Street apartment with George, who would not be divorced until December but had been separated for a few years by this point from his first wife (also named Barbara). "My home was always open to people who needed a place to stay for a night or two," George recalled two decades later. "So, I told her to stay until she found something on her own and she stayed, and stayed, and stayed."[65]

While most of the remaining members of the Melville Collective—Robin, Sharon, Lester, and Lester's fiancée—argued that the group should not steal any thunder from the upcoming march in Washington, Jane did not care. In fact, their reluctance to taking part in another bombing at this time suited her just fine. With the four of them out of the picture and Sam out of town, she could finally work with Pat and Dave—and she knew exactly what she wanted to do.

Chapter 14

Join the Conspiracy

GEORGE DEMMERLE HAD planned to parade a turkey around Lower Manhattan on election day but ended up having to go to Chicago instead. In preparation for the Chicago Seven trial scheduled to begin later in the month, the district attorney had put George's name on the witness list.[1] Having spent three years creating his Prince Crazie alter ego and infiltrating the most extreme edge of the New Left, George was determined not to have his cover blown now and planned to plead his case in person with prosecutors in Chicago.[2] The intelligence he was gathering as an undercover informant in New York would, he hoped, trump prosecutors' desire to nail Robin Palmer for his riotous behavior at the Democratic National Convention.

The prospect of being outed terrified the undercover Crazie, and with good reason. Another informant named Louis Salzberg had just been unmasked in court. A short man with glasses and long sideburns, Salzberg had been a fixture at protests and street theater skits over the past couple of years. As a staffer at the Spanish-language daily *El Tiempo* covering the antiwar beat, Salzberg had provided a steady stream of photos to the FBI since early 1967. When he had been fired from the paper in January 1969, the bureau helped him set up his own shop. "For years, there was hardly a demonstration in the greater New York area that I didn't attend: Madison Square Garden, Central Park, Fifth Avenue, Union Square, the U.N. You name it," Salzberg said.[3] He played the part too, decorating his new office at 41 Union Square West with a poster of Che Guevara and reaching out directly to the leftist groups he had gotten to know while a staffer at *El Tiempo* and asking them to let him know when they had events planned that they'd like him to cover."[4] By the time the Chicago trial began in October 1969, Salzberg had given thousands of photographs of Movement members to the Feds. Salzberg ended up admitting under oath at the trial that the FBI had paid him about $7,000 and covered another $2,000 of expenses since 1967, leading Dave Dellinger to comment from the defense table, "That's quite a letdown, Louis," while fellow defendants made pig noises in the photographer's direction.[5] (A number of Salzberg's photos appear in this book courtesy of his surviving relatives.)

But Demmerle would suffer no such indignity, not yet at least. The DA not only released him from being a witness but also, after pressure from the FBI, agreed to strike his name from the record, blaming his dismissal on his "background of being AWOL . . . therapy treatments and past involvement with the Minutemen."[6] This was particularly beneficial to Robin Palmer, since the case against him had to be dropped without Demmerle as a witness.[7] If he had been forced to testify, Demmerle said, he had been planning to "sit down on the floor in front of the defendants' table and say, 'Try me as well because I was part of it.'"[8]

On Thursday, November 6, a relieved George Demmerle returned to New York City with a short haircut and the tantalizing cover story to explain his absence that he had been away taking part in "clandestine activities in Chicago."[9] Over the weekend, most likely on Saturday, November 8, Demmerle received a phone call from Sam Melville, himself just back from the Midwest. Alpert recollected that the two men might have seen each other one other time since Woodstock; an FBI report says that Melville had attended "two or three" Crazies meetings and another report said he had attended "three or four" Crazies meetings.[10] How is it that Sam might have not harbored the same suspicions that many others in the Collective, or the Movement for that matter, did? Pat Swinton, who recalled that Demmerle had been at her apartment "a number of times," chalked it up to Sam being a "different kind of activist from the rest of us." As she explained it, "Because he wasn't going to all these meetings, Sam didn't have this built-up picture of George as a funny guy with a cape [so] all George had to do was say 'I did blah, blah, blah,' and Sam believed him."[11]

When the two men met up in the East Village that weekend, Melville not only invited Demmerle to join him in a bombing action in the upcoming days but also spilled the beans about what he had been up to for the past few months—details on the Explo robbery and all the bombings to date. "The only thing he didn't give me was names of the members," recalled George.[12]

One would think that after three years of undercover work, being invited into the fold of the headline-grabbing conspiracy would have felt like the big payoff for Demmerle. In reality, it was far more complicated. It presented two dilemmas in particular. First, blowing the whistle on Sam would mean George's own unmasking and ostracism from a group of people who had grown to be the closest thing he'd ever had to family. "I was trapped. That was the hardest part of all," Demmerle said three decades later. "There was a real sense of community there, people cared for one another, a real coming together of people and I loved it."[13] Deciding whether to report Melville to the FBI was complicated for a second possible reason. "I thought that he [could be] a federal agent . . . and they were testing me," said George.[14] But he had it backward. Demmerle was being subjected to a loyalty test, only not by the Feds. According to comments Robin Palmer made later to author Larry Sloman, "[Sam] was going to do these bombs in the vehicles as a way to test George," he said. [15] Ultimately, Demmerle felt he had no choice. "I admired Sam," George told the *Dallas Observer*. "But Sam needed to be caught. Eventually he would have killed someone."[16]

When George reached out to report his meeting with Sam to the FBI, his regular contact, Special Agent Robinson, was out of town for the weekend, so he met up with Special Agent George Twaddle.[17] The information he passed along ended up in this November 15 FBI report:

> SAM stated that he and his group have been involved in six bombings which included the bombing of the United Fruit Company, New York City, the Federal Building and the Whitehall Induction Center. One of the jobs in Milwaukee included the bombing of the National Guard Office. SAM gave the impression that six individuals were involved in the bombings.
>
> SAM stated that he has a tie-in with a group in Canada who have also been involved in bombings.
>
> SAM invited DEMMERLE to participate in a bombing on November 12, 1969, involving six Army trucks located at a National Guard Armory near Grand Central Station, New York City. SAM stated that three sticks of dynamite would be placed in six different trucks.
>
> SAM state that he had been involved in the robbery of Explo, Incorporated, Bronx, New York, where dynamite and blasting caps

> were stolen. He stated that he had taken part in this robbery and used .22 caliber pistol. He commented there was only one guard on duty at the time and this individual was an old man.
>
> SAM told DEMMERLE that when he makes bombs he uses two timers to insure that the bomb explodes. He further related that he uses the "hand method" referring to a clock hand. He commented he also used gelatin with the dynamite.
>
> SAM commented that SHARON KREBS of the Crazies has knowledge of the various bombings which have taken place but has not directly participated in these bombings.[18]

It was the detail about where the dynamite had been stolen from—information that had not been made public—that confirmed to the FBI that Melville was indeed their man. The FBI encouraged George to arrange a follow-up meeting for November 11.[19] According to the FBI file at the time and an interview George did much later, the two men met "several" other times over the next few days to prepare for an attack on the unspecified armory.[20] When Hughey learned of Melville's loose talk he was furious. Swinton appeared less angry. Nonetheless, the two of them decided to join Jane Alpert in their own plan for a massive, multiprong strike at the corporate imperialists.

On the afternoon of Monday, November 10, Jane, Pat, and Dave gathered at the East Second Street bomb factory. It was Jane's first time there, and she was shocked at what she saw. In addition to the alarm clocks, wires, and batteries there was a pistol, a rifle, and a couple of submachine guns. After Dave assembled three bombs, the three of them changed clothes and departed one at a time, parading past a team of undercover agents dressed as vagrants who did nothing to stop them.[21] Pat headed downtown while Jane and Dave boarded an uptown subway. Following the Melville playbook, each found a discreet location on an upper floor of the target building and left a bomb set to go off in the middle of the night. Returning home that afternoon, Jane typed up a communique and sent it out to the newspapers.

Deputy Inspector Seedman had just gotten home to Long Island at 2:00 a.m. when he turned on the radio. Shortly after 1:00 a.m., he learned, explosions had gone off almost simultaneously at the offices of Standard Oil in the RCA Building at Rockefeller Center and at One Chase Manhattan Plaza in Lower Manhattan; five minutes later, a similar blast occurred at IBM offices in the GM Building at Fifty-Ninth Street and Fifth Avenue.[22] Seedman put his tie back on and jumped in his car. After visiting all three sites, he established a command center outside Rockefeller Center, not far from where the tuxedoed revelers from the Rainbow Room had had to exit the fire stairs a few hours earlier. As the morning progressed, details started to trickle in: At the GM building, the bomb had been planted between two vending machines near the service elevators on the nineteenth floor; at the Chase building, the bomb had been left in a locker near the elevators on the sixteenth floor; the bomb at Rockefeller Center had also been deposited near the elevator bank on the twentieth floor.[23] By far the most damage from a financial perspective occurred at Chase Manhattan, where the destruction of walls, ceilings, elevators, and equipment was estimated to be almost $800,000. Total damage estimates from the seven bombings to date exceeded $1.5 million, according to FBI reports.[24] Seedman immediately received authorization for another twenty-five officers to blanket the streets of the Lower East Side.

The Popular Front for the Liberation of Palestine initially tried to claim responsibility for the bombings from their headquarters in Jordan, but the letter from Jane that the AP received that morning debunked that unlikely story.[25]

> During this week of antiwar protest, we set off explosives in the offices of Chase Manhattan, Standard Oil, and General Motors . . .
>
> The Vietnam War is only the most obvious evidence of the way this country's power destroys people. The giant corporations of America have now spread themselves all over the world, forcing entire foreign economies into total dependence on American money and goods. Spiro Agnew may be a household word, but it is the rarely seen men, like David Rockefeller of Chase Manhattan, James Roche of General Motors and Michael Haiden of Standard Oil, who run the system behind the scenes.
>
> The empire is breaking down as peoples all over the globe are rising up to challenge its power. From the inside, black people have been fighting a revolution for years.
>
> And finally, from the heart of the empire, white Americans too are striking blows for liberation.

That morning Seedman received a call from the FBI New York Bureau Chief, John Malone, with big news. They had a name: Sam Melville. The

FBI and NYPD now knew both the East Second Street and East Fourth Street addresses; they knew of Melville's connection to Alpert and about the underground newspaper she worked at. Acknowledging that the only basis they had to make an arrest at that point was the word of an informant, Malone and Seedman agreed to wait to try to catch Melville in the act. "If Melville really was our man, his line of work [plumbing engineer] explained his expertise at messing up those buildings," Seedman said later. "This was the work of a guy who understood the vital systems of an office building the way a doctor understands the body."[26]

That day, Tuesday, November 11, a couple of hundred copycat bomb threats were called in around the city to places like the New York Stock Exchange and Lincoln Center, necessitating the evacuations of the Pan Am building and the CBS building, among others. Meanwhile, the FBI and NYPD began surrounding Melville's apartment. In the early evening Sam called to say he was on his way over to George's apartment. When Sam arrived on East First Street ten minutes later, packing a .38 revolver, he went straight over to the phone and removed the mouthpiece and earpiece. Melville asked whether Demmerle was prepared for a shootout, and Demmerle replied that he was not unless it was absolutely necessary. He then complimented Melville on the previous night's bombings. "They went pretty good, didn't they?" said Sam. George also brought up the press release and, fishing, said it sounded like Pat Swinton. Sam, who had avoided mentioning any of the Collective members' names, was clearly caught off guard and said she had just been involved in the group's communications but was not part of the bombings.[27] Getting back to business, Melville said the two of them should meet outside George's apartment the following day at 3:00 p.m. and that they would go from there to the East Second Street studio to pick up the bombs. Sam had yet to tell George the specific target, but law enforcement was able to narrow down the list of likely targets to three armories, two in the general vicinity of Grand Central Station and one in Jamaica, Queens. Between the FBI and NYPD, they had the manpower to cover all of them; in fact, they even encouraged the National Guard to make sure they parked plenty of trucks outside as bait.[28]

Later that evening Robin Palmer, who had yet to take part in any of the bombings and had claimed to be busy with plans for the Mobe march, showed up at Sam and Jane's apartment, energized by the success of the triple bombing. He asked Sam if he would help him with an action the next day.[29] Melville's answer, of course, was yes.

Meanwhile, Seedman's new crew of twenty-five officers was doing its best to keep tabs on Sam and Jane. Staking out their apartment building, the detectives had become aware of some sort of connection between the couple and three other people—Swinton, Hughey, and Demmerle—but didn't know any specifics beyond that, including the role of Demmerle. Palmer's and Krebs's efforts to avoid being seen with Alpert and Melville were working. The Collective members were not making it easy on their tails either, keeping the shades drawn and lights on twenty-four hours a day and, according to Seedman, "avoiding the front entrance, skittering across rooftops and dropping into the hallways of other buildings."[30]

The next morning, as Sam and Robin met up at the bomb factory, two FBI agents calling themselves Terry and Mickey entered the ABCO air conditioning office at 240 East Fourth Street and asked to use the space to keep watch on the apartment building across the street. The owner agreed. At 2:00 p.m. , according to an account in the *Daily News*, the agents were replaced by "two Ivy League types in chino pants and bulky sweaters" who brought with them a radio transmitter-receiver, two walkie-talkies, and a pair of binoculars. They shaved two peepholes into the painted window and kept their eyeballs glued to the openings for the next ten hours.[31]

At 3:00 p.m., as planned, Sam and George met outside the new recruit's East First Street apartment and then walked to a bar on East Seventh Street. Once seated, Melville, dressed in a well-worn Air Force jacket with sergeant's stripes on the sleeves and still packing his revolver, told Demmerle that a bombing was already in motion to go off at 9:00 that night but did not disclose the location. Sam told George to return home and change into clothes with big pockets before coming back to meet him at East Second Street at 8:00 p.m. He also asked him to swing by the Department of Motor Vehicles to pick up some driver's license applications, since the Collective was planning to create some fake identities in advance of a fundraising crime spree. The group's savings, Sam said, had dwindled to $1,200.[32]

That afternoon Robin, with Sam along for moral support, deposited a bomb in a fifth-floor men's room of the Criminal Courts Building, which, as any New Yorker who read the newspaper knew, was where the Panther 21 trial was taking place.

There were twenty-eight agents posted in the surrounding blocks when Jane left her apartment building at 5:00 p.m. One of them trailed her on his motorcycle as she hailed a taxi at First Avenue and East Fourth Street and took it to Twenty-Fifth Street and Park Avenue South, a block from one of the armories. The FBI decided not to pick her up, settling instead for a strong clue as to that evening's target. At 6:00 p.m. the owner of the air conditioning store across from Jane and Sam's place went through the motions of closing the shop, leaving the agents inside.

Around this time Demmerle heard from Melville again, with some more big news. Melville told him the location of the bomb that was set for 9:00 p.m.—the Criminal Courts Building. This felt like a test to George. "I phoned the report in and I told them, 'If you touch this one, they're going to know that I'm an agent,'" Demmerle said later. The ball was now in Malone's court: he had to decide whether to move on Melville based on this secondhand information or wait to try to catch him in the act at one of the armories that night. He decided to wait. "They had no idea where in the building the bomb was," George recounted, "but they took the chance."[33]

George left his apartment for Sam's place at 7:55 p.m. and arrived at Sam's place five minutes later. Sam, who had just said goodbye to Jane at the East Fourth Street apartment, arrived at the bomb factory shortly thereafter. Entering the studio, George noticed two bags on the floor—one blue canvas with leather trim, the other khaki—with sticks of dynamite visible in them. Four alarm clocks, each with a small piece of wood glued to its face and a wire leading out of its mechanical parts, were set out on the floor. Using a supply of blasting gelatin, Sam began assembling the four bombs, attaching two of the clocks to four sticks of dynamite each and two of them to five sticks apiece.[34]

At 8:42 p.m. Seedman, who was at a banquet in Lower Manhattan, received a phone call: a bomb had just gone off at the Criminal Courts Building, blowing out windows, leveling a seventy-foot wall, and ejecting one woman off a toilet seat below—but injuring no one.[35] Only blocks away, the detective ran to the scene with just one thought racing through his head. *If the FBI's source was wrong, then we're back to square one.* As for Demmerle, he had passed the loyalty test. "The bomb went off and that proved to Sam that I was cool," he said.[36]

Back at the bomb factory, Melville had worked up an appetite and declared that they should get some food on the way to the armory. Following Melville's instructions, Demmerle left the apartment first and headed to the B & H Sandwich Shop at 127 Second Avenue near St. Marks Place. Three minutes later Melville followed. "The package is leaving the residence, carrying a bag in his left hand. All units begin operation," crackled the channel being shared by the police and FBI.[37]

George entered the deli, sat down, and ordered a sandwich. Sam, who'd walked west on Second Street and north on the west side of Second

Avenue, arrived with a duffel bag, sat down near the front door, and ordered a bowl of soup. Fifteen minutes later Sam got up and headed to the Astor Place subway, waiting at the north end of the platform for the 6 local train; George, a small backpack over one shoulder, left the deli shortly after Sam. He walked up Second Avenue, went west on Eighteenth Street, and then turned up Third Avenue.[38] On the subway now, Melville was observed by an undercover cop holding an "olive drab satchel" in his lap and "humming a tune."[39]

Emerging from the 6 train at Twenty-Third Street and Park Avenue at 10:00 p.m., Sam failed to notice a blue Chevrolet with two federal agents and an NYPD officer inside. The car trailed Sam as he walked east on Twenty-Third Street. As the target turned north onto Lexington Avenue, the police officer, a young-looking guy with blond hair named Sandy Tice, slipped out of the back seat and set off on foot. Moments later, Sam approached three U.S. Army trucks parked on the north side of the street between 117 and 129 East Twenty-Sixth Street; after examining them closely, Sam proceeded to Lexington, bag still in hand, and turned down toward Twenty-Fifth Street, where George was waiting. "There are three big beauties on Twenty-Sixth Street," he allegedly said, in reference to the trucks they had targeted. Sam instructed George to make sure the truck doors were unlocked. George headed back up Lexington and onto Twenty-Sixth Street, Sam close behind.

> *All units proceed to the armory. He's at the armory. It is not necessary for him to set that thing. It could be all set to go.*[40]

Tice followed twenty steps or so behind as Melville and Demmerle neared the trucks. While Tice stalled for time by speaking to a man walking his dog, Melville crossed to the south side of the street and Demmerle approached the trucks on the north side of the street in front of the Elton Hotel at 101 East Twenty-Sixth Street.[41] Tice was considering his next move when he heard the pounding of feet on the pavement behind him. "Drop it!" two FBI agents, guns drawn, yelled. Melville stopped digging in his bag as Tice shouted, "Don't drop it, for Christ's sake!" Melville and Demmerle were thrown against the wall and frisked. In addition to a loaded .22 caliber revolver in Demmerle's jacket pocket, the agents found two bombs in the green knapsack he was carrying.[42] As the agents handcuffed the two men, Tice was left with the bombs. Seeing his look of panic, Melville said, "Relax, they're not set to go off until two o'clock."[43] The time was 10:10 p.m.[44]

The police radio crackled:

Clear the inside of the armory and both sides of the street. The bomb squad is on the way. No one, repeat, no one is to touch the duffel bag or what was thrown inside the truck. Bring the two prisoners back to FBI headquarters. To other units: Begin search of all suspects' apartments. No papers (search warrants) are needed if suspect material may be found endangering lives of others.[45]

Minutes later, as George and Sam were taken to FBI headquarters on Sixty-Ninth Street, at least two dozen police officers burst into Jane Alpert's apartment, where she and Dave Hughey were in the bedroom listening to the radio, waiting for Sam to return. When it was clear that the officers were intent on smashing in the door, Jane opened the bolt. They slammed her up against the wall and grabbed Dave as he came out of the bedroom. Jane refused to admit her identity. Handcuffed, the pair watched as the police, without a warrant, tore apart the apartment, emptying shelves and drawers onto the floor in the process. Alpert and Hughey were taken to FBI headquarters on East Sixty-Ninth Street, where Melville and Demmerle already were. After being allowed to call her attorney, Jane confirmed her identity and allowed herself to be fingerprinted.[46] A few hours later she was going through the dehumanizing intake process at the Women's House of Detention, a site she had spent countless hours outside as a protester.[47]

Inside the FBI interview room Melville, who would soon be transported with Hughey and Demmerle to the Federal House of Detention for Men on the West Side Highway in the early morning (figure 59), was telling all, at least according to FBI records. His interrogators, who were relieved to hear that he had used up his entire supply of dynamite with the bombs intended for the armory, went through the laundry list of bombings from the past four months, taking care to shoulder all of the responsibility.[48]

Federal Office Building, Foley Square, September 19, 1969:
"Yes, I placed that bomb."

Selective Service Headquarters, 39 Whitehall Street, October 7, 1969:
"Yes, I did that one too."

Marine Midland Grace Trust Company, 140 Broadway, August 20, 1969:
"I previously told you about that one. I did it."

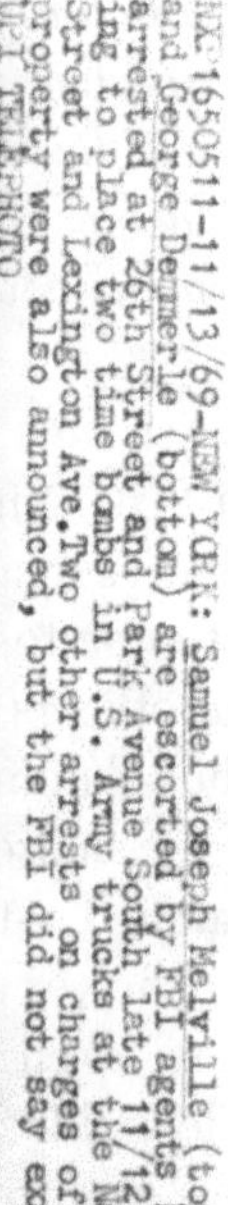

59. Sam Melville and George Demmerle arrests, early morning, November 13, 1969. UPI.

United States Courthouse, Foley Square, September 19, 1969:
"No, I did not place the bomb there. I know nothing about that one."

Manhattan Criminal Court Building, 100 Centre Street, November 12, 1969:
"Yes, I told you I placed that bomb this morning. It was scheduled to go off around 9:00 p.m."

1 Chase Manhattan Plaza, General Motors Building, and Rockefeller Center, November 10, 1969:
"I placed all three bombs in those buildings."

The Pen Fruit Bombing in August 1969:
"No, I had nothing to do with that. I know nothing about it."

United Fruit Company, Pier 3, North River, July 27, 1969:
"Yes, I was responsible for that one."

Noticeably absent from FBI headquarters that night and the arraignment the next morning was Pat Swinton. With her daughter in Chicago for the week, Pat had holed up for twenty-four hours with her sometime lover—a "Puerto Rican revolutionary," as she described him—doing acid and "screwing our brains out." At one point around midnight, they came up for air and turned on the radio. When she heard the news, she had to sober up quickly and start making calls. She managed to rustle up some cash, and a close friend brought her van around. Putting Pat on the floor in the back covered by a mattress, the friend drove her to the Philadelphia airport, where she caught a plane to California. Pat Swinton would stay underground for the next five years.[49]

Chapter 15

The Trial

AFTER WHAT SEEMED LIKE only an hour of sleep, Jane Alpert awoke to the buzzing, clanking, and yelling that was part of the morning ritual at the Women's House of Detention, where she'd been taken after her arrest the night before. A breakfast tray was slid through a slot in the door of her cell, and she was told to hurry: she was due in court with Melville, Demmerle, and Hughey in an hour to face a federal charge of conspiracy to bomb the Federal Building in September, the Whitehall Induction Center in October, and the army trucks outside the Twenty-Sixth Street Armory the previous night. It was Thursday, November 13.

The initial bail hearing was held at the U.S. Courthouse in the financial district. "The tiny room at the Federal Court Building, Foley Square, is packed with FBI agents, prosecuting attorneys, and security guards," reported *The Seed*. "A small, 8-man contingent of movement freaks sits excitedly in the back. The handcuffed prisoners are escorted in. They are unhandcuffed; Janie raises the clenched fist and smiles at us."[1] Also in the room were the entire staff of *Rat* as well as Jane's father and the Park Avenue lawyer he had hired to defend her, Mortimer Todel.

Arguing that the defendants had exhibited "wanton disregard for the safety of their fellow citizens," District Attorney Robert Morgenthau demanded bail of $500,000 apiece. The judge agreed. In the indictment papers Morgenthau also revealed that part of his case was based on "admissions made by one of the defendants." As the four accused bombers—Melville, Demmerle, Hughey, and Alpert (figure 60)—were led away in cuffs, a group of supporters raised their fists and chanted "Right on!"[2]

The next morning, Friday, November 14, prosecutors agreed to reduce bail to $150,000 for Hughey, $100,000 for Alpert, $300,000 for Melville, and $200,000 for Demmerle, whose undercover status was still unknown to prosecutors (though Malone had let Seedman in on the secret shortly after the arrest).[3] In the afternoon District Judge Marvin Frankel heard the defense's application for a further reduction in bail. Hughey's lawyer, William Crain, pointed to that the lack of evidence against his client as well as his lack of financial resources. "The only reference to my client is that Mr. Hughey and one of his co-defendants, Miss Alpert, are close at the heart of the conspiracy . . . but there is no indication whatsoever that they have committed an overt act or that they had any connection to the crime other than that an informant said they did," Crain said. As for reducing his bail, "Mr. Hughey is indigent . . . $150,000 is as impossible as $500,000."[4] Crain suggested that $5,000 might be "ascertainable" by his Baptist minister father.

Crain also argued on behalf of all the defendants that Morgenthau's pervasive presence in the press in the last two days would make it extremely difficult to find an impartial group of jurors and that the defense should therefore be allowed to screen candidates through the process known as *voir dire*. "It is our position that no grand juror of this county who has been exposed to these inflammatory and improper statements to the press

NXP1650572-11/13/69-NEW YORK: FBI agents and police arrested 11/13 these three men and this woman accused of attempting to plant dynamite time bombs in an army truck outside a midtown Manhattan armory. The FBI declined to say whether the suspects were responsible for the 11/12 blast in New York's Criminal Courts Building or any other of the recent skyscraper bombings terrorizing the city. The four suspects, shown in FBI photos, are (L-R) Samuel Joseph Melville,34; George Demmerle,39; John David Hughey III; and Jane Lauren Alpert,22. UPI TEL PHOTO 1d

60. Melville Collective mug shots, November 13, 1969. UPI.

would be able to return a true bill impartially," he said. Assistant U.S. Attorney John Doyle III objected, and the judge concurred. "The application is denied . . . on the ground that at least in its historical roots the grand jury is very different from the petit jury and is allowed to know things in ways that petit juries are not."[5]

Wall Street attorney Ernest Rosenberger, representing the still-undercover Demmerle, made arguments like Crain's for reducing his bail from $200,000 to $5,000, emphasizing George's roots in the community and record of showing up promptly to past court dates. Referring to the prosecuting attorneys for the government, Rosenberger said, "They were improper. They were unreasonable. They were improvident."[6] Jane's lawyer told the judge he believed that $10,000 bail was realistic in her case. Finally, Robert Projansky, proposing bail of $15,000 for Sam, reiterated the concept that "to set bail which we all know in advance is out of reach of this defendant, I submit that is tantamount to setting no bail at all."[7] The next morning Judge Frankel, noting that the evidence against Sam and George was "substantial" but "far less" against Jane and Dave, ended up lowering bail to $50,000 for the older men; $25,000 for Dave; and $20,000 for Jane.[8]

Within twenty-four hours of the arrests the New York newspapers had all released profiles of the four defendants and their on-the-run accomplice. The *New York Post* managed to track down one of George's younger brothers, who spoke on the condition of his first name being withheld. "I don't know too much about him. He must have had a hard life. I was only close to him for maybe two years. Once I got to know him, he was a polite person . . . nice to talk to . . . smarter than I am."[9] His older brother, Walter, who had also been sent away to the same group home with George as a young child, was reached by the *New York Times* for comment: "I thought he was to the right from the way he talked. How, if he got to the left, I don't know."[10] As for Melville, the *Times* could only get his landlord on record calling him "a quiet one" and commenting on his predilection for weightlifting and health food.[11] Meanwhile, *Newsweek* noted that the alleged bombing ringleader "had been questioned previously about bombings in Toronto and Chicago."[12]

On the morning of November 14 a search warrant was obtained from Commissioner Earle Bishopp of the U.S. Southern District of New York for the bomb factory at 67 East Second Street. Upon entering, police found a .30-caliber carbine M-1 rifle, two 9-millimeter pistols, a few dozen blasting caps, some identification papers in the name of David McCurdy, and a map of the Bronx with the Explo Industries warehouse circled. The

NYPD bomb squad also determined that there were no explosive devices left in the apartment.[13]

While the arraignments were taking place on the morning of November 15, some 250,000 people—the biggest crowd to date—were gathering to march down Pennsylvania Avenue to the Washington Monument in the Mobe-organized antiwar protest. While accounts of the march itself describe a largely peaceful event, the most militant of marchers did make their presence known. "At dusk, after the mass demonstration had ended, a small segment of the crowd, members of radical splinter groups, moved across Constitution Avenue to the Labor and Justice Department buildings, where they burned United States flags, threw paint bombs and other missiles and were repelled by tear gas released by the police," reported the *New York Times*.[14] When asked about the Melville bombings, Ron Young, one of the organizers of the Mobe march, replied, "If you're concerned about bombs, then think about the thousands of bombs dropped on Vietnam every day."[15]

The Melville Collective federal indictment, which was recorded on November 18, alleged that the defendants "would and did place and cause to be exploded explosive devices in buildings and vehicles owned by the United States and departments and agencies thereof, including the Federal Office Building located at 26 Federal Plaza, New York, New York, the United States Armed Forces Examining and Entrance Station located at 39 Whitehall Street, New York, New York, and a United States Army truck located in the vicinity of 26th Street and Lexington Avenue, New York, New York."[16] The DA held another potential charge—destruction of property—over their heads as well.

Alpert, Melville, and Hughey all pleaded not guilty.[17] In true revolutionary spirit, the three prisoners had agreed that they would refuse to get out on bail until the Panther 21 were freed. For Melville, this was an easy opportunity to burnish his already impeccable stature within the Movement (he could not have made bail if he wanted to), but for Alpert and Hughey it was a real choice—and real sacrifice—to make. "It really disgusted us to think of taking advantage of the racism that would enable at least two of us to get out while black people could rot in prison on totally unraisable ransoms," Jane said. She changed her mind when another inmate at the Women's House of Detention, a twenty-two-year-old Black Panther named Afeni Shakur, less than two years shy of giving birth to her future rap star son Tupac, sent word that Jane should leave if she could: "Revolutionaries belong on the streets, not in the jails," Shakur said.[18]

Support on the outside among the left was strong. One flyer that was distributed at the time summed up the radical consensus: "Either the accused did strike a magnificent blow against those who make profit through the destruction of our lives and our world, and they are our most courageous and beloved comrades; or they are being framed by a government bent on destroying our movement of hope and resurrection. In both cases they deserve our total support."[19]

With much of New York still shellshocked and confused by the rash of bombings, *Rat* editor Jeff Shero attempted to put the Melville Collective's actions into the context of growing frustration within the New Left over the past couple of years.

> The recent bombings in New York are not really a new phenomenon. They are merely a new stage in the existing trend. Instead of attacking draft boards and centers of campus war research, the bombers chose corporate headquarters at the Empire's heart. The letters from the bombers made their intentions clear. Their actions were not designed to injure people, only institutions which profit from and perpetuate the War Machine. . . . If the destruction of Vietnam couldn't be halted by choosing between Nixon and Humphrey, or by staging the largest peace marches in history then the hour had arrived that the machine itself must be shut down.[20]

On November 17 prosecutors brought a new indictment against the Panther 21—who had already been locked up for more than seven months—that added a twenty-second name to the list of defendants and a subway switch room to the list of targets that already included the New York Botanical Gardens, Macy's, and the Long Island Railroad, among others. With seven hundred protesters outside the courthouse, the defendants stood in front of the judge and said, "We plead guilty to being black in a racist America." That same day, twenty-three Weathermen were arrested in connection with a shootout with Boston police nine days earlier.[21]

On November 18, during the graveyard shift, George Demmerle was quietly released on his own recognizance without bail; the proceedings of the release hearing were sealed.[22] On the morning of November 19 Alpert and Hughey pleaded innocent. Bail having already been set at $20,000 apiece, Judge Milton Pollack ordered both defendants to surrender their passports and set December 15 as the next date for arguments on legal motions. Melville, who did not have a lawyer at this point, let alone bail money, was unable to enter a plea.[23] The following day, November 20, Jane (figure 61) posted bail and was released from the Women's House of

61. After being released on bail, Jane Alpert receives a hero's welcome. AP Photo/*New York Times*.

Detention. She emerged into a world where she was a cause célèbre. According to her memoir, she relished the attention. The *Rat* staff welcomed her back with open arms, and she immediately began getting front-page assignments. "I soon discovered I could do no wrong," she recalled. "I no longer had to sweep or file or type. I didn't even have to come to the office. The telephone rang for me twenty times a day—reporters, old friends, movement stars from other cities hoping to meet me—and the Rat staff dutifully took all the messages and never once complained."[24]

On November 23, some 350 people—including Allen Ginsberg, Andy Warhol muse Ultra Violet, and Paul Krassner—turned out for a rally in the ballroom of the Hotel Diplomat to raise funds for the Melville Collective defense. Dave Hughey, who along with Jane Alpert was a guest of honor, told a *New York Post* reporter on hand that "challenging the system means putting that thing called life on the line. If the movement is going to join the revolution it has to start letting go."[25]

George's release, meanwhile, was starting to raise eyebrows. There could be only one rational explanation for the sweetheart treatment: "The circumstances of his release strongly suggest that he may turn up at the trial as 'state's evidence' against the other defendants," according to a November 20 story in the Liberation News Service. "The FBI refuses to discuss whether it had undercover agents working to uncover—or to create—the bomb plot. But even in the eyes of the *New York Times* everything points to at least one of the defendants being an informer."[26] If only the public had known the half of it. According to an FBI report at the end of November, George had attended fifty-five meetings (including one Black Panther study group and a half dozen Young Patriots gatherings), submitted sixty-eight written reports and nine oral reports, and provided information on a hundred and twenty-five people in the past six months.[27] This doesn't exactly sound like the work of someone dialing back his intelligence reporting, as George later claimed he was doing during these final months. One of the many Movement members who would be stunned by the news of his role was George's new girlfriend, the ex-Weathermen member who'd moved in with him in the fall and never moved out. "I didn't confide in her," George said. "I didn't trust her enough to tell her."[28]

As chatter about George's involvement evolved from theory to fact within a couple of weeks of the bust, public discourse examined the tactics and ethics of law enforcement's infiltration and entrapment of radical groups. "Who or What Is George Demmerle?" read the headline in the *Daily World* on November 29. "How does a jobless die-maker manage to retain an expensive attorney whose offices are located at 37 Wall Street?" the article continued. "And how does a man without any visible means of support for more than a year maintain his apartment?"[29]

"As soon as I heard that four people were arrested for these bombings, it struck me that if any one of them actually was guilty, it would have to be Crazie George, cause he was the craziest person I had ever met," *Rat* photographer Paul Simon told Claudia Dreifus, the same reporter who'd confronted George at the Nagasaki Day demonstration in Central Park, for an article she wrote for the *East Village Other* three weeks after the arrests. "But as soon as I learned that there was a police informer among the defendants, I immediately thought of George—for the very same reason." Simon's editor, Jeff Shero, who remembered attending a few Yippie meetings with George, recalled to Dreifus, "He'd get up and say to people. 'Anyone who wants to get arrested, come with me.' A lot of people thought he was cool and radical. In retrospect, it appears that George was trying to get a lot of people busted." A third *Rat* employee quoted in the article, a photographer named Bill Etra, was truly surprised. "It's really hard for me to conceive of a police agent being tripped-out constantly," Etra said. "And George always went around as if he was on one big, big trip."[30]

The *New York Post* found a couple of Movement members who had known George to speak about him without attribution. "Old George . . . was always talking about coming 'round and bombing someplace," one said. "He was the most adventurous of all. He did the nuttiest things."[31] And another: "He was always conspiring with someone on some level. He had blueprints for sub-machine guns, and he had a detailed breakdown of how to make sub-machine guns for $12 each. He also had this thing worked out where he wanted to blow up the Brooklyn Bridge with a garden hose. He wanted to hook the hose up to a gas line."[32]

The pervasiveness of undercover agents in the Movement was taking its toll in general. In his regular column in the *East Village Other*, Allan Katzman described the decision by the Veterans & Reservists to call it quits because of the level of infiltration within the group. "We decided to disband because of our potential threat to the movement itself and because we understood that when the police force themselves into organizations like ourselves, they force us to become totalitarian to plug up the leak," a spokesman explained. The implications for the Movement, concluded Katzman, were ominous: "Because of this natural outgrowth to survive as a well functioned organization, the New Left will become more paranoid and suspicious of its people if they are not willing to die at a moment's notice for party policy. . . . A true believer will be one who lives, eats, breathes the revolution for twenty-four hours a day."[33]

A few days later an editorial in the *Seed* was a bit more defiant. "The bombings and arrests have unleashed a brief wave of confusion and paranoia through the movement here," wrote a staffer with the pen name "The Black Rat." "The government is precisely seeking that: to intimidate us and to breed fear and distrust among brothers and sisters. . . . Whether or not some bombers are in jail today, this is not the end of bombing in Amerika."[34]

Even the conservative columnist, James A. Wechsler, writing a few months later in the *New York Post*, questioned the tactics and ethics of such widespread use of informant provocateurs by law enforcement. "Both the scope and the character of such secret exercises have too long been unquestioned and unexplored by any Congressional committee. . . . How many such 'nuts,' as Demmerle so cheerfully portrayed himself, are on the FBI payroll?"[35]

Leftist quarterly *Dissent* did some soul-searching from the other end of the political spectrum: "How many other acts of violence and disruption, undertaken by far-out elements of the New Left, were in fact provoked by agents of the FBI or the police? When will the more serious people on the New Left learn that if someone starts shouting for bullets and blood he is as likely to be a secret agent as a sincere nut? And might not institutions that have suffered damage from recent riots consider the possibility that they were provoked by police agents?"[36] If the FBI had publicly denied knowledge of these incitement techniques, it would have been disingenuous. A report written in the wake of the bombing arrests notes that Demmerle "dropped hints that he was involved in 'heavy stuff' and had contacts throughout the US that could obtain almost any kind of explosive material if the need arose. . . . [He] also dropped hints that his contacts were involved in a bombing in Chicago and an oil line in NJ."[37]

In December, John Cohen, Sam's friend from their days at the Columbia Action Committee who, like Wolfe Lowenthal, had managed to extract himself from the bombing collective before things got too serious, provided an update on Melville's quality of life in the Federal House of Detention, where he was still being held on $50,000 bail. "About three weeks after his arrest he was severely beaten by his cellmates, and since then he has been isolated with one other prisoner in a maximum-security cell block," wrote Cohen in *Rat*. "He is not permitted to leave the cell to exersize [*sic*]. He is not permitted to watch television. Once a week he is permitted visitors for one hour." Cohen went on to question the case against Sam, which he claimed was based on a forced confession and "the testimony of crazy George Demmerle, a notably unstable human being, a police agent, and a refugee from mental institutions and the Minutemen."[38]

In early December, the same week that Black Panther leader Fred Hampton was murdered in his bed by Chicago police and a teenage concertgoer was killed by the Hells Angels during a Rolling Stones performance at the Altamont rock festival in California, the Melville Collective case was transferred to the court of the notoriously reactionary judge Milton Pollack, a negative development for the defense. Jane had also decided to switch attorneys by this point, jettisoning her corporate lawyer in favor of the more countercultural Sanford Katz. Her plan was to use the money she saved to help pay for Sam and Dave's legal representation.[39]

After a month of fundraising, a group of twenty or so of Melville's supporters had finally raised the down payment necessary to obtain the $50,000 bond to get him out on bail. On December 29, as part of a hearing on a motion by his lawyer to suppress a statement written down by an agent on the night of the arrest but never signed by the accused bomber, the ragamuffin crew piled into Pollack's courtroom, bond in hand, only to run into an unexpected wall: Since "[Melville has] no normal social or financial ties which would act as a reasonable influence," the judge said, he would require a single individual who not only could come up with the entire $50,000 himself but also would agree to take Sam into custody. And then he doubled the bail to $100,000.[40]

On the second day of the hearing Special Agent Robinson confirmed on the witness stand what was already by now obvious: that George Demmerle was an undercover agent.[41] Two weeks later, on January 14, Morgenthau filed a new indictment in Manhattan Federal Court to replace the original one from November. The twenty-three-count indictment dropped Demmerle's name and added additional charges for Melville relating to the production and possession of explosives. With the additional charges, Melville was potentially looking at a sentence length of more than a hundred years.[42]

The arraignment the next morning was chaotic. "Cries of 'pig,' shouts and stomps broke the decorum of Federal Court in Foley Square yesterday morning," reported the *Daily News*. When U.S. attorneys asked that Sam's bail be tripled from $100,000 to $300,000, one of the hundred or so supporters in the gallery shouted, "With $300,000 we could buy up an entire black ghetto and renovate it!" Pollack responded, "You are not going to help the defendants by making a circus of this courtroom." Hughey, whose current address was noted as being 228 East Third Street, stood up, raised a clenched fist, and bellowed, "Yes, it will! Yes, it will!" At this point, Pollack adjourned the case until the afternoon. At this much calmer session the judge ruled to keep Sam's bail at $100,000.[43]

A month later, during pretrial motions, the issue of the defense attorneys' bandwidth was raised. The three lawyers involved in the Melville case were concurrently working on the high-profile Panther 21 trial that had been dragging on for nine months. At the same hearing Pollack asked Sam why he was still sitting in jail even after raising his $100,000 bail. "I don't have half a million dollars," Sam sneered. "How the hell am I going to get out of jail, jackass?" Jane, who was seated close to Sam, started giggling.[44] Turns out that word had made it to Sam that he would be hit with state charges if he did get out of jail and that that this time his bail would be raised to $500,000. Melville was right, but it would turn out to be worse than that.

When State Supreme Court Justice Irving Lang weighed in three weeks later on the bail relating to the state charges that had been filed against Melville in the meantime, he slammed the door on Melville getting out. "If a court determines that a defendant would be a threat if released prior to trial, its duty is to remand him rather than set an extremely high bail," Lang wrote in the thirteen-page decision on March 10 that denied the accused bomber any bail at all. According to the *New York Times*, this concept of "preventative detention" had never been applied in New York State before, at least not in a noncapital case.[45]

A day after Judge Lang's decision, the U.S. Attorney's office leaked a story to the *New York Post* about an escape attempt by Melville the previous Saturday. According to the story Melville had been in the Federal Courthouse for a private meeting with his lawyer when he had overpowered an unarmed guard, tied him up with a belt, and fled down a staircase, only to be apprehended by an armed guard a few moments later. According to the *Post*, Judge Lang was unaware of the escape attempt when he made his ruling denying bail.[46]

Demmerle, in fear for his life since his unmasking, was in frequent contact with both the FBI and Assistant District Attorney Doyle during this time, though Doyle had already decided not to use Demmerle as a witness. "They would not put me on the stand because they were afraid of what I would say," he said later. "The defense wanted me in the worst way [but] the government blocked every attempt." Low on funds, George was also eager to get back to work. He came out of hiding once around this time to attend the Bronx funeral of a member of the Yippies named Michael "Mitch" Diamond. At the ceremony, a man George had known from his time in the Movement came up to him and said, "There's a $2,000 price on your head. I would get away from here as quick as you can." George skipped the burial.[47] Describing the run-in later to a reporter, Demmerle defended himself. "What I wouldn't reveal I was never questioned on—it was that I tried to help a lot of people out. If they needed food, a place to sleep, if they needed a shirt—it was there."[48]

One person who did forgive Demmerle when his identity was revealed was Charlotte Polin, the mentally ill woman who had written the letter of recommendation to Ho Chi Minh two years earlier. Her forgiveness was ultimately bittersweet. Just a week after the arrests of the Melville Collective, Polin, who by late 1969 had changed her name to Lan (the Vietnamese word for orchid), and her boyfriend Walter Petersen wrote George a letter in which they thanked him for all the kindness he had shown her. "We understand that you did what you had to do, and we do not blame you one bit for anything that happened. [Lan] has always had a special loving feeling for you because of how you did your best to help her when she needed help so badly."[49] The pair, who had recently started a group called Aid to Vietnamese Victims of US Bombings, even invited George over for dinner.[50]

The letter was the last George would hear from Polin.[51] Six weeks later, Walter Teague (for whom she worked as a researcher for a spell) received a call from the police asking him to come to the Brooklyn apartment she shared with Petersen. When Teague arrived, he was confronted with a shocking scene. The cops had torn the place apart. It was a mess, and there were busted statuettes of Ho Chi Minh on the floor. There were no bodies, but the traces of what Teague believes was a suicide pact were everywhere. "He had shot her and then shot himself and the brains were all over the wall," surmised Teague.[52] According to a newsletter called *Combat*, Petersen had shot Charlotte with a 12-gauge shotgun and then killed himself.[53]

The list of people who should not have been surprised by Polin's death included both Demmerle and Special Agent Robinson at the New York Office of the FBI. A January 1969 report by George—redacted but undoubtably about Polin—notes that "she has been dwelling on committing suicide as she is unable to fulfill her commitments to [the] North Vietnamese."[54] George also claimed that the cops told him that the news of his betrayal had prompted her to kill herself, her forgiveness letter not withstanding. "The pig turned out to be the good guy," George said. "Her belief system was totally destroyed."[55] Teague was a little more philosophical about the double suicide. "I think they were both victims of the war," he said. "Just as when she cried in Vietnam and the Vietnamese had to send her home, I think they were both being overwhelmed by the war and their inability to do anything [about it]."[56]

A few days later Hughey, Alpert, and Melville were hit with a third indictment that also layered on charges for Sam's attempted escape, and on March 24 a new name entered the mix when eighteen-year-old Bronx native Jonathan Grell, described by the FBI as a "fugitive who had been arrested in October 1969 for barking at a dog and causing a disturbance," was picked up in Canjilon, New Mexico.[57] According to the warrant, the FBI claimed to have statements from "three persons to whom the defendant admitted his membership in the [Melville] conspiracy . . . and predicted certain bombings in advance." In addition, he reportedly had been arrested two other times in November, once for possession of a handgun and once for the attempted sale of two rifles and a shotgun and had failed to show up at his court dates for any of the charges.[58]

Grell, a Bronx High School of Science dropout, was originally detained as a material witness, according to the Albuquerque FBI office, but was charged on March 27 while still in New Mexico on three counts: conspiracy, destruction of government property, and using a firearm in the commission of a felony.[59] The charges related to the same three buildings cited in the Melville case.[60] Grell waived extradition, and on March 30 he was brought back to New York City, where on April 2 he was included in a fourth indictment in the Melville Collective case and had bail set for him at $75,000.[61] A trial date of April 29 was set at that time.[62]

Nineteen days before the new trial, Melville was moved from the Federal House of Detention to the Manhattan Detention Complex (aka the Tombs), where he was placed in solitary confinement and denied all privileges, including visitors and even books.[63] During pretrial motions, near the end of the month, Judge Pollack severed Grell's case from the other three defendants, and the teenager was sent to Bellevue Hospital for psychiatric review.[64] As part of the same pretrial hearing the judge denied three other motions from the defense: one to rule out the use of Melville's confession; one to declare inadmissible some of the evidence found in Alpert and Melville's apartment on the grounds that a warrant was not obtained until two days after the fact; and one to sever Melville's case from the others.[65] Meanwhile, Robin and Sharon, miraculously unscathed by the bombing inquiries, announced to Jane that they were planning to go underground with the Weathermen. Soon after, Jane, living in a new apartment at 196 East Third Street, forged her own connection with the Weathermen by embarking on a clandestine affair with the increasingly paranoid Mark Rudd.[66]

On March 6 a series of blasts tore through 18 West Eleventh Street, leveling the Greenwich Village townhouse and severely damaging actor Dustin Hoffman's house next door. The house where the explosions occurred belonged to the family of Cathy Wilkerson, who, along with four other Weathermen, had turned the basement into a bomb factory. Three of them—Ted Gold, Terry Robbins, and Diana Oughton—were killed, while Wilkerson and Kathy Boudin escaped in the chaotic aftermath of the explosion. The bombs were being assembled for actions planned that night at Fort Dix and Columbia University. "We're going to kill the pigs at a dance at Fort Dix," Robbins had told Rudd.[67]

Only days earlier Robbins, along with New York Weathermen head J. J. Jacobs, had been interrogating Robin and Sharon as part of their recruitment process into the cultlike group. "I didn't know that he was over there in Kathy Wilkerson's house building these bombs," Palmer said later. "But Terry Robbins scared the shit out of me that night. I predicted to him, with J. J. present, that he was going to kill himself."[68] Even Rudd, who admitted later that he had signed off on the plan to bomb Fort Dix, knew that something was off with Robbins. "Part of the problem was that Terry was doing all the thinking," Rudd wrote. "He was just twenty-one years old, small, wiry, and smart as a whip, though by the time of the explosion his thinking had become twisted."[69]

The townhouse explosion would, nine months later, result in a rare moment of humility for the Weathermen when Bernadine Dohrn wrote a mea culpa in a missive known as the New Morning Statement: "This tendency to consider only bombings or picking up the gun as revolutionary, with the glorification of the heavier the better, we've called the military error."[70] The explosion also almost certainly accelerated the migration underground. By the spring it became clear that the true believers—those committed to the Weatherman mantra of "Bringing the War Home"—were all headed there. In addition to Boudin and Wilkerson, Bernadine Dohrn, Bill Ayers, and Mark Rudd dropped out of sight. H. Rap Brown did not show up for his court appearance in Maryland in March, either. Closer to home, Sharon Krebs and Robin Palmer, who had been spending a lot of time with Jeff Jones, were preparing to join the underground movement. Because of the group's ban on monogamy, they were headed to separate cells—Palmer to Boston, Krebs to San Francisco.[71] Even though they were separated physically, they still were joined by their underground codenames given to them by Weatherman leadership: Robin was Creedence, and Sharon was Clearwater.[72]

George had quite a scare on March 14 when two fires broke out in the middle of the night at the Brooklyn Heights Hotel where he had been living with his girlfriend for the past few weeks, legitimizing his fears that Melville was coming after him from jail.[73] A couple of years later, though, he started to think it may have been the government trying to scare him.[74] Assistant U.S. Attorney Doyle moved George to another hotel while he considered whether to put him in protective custody. Not wanting to lose his job at Jade Engraving in Sunset Park, however, George resisted, even when the Fire Department issued its verdict that the fires had mostly likely been a case of arson. After further discussion between Doyle and his assistant, Silvio Mallo, George was allowed to continue to go to work on the condition that he find new lodging.[75]

In April, Alpert had a pay-phone-to-pay-phone call with Pat Swinton, the first time she had heard the voice of her fugitive friend since November 12. With Rudd's encouragement, by the end of April Jane had decided that she would jump bail and go underground herself. According to Teague, who barely knew the accused bomber, Alpert invited him out to coffee around this time. "For whatever reason, Jane decided she was interested in me and wanted me to go with her when she jumped bail," Teague remembered. He turned her down. "I have a group and a purpose, and it wouldn't make any sense for me to go underground anyway, not just with you," he said to her.[76]

On the night of Thursday, April 30, the eve of her planned departure, Jane returned to her apartment after dropping her two dogs off with a friend. There was a message from Sam's lawyer, William Crain. She raced up to his townhouse in Murray Hill, where he delivered the news: if Dave, Jane, and Sam all agreed to plead guilty to lesser charges, Sam's sentence would be reduced from as much as 195 years down to fifteen, and Dave and Jane's term would be capped at five years.[77] She did not like the idea at first, but both Melville and Hughey were so strongly in favor that she pushed back her departure until the following week.

On Monday, May 4, the same day that the Ohio National Guard killed four students at Kent State, Jane appeared with her two coconspirators in court. After all the headline-grabbing drama, the end game was a bit of an anticlimax. "The defendants calmly admitted their guilt before a hushed and undemonstrative group of spectators—mostly female supporters of Miss Alpert," the *New York Post* reported. "I conspired with others to destroy federal property," Jane said to the judge matter-of-factly.[78] Throughout the forty-five-minute hearing Melville, wearing blue denim pants and shirt, and Alpert, in a green T-shirt and jeans, "repeatedly embraced" while Hughey sat impassively.[79] Just as Jane had, the two men pled guilty to conspiring to destroy government property, with Sam copping to an extra charge for assaulting an officer while trying to escape from the Federal Detention Center in Lower Manhattan.

With sentencing still more than a month away, Jane, sporting a blond wig and a decidedly unradical outfit, walked out of her parents' Forest Hills home the next day without so much as a suitcase. Arriving at the train station, she found herself in a swarm of antiwar activists heading to the same place she was—Washington, DC. "They looked at me contemptuously," she said. "I looked like a secretary for an accounting firm and I felt repulsive." From Washington she took a plane to California and faded into the underground.[80] When she failed to show up at her next thrice-weekly check-in at the U.S. Attorney's office, authorities declared her a fugitive; they also revoked Dave Hughey's bail privileges, sending him to Federal Detention Headquarters to await sentencing.[81]

On May 23 Demmerle made his first public appearance since his unmasking, attending a prowar rally at the Manhattan Center organized by the conservative group Silent Majority for a United America. "In a dark suit, his hair neatly trimmed, he looked a far cry from the wild-eyed, uncropped 'radical' in green laborer's uniform arrested last November with Sam Melville," the *Post* reported. When the master of ceremonies read out George's list of achievements, the crowd cheered as the former agent stood up, waving and smiling. Asked by a reporter if he felt guilty about turning in his friends, George said, "Yeah, yeah, but you do it because you know where they're heading. You know they're going to pick up a gun some day and shoot."[82] Twenty-two years later George explained that his appearance at this event and a dinner in his honor soon after had been largely performative, a way to signal to the FBI that he was staying in line. "The indictment was held over my head for two more years," he said, "and I knew damn well that I better be a good boy, or I could be charged as a double agent."[83]

May 1970 ended up being one of the most violent months on record in the United States. On the heels of the Kent State and Jackson State massacres, not to mention the U.S. invasion of Cambodia, there were 149 domestic bombings and another seventeen attempts. This suited the Weathermen just fine, but their antics antagonized more mainstream Movement members. As Tom Hayden wrote in *Ramparts*, "To us, revolution was like birth: blood is inevitable, but the purpose of the act is to create life, not to glorify blood. Yet to the Weathermen bloodshed as such was 'great.'"[84] Herbert Marcuse, still one of the guiding if grandfatherly lights of the New Left, was even more dismissive, calling out the "acts of violence by pseudo-political radicals" as "stupid, criminal and only play[ing] into the hands of the establishment."[85]

On June 19 Judge Gerald Caulkin sentenced Melville, who was sporting a beard again, to a minimum of six years in state prison, and an hour later Judge Pollack sentenced him to thirteen to eighteen years in prison on federal charges.[86] The sentences were ordered to be served concurrently.[87] Security at the federal sentencing was heavy, reported the *New York Times*,

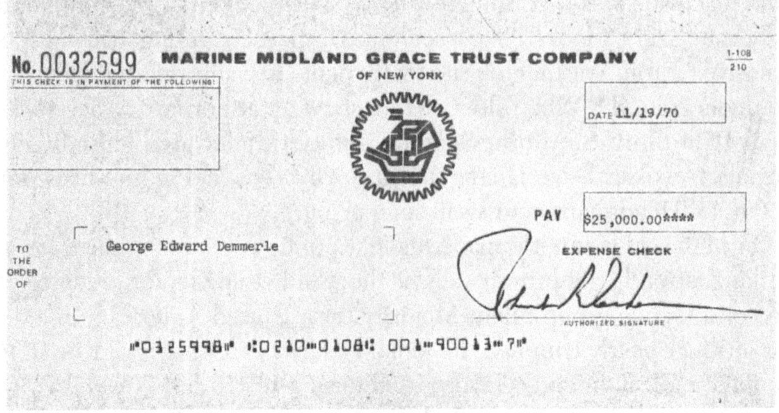

No.0032599 MARINE MIDLAND GRACE TRUST COMPANY
OF NEW YORK

1-108
210

THIS CHECK IS IN PAYMENT OF THE FOLLOWING:

DATE 11/19/70

PAY $25,000.00****

TO THE ORDER OF George Edward Demmerle

EXPENSE CHECK

AUTHORIZED SIGNATURE

62. George Demmerle's reward from Marine Midland bank. Estate of George Demmerle.

and the atmosphere "tense but orderly."[88] During the sentencing, as Judge Pollack was noting that the damage to the induction center had grown to over $90,000, Sam interrupted him, saying "that's about two Viet Cong."[89] On his way out of the courtroom, headed back to the Tombs temporarily before being sent to Attica, Sam gave the gallery a clenched-fist salute.[90]

Meanwhile Hughey's prospects were looking a little better. Pollack stated that he had been ordered to receive a psychiatric examination "to determine whether he is fit to be returned to society as a useful citizen" and that the findings would be released in a presentencing report within sixty days.[91] Pollack held out the possibility that Hughey could ultimately be sentenced under the youthful offender act, which would likely end up falling well short of the maximum sentence of four to six years. It would also give him the opportunity to have his record cleared.[92] In the end, he was sent to a federal reformatory in Petersburg, Virginia.[93]

On November 20, 1970, four years and four months after he had placed his original cold call to the FBI, George Demmerle took a couple hours off work to take the subway to Lower Manhattan, where he passed by the red Noguchi cube and entered the lobby of 140 Broadway. He took an elevator upstairs and with no fanfare whatsoever collected the reward that Marine Midland had offered for information leading to the capture of the person responsible for bombing the bank fifteen months earlier.[94] The amount, $25,000 (figure 62), was almost five times as much as he'd earned during his two and a half years on the FBI payroll.[95]

Chapter 16

Aftermath

STEVE WEINER, A TWENTY-TWO-YEAR-OLD undercover cop who'd joined the NYPD in early 1969 to avoid the draft, was walking home to his small apartment on Stanton Street one afternoon in June 1970 when someone tapped him on the shoulder. After a few months of attending Movement meetings and protests, Weiner had established his radical credibility the previous October by taking part in the Days of Rage in Chicago and afterward back in New York "hanging out in cafes, talking to the Crazies, who would wear red buttons with a machine gun on it." Weiner showed a knack for the craft. "I'd make friends, socialize, get arrested with people," he described in a *Newsday* profile more than a decade later. "The only way I can describe it—I was a camera, taking in everything."[1] In recent weeks, however, as the Weathermen had scattered in the wake of the townhouse explosion in March, his network had begun to dry up.

Turning around, Weiner was relieved to see one of his old contacts, Robin Palmer. Recently back from Boston where he had been part of a five-person underground cell for the past three months, Palmer had a beard and looked older. The rambunctious former Yippie and Crazie with more than a dozen arrests under his belt had been forced to come back aboveground days earlier because Sharon Krebs, his girlfriend and radical co-conspirator for the past three years, had experienced a manic-depressive episode during her immersion in a separate underground cell and "become unable to carry her load . . . on the west coast," according to Robin. The Weathermen, Robin said later, "were scared that she'd fuck up in some way . . . and they'd all get busted." Since Sharon was in no shape to return to their Bedford Street apartment alone (and no one trusted her not to spill the group's secrets), it was agreed that Robin should join her.[2]

With the downtown radical scene so splintered in the wake of the Melville arrests and the townhouse explosion, both men were excited to see each other, though for different reasons. It didn't take long for the unsuspecting Palmer to tell Weiner that he was planning to form a new bombing cell and invite him to join on the condition that Weiner be ready to give up everything at a moment's notice to go underground. Not wanting to look too eager, Weiner said he would think about it. A few days later Weiner bumped into another former Crazie named Marty Lewis, also back in town after lying low in California for a few months. Lewis "wasn't a media personality, just a guy people trusted, committed to the movement but just a spear carrier like me," Weiner recalled. Palmer had already spoken with Lewis, and the three men decided to move ahead together; not wanting to be chauvinists, they invited Krebs and three other women—Claudia Connine, Joyce Plecha, and Leslie Bacon—into the group. In the subsequent weeks, Bacon would drop out and a twenty-year-old man named Christopher Trenkle would join.[3]

Weiner had first met Palmer and Krebs at a rally for the Panther 21 in front of the Criminal Courts building a year earlier. Weiner had noticed the couple—they both were carrying pigs' heads on sticks—before the cops charged the crowd. When Krebs tripped trying to get away, Weiner picked her up and the three of them escaped into Chinatown. A week later, Palmer invited Weiner, who'd come to the force without any strong political convictions, to come to a Crazies meeting.[4]

Over the six months after Palmer and Weiner reconnected in mid-1970, the seven cell members met frequently to brainstorm on the how and where of their first action and, as the fall got underway, to practice building bombs, which they soon decided should be made of gasoline and not dynamite. Unfortunately for the real radicals, many of these meetings were held in Weiner's apartment on the Lower East Side, which was tapped by the police.

After deciding on a target—the First National City Bank at 1275 Madison Avenue—the group agreed that Weiner, whom they believed drove a taxi for a living, would ferry the bombers and their equipment to the site and serve as a lookout. Weiner's tensest moment as an undercover came with just two weeks to go before the bombing they'd planned to commemorate the December 4 anniversary of the killing of Black Panther chairman Fred Hampton. Arriving at one of the group's meetings in the East Village, Weiner was met with silent glares. "We know you're a pig," said one of the women, nodding to her backpack where she claimed to have a gun.

"Defend yourself. . .and you better say the right things!" Weiner's mind was racing, trying to figure out how he might have given himself away. He decided to try sarcasm. Gesturing to two German shepherds sleeping in the corner, he said, "Yeah, there are my partners." No one laughed. He tried again. "Yeah, you're 100 percent right." Standing up, the undercover policeman pulled his wallet out of his back pocket and flipped it open, as if it were a badge. "You're all under arrest!" A long silence followed until Robin let out a laugh, and everyone else followed suit. Tragedy narrowly averted.[5]

Sometime after midnight on December 4, the crew met up at an apartment on East Thirteenth Street. The bombing materials—gasoline, milk cartons, and fuses—were laid out. Weiner, the driver and lookout for the night, had to steady himself. "These people weren't friends, but in a way, they were," he recalled later, echoing some of the same mixed emotions expressed by George Demmerle. "These people were opposed to oppression and war [but] I had to remind myself that their plan was to assassinate people, and in the end, they were becoming the same thing they were fighting."[6]

Weiner drove Palmer and Lewis uptown in his cab, which had been bugged with a microphone and transmitter so police could hear what was going on in real time. He dropped the men and began circling the block. The other four cell members arrived at Madison and Ninety-First Street, oblivious to the number of derelicts on the block. It was after 3:00 a.m. when the four milk cartons full of gasoline were lined up on the windowsills of the bank; two of the cell members stood ready with hammers to shatter the windows.[7]

At 3:20 a.m., according to news reports, plainclothes policemen posing as drunks staggered up the block and worked their way between the Weathermen and their bombs. Uniformed cops descended. The gig was up. All six cell members were handcuffed and arrested. Weiner, who'd remained in his cab, opted not to go through the charade of being booked, and in less than two weeks his name had been published in the alternative press as the whistle-blowing pig, setting off the predictable soul-searching and second guessing within the Movement.[8] "Many of the people who remember him hanging around movement groups say now that they had suspicions about him but never checked him out thoroughly," according to a *Rat* article. "He used to go to meetings and demonstrations, but never talked much, and though superficially friendly, never got really close with anyone."[9] Palmer, suckered for a second time in a year, was philosophical. "Steve Weiner was very good at conning us and particularly conning me," Palmer reflected. "He had a lot of sympathy for us and our politics but when we started advocating getting guns and shooting police, he shed some of his qualms in regard to turning us in," he rationalized.[10]

On December 8, 1970, all six members of Robin Palmer's Weather Underground cell were charged with attempted arson in the first degree as well as conspiracy to commit criminal mischief. The seven-count indictment also alleged that other targets in the "escalating series of attacks" the group had planned for the future included two police stations as well as the Bolivian consulate, Nixon's former law firm, and the Math and Science Building at NYU.[11] Palmer, with fifteen arrests under his belt at that point, was given an initial bail of $250,000 but ended up being released from the House of Detention on Centre Street for $60,000 on March 10; bail for Sharon and the other four defendants had been set at $50,000 apiece. On March 18 Robin entered a plea of guilty to the felony of conspiracy to commit arson, second degree.

For Robin and Sharon, both out on bail, the next two months were personally tumultuous. According to Robin, Sharon became fixated on a plan to marry him while also getting pregnant with the child of a Black man; she started wearing dashikis and taking Swahili classes, too. With only days to go before the wedding, however, Sharon called it off. They still threw a party but Palmer ended up spending the final days leading up to his imprisonment having a fling with one of the other women from the cell, Joyce Plecha.[12]

At the sentencing on May 7, 1971, defense lawyers tried to emphasize the political nature of their clients' crime, noting also that there had been 169 political bombings in the prior two years in New York City. Justice Harold Birns did not buy it. "All were partners in a criminal enterprise, and their political beliefs in no way mitigate the enormity of the crime," he said.[13] Robin, Sharon, and Marty Lewis received the maximum sentence of four years in prison, while Joyce Plecha and Claudia Conine were sentenced to three years apiece. The sixth member of the group, Christopher Trenkle, was referred for psychiatric examination.[14]

By the time Robin and Sharon were sentenced, George Demmerle was still in New York, looking for work as a private investigator and trying to get a book deal.[15] Meanwhile, Jane Alpert was on the run in San Diego, where she had befriended a doctor and his wife and found work as a medical assistant in their office. While in Southern California she had joined a weekly women's group that began to have a profound effect on how she viewed her time with Melville and in the Movement.[16]

In the late afternoon of Thursday, September 9, 1971, Jane was leaving the beach when she passed a newsstand and saw the headline in an evening edition of the newspaper: "Inmates Riot at New York's Attica Prison." Her heart sank. After a fitful weekend with no news about Sam's status, Jane was in a friend's car on the way to a job interview when she heard the news on the radio. The standoff had escalated, and helicopters were circling the prison. At 6:00 the next morning Jane was awakened by a phone call. It was John Cohen. Melville was dead.[17]

The details of Sam's killing are not clear to this day. A contemporaneous article in the *New York Times* quoted a Department of Corrections official claiming that "one prisoner, known as Mad Bomber Melville, was killed by a sharpshooter as he was running with four home-made bombs ready to blow up a 500-gallon fuel tank on the grounds."[18] Years later Palmer, who ended up serving about half of his 2.5-year sentence in Attica, would claim that Melville had only been injured by the sharpshooter and that, as Robin held his wounded friend in his arms, another guard had executed him.[19] A photo of Sam's body in the morgue, included in Joshua Melville's book, shows four gunshot wounds, none more than a couple of inches apart from another, just below Sam's left shoulder. "According to [the ballistic report], buckshot used that day had a diffusion of five to eight inches when fired from more than thirty feet [but] the diffusion of [Sam's] wounds was only four inches," wrote the younger Melville. "And according to the state itself, the distance needed for buckshot with a diffusion of only four inches was less than fifteen feet." The conclusion, to Joshua Melville, is obvious: "Dad was murdered at point-blank range."[20]

Three days before he was killed, Sam had written a short letter to be shared with his supporters in the Movement:

Power People!

We are strong, we are together, we are growing. We love you all, we need your continuing love & support. Brother Huey is on his way and Counselor Kunstler, too. YAWF is storming the walls. What shall we do? Cha cha cha.

Ho Ho Ho Chi Minh

Please Inform our next of kin.[21]

The following week Melville's body lay in state at the Washington Square Methodist Church, which had become an important hub for antiwar radicals, women's libbers, and gay rights activists in New York. For three days, Movement members—Black Panthers, Yippies, Young Lords, and others—floated through the space, culminating in a speech by leftist attorney William Kunstler:

> I was probably the last person to see Sam alive. On Sunday evening, seven or eight members of the negotiating committee went into the prison . . . when we were about to leave we went over to see Sam. I went over to a line of 100 prisoners who had formed a human barricade by linking their arms together. Sam was standing with his brothers. I can't remember what I said, but I can remember him saying to tell everyone 'I'm at peace with the world.'"[22]

Despite the great risk, Jane decided to go to New York. "I knew I had to be with Sam's body," she wrote in her autobiography. "Nothing else would make his death real to me." In disguise, she boarded a flight, and the next night at 2:00 a.m., after the throngs had cleared out of Washington Square Methodist, she was able to see Sam a final time. "The bombings may have been wrong, but our impulse to defy the American establishment, especially at the height of the Vietnam War, had been right, and without Sam I would never have acted on it," she wrote a decade later.[23]

On her last night in New York John Cohen took Jane out to a Chinese restaurant to pitch an idea: What if they published a book of Sam's letters from prison? Cohen had already lined up a publishing deal and that evening offered Alpert half of the $7,500 advance to write a ten-thousand-word introduction. *Letters from Attica*, which comprised Sam's correspondence with his son, his ex-wife, and Cohen and included forewords by both Cohen and Alpert, was published in March 1972.

A month after Sam's killing George Demmerle was honored by another conservative group called the Silent Majority for a United America at its annual fundraising dinner at the Safari Club in College Point, Queens. In the view of these right-wingers, Demmerle's sacrifice and achievements had gone woefully unrecognized. "When he was acting out his role as a hard-core subversive, he received all kinds of publicity," the Silent Majority's publicity director, Paul Seufert, said. "Then, when he exposed his 'fellow travelers,' the New York Bombers, etc. and pointed up the communist controlled or inspired activities of the Bernardine Dohrns, the Jerry Rubins, and others, he received an awesome 'publicity silence.'" Still craving the love and attention he failed to get as a child, George accepted the invitation to the dinner without apology, despite the FBI's misgivings about him appearing in public. "If these people want to throw a dinner on my behalf—fine," he told a local reporter.[24]

In early November George, hoping for more affirmation as well as collateral to help him clear his police and army records, reached back out to the FBI to ask why he'd never received a bonus or a letter of thanks. The issue was elevated all the way to the director's office, which responded in mercenary fashion. "While there is no dispute concerning the value of this informant, the Bureau feels a personal letter to him might serve as an endorsement of any future actions on the part of Demmerle, thus affording him an opportunity to capitalize on his connection with the Bureau without any control," read the response. "Continue your efforts to maintain complete control of this former informant."[25]

Just before Thanksgiving Demmerle was nominated for the George Washington Award, an annual prize given by a conservative organization called Freedom's Foundation. In addition to touting Prince Crazie's greatest-hits reel of groups infiltrated, bad guys brought down, and stray youths saved ("said by several agents of the F.B.I. to have been the best subversive intelligence agent ever"), the five-page nomination letter highlighted three noteworthy accomplishments of Demmerle's. It celebrated the fact that "the obscene underground revolutionary newspaper, *Rat*, ceased publication" and spun Charlotte Polin's suicide as a bright spot on George's résumé. The letter also claimed that "During the 'Four Days of Rage' in Chicago, the Weathermen chose George Demmerle to head up their security to keep out undercover agents," a claim difficult to prove but not inconsistent with the detailed reporting George provided during those days and what we know now about his martial arts skills.[26]

The nomination, which was supported by members of other conservative groups like the National Committee for Responsible Patriotism and the Women's National Republican Club, also included this surprise: "Over a year after Melville's arrest, Demmerle again aided the forces of justice in pinpointing a second bomb group and gave information leading to its capture. The group included Leslie Bacon, on trial now for bombing the Capitol Building in Washington, D.C."[27] Decades later Palmer himself later explained that Bacon, all of eighteen at the time, had originally committed to joining his Weather Underground cell before deciding in the fall of 1970 that she did not want to go underground.[28] Instead she joined a commune in Washington State that was implicated in the bombing of a Capitol Building bathroom in protest of the U.S. invasion of Laos.[29] It is hard to imagine that Demmerle could have had much of a hand in cracking either her or Palmer's case, though he might have supplied background information that was helpful.

In early 1972, shortly after Demmerle began working for the Burnes Detective Agency in New York at a salary of $200 a week, an advance copy of *Letters from Attica* was delivered to Jane Alpert at her new hideout in a small town in New Mexico.[30] By this point she was regretful, if not embarrassed, about the introduction that now had her name on it, despite some last-minute edits she had made "to reflect my entirely changed interpretation of Sam." Though written only a few months earlier, her take on the events of 1968 and 1969 were already out of step with her rapidly evolving feminist consciousness.[31]

Between her weekly meetings with her women's group in San Diego and frequent phone calls with the feminist writer/activist Robin Morgan, Jane's feminist reorientation was fully under way. "Everything I read during those early months of 1972 became text for the same subject: the age-old oppression of women by men," she wrote later.[32] That evolution, combined with a handful of dispiriting run-ins with Weathermen who were not receptive to her revisionist history, only hastened her transformation and hardened her resolve to write her own story.[33]

One of these encounters was with Mark Rudd, the former SDS and Weatherman star with whom Jane had had a fling back in New York in the spring of 1970 before she went underground. Still on the run after quitting the Weathermen, Rudd had moved to Santa Fe in 1971. On this evening in April 1972 both Alpert and Rudd had decided to attend a lecture in a downtown church by an English doctor about his years working in China. When Rudd spotted Alpert he was stunned by her lack of disguise, which only confirmed the periodic reports he had received about her that she was "Not Doing Well," which in Weathermen-speak could mean anything from losing political faith to losing her mind.[34]

The sight of her former lover in the small church spooked Jane, and she snuck out before the lecture ended. Rudd managed to get a message to her through the friend she had been sitting with, and the two on-the-run radicals met up in a deserted strip mall parking lot. As soon as Rudd complimented her on what she had written for *Letters from Attica*, he knew something had changed in her. "I'm sorry I wrote it," she told him. 'I've been getting in touch with my own oppression as a woman and I don't have much sympathy for an oppressor like Melville." Before they packed up and headed back to the East Coast, Rudd and his girlfriend ended up hanging out with Jane a few more times.[35]

In addition to having become Alpert's closest friend, Robin Morgan was by this point a well-known figure in not only feminist circles but on the left in general. Active with SNCC and CORE earlier in the decade, Morgan had been a founding member of New York Radical Women and Women's International Terrorist Conspiracy from Hell (WITCH). In 1970 Alpert and Morgan had led a women's takeover of *Rat*, a move that had proved impossible for editor Jeff Shero to block in the political climate of the time. "This takeover had to happen. The blatant sexism of *Rat* in the past is only part of what made it necessary," the new editors wrote in the February 6 paper. "*Rat* has been moving no one to action, has failed to even suggest directions for action."[36]

On page 6 of this inaugural issue Morgan penned an article called "Goodbye," a full-fledged kiss-off to the patriarchy: "Goodbye, goodbye forever, counterfeit Left, counterfeit, male-dominated cracked-glass-mirror reflections of the Amerikan nightmare," began the final paragraph. "Women are the real Left. We are rising, powerful in our unclean bodies; bright, glowing mad in our inferior brains; wild hair flying, wild eyes staring, wild voices keening; undaunted by blood we hemorrhage every twenty-eight days. . . . We are rising with a fury older and potentially greater than any force in history, and this time we will be free or no one will survive."[37]

Stung by the Weathermen's refusal to adapt their imperialism-centric world view to sufficiently include feminism and egged on (and edited) by Morgan, Jane embarked on a new writing project. In the early months of 1973, against the backdrop of the historic *Roe v. Wade* decision in January, Jane composed a lengthy treatise called "Mother Right: A New Feminist Theory" that would change the next few years of her life and ultimately create divisions not only in the feminist world but the broader Movement as well. In early May 1973, a few months after moving to Denver under an assumed identity and starting to teach at an Orthodox Jewish school for girls, Alpert mailed her manuscript to *Off Our Backs*, the feminist paper founded by Marilyn Webb, the speaker who had been so shockingly cat-called during her speech at the counter-inaugural in 1969. "Having gone underground three years ago as a committed leftist, and since become a radical feminist, I regard this piece as a distillation of what I have learned," Jane wrote in the introduction. "[It] describes the process by which I became a feminist and devoted a fair amount of space to my vision of the future, for you, for myself, for the planet."[38]

The body of the essay, published within a few days of being submitted, attacked the chauvinism and ideological priorities of the left in general and the Weather Underground, as the group had been called since 1970, in specific. "I have some hope that the impact of a public statement may do what none of my private arguments have succeeded in doing: persuade you to leave the dying left in which you are floundering and begin to put your immense courage and unique skills to work for women—for yourselves." Alpert's tone toward Melville had changed meaningfully too in the year since she had written her essay for *Letters from Attica*. "What he valued in me, besides having a dependable sexual partner and housekeeper, was what he took be my 'independence' and 'self-sufficiency' [which] made me useful to him as an ally, and further assured that I had the quality he prized above all else: the capacity to love him devotedly yet get along without him uncomplainingly whenever he chose to leave," she wrote.[39]

Alpert went after not only Sam but also the male leaders of the Weathermen Central Committee, including Bill Ayers for his "generally fickle and high-handed treatment of women" and Jeff Jones, "who once told me that dull-witted misogynist Robert [*sic*] Palmer said that if I thought Weatherman was a male supremacist organization, I could 'suck his dick.'"[40] Regarding this public slight, Palmer later commented, "I was always hurt by Jane's hostility because I always felt it began with her. At one point we were lovers, which she initiated, so for her to do this was a real drag." He also thought that Alpert treated Melville unfairly in her piece. "I'm sure Sam was a male chauvinist, which I think is wrong but not a crime."[41]

Alpert left the most controversial part for the end: "And so, my sisters in Weathermen, you fast and organize and demonstrate for Attica. Don't send me news clippings about it, don't tell me how much those deaths moved you. I will mourn the loss of 42 male supremacists no longer."[42] To say such things about Movement martyrs at this time was nothing short of apostasy among the left.

On August 12, 1972, George Demmerle, recently married for the second time to the ex-Weatherman who'd moved in with him in the fall of 1969, left New York City for good, moving to a small town outside of Huntsville, Alabama, called Guntersville and putting an end to his official relationship with the FBI.[43] The Bureau closed his file three days later.[44] He divorced his second wife in 1974 and married his third, a woman named Ann Frankie Vunkanon, in 1975. This marriage ended eight years, one affair (by George), and five miscarriages later. In a 2003 interview, his third wife explained how George could have done such a good job infiltrating a group that held such opposite beliefs. "He is self-centered and likes the attention," she said. "Any kind of group that is meeting his social needs is where he feels he belongs."[45]

In September 1972 Robin Palmer was moved from Attica to the Great

Meadow Correctional Facility in Comstock, New York. On November 28, 1973, he was paroled fourteen months early, despite his refusal on two occasions to be interviewed by the FBI. Before his release he received a full psychological evaluation by Ralph Freedman, chief of psychiatric services at the prison, who gave him a clean bill of mental health—"no volubility . . . no delusional trends of thought . . . judgment not impaired"—while noting that "[Palmer] would like to do away with our way of life and replace it with his brand of government." But, Freedman felt, there was no point in keeping him locked up. "I don't think that staying in prison will affect any change in his way of thinking," wrote the doctor.[46]

Palmer returned to his apartment at 151 West Tenth Street, the same one he had sublet to the staff of *Crazie* magazine in 1969 and would hold onto for many more years before decamping back to the Ithaca area. In the months leading up to her own parole in late 1972, Sharon Krebs, who ended up serving just a year and a half, had told her parole board that she and Robin were planning to get married, but by the time of Palmer's second and final parole board hearing (his first attempt, in October 1972, had been rejected) he not only denied that this was in the cards but requested permission to live with Joyce Plecha, the cell member with whom he had had his fling before entering Attica. This request was denied.[47]

On November 14, 1974, after more than four years on the run, Jane Alpert turned herself in to federal authorities. "The strain of living a lie, of being unable to form close friendships, of knowing that you might have to pack up at a moment's notice had become unbearable," she told the *New York Times*. "Besides, the reasons I had gone underground no longer existed: Melville was dead and so was the movement."[48] On January 13, 1975, the same judge who had overseen her original case, Milton Pollack, sentenced Alpert to twenty-seven months in federal prison—eighteen months for the original conspiracy charge plus nine months for jumping bail.[49] She began serving her time in a Muncie, Pennsylvania, penitentiary two weeks later.[50]

In an interview two months after entering prison, Alpert summarized succinctly the ideological point she had arrived at. "The Left is hopelessly male in outlook," she said. "The Left does not deal with, cannot deal with, the essential paradigm of power in human society, which is the sexual relationship between men and women."[51] Yet her dismissal of the deaths at Attica, her shrugging off all personal responsibility for her role in the bombings, and her provision of personal details about Movement members who were still underground had earned her the disapprobation of a segment of the women's movement.[52]

"There are two kinds of justice in this country. The system of justice for people like Jane Alpert, and the system of justice for people like [Black Panther] Assata Shakur," wrote Flo Kennedy, Susan Sherman, Ti-Grace Atkinson, and Joan Hamilton, card-carrying feminists all, in a joint statement circulated somewhere at the beginning of March 1975. "Is this what we want the women's movement to represent? The kind of movement Jane Alpert represents. A movement based on class privilege, on white privilege. A racist movement completely cut off from our real needs."[53] Alpert's attitude toward Melville's killing in prison, as if he deserved it, was particularly upsetting to the women. "Maybe he was a sexist pig but that's not a death sentence—they murdered him at Attica," Susan Sherman later said.[54]

The letter by the four feminists set off "a furor greater than anything we could imagine," Sherman wrote.[55] In the March 8 issue of *Majority Report*, a lacerating defense of Jane signed by eighty-nine people, including Gloria Steinem, was published next to the original letter. "[Jane's] conduct under enormous pressure was and continues to be that of a woman with great integrity and strong feminist commitment. . . . We have an organic commitment to all oppressed peoples—but we affirm our own priorities as women. To do otherwise is indeed a betrayal of feminism."[56]

Although her name was lost in the sea of signatures, the driving force behind the swift and harsh rebuttal was Robin Morgan. According to Palmer, Morgan's motivations in leaping to Alpert's defense were more personal than political. "I knew that [Morgan] was desperately in love with Jane and that she was doing this as a gesture, a very dramatic act of love for Jane," he said. In fact, Palmer said, Morgan tried to blackmail him and Sharon Krebs into signing the group letter in defense of Jane. "[Morgan] sent word to me and Sharon through a lawyer that if we did not sign this petition, she was going to turn state's evidence on us with information that she knew about us in connection with the [Melville] bombings." The pair refused to sign. "I knew she was bluffing," claimed Palmer.[57]

Part of the rebuttal by Morgan and others included taking offense at the suggestion that Jane's many hours of conversations with law enforcement in the wake of her surrender could have jeopardized the Movement members living underground. Morgan argued, and Alpert confirmed years later, that she had fabricated a good deal of what she'd told the FBI and her own lawyer. However, the nuggets of truth buried in her tale were enough to do real damage. "Alpert now admits that the strategy of trying to outsmart the FBI was 'bad for the movement, Pat and me,'" wrote the historian Alice Echols, who interviewed Jane for her book *Daring to Be Bad* in the late 1980s.[58]

Passing her cooperation off as harmless became a little harder to do after March 12, 1975, the day Pat Swinton, then thirty-three and going by the name of Shoshana Rihn, was arrested in Brattleboro, Vermont, where she had been living on a commune known as the Packer Corner Farm and working in a health food store.[59] As Jane admitted in her 1981 autobiography, she knew exactly where Pat lived and had had a falling out with her on the phone sometime after the publication of "Mother Right."[60] Moreover, the sworn testimony of Assistant U.S. Attorney David Cuttner in Swinton's case made Alpert's cooperation sound extensive. Over six hours of interviews with the FBI, Cuttner said, Alpert, "provided detailed information about the bombing conspiracy . . . and about her years of fugitivity, including her contacts with the 'Weather Underground' and other federal fugitives." In Jane's defense, however, Cuttner did point out in his affidavit that she had been asked about Swinton specifically and professed not to have had any contact with her since the day of the original arrests in November 1969, an assertion that Swinton's own lawyer undercut weeks later at Swinton's bail hearing.[61]

Unlike the other members of the Melville Collective, Swinton entered a plea of not guilty and was released in mid-April on $200,000 bail, ponied up by her family and commune members, who posted the farm as collateral. Less than a week later Pat Swinton, or Shoshana Rihn as she continued to go by for the rest of her life, was weighing in on the feminist schism over Jane Alpert. Speaking with *Majority Report*, Pat tried to walk a calming, middle path. "[I don't believe] Jane would knowingly collaborate with the authorities," she said at one point. "[But] they can use everything you say in some way [so] there's no such thing as a little cooperation with the FBI."[62]

Two weeks later, ex–Weather Underground member Mary Moylan chimed in with her own withering takedown of Alpert. "Wherever she looks not only here but around the world, she sees women as passive tools. Women trusted her . . . she broke their trust," she wrote in *Off Our Backs*. "When Jane turned herself in the same issues were again raised. Sam Melville was again the fall guy. Politics, in general, & the left, in particular were denounced." Moylan also condemned Jane's cooperation with law enforcement. "There's no such thing as useless information," she said, adding, "At this time there is no way we consider Jane a sister. We have too much respect for sisterhood for that."[63]

Perhaps most damning of all was an article by the "Women of the Weather Underground" in the April 10 issue of *Majority Report* and reprinted in the May/June issue of *Off Our Backs*:

> By her collaboration, Alpert has made herself an enemy of the people, and especially women, for it is our struggle in particular she seeks to destroy and confuse. Millions of women must fight for unity and solidarity if they are to win the battles against racist schools, against the exploitation of our labor, against the cruel and oppressive health care and welfare systems. Her acts and words justify divisions among us and demean the difficulties women have endured in the struggle for liberation. To our culture of sisterhood and resistance she has contributed only her example of back-stabbing and hypocrisy.[64]

By late June, approximately the midpoint between Swinton's arrest and her trial date, her take and tone on the Alpert controversy had become less forgiving. "As part of becoming more one with that respectable society, she decided to be as cooperative as she could, in terms of giving a lot of details about where she had been and what she had been doing. And that was enough to lead to me," she said in *Off Our Backs*. "I don't say that she deliberately named names . . . but she gave a good rundown of what her life had been like for the last five years [and] that was enough."[65]

On September 22, 1975, the opening day of Swinton's trial, both Alpert and Hughey, who had finished serving his own sentence two years earlier, refused to testify against her. "My life may be in danger if I testify in these proceedings," Alpert told Judge Pollack, who held Alpert and Hughey in contempt of court, something they both would be indicted for afterward.[66] The judge also sequestered the jury after learning of the swarm of protesters outside handing out leaflets describing Pat as a victim of "a system of oppressive hierarchies—sex, race and class."[67]

George Demmerle, who had been spent the last three years in Alabama working in a scrap metal yard, getting divorced for the second time, and marrying for the third, was forced to come back to New York to testify and managed, in his own way, to help scuttle the U.S. Attorney's case against Swinton. Once he had been sworn in, George, looking, as the *LA Free Press* called it, "unkempt and unstable," recounted what he was already on record for—that Melville had told him that Swinton "helped write the communiques but she had nothing to do with the bombings."[68] But when he was asked to identify her in the courtroom, Demmerle hedged, on purpose he later said. "That's hard to say. It was seven years ago."[69] And when the government prosecutors tried to place her at weapons training sessions, George said he could not remember if she had been at the gatherings where guns and explosives were discussed.[70] During the lunch break an enraged U.S. attorney berated and threatened his witness. Cross-examined later by Pat's lawyer, Frederic Cohn, George said, "In all my time in the movement I never saw Pat Swinton engage in an act of violence."[71]

The government struck out as well with its next two witnesses, a pair of hitchhikers whom Jane and Pat had picked up while on the lam. One said he was on LSD the whole time and could not remember anything other than that the two women had said they were living underground. The other recanted earlier statements he had made to prosecutors about Swinton's hand in the communiqués, leaving government lawyers and the judge fuming.

With Pat sitting there in her purple vest, blue jeans, and tan boots, the government called its last witness on the fourth and final day of the trial. The man who took the stand, Jack Godoy, would likely have been recognizable to anyone who had been at the Gansevoort Pier on that Saturday in September 1968 when George was tossed into the Hudson River after his mock assassination attempt of Pigasus. Under oath Godoy admitted that he had been an undercover agent and infiltrated several radical groups that Swinton had belonged to but offered little else to pin on her.[72] Although in retrospect it made sense—Godoy oozed straightness—his duplicity was news to Movement members.

Godoy's testimony was not enough to make up for the flimsiness of the other witnesses—Swinton's lawyer did not call a single person to the stand.

63. Pat Swinton after being acquitted, New York, September 26, 1975. AP Photo.

After one day of deliberating, the jury of nine men and three women acquitted her. "We all felt the government had no case," one of them told the *Brattleboro Reformer*.[73] There were shouts of joy from the gallery when the verdict was announced, and Swinton teared up. As the jury filed out of the room, she clapped softly and then ran to hug her parents. Swinton left the courthouse to find a crowd of supporters waiting for her in the rain (figure 63). She returned to Vermont in time to perform in *The Crucible* under her new name Shoshana Rihn.[74] As of 2023 she was living in Brattleboro and continued to go by that name.

George Demmerle would go on to reinvent himself a few more times as an artist, a hippie, and, marrying for a fourth and final time in 1988, a husband. He spent the final two decades of his life with his last wife, Carol Barnes Price, living outside Dallas and devoting himself to his artwork. He died at Arlington Memorial Hospital in Texas on October 27, 2007, of colon cancer and lung failure, leaving behind boxes of flyers, photographs, and banners from the more than three years he spent embedded in the Movement.

64. George Demmerle, Crazie to the end. Estate of George Demmerle.

In middle age, George got a kick out of occasionally donning his colorful old costumes and reprising his Prince Crazie persona (figure 64). In his later years he attained modest recognition for his sculptures, which owed at least a nod to the psychedelic sixties. He was always happy to speak to an occasional curious member of the press, and his close friends knew all about his former life. For the most part, though, he lived a quiet suburban existence, beloved by his wife Carol and a small circle of friends and grateful that the onetime foster child had ended up with a sense of meaning and belonging. "He's an oddity, but he's got so much love in him," said Price. "He's very moldable, and relishes the experience of existing in new contexts," she added. George probably would have agreed with that assessment. "My thinking is quite broad. I'm not putting myself in anybody's bag," he said in 1970. "I disagree with a lot of points of view—left and right. I'm my own man."[75]

Epilogue

Heroes and Villains

HALF A CENTURY LATER, what to make of George Demmerle and fellow agents in the Movement like Lou Salzberg, Jack Godoy, Myron Kopchynsky, Steve Weiner, and plenty of others? While their backgrounds tend to differ, they appear to have reached similar conclusions by the end of their undercover service: unlike their handlers at the FBI or NYPD, the undercover agents often felt an appreciation for the motives of and even a sense of camaraderie with the radicals they were embedded with while disapproving of their means and methods.

"I was never against the things they stood for, like stopping the war in Vietnam. A lot of what they did changed the country for the better," said Steve Weiner, who brought down Robin Palmer and Sharon Krebs's Weathermen cell in 1970. "But I could never justify murder in the name of a moral cause. I came out believing that if you're going to change anything, you've got to do it within the system."[1] Louis Salzberg, who photographed much of the street theater and protests staged by the Yippies, Crazies, and others, said he had no regrets. "I did what I considered my patriotic duty," he told the *Daily News*. "The overriding fact is that the country [was] being threatened by revolutionaries."[2] Even some of the radicals who were in theory betrayed by these men have enough perspective to see the gray areas. "[Jack] Godoy would come over to our apartment each Friday evening to watch *Star Trek*," Veterans and Reservists to End the War in Vietnam (V&R) member Michael Spector recalled. "Was it undercover business or pleasure?"[3]

Although George's journey began on the far right, he ended up somewhere in the middle, wary of any kind of ism, left or right. "I'm a free thinker. I've met many people in life and gotten a broad outlook," he told an interviewer in 1971. "Because somebody is against the war, am I supposed to hate them? Hell no."[4] A *Newsday* profile of Weiner revealed a similar dynamic. "During the months of undercover work, Weiner felt a personal bond with some of the cell members. He had become their friend and had won their confidence. And he found some of their ideas were valid." But, the article continued, "they had taken their beliefs to an extreme he could not accept, that was repugnant."[5]

Another redeeming aspect of his undercover work, Demmerle emphasized, was how he used his position inside the Movement to help the many young and vulnerable people it attracted, providing food, housing, and clothes.[6] "In my relations with the kids in the Village my approach was always one of affection and honesty," George wrote after being unmasked. "If there was no information about subversive activities [at stake] I could open up and the relationship that was established remained so far as I was concerned."[7] And, especially during his final year undercover, Demmerle could act in a very empathetic or compassionate manner toward his marks. "In Chicago, when the shit hit the fan, when gas was thrown at us, George hustled us away," remembered V&R member Lew Friedman.[8] Others could think of instances where Demmerle's actions had been protective and appreciated. Stew Albert, the Yippie founding member and, like Robin Palmer, an unindicted coconspirator in the Chicago Seven trial, had a take on Demmerle that was evenhandedly philosophical. "He was just playing his part in the drama going on, a drama that took on consequences he probably hadn't thought of."[9]

All the undercover agents who were unmasked had to contend not only with ostracization but also threats to their safety. Salzberg told of being snubbed not only by journalist friends but also by teachers at his kids' school in suburban Long Island.[10] Weiner's wife recalled that in the wake of the trial of the Palmer Weathermen cell, they had a bodyguard stationed outside their home. "I was afraid to leave the house," she said.[11] George Demmerle died in 2007 believing that two attempts had been made on his life in the months after he was outed.

How did George get away with his act, which was particularly brazen compared to most undercover agents? While plenty of people claimed after the fact to have sensed something fishy about Prince Crazie, their reservations were clearly not enough to have hindered his ability to stay close to Movement leaders. "None of us liked or respected Demmerle," wrote Jane Alpert in her autobiography, adding that Dave Hughey "believed he was actually an undercover agent."[12] Stew Albert told journalist David Bonner in 2008, "I suspected him, so we didn't hang out."[13] And some of those who had not suspected him felt anger and disgust. "[George] had a lot of us fooled," said *Rat* writer Lee Merrick after the Melville Collective bust. "It is depressing and disgusting that good people all over the movement were tainted by him."[14]

While he will always be a pig to many in the Movement ("George Demmerle doesn't deserve a book," Wolfe Lowenthal replied in his email refusing to be interviewed for this account), still others had a grudging respect for what he had pulled off. An ability to handle his drugs seems to have helped. "[The Yippies] never suspected he was a spook; after all, marijuana was a revolutionary drug and no pig could maintain his cover while under the honest influence of the herb," wrote Martin Lee in his history of LSD in the 1960s.[15] "No one could outdo him in his verbal readiness to smite the Establishment with fire and sword," according to a 1970 *Dissent* article. "There was a certain sweetness about him," Krassner told the *Dallas Observer*. "I never suspected he was some kind of spy."

Of all the Movement heavies, perhaps Jerry Rubin was the one with the most enduring, albeit grudging, respect for what George had pulled off: "We knew pigs could memorize a lot of ideological crap and mechanically rap revolution. But no pig would grow his hair long. No pig would smoke dope and maintain his cover. No pig could run with the outrageous antics of the street theater Yippies and Crazies. Then came George Demmerle."[16] "Few people on either side trusted him . . . they simply didn't believe him coming or going," said Steve Aydt, a friend of George's later in life. "In some respects, he's a living cautionary tale about the dysfunction of the intelligence state and the havoc it can wreak on human lives. But his story is also a hopeful one. People can change in profound ways."[17]

GROUPS AND PEOPLE

Groups

Alternate U.—Started in early 1969 by Tom Wodetzki as the successor to the recently closed Free School, the Alternate U. offered a variety of classes on political and cultural topics and its classroom space at 69 West Fourteenth Street doubled as a meeting spot for many of the leftist organizations in New York City, from the *Black Panthers* to the *Yippies*.

Black Mask—*Ben Morea*, Ron Hahne, and Dan Georgakas published the first issue of *Black Mask* in 1966, and over the next two years a group of anarchists and artists on the Lower East Side coalesced around the magazine. Under the charismatic, take-no-prisoners leadership of Morea the group pioneered a unique mix of street theater, art, and political commentary until, in early 1968, it morphed into a new cadre of wild men named *Up Against the Wall, Motherfucker*, a line from the poem "Black People!" by Amiri Baraka.

Black Panthers—Founded in Oakland in October 1966 by Huey Newton and Bobby Seale, the Black Panthers preached a Marxist message of Black Power as they expanded to major cities around the country and became a north star not only to the Black community but to a generation of white radicals as well. In 1968 and 1969 there was very little action taken on the white left that was not filtered through the prism of "What would the Panthers think?"

Coalition for an Anti-Imperialist Movement (*Co-Aim*)—*Co-Aim* formed in the spring of 1968 as an umbrella group for several radical organizations, including the *U.S. Committee to Aid the National Liberation Front of South Vietnam*, the *Veterans and Reservists to End the War in Vietnam* and *Youth Against War and Fascism*. In particular, the group, under its de facto leader, *Walter Teague*, sponsored two antiwar marches in Washington Square Park in April and May 1968 that unified and helped radicalize the Movement downtown.

Crazies—In the wake of Nixon's inauguration, a group of *Yippies* that had been staging "zaps" of liberal politicians since returning from the Democratic National Convention began meeting regularly to plan more over-the-top disruptions, many of which included their signature move of stripping naked and presenting the unlucky target of their disapprobation with a raw pig's head on a silver platter. The Crazies' mascot was the alter ego of undercover agent *George Demmerle*, Prince Crazie.

Free School—Launched in July 1965 as the Free University by two professors who had been fired for their communist affiliations, the *Free School* (as it was later called) became the hub for the New Left in New York as resistance to the war abroad and to racism at home hardened. The school collapsed in the summer of 1968 but was reborn again a few months later as the *Alternate U.* under different leadership.

John Birch Society—*JBS* is a far-right group founded in 1958 to counter the perceived threat of communism to the American way of life. The group spread quickly across the country and, through its highly organized structure and propaganda machine, continued to crusade against communism long after McCarthyism had waned. *George Demmerle* was a member of the group in Brooklyn until 1965.

Melville Collective—Named for its charismatic and unpredictable leader, Sam Melville, the Collective set off seven dozen bombs in New York City between July and November 1969 and created the playbook for the Weathermen and other left-wing extremists that followed. In addition to Melville, its members included *Jane Alpert*, *Robin Palmer*, and *Sharon Krebs*.

Minutemen—The *Minutemen* were an even more militant conservative group than the *John Birch Society*, emphasizing guerrilla warfare training and shooting practice for its members in preparation for the impending communist uprising on U.S. soil. *George Demmerle* was a member for a short period in 1965 but quit when his troop commander threatened to kill him.

Progressive Labor—Formed in 1962 out of a split in the Communist Party USA, *Progressive Labor* was the overtly (and, many would say, overly) serious set of Marxist true believers who did a surprisingly effective job, given their small numbers, of infiltrating *SDS* and trying to slow the *New Left* drift away from a focus on the working class toward civil rights and student-led revolution. In the end, its clash at the end of the decade with the *Weathermen* faction within *SDS* would be the undoing of the student group.

Revolutionary Contingent—Formed in the run-up to the Mobe march in Central Park in April 1967, the Revolutionary Contingent was an umbrella group that attracted and attempted to organize some of the most radical people and groups in New York. Bringing together key players from the *U.S. Committee to Aid the National Liberation Front of South Vietnam*, *Veterans and Reservists to End the War in Vietnam*, and *Youth Against War and Fascism*, the RC introduced a more hardline and physical resistance to the left, whether sacking the military recruitment office in Times Square or burning General Westmoreland in effigy in front of the Waldorf Hotel.

Student Nonviolent Coordinating Committee (SNCC)—*Snick*, as its commonly pronounced, along with Martin Luther King Jr's *Southern Christian Leadership Conference* (SCLC), was the primary vehicle for civil rights protest by young people in the South in the early 1960s. Famous sit-ins in Greensboro, North Carolina, Orangeburg, South Carolina, and elsewhere transfixed the nation and galvanized a generation of white students from the North to join in the struggle for racial equality. As the decade progressed its leadership became more radical, and the group pushed away many of the white volunteers like *Abbie Hoffman* who had joined the struggle.

Students for a Democratic Society (SDS)—Created as the youth division of the *League for Industrial Democracy* in 1960, *SDS* really picked up steam at its convention in the summer of 1962 when the Port Huron Statement, written by a young Tom Hayden, introduced the idea of "participatory democracy." As the United States sent troops to Vietnam in 1965, *SDS* grew into the most important antiwar and New Left organization in the country until it collapsed under the weight of its own infighting at the end of the decade.

Up Against the Wall, Motherfucker—Inspired by a line by the Black poet Amiri Baraka, the *Motherfuckers* were angry anarchists dedicated to battling capitalists and communists alike through a mix of street theater and sometimes violent confrontation. Though best known for a series of attention-grabbing stunts like dumping garbage in the fountain at Lincoln Center and staging a mock assassination of a Columbia poetry professor, the group was also one of the most active when it came to organizing community resources for the poor on the Lower East Side in the late 1960s.

U.S. Committee to Aid the National Liberation Front of South Vietnam (USCANLF)—In late 1964 *Walter Teague* looked around and realized that although there were plenty of voices for peace, there wasn't anyone advocating for the Vietnamese people, so he started USCANLF and quickly became a skilled activist with the best collection of Vietnamese literature and films in the country. He spent the next decade fighting for and humanizing the Vietnamese with his megaphone, marching, and media savvy.

Veterans and Reservists to End the War in Vietnam (V&R)—Started in late 1965 to give Vietnam veterans and reservists a distinct voice, V&R called for immediate withdrawal from Vietnam, not just a peaceful end to the war. The group played an active role in organizing antiwar marches and its members overlapped with, and participated alongside, the *Yippies* and *Crazies* in many of their most memorable protests and skits. *George Demmerle* and *Robin Palmer* both traveled to Chicago for the Democratic National Convention of 1968 with the V&R contingent.

Weathermen—Formed in 1969 as the most radical contingent within SDS, and named after a line in Bob Dylan's song "Subterranean Homesick Blues," the *Weathermen* (alternately called the Weatherman or the Weather Underground) went down a path of extremist self-destruction, tearing the student group apart in the process. Best known for the unintended explosion of an Eleventh Street townhouse, Weathermen members went underground in 1970 and ultimately imploded in a morass of bombs, orgies, and LSD.

Women's International Terrorist Conspiracy from Hell—WITCH was formed on Halloween night 1968 after a rupture in the feminist group New York Radical Women. WITCH adopted many of the flamboyant tactics popularized by the Yippies in their effort to bring down the patriarchy, including a costumed march on Wall Street and a protest outside a bridal convention at Madison Square Garden.

Young Lords—Begun as a Puerto Rican street gang in Chicago in 1960, the Young Lords evolved into a political consciousness-raising and community-support group in the last two years of the decade, mimicking many of the *Black Panthers'* programs and structure in the process. In New York, the Lords drew a lot of attention in the summer of 1969 for dragging mounds of garbage into the middle of Third Avenue in Harlem and setting it on fire to protest the lack of attention to poor neighborhoods from the Department of Sanitation.

People

Jane Alpert—A recent Swarthmore graduate working at Cambridge University Press when she met Sam Melville in the fall of 1968, Alpert became an active participant in the *Melville Collective*'s bombing spree before going underground and having a feminist awakening that made her reassess her entire time in the radical left. Her autobiographical account of the era, *Growing Up Underground*, is the most relevant first-person account of the period and events covered by this book.

George Demmerle—A right-wing machinist from Brooklyn and member of both the *John Birch Society* and the *Minutemen*, Demmerle hatched his own plan to move to the East Village and spy on the radical left in 1966. On his way to infiltrating the *Revolutionary Contingent*, the *Yippies*, and finally the *Melville Collective*, Demmerle created an alter ego known as Prince Crazie who would parade around the Village in a purple cape and orange-plumed centurion's helmet and help disrupt numerous political events.

Abbie Hoffman—The cofounder, with Jerry Rubin, of the *Yippies* and the brilliant jester in chief of the far left, Hoffman was responsible not only for some of the greatest political pranks of all time but also for organizing the Festival of Life at the 1968 Democratic National Convention in Chicago, which ended, famously, in a conflagration of unrest and police brutality.

Carola Hoffman—A New Jersey native, Carola Hoffman was still a teenager when she left home for the Lower East Side in 1968 and quickly fell in with members of the *Veterans & Reservists* and the *Yippies* and was there for the founding of the *Crazies*. Present at many of the Crazies' protests and zaps, Hoffman (no relation to Abbie) and her teenage pal Vincent Tsao had a front row seat for the New York revolution in the last couple of years of the 1960s.

David Hughey—A Duke dropout and Baptist minister's son, Hughey sported a lanky build and low-key demeanor that belied a ferocious devotion to Movement causes. Not technically a member of the *Melville Collective*, he ended up playing an important role in the bombings of 1969 after earning respect for his role in the *U.S. Committee to Aid the National Liberation Front of South Vietnam*.

Sharon Krebs—A book-smart, dauntless organizer, Sharon went from helping her husband Allen open the *Free University* to stripping naked at political luncheons alongside *Robin Palmer* and planning bombings with the *Melville Collective*. Like many in the most extreme reaches of the Movement, Krebs's mental illness manifested itself as the weight of the war and her own actions mounted.

Sam Melville—At once charismatic and mercurial, Melville became interested in Movement politics while living with a girlfriend near Columbia University in the late 1960s and later, in the final year of the decade, moved downtown with *Jane Alpert*, where he proceeded to dabble in LSD and become increasingly radicalized, ultimately becoming convinced that the only way to change the system was to blow it up.

Ben Morea—The artist and anarchist first made his mark with the publication of a monthly magazine called *Black Mask* and Diggers-inspired marches on Wall Street, but by 1968 he had evolved into the leader of a band of seemingly fearless Lower East Side radicals called the *Motherfuckers* who bullied the established members of the community while working tirelessly to provide free meals, clothing, and legal advice to the neighborhood poor.

Robin Palmer—English teacher, deep sea diver, and part-time porno actor, Palmer turned his back on his middle-class roots to become one of the most rambunctious and most arrested radicals in town. A member of the *Veterans & Reservists*, the *Yippies*, and the *Crazies*, Palmer relished hoisting the Vietcong flag and joining his girlfriend *Sharon Krebs* in disrobing and serving pig's heads to liberal leaders.

Albert Seedman—Albert Seedman, the lead inspector on the Kitty Genovese murder of 1964, was pulled in to investigate the rash of bombings that occurred in New York City in late 1969. In the final weeks of the case, the cigar-chomping veteran detective worked closely with the FBI to tighten the noose around the bombers' necks.

Pat Swinton—Staffer at the *Guardian* and researcher at the North American Congress on Latin America, Swinton helped steal President Grayson L. Kirk's records during the Columbia University uprising of 1960 and a few months later fell in with *Sam Melville* and *Jane Alpert*. By the time the couple had moved into her building,

Swinton had slept with both and become their confidante, although neither she nor her sometime boyfriend *Dave Hughey* was ever officially invited to join the *Melville Collective*.

Walter Teague—The studied and presentable Teague may have not looked the part, but in 1964, when he started the *U.S. Committee to Aid the National Liberation Front of South Vietnam*, he staked out as far left a position on the war as was possible. Over the next decade, while interacting with all the key antiwar players in New York, he squared off with the House Un-American Activities Committee, distributed countless Vietnamese films and books, and brought an element of care and deliberation to what was often a harried, ad hoc process.

NOTES

1. Born under a Bad Sign

1. George Demmerle interview, Irving (TX) Community Television, March 29, 1999.

2. Some of the quotations and details relating to Demmerle's early life come from printed transcripts given to the author by Demmerle's widow that appear to have been conducted by students from the University of North Texas circa 2002. The documents will be cited as "UNT interviews, 2002" hereafter.

3. Demmerle interview, Irving (TX) Community Television.

4. Matthew Milliken, "Gould Foundation Carries Out Work of Its Founder," *The Journal News*, September 29, 2001.

5. Madeline Sward, "How I Was Parented," George Demmerle Archives.

6. UNT interviews, 2002.

7. Letter from Nelson Drimalas to George Demmerle, March 1, 1999, George Demmerle Archives.

8. Demmerle interview, Irving (TX) Community Television.

9. Ibid.

10. UNT interviews, 2002.

11. Ibid.

12. Jorge Demmerele, interview with the author, August 4, 2023.

13. Demmerle interview, Irving (TX) Community Television.

14. "Births," *American Foreign Service Journal* 25, no. 6 (June 1948): 44.

15. Demmerle interview, Irving (TX) Community Television.

16. UNT interviews, 2002.

17. Ibid.

18. Military Records, George Demmerle Archives.

19. UNT interviews, 2002.

20. William Conrad Gibbons, *The U.S. Government and the Vietnam War: Executive and Legislative Roles and Relationships, Part I* (Princeton, NJ: Princeton University Press, 2014), 75.

21. UNT interviews, 2002.

22. Ibid.

23. Jorge Demmerele interview.

24. An FBI memorandum from the director of the FBI to the special agent in charge (New York) on February 23, 1967, refers to George as being the "father of a 13-year-old boy." The affair was confirmed by an interview with Jorge Demmerele, George's adopted son, who tweaked the spelling of his last name for privacy and safety issues in the 1960s.

25. Jorge Demmerele interview.

26. Ann Zimmer, "Yippie Spy," *Dallas Observer*, March 16, 1995, 17–23.

2. Right-Wing Seduction

1. Richard Hofstadter, *The Paranoid Style in American Politics, and Other Essays* (New York: Vintage Books, 2008), 111.

2. Neil Genzlinger, "John Stormer, 'None Dare Call It Treason' Author, Dies at 90," *New York Times*, July 17, 2018.

3. Jorge Demmerele, George Demmerle's adopted son, recalls his father being a member of the John Birch Society earlier than 1964, but there is nothing in his FBI files or interview transcripts to back that up.

4. George Demmerle interview, Irving (TX) Community Television, March 29, 1999.

5. UNT interviews, 2002.

6. Jorge Demmerele, interview with the author, August 4, 2023.

7. Walter Teague, interview with the author, December 28, 2022.

8. Rosemary Ruether, "The New Left: Revolutionaries After the Fall of the Revolution," *Soundings: An Interdisciplinary Journal* 52, no. 3 (Fall 1969): 247.

9. The historian Van Gosse has made the point that the New Left base was much broader than a bunch of middle-class white kids, describing it as a "movement of movements" that encompassed "all the struggles for fundamental change from the early 1950s roughly to 1975," including but not limited to the civil rights, antiwar, and feminist movements. As resistance to the war gained mindshare among the New Left, there was a reluctance on the part of many Black activists to throw in with predominantly white groups. Van Gosse, *Rethinking the New Left: An Interpretative History* (New York: Palgrave Macmillan, 2005), 5.

10. John A. Lynn, *Another Kind of War: The Nature and History of Terrorism* (New Haven, CT: Yale University Press, 2019), 210.

11. Richard J. Ellis, "Romancing the Oppressed: The New Left and the Left Out," *Review of Politics* 58, no. 1 (Winter 1996): 128.

12. Irwin Unger, "The 'New Left' and American History: Some Recent Trends in United States Historiography," *American Historical Review* 72, no. 4 (July 1967): 1242.

13. John Patrick Diggins, *The Rise and Fall of the American Left* (New York: W. W. Norton, 1992), 228.

14. "Port Huron Statement" from http://www.progressivefox.com/misc_documents/PortHuronStatement.pdf

15. Gosse, *Rethinking the New Left*, 43.

16. Richard Rothstein, "A Short History of ERAP," *SDS Bulletin*, February–March 1965, 2; Students for a Democratic Society, "ERAP Projects," *SDS Bulletin*, June 1964.

17. Rothstein, "A Short History of ERAP," 2.

18. Jonathan Eig, *King: A Life* (New York: Farrar, Straus and Giroux, 2023), 487.

19. Becky Thompson, *A Promise and a Way of Life: White Antiracist Activism* (Minneapolis: University of Minnesota Press, 2001), 60.

20. Stokely Carmichael, speech at the University of California, Berkeley, October 29, 1966, https://americanradioworks.publicradio.org/features/blackspeech/scarmichael.html

21. Larry Sloman, *Steal This Dream: Abbie Hoffman and the Countercultural Revolution in America* (New York: Doubleday, 1998), 47–48.

22. Diggins, *Rise and Fall of the American Left*, 216.

23. Philip Foner, *U.S. Labor and the Vietnam War* (New York: International Publishers, 1989), 12–13.

24. Ibid., 19, 22–23.

25. Ibid., 20.

26. Carola Von Hoffmannstahl, "Robin Palmer: Weatherman Yippie Right Wing Rebel Forever," *OpEdNews.com*, October 18, 2010.

27. Robin Palmer, interview with Jeremy Varon, October 31, 1994.

28. Gosse, *Rethinking the New Left*, 90.

29. Paul Potter, "Naming the System," speech, https://www.sds-1960s.org/sds_wuo/sds_documents/paul_potter.html

30. Todd Gitlin, *The Sixties: Years of Hope, Days of Rage* (New York: Bantam Books, 1987), 183.

31. Harold Jacobs, ed., "Chronology of Events," *Weatherman* (New York: Ramparts Press, 1970), xv.

32. David Farber, *The Age of Great Dreams: America in the 1960s* (New York: Hill and Wang, 1994), 156.

33. Gitlin, *The Sixties*, 191.

34. John McNaughton, "Action for South Vietnam," March 10, 1965. Department of State, Vietnam Negotiating Files: Lot 69 D 412, Project Mayflower.

35. William Borders, "Marchers Heckled Here—Eggs and a Can of Paint Are Thrown," *New York Times*, October 19, 1965.

36. Harry Ring, "Thousands Protest U.S. War in Vietnam," *The Militant*, October 25, 1965.

37. Jorge Demmerele, interview with the author, August 4, 2023.

38. UNT interviews, 2002.

39. Jorge Demmerele interview.

40. Gosse, *Rethinking the New Left*, 23–24.

41. Borders, "Marchers Heckled Here."

42. Stuart Dim, "Vets Day Rally 'Round the Platform," *Newsday*, November 12, 1965, 5.

43. Ibid.

44. Walter Teague, interview with the author, December 22, 2022.

45. Ibid.

46. Fred P. Graham, "Vietcong Flags Are Sold in Washington as Groups Arrive for March," *New York Times*, November 26, 1965.

47. FBI Memorandum from C. D. Brennan to W. C. Sullivan, August 15, 1967.

48. Interview with George Demmerle, Irving (TX) Community Television.

49. UNT interviews.

50. Jorge Demmerele interview.

51. UNT interviews.

52. "Minutemen Training Program, Phase I, Work Project No. 6," Demmerle FOIA files, noted March 17, 1965.

53. FBI Memorandum from Special Agent John W. Robinson to Special Agent in Charge, "George Demmerle, Possible PSI," September 19, 1966.

54. Ann Zimmer, "Yippie Spy," *Dallas Observer*, March 16, 1995, 19.

55. FBI Memorandum from Special Agent in Charge, New York, to FBI Director, "George Demmerle, PSI," December 20, 1966, 2.

56. Mike Spector, email to the author, August 9, 2023.

57. Lew Friedman, interview with the author, December 7, 2022.

58. "Veterans and Reservists to End the War in Vietnam" flyer, November 1965, Lew Friedman Archives.

59. "Action Call for Veterans and Reservists" flyer, February 1966, Lew Friedman Archives.

60. "Veterans for Peace in Vietnam: What's Being Done" flyer, March 1966, Lew Friedman Archives.

61. David Lewis Stein, *Living the Revolution: The Yippies in Chicago* (New York: Bobbs-Merrill, 1969), 11.

62. Douglas Robinson, "Antiwar Protests Staged in U.S.; 15 Burn Discharge Papers Here," *New York Times*, March 26, 1966.

63. "Veterans and Reservists to End the War in Viet Nam" newsletter, April 5, 1966, Lew Friedman Archives.

64. "Press Supplement: Veterans & Reservists' Washington's Birthday Parade for Peace" flyer, February 1967.

65. Palmer interview with Varon, October 31, 1994.

66. FBI Memorandum, Special Agent in Charge, New York, to FBI Director, December 26, 1968.

67. The group closed its April 18 newsletter with a practical issue that would plague many of the more radical groups throughout the rest of the decade: "We are still substantially in debt—and so must once again urgently request contributions."

68. "Veterans and Reservists to End the War in Viet Nam" newsletter, July 27, 1966.

3. Getting Inside

1. FBI Memorandum from Special Agent James F. Reilly to Special Agent in Charge, "George Demmerle," August 9, 1966.

2. Roger Vaughn, "The Anti-University is the Newest Meeting Place for Young Radicals," *Life*, May 20, 1966, 119–120.

3. Free University of New York, Fall Course Catalog 1965, https://www.jstor.org/stable/community.33282050.

4. "Radicals Set Up Own 'University,'" *New York Times*, July 11, 1965.

5. House Committee on Un-American Activities, August 16–19, 1966, 45.

6. Vaughn, "The Anti-University," 119–120.

7. Edward Grossman, "New York's Schoolhouse for the Left," *Harper's*, April 1966, 81.

8. Ibid., 75.

9. "House Passes Bill to Punish Those Aiding the Viet Cong," *CQ Almanac 1966*, 623–627.

10. "HUAC Won't Act Against 2 Who Defied Subpoenas," *Tucson Daily Citizen*, August 30, 1966, 10.

11. Robin Palmer, interview with Jeremy Varon, October 31, 1994.

12. Walter Teague, interview with the author, December 9, 2022.

13. "CLU Moves to Fight Book Ban," *Miami Herald*, December 2, 1966.

14. "Walter D. Teague III, Charlotte Polin, United States Committee to Aid the National Liberation Front of South Vietnam, Liberation, Fifth Avenue Peace Parade, and Free School of New York, Inc., Plaintiffs-appellants, v. Regional Commissioner of Customs, Region II and Secretary of the Treasury of the United States, Defendants-appellees, 404 F.2d 441 (2nd Cir. 1969), https://law.justia.com/cases/federal/appellate-courts/F2/404/441/225140/

15. "North Viet, Red Chinese Periodicals Barred," *Passaic Herald-News*, August 8, 1967, 3.

16. Teague interview with the author, December 9, 2022.

17. Toru Umezaki, "The Free University of New York: The New Left's Self-Education and Transborder Activism," PhD diss., Columbia University, 2013.

18. Peter Kihss, "Westmoreland Decries Protests," *New York Times*, April 25, 1967, 14.

19. Palmer interview with Varon, October 31, 1994.

20. Paul Krassner, *Confessions of a Raving, Unconfined Nut* (New York: Simon & Schuster, 1993), 152.

21. Abbie Hoffman, *The Autobiography of Abbie Hoffman* (New York: Four Windows Eight Walls, 1980), 81.

22. Ibid., 88.

23. Osha Neumann, *Up Against the Wall, Motherfucker: A Memoir of the '60s, With Notes for Next Time* (New York: Seven Stories Press, 2008), 41.

24. Larry Sloman, *Steal This Dream: Abbie Hoffman and the Countercultural Revolution in America* (New York: Doubleday, 1998), 62.

25. Vincent J. Cannato, *The Ungovernable City: John Lindsay and His Struggle to Save New York* (New York: Basic Books, 2001), 143.

26. Ronald Sukenick, *Down and In: Life in the Underground* (New York: Collier Books, 1987), 188.

27. Sloman, *Steal This Dream*, 76.

28. Steven R. Weisman, "Book Review: The Mayor's Man," *New York Times*, March 16, 1975, 69.

29. In fact, Gottehrer put such faith in Abbie's ability to serve as a liaison to the hippies and disaffected youth ("one of the most creative public advocates I had ever met") that he later came up with a way to funnel money to Abbie through a minister at a Greenwich Village church to compensate him for writing a safety guide for runaways and other homeless or clueless youth; this effort became Abbie's 1967 book *Fuck the System*. Cannato, *The Ungovernable City*, 221, 223–225.

30. Sloman, *Steal This Dream*, 78.

31. FBI Memorandum from Special Agent John W. Robinson to Special Agent in Charge, "George Demmerle—Possible PSI," September 19, 1966.

32. CCAN meetings were held on September 7 and 14 at 44 Butler Street in Brooklyn and involved approximately a dozen attendees.

33. Teague interview with the author, December 2, 2020.

34. Jim Dann and Hari Dillon, "The Five Retreats: A History of the Failure of the Progressive Labor Party," *Encyclopedia of Anti-Revisionism On-Line*, 1977, https://www.marxists.org/history/erol/1960-1970/5retreats/.

35. Irwin Unger, *The Movement: A History of the American New Left, 1959–1972* (New York: Dodd, Mead & Company, 1974), 86.

36. Kirkpatrick Sale, *SDS* (New York: Random House, 1973), 122.

37. Ann Zimmer, "Yippie Spy," *Dallas Observer*, March 16, 1995, 19.

38. FBI Memorandum from Special Agent John W. Robinson, October 31, 1966.

39. FBI Memorandum from Special Agent John W. Robinson, November 16, 1966.

40. FBI Memorandum from Special Agent in Charge, New York, to FBI Director, "George Demmerle, PSI," December 20, 1966.

41. Lawrence Van Gelder, "Columbia Students Help Occupy Flats Run by University," *New York Times*, May 19, 1968.

42. "Investigation Regarding Samuel Joseph Melville," FBI File Number 117 506 H, Report Number NY 52-9441, December 1969, 118–121.

43. Joshua Melville, *American Time Bomb: Attica, Sam Melville, and a Son's Search for Answers* (Chicago: Chicago Review Press, 2021), 31.

44. Ibid., 31.

45. *Answer to the Letter of Allegations and Supporting Affidavits and States,* Headquarters First Army, Field Board of Inquiry, December 3, 1954, 2–3.

46. Ibid., 5.

47. Ibid., 7.

48. Joshua Keeran, "US Military Relied on Draft-Induced Volunteerism," *Delaware Gazette*, March 11, 2021.

49. FBI Memorandum from Vincent A. Alvino, File #100-417090, April 25, 1969.

50. *Answer to the Letter of Allegations*, 14.

51. Ibid., 1.

52. Ibid., 15.

53. FBI Memorandum from Special Agent in Charge, New York, to FBI Director, "Richard Robin Palmer," June 21, 1973.

54. FBI Memorandum from Joseph Furrer to Secret Service, "Richard Robin Palmer," July 25, 1968.

55. Email from Carola Hoffman to the author, February 27, 2020.

56. FBI Memorandum, "Richard Robin Palmer."

57. Arthur Knight and Hollis Alpert, "The History of Sex in Cinema," *Playboy*, November 1967, 157.

58. Jeremy Varon, *Bringing the War Home: The Weather Underground, the Red Army Faction, and Revolutionary Violence in the Sixties and Seventies* (Berkeley: University of California Press, 2004), 139.

59. Melville, *American Time Bomb*, 31–32.

60. Cannato, *The Ungovernable City*, ix–x.

61. Douglas Robinson, "Parades and Ceremonies Honor the Nation's Past and Present Fighting Men," *New York Times*, November 12, 1966.

62. "Discharges Burned at Antiwar Rally," *Long Island Press*, November 2, 1966.

63. FBI Memorandum from Special Agent John W. Robinson, November 16, 1966.

64. FBI Memorandum from Special Agent John W. Robinson, December 8, 1966.

65. FBI Memorandum by Special Agent John W. Robinson, December 20, 1966.

66. FBI Memorandum to Special Agent John Robinson, November 21, 1966.

67. FBI Memorandum by Robinson, December 20, 1966.

68. FBI Memorandum from the FBI Director to the Special Agent in Charge, January 18, 1967.

69. The only reference to Creedmoor came from George's son, Jorge, who mentioned it in an interview with the author, August 4, 2023.

4. The Revolutionary Contingent

1. John McMillian, "Ben Morea, Garbage Guerilla," *New York Press*, May 5, 2006.

2. Ben Morea, interview with the author, December 9, 2022.

3. Ibid.

4. Timothy Scott Brown, "The Sixties in the City: Avant-gardes and Urban Rebels in New York, London and West Berlin," *Journal of Social History* 46, no. 4 (Summer 2013): 825.

5. *Black Mask & Up Against the Wall Motherfucker: Flower Power Won't Stop Fascist Power*, unknown author, publisher, and date.

6. "Angry Arts Weeks," https://rokantyfaszystowski.org/en/angry-arts-week/

7. Morea interview.

8. Malav Kanuga, "The Many Recurring Dreams of Reason: The Motherfuckers and the Art of Rebellion," in *Jews: A People's History of the Lower East Side* (New York: Clayton Press, 2012), 3:135.

9. Morea interview.

10. John P. Callahan, "Parades for Peace, Brotherhood . . . (And Washington) Mark Holiday Here," *New York Times*, February 23, 1967.

11. FBI Memorandum from Special Agent John W. Robinson, January 18, 1967.

12. FBI Memorandum from Special Agent John W. Robinson to Special Agent in Charge, "Committee for Independent Politics," February 1, 1967.

13. FBI Memorandum from the FBI Director to the Special Agent in Charge, New York, "George Edward Demmerle—PSI," February 23, 1967.

14. FBI Memorandum from Special Agent in Charge, Newark to Special Agent in Charge, New York, "George Demmerle—PSI," January 31, 1967.

15. FBI Memorandum by Special Agent John W. Robinson, December 20, 1966.

16. Jorge Demmerele, interview with the author, August 4, 2023.

17. FBI Memorandum, February 23, 1967.

18. FBI Memorandum from Special Agent John W. Robinson to Special Agent in Charge, New York, March 22, 1967.

19. FBI Memorandum from Special Agent John W. Robinson, March 28, 1967.

20. FBI report "Investigation Regarding Samuel Joseph Melville," File Number 117 506 H, Report Number NY 52-9441, December 1969, 120.

21. Joshua Melville, *American Time Bomb: Attica, Sam Melville, and a Son's Search for Answers* (Chicago: Chicago Review Press, 2021), 60.

22. Jane Alpert, *Growing Up Underground* (New York: Morrow, 1981), 59.

23. Ibid., 119.

24. Melville, *American Time Bomb*, 2.

25. Alpert, *Growing Up Underground*, 119–121.

26. Melville, *American Time Bomb*, 4. See also FBI report "Investigation Regarding Samuel Joseph Melville," 122.

27. FBI report "Investigation Regarding Samuel Joseph Melville," 120.

28. Melville, *American Time Bomb*, 33.

29. NYPD report, B.S.S. #151-M (Supplementary #2), April 17, 1967, 3–4, Walter Teague FOIA Archives.

30. Brent Sharman, interview with the author, January 7, 2023.

31. NYPD Memo, B.S.S. #252-M (First and Final Report), April 7, 1967.

32. "My First Antiwar Protest," *New York Times*, April 14, 2017.

33. Flo Kennedy, "Harlem Against the Draft," *Movement*, May 1967.

34. NYPD report, April 7, 1967, 3. Note that the Black Panthers did not have a presence in New York City, or anywhere outside of Oakland, yet.

35. Kennedy, "Harlem Against the Draft."

36. V&R Newsletter, April 1967, Lew Friedman Archives.

37. National Renaissance Party counterdemonstrators listed in NYPD report, B.S.S. . . #151-M (Supplementary Report), April 17, 1967, Walter Teague Archives.

38. NYPD report, April 17, 1967, 3; Douglas Robinson, "100,000 Rally at U.N. Against Vietnam War," *New York Times*, April 16, 1967.

39. NYPD report, April 7, 1967, 3.

40. "Guerrilla Warfare Advocates in the United States," Committee on Un-American Activities, House of Representatives, 90th Congress, 2nd Session, May 6, 1968, 41.

41. Jonathan Eig, *King: A Life* (New York: Farrar, Straus and Giroux, 2023), 513–519.

42. Address by Dr. Martin Luther King Jr., April 15, 1967, https://www.crmvet.org/docs/mlkviet2.htm

43. Frank Gillette, "On the Revolutionary Contingent," *Treason!*, Summer 1967, 15.

44. "Guerrilla Warfare Advocates in the United States."

45. Gillette, "On the Revolutionary Contingent," 15.

46. "Guerrilla Warfare Advocates in the United States," 41.

47. Jack A. Smith, "SDS Sets Out on a Radical Path," *National Guardian*, July 15, 1967.

48. "Guerrilla Warfare Advocates in the United States," 45.

49. Lee Merrick, "Life with 'Crazie' George," Liberation News Service, January 24, 1970, 18.

50. Peter Kihss, "Westmoreland Decries Protests," *New York Times*, April 25, 1967, 1; HUAC, 44.

51. FBI Memorandum from FBI Director to Special Agent in Charge, New York, April 26, 1967.

52. "Revolutionary Contingent," Melville Case Report, NY Office, January 14, 1970, 190.

53. FBI Memorandum from Special Agent John W. Robinson to Special Agent in Charge, May 25, 1967.

54. Tom Wells, *The War Within: America's Battle Over Vietnam* (Berkeley: University of California Press, 1994), 141.

55. "The Veteran," Vietnam Veterans Against the War, https://vvaw.org/veteran.

56. Andrew E. Hunt, *The Turning: A History of Vietnam Veterans Against the War* (New York: NYU Press, 1999), 57.

57. Email from Michael Spector to the author, December 21, 2022.

58. Email from Lew Friedman to the author, December 22, 2022.

59. Maryland State Archives, https://msa.maryland.gov/megafile/msa/speccol/sc2200/sc2221/000012/000008/html/speech1.html

60. Lorraine Boissoneault, "Understanding Detroit's 1967 Upheaval 50 Years Later," *Smithsonian*, July 26, 1967.

61. Rick Rojas and Khorri Atkinson, "Five Days of Unrest That Shaped, and Haunted, Newark," *New York Times*, July 11, 2017.

62. Eig, *King*, 468.

63. Milton Viorst, *Fire in the Streets: America in the 1960's* (New York: Simon & Schuster, 1979), 337–338.

64. James Miller, *Democracy Is in the Streets: From Port Huron to the Siege of Chicago* (Cambridge, MA: Harvard University Press, 1994), 277.

65. Ronald Sukenick, *Down and In: Life in the Underground* (New York: Collier Books, 1987), 194–195.

66. Abbie Hoffman, *The Autobiography of Abbie Hoffman* (New York: Four Windows Eight Walls, 1980), 99.

67. Sukenick, *Down and In*, 181.

68. Vincent J. Cannato, *The Ungovernable City: John Lindsay and His Struggle to Save New York* (New York: Basic Books, 2001), 141–142.

69. FBI Memorandum from Special Agent John W. Robinson to Special Agent in Charge, New York, June 20, 1967.

70. Cannato, *The Ungovernable City*, 132–138.

71. Ann Zimmer, "Yippie Spy," *Dallas Observer*, March 16, 1995, 20.

72. FBI Memorandum from Special Agent in Charge, New York, to the FBI Director, June 22, 1967.

73. FBI Memorandum from Special Agent John W. Robinson, April 27, 1967.

74. Toru Umezaki, "The Free University of New York: The New Left's Self-Education and Transborder Activism," PhD diss., Columbia University, 2013, 254.

75. "Uncle Ho to Polin, 25 November 1965," McCombs Exhibit No. 2-C, in *Bills to Make Punishable Assistance to Enemies of U.S. in Time of Undeclared War*, 1053.

76. Charlotte Polin, "Letter to the Committee for Cultural Relations with Foreign Countries, Hanoi," June 7, 1967 (FBI files).

77. FBI Memorandum from Special Agent in Charge, New York, to FBI Director, June 26, 1967.

78. FBI Memorandum from Special Agent John W. Robinson, July 18, 1967.

79. George Demmerle, "Letter to the Committee for Cultural Relations with Foreign Countries, Hanoi," July 7, 1967 (FBI files).

80. USCANLF Archives, 1967.

81. FBI Memorandum from Special Agent James F. Reilly to Special Agent in Charge, New York, July 10, 1967.

82. FBI Memorandum from Special Agent in Charge, New York, to FBI director, November 22, 1967.

83. FBI Memorandum from Special Agent James F. Reilly, July 19, 1967.

84. FBI Memorandum from Special Agent in Charge, New York, to FBI Director, July 28, 1967.

85. FBI Memorandum, "Correlation Summary, Subject Richard Robin Palmer," March 2, 1972.

86. FBI Memoranda, July 31, 1967, and August 15, 1967.

87. FBI Memorandum from Special Agent John W. Robinson, August 14, 1967.

88. FBI Memorandum from Special Agent in Charge, New York, to FBI Director, August 21, 1967.

89. FBI Memorandum from Special Agent John W. Robinson, August 28, 1967.

90. Zimmer, "Yippie Spy," 19.

91. FBI Memorandum, File Number NY 100-160251, September 26, 1967.

92. FBI Memorandum, "Revolutionary Contingent," October 10, 1967.

93. FBI Memorandum from C. D. Brennan to W. C. Sullivan, "George Edward Demmerle—Potential Security Informant," August 15, 1967.

94. FBI Memorandum from FBI Director to Special Agent in Charge, New York, August 16, 1967.

95. FBI Memoranda, August 21, 1967, and September 1, 1967.

96. FBI Memorandum from Special Agent in Charge, New York, to FBI Director, August 25, 1971.

97. FBI Memorandum from the Special Agent in Charge, New York, to the FBI Director, October 3, 1967.

5. The Pentagon

1. Michael S. Foley, Ed., *Dear Dr. Spock: Letters about the Vietnam War to America's Favorite Baby Doctor* (New York: New York University Press, 2005), 112.

2. Nguyen Van Luy, Speech at the Lincoln Memorial, October 21, 1967, http://www.redandgreen.org/Vietnam/NVL_docs/Nguyen_Van_Luy_10-21-1967.pdf

3. William Chapman, "179 Arrested as Violence Takes Over," *Washington Post*, October 22, 1967.

4. Tom Wells, *The War Within: America's Battle Over Vietnam* (Berkeley: University of California Press, 1994), 176.

5. Larry Sloman, *Steal This Dream: Abbie Hoffman and the Countercultural Revolution in America* (New York: Doubleday, 1998), 96.

6. FBI Memorandum, September 20, 1967.

7. Robin Palmer, interview with Jeremy Varon, October 31, 1994.

8. Sloman, *Steal This Dream*, 103.

9. Chapman, "179 Arrested."

10. Wells, *The War Within*, 197.

11. Johnny Black, "What Happened the Day the Fugs Attempted to Levitate the Pentagon," *Classic Rock*, December 13, 2016.

12. *The Nation* says the number was a half dozen; the *Washington Post* says twenty to thirty.

13. Joseph A. Loftus, "Guards Repulse War Protesters at the Pentagon," *New York Times*, October 22, 1967.

14. Ben Morea, interview with the author, December 9, 2022.

15. In an interview with the author, Teague said that other people in the holding cell wrote up the statement and gave it to him.

16. USMarshals.gov at https://www.usmarshals.gov/who-we-are/history/historical-reading-room/us-marshals-and-pentagon-riot-of-october-21-1967

17. Palmer interview with Varon.

18. "Meeting of the Rev. Con., October 31, 67," handwritten notes, FOIA documents.

19. FBI Memorandum from Special Agent in Charge, New York, to FBI Director, February 5, 1968.

20. Osha Neumann, *Up Against the Wall, Motherfucker: A Memoir of the '60s, With Notes for Next Time* (New York: Seven Stories Press, 2008), 76.

21. "Some Notes on Our Activities," USCANLF Newsletter, December 1967.

22. Homer Bigart, "War Foes Clash with Police Here as Rusk Speaks," *New York Times*, November 15, 1967.

23. USCANLF newsletter, December 21, 1967.

24. Vincent J. Cannato, *The Ungovernable City: John Lindsay and His Struggle to Save New York* (New York: Basic Books, 2001), 151.

25. Ibid.

26. "Police Frame-Up!" Insert, USCANLF newsletter, December 21, 1967.

27. Cannato, *The Ungovernable City*, 152.

28. Martin Jezer, "A Happening for the Birds," *WIN*, January 15, 1968.

29. "The Great Christmas Mill-In," *WIN*, January 15, 1968.

6. Yippies and Motherfuckers

1. David Lewis Stein, *Living the Revolution: The Yippies in Chicago* (New York: Bobbs-Merrill, 1969), 10.

2. Paul Krassner, *Confessions of a Raving, Unconfined Nut* (New York: Simon & Schuster, 1993), 156.

3. "The Politics of Joy," *The Movement*, November 1968, 10.

4. David Farber, *Chicago '68* (Chicago: University of Chicago Press, 1988), 212.

5. Ibid., 16.

6. Abbie Hoffman, "The Yippies Are Going to Chicago," *The Realist*, September 1968.

7. Abbie Hoffman, *The Autobiography of Abbie Hoffman* (New York: Four Windows Eight Walls, 1980), 102.

8. Stein, *Living the Revolution*, 8.

9. Ben Morea, interview with the author, December 9, 2022.

10. Peter Werbe, "Surreal Life," *Detroit Metro Times*, January 5, 2005.

11. Iain McIntyre, "Ben Morea: An Interview," https://theanarchistlibrary.org/library/Iain-mcintyre-ben-morea-an-interview.

12. Werbe, "Surreal Life."

13. Ron Porambo, "What Really Happened with LeRoi Jones in Newark," *The Realist*, September 1968.

14. "LeRoi Jones Seized in Newark After Being Hurt," *New York Times*, July 15, 1967.

15. FBI Memorandum from Special Agent in Charge, New York, to FBI Director, February 5, 1968.

16. Student Nonviolent Coordinating Committee, *Fact Sheet: Orangeburg, South Carolina*, February 9, 1968.

17. NYPD report, B.S.S. 92-M, February 7, 1968, Walter Teague Archives.

18. "Sanitmen Defy Injunction, Continue Walkout," *New York Daily News*, February 3, 1968, 7.

19. McIntyre, "Ben Morea: An Interview."

20. Hoffman, *Autobiography*, 102.

21. Andrew Cornell, *Unruly Equality: U.S. Anarchism in the Twentieth Century* (Berkeley: University of California Press, 2016), 244.

22. Todd Gitlin, *The Sixties: Years of Hope, Days of Rage* (New York: Bantam Books, 1987), 239.

23. Herbert Marcuse, Barrington Moore, Jr., and Robert Paul Wolff, *A Critique of Pure Tolerance* (Boston: Beacon Press, 1965), 81.

24. Hoffman, *Autobiography*, 84.

25. Ibid., 85.

26. Peter Stansill, "Affinity Group: A Street Gang with an Analysis," in *BAMN (By Any Means Necessary: Outlaw Manifestos and Ephemera 1965–1970)*, ed. David Zane Mairowitz (New York: Autonomedia, 1999), 144–146.

27. McIntyre, "Ben Morea: An Interview." Church was the Judson Church.

28. Ronald Sukenick, *Down and In: Life in the Underground* (New York: Collier Books, 1987), 156.

29. Larry Sloman, *Steal This Dream: Abbie Hoffman and the Countercultural Revolution in America* (New York: Doubleday, 1998), 77.

30. Ben Morea, interview with the author, January 18, 2023.

31. Stein, *Living the Revolution*, 12–13.

32. Ibid., 17.

33. Krassner, *Confessions*, 157.

34. FBI Memorandum, File Number NY 100-162260, March 16, 1968.

35. David Caute, *The Year of the Barricades: A Journey Through 1968* (New York: Harper & Row, 1988), 302.

36. FBI Memorandum, March 17, 1968.

37. "Interview with Osha Neumann," *Datacide Magazine*, April 1, 2017, https://datacide-magazine.com/interview-with-osha-neumann/

38. James Carr, *Bad: The Autobiography of James Carr* (Oakland: AK Press/Nabat, 2002), 230–231.

39. Morea interview, January 18, 2023.

40. Marty Jezer, *Abbie Hoffman: American Rebel* (New Brunswick, NJ: Rutgers University Press, 1993), 130.

41. Martin Jezer, "Yip!," *WIN*, April 15, 1968, 8.

42. Lew Friedman, interview with the author, December 3, 2020.

43. "Youth: The Politics of Yip," *Time*, April 5, 1968.

44. "Yip-In Stops Trains at Grand Central," *New York Free Press*, March 28, 1968.

45. Jezer, "Yip!," 8; Sloman, *Steal This Dream*, 115.

46. Jezer, "Yip!," 8.

47. Morea interview, December 9, 2022.

48. Jezer, *Abbie Hoffman*, 133.

49. Tony Ortega, "Yip-In Turns into Bloody Mess as Police Riot at Grand Central," *Village Voice*, March 28, 1968.

50. Sloman, *Steal This Dream*, 116.

51. Morea interview, December 9, 2022.

52. Grace Glueck, "Hippies Protest at Dada Preview," *New York Times*, March 26, 1968, 21.

53. By this point the group was widely being referred to as the Motherfuckers, but Katzman's use of Black Mask also shows that names, terminology, and so on could be more fluid in the moment than historians might prefer.

54. Allan Katzman, "Poor Paranoid's Almanac," *East Village Other*, March 28, 1968.

55. Philip Leider, "Dada, Surrealism and Their Heritage," *Art Forum*, May 1968, 22.

56. FBI Memorandum, "Meeting of YIPPIES," March 30, 1968.

57. Farber, *Chicago '68*, 38.

58. Krassner, *Confessions*, 159.

59. Stein, *Living the Revolution*, 25.

7. Riots of Spring

1. "The Siege of Columbia," *Ramparts*, June 1968, 28.

2. Irwin Unger, *The Movement: A History of the American New Left, 1959–1972* (New York: Dodd, Mead & Company, 1974), 105.

3. "The Siege of Columbia," 28.

4. Jeremy Avorn, *Up Against the Ivy Wall: A History of the Columbia Crisis* (New York: Atheneum, 1969), 18.

5. Unger, *The Movement*, 113.

6. Avorn, *Up Against the Ivy Wall*, 20.

7. Ibid., 19.

8. Columbia Strike Committee, *Why We Strike*, 1968, 6.

9. Avorn, *Up Against the Ivy Wall*, 9.

10. Paul Cronin, ed., *A Time to Stir: Columbia '68* (New York: Columbia University Press, 2018), 295.

11. Mark Rudd, *Underground: My Life with SDS and the Weathermen* (New York: William Morrow, 2009), 44–45.

12. "Draft Official Hit in Face with Pie During Talk Here," *Columbia Spectator*, March 21, 1968, 1.

13. Mark Rudd, "Notes on Columbia," *The Movement*, March 1969, 7.

14. Ben Morea, interview with the author, December 9, 2022.

15. Avorn, *Up Against the Ivy Wall*, 27.

16. Mark Rudd, "Notes on Columbia," 7.

17. Joshua Melville, *American Time Bomb: Attica, Sam Melville, and a Son's Search for Answers* (Chicago: Chicago Review Press, 2021), 36.

18. Palmer's widow provided a photo of him scaling the facade to Jeremy Varon. Joshua Melville, who interviewed Palmer extensively, claims in *American Time Bomb* that the two were together (36).

19. James Simon Kunen, *The Strawberry Statement: Notes of a College Revolutionary* (New York: Random House, 1968), 25.

20. Melville, *American Time Bomb*, 37. Joshua Melville's book takes certain editorial liberties with characters and quotations that he is forthright about; nevertheless, it can sometimes be difficult to tell where creative license is being used, so specific details need to be taken cautiously.

21. "Here We Are: Brattleboro's Community Talk Show," *Brattleboro Community Television*, February 3, 2020.

22. "Introduction," *Who Rules Columbia*, North American Congress on Latin America, June 1968, 2.

23. Walter Teague, interview with the author, December 28, 2022.

24. Kunen, *The Strawberry Statement*, 26.

25. Robin Palmer, interview with Jeremy Varon, October 25, 1994.

26. Kunen, *The Strawberry Statement*, 29.

27. Palmer interviews with Varon, November 14, 1994, and December 8, 1994. See also Kunen, *The Strawberry Statement*, 28.

28. Robin Palmer, interview with Jeremy Varon, December 4, 1994.

29. Michael A. Baker, Bradley R. Brewer, Raymond DeBuse, Sally T. Hillsman, Murray Milner, and David V. Soeiro, *Police on Campus: The Mass Police Action at Columbia University, Spring 1968* (New York: Temco Press, 1969), 20, 57.

30. Morea interview, December 9, 2002.

31. "Interview with Osha Neumann," *Datacide Magazine*, April 1, 2017, https://datacide-magazine.com/interview-with-osha-neumann/

32. "The Siege of Columbia," 37.

33. Osha Neumann, *Up Against the Wall, Motherfucker: A Memoir of the '60s, With Notes for Next Time* (New York: Seven Stories Press, 2008), 82.

34. Morea interview, December 9, 2002.

35. Abbie Hoffman, *The Autobiography of Abbie Hoffman* (New York: Four Windows Eight Walls, 1980), 139–140.

36. Morea interview, December 9, 2002.

37. Neumann, *Up Against the Wall, Motherfucker*, 99.

38. Cronin, *A Time to Stir*, 379.

39. Baker et al., *Police on Campus*, 57, 61–64.

40. FBI Memorandum from J. Edgar Hoover, May 14, 1968, via Chicago68.com.

41. Frank Da Cruz, "Columbia University 1968," April 1998, http://www.columbia.edu/cu/computinghistory/1968/

42. Lawrence Van Gelder, "Columbia Students Help Occupy Flats," *New York Times*, May 18, 1968.

43. Melville, *American Time Bomb*, 37.

44. On May 19 rallies sponsored by the National Day for Black Unity and took place simultaneously in Bedford Stuyvesant and Harlem. NYPD memo, B.S.S. Comm. #358, May 21, 1968, Walter Teague Archives.

45. Jane Alpert, *Growing Up Underground* (New York: Morrow, 1981), 112.

46. NYPD memo, B.A.A 391-M, May 23, 1968, Walter Teague Archives.

47. Paul Cronin, ed., *A Time to Stir: Columbia '68* (New York: Columbia University Press, 2018), 295.

48. Melville, *American Time Bomb*, 44.

49. FBI Memorandum, "TPF Dinner," May 2, 1968.

50. FBI Memorandum from Special Agent in Charge, New York, to FBI Director, June 4, 1968.

51. "Statement of Purpose" flyer, 1968, Walter Teague Archives.

52. "We're Going Back to Washington Square Park," Co-Aim Flyer, May 1968.

53. Co-Aim Flyer, April 27, 1968, USCANLF Archives.

54. USCANLF Newsletter, July 21, 1968.

55. Carola Hoffman, interview with the author, December 11, 2022.

56. Walter Teague, interview with the author, December 9, 2022.

57. Homer Bigart, "Leftist Protesters Elude Police During Lower East Side March," *New York Times*, May 19, 1968.

58. Carola Hoffman, email to the author, December 15, 2022.

59. "80 Reserves March in Antiwar Parade," *New York Times*, April 14, 1968.

60. "150 Picket Opening of 'Green Berets'; Signs Score Wayne," *New York Times*, June 20, 1968.

61. Renata Adler, "Screen: 'Green Berets' as Viewed by John Wayne," *New York Times*, June 20, 1968.

62. FBI Memorandum, "Meeting at the Brooklyn Botanic Gardens," June 21, 1968.

63. Teague interview, December 9, 2022.

64. FBI Memorandum from Special Agent in Charge, New York, to the FBI Director, June 4, 1968.

8. Summertime Blues

1. Robin Palmer, interview with Jeremy Varon, October 31, 1994.

2. Larry Sloman, *Steal This Dream: Abbie Hoffman and the Countercultural Revolution in America* (New York: Doubleday, 1998), 49–50.

3. Carola Von Hofmannsthal-Solomonoff (a.k.a. Carola Hoffman), "Robin Palmer: Weatherman Yippie Right Wing Rebel Forever, Part Two," Blogger News Network, October 18, 2010.

4. David Farber, *The Age of Great Dreams: America in the 1960s* (New York: Hill and Wang, 1994), 86–87.

5. David Gilbert, Robert Gottlieb, and Gerry Tenney, "Toward a Theory of Social Change: The 'Port Authority Statement,'" *Lost Writings of SDS*, 108, https://www.sds-1960s.org/PortAuthorityStatement.pdf.

6. Harold Jacobs, ed., "Chronology of Events," *Weatherman* (Berkeley, CA: Ramparts Press, 1970), xv.

7. Ann Gordon, "SDS Convention—Marriage of Convenience," *SF Express*, July 17, 1968.

8. Jeff Gordon, "SDS: An Analysis," *Progressive Labor*, October 1968.

9. Osha Neumann, *Up Against the Wall, Motherfucker: A Memoir of the '60s, With Notes for Next Time* (New York: Seven Stories Press, 2008), 88–89.

10. Jeff Gordon, "SDS: An Analysis," Progressive Labor, Vol. 6, No. 5, October 1968. https://www.marxists.org/history/erol/1960-1970/pl-sds.htm

11. Jacobs, "Chronology," 3.

12. Ann Gordon, "SDS Convention—Marriage of Convenience," *SF Express*, July 17, 1968.

13. Co-Aim Flyer, USCANLF Archives, 1968.

14. FBI Memorandum, "Meeting of CO-AIM," July 17, 1968.

15. "Old News," *Bedford Barrow Commerce Block Association Newsletter*, November 2017.

16. "36 Youths Held in Tie-Up After Humphrey Protest," *New York Times*, July 24, 1968, 24.

17. FBI Memorandum, Vincent Alvino to Secret Service, April 25, 1969.

18. Robin Palmer, interview with Jeremy Varon, December 8, 1994.

19. "36 Youths Held."

20. Homer Bigart, "Derelicts and Hippies Are Making Washington Square a Nightmare Area," *New York Times*, August 9, 1968, 23.

21. "Counterintelligence Program Internal Security Disruption of the New Left," *Cointelpro*, July 5, 1968.

22. Robert D. McFadden, "Police-Black Panther Scuffles Mark Brooklyn Street Rally," *New York Times*, August 2, 1968.

23. Sidney E. Zion, "5 Black Panthers Held in Brooklyn," *New York Times*, September 13, 1968.

24. David Burnham, "Off-Duty Police Here Join in Beating Black Panthers," *New York Times*, September 5, 1968.

25. Sidney E. Zion, "5 Black Panthers Held in Brooklyn," *New York Times*, September 13, 1968.

26. USCANLF Archives, 1968.

27. David Farber, *Chicago '68* (Chicago: University of Chicago Press, 1988), 49.

28. FBI Memorandum from Special Agent in Charge, New York, to FBI Director, August 9, 1968.

29. Martin A. Lee and Bruce Shlain, *Acid Dreams: The Complete Social History of LSD—The CIA, The Sixties, and Beyond* (New York: Grove Press, 1985), 173.

30. FBI Memorandum from the FBI Director to the Special Agent in Charge, New York, "DEMCON," August 15, 1968.

31. Joshua Melville, *American Time Bomb: Attica, Sam Melville, and a Son's Search for Answers* (Chicago: Chicago Review Press, 2021), 45.

32. FBI Memorandum, "V&R Involvement in Chicago Demonstration," August 24–30.

33. Ben Morea, interview with the author, December 9, 2022.

34. Neumann, *Up Against the Wall, Motherfucker*, 102.

35. Farber, *Chicago '68*, xiv.

36. Ibid., 52, 84.

37. FBI Memorandum, July 5, 1968.

38. FBI Memorandum, November 25, 1968.

39. FBI Memorandum, June 5, 1968.

40. FBI Memorandum, July 17, 1968.

41. Judy Gumbo, *Yippie Girl: Exploits in Protest and Defeating the FBI* (New York: Three Rooms Press, 2022), 84–85.

42. Merriman Smith, "Yippies' Pig Candidate 'Bores' Chicago Police," *Indianapolis Star*, August 24, 1968.

43. Gumbo, *Yippie Girl*, 86–87.

44. Abbie Hoffman, *The Autobiography of Abbie Hoffman* (New York: Four Windows Eight Walls, 1980), 153.

45. Jonah Raskin, *For the Hell of It: The Life and Times of Abbie Hoffman* (Berkeley: University of California Press, 1996), 157.

46. Gumbo, *Yippie Girl*, 82.

47. Ed Sanders, *Shards of God: A Novel of the Yippies* (New York: Grove Press, 1970), 112; Gumbo, *Yippie Girl*, 93–94.

48. Wolfe Lowenthal, *Gateway to the Miraculous: Further Explorations in the Tao of Cheng Man-ch'ing* (Berkeley: Frog, Ltd., 1994), 43.

49. David Caute, *The Year of the Barricades: A Journey Through 1968* (New York: Harper & Row, 1988), 313.

50. Farber, *Chicago '68*, 178.

51. Gumbo, *Yippie Girl*, 97.

52. Farber, *Chicago '68*, 180.

53. Gumbo, *Yippie Girl*, 99.

54. David Lewis Stein, *Living the Revolution: The Yippies in Chicago* (New York: Bobbs-Merrill, 1969), 77.

55. Farber, *Chicago '68*, 183.

56. FBI Memorandum, "V&R Involvement in Chicago Demonstration," August 24–30.

57. Stein, *Living for Revolution*, 81.

58. Paul Krassner, *Confessions of a Raving, Unconfined Nut* (New York: Simon & Schuster, 1993), 164.

59. FBI Memorandum, "V&R Involvement in Chicago Demonstration," August 24–30.

60. Ibid.

61. Stein, *Living for Revolution*, 86.

62. FBI Memorandum, "V&R Involvement."

63. Stein, *Living for Revolution*, 91, 95.

64. "The Case of the Defendant Who Was Bound and Gagged," Constitutional Rights Foundation, *BRIA Archives*, https://www.crf-usa.org/bill-of-rights-in-action/bria-6-4-the-case-of-the-defendant-who-was-bound-and-gagged.

65. Stein, *Living for Revolution*, 100–101.

66. Caute, *The Year of the Barricades*, 315.

67. FBI Memorandum, Vincent Alvino to Secret Service, April 25, 1969.

68. *Testimony of Allen Ginsberg*, Chicago 7 Trial, http://law2.umkc.edu/faculty/projects/ftrials/Chicago7/Ginsberg.html.

69. R. C. Baker, "A Visit to Chicago: Blood, Sweat & Tears," *Village Voice*, September 5, 1968.

70. Stein, *Living for Revolution*, 102.

71. Baker, "A Visit to Chicago."

72. Sloman, *Steal This Dream*, 153.

73. Jeremy Varon, *Bringing the War Home: The Weather Underground, the Red Army Faction, and Revolutionary Violence in the Sixties and Seventies* (Berkeley: University of California Press, 2004), 329.

74. Robin Palmer, interview with Jeremy Varon, December 4, 1994.

75. Farber, *Chicago '68*, 192.

76. Hugh Hough, "Battle of Grant Park," *Chicago Sun Times*, August 29, 1968.

77. FBI Memorandum, "V&R Involvement."

78. Stein, *Living for Revolution*, 114–116.

79. Gumbo, *Yippie Girl*, 105.

80. FBI Memorandum, "V&R Involvement."

81. *Testimony of Linda Hager Morse*, Chicago 7 Trial, http://law2.umkc.edu/faculty/projects/ftrials/Chicago7/Morse.html.

82. Farber, *Chicago '68*, 199.

83. Stein, *Living for Revolution*, 118.

84. Jack Newfield, "Chicago 1968: A Riot by the Cops," *Village Voice*, September 5, 1968.

85. FBI Memorandum, "V&R Involvement in Chicago Demonstration," August 24–30.

86. FBI Memorandum from Special Agent Paul A. Zolbe, File Number NY 100-160649, September 24, 1968.

87. Caute, *The Year of the Barricades*, 322.

88. Lewis S. Feuer, "Student Unrest in the United States," *Annals of the American Academy of Political and Social Science* 404 (November 1972): 175; Farber, *Age of Great Dreams*, 224.

9. Let's Go Crazie

1. Todd Gitlin, *The Sixties: Years of Hope, Days of Rage* (New York: Bantam Books, 1987), 326.

2. *Testimony of Linda Hager Morse*, Chicago 7 Trial, http://law2.umkc.edu/faculty/projects/ftrials/Chicago7/Morse.html.

3. Tom Wells, *The War Within: America's Battle Over Vietnam* (Berkeley: University of California Press, 1994), 284.

4. Ibid., 283.

5. Steve Lerner, "The Lower East Side: Radicalization of the Hip," *Village Voice*, November 28, 1968.

6. Todd Gitlin, "New Left, Old Traps," *Ramparts*, September 1969.

7. *Black Mask & Up Against the Wall Motherfucker: Flower Power Won't Stop Fascist Power*, unknown author, publisher, and date.

8. Larry Sloman, *Steal This Dream: Abbie Hoffman and the Countercultural Revolution in America* (New York: Doubleday, 1998), 55.

9. Gitlin, *The Sixties*, 338.

10. Milton Viorst, *Fire in the Streets: America in the 1960's* (New York: Simon & Schuster, 1979), 461.

11. Abbie Hoffman, *The Autobiography of Abbie Hoffman* (New York: Four Windows Eight Walls, 1980), 160.

12. Robin Palmer, interview with Jeremy Varon, October 25, 1994.

13. Harold Jacobs, ed., "Chronology of Events," *Weatherman* (Berkeley, CA: Ramparts Press, 1970), 4.

14. Andrew Kopkind, "The Real SDS Stands Up," *Weatherman*, 17.

15. Palmer interview with Varon, October 25, 1994.

16. Sloman, *Steal This Dream*, 156, 152.

17. Ann Zimmer, "Yippie Spy," *Dallas Observer*, March 16, 1995.

18. UNT interviews, 2002.

19. Lew Friedman, interview with the author, December 3, 2020.

20. Interview with George Demmerle, *Irving (TX) Community Television*, March 29, 1999.

21. UNT interviews, 2002.

22. Ibid.

23. Ken Wachsberger, interview with the author, December 22, 2022.

24. Jane Alpert, *Growing Up Underground* (New York: Morrow, 1981), 14, 109.

25. Ibid, 109.

26. Ibid.

27. Carola Hoffman, email to the author, May 4, 2020.

28. Walter Teague, email to the author, February 11, 2020.

29. *Stenciling Tips Flyer*, Demmerle FOIA files, November 3, 1968.

30. Joshua Melville, *American Time Bomb: Attica, Sam Melville, and a Son's Search for Answers* (Chicago: Chicago Review Press, 2021), 85.

31. NYPD Memo, B.S.S. Case #729-M, September 10, 1968, Walter Teague Archives.

32. Flo Kennedy, *My Hard Life and Good Times* (Englewood Cliffs, NJ: Prentice-Hall, 1976), 2, 5, 27.

33. NYPD Memorandum, September 28, 1968, from Walter Teague Archives.

34. Carola Hoffman, email to the author, January 27, 2020.

35. Palmer interview with Varon, October 25, 1994.

36. NYPD Memorandum, September 28, 1968.

37. FBI Memorandum, September 28, 1968.

38. Jerry Rubin, *We Are Everywhere* (New York: Harper & Row, 1971), 216–218.

39. Timothy Scott Brown, "The Sixties in the City: Avant-gardes and Urban Rebels in New York, London and West Berlin," *Journal of Social History*, Vol. 46, No.4 (Summer 2013), 827.

40. Carola Hoffman, interview with the author, December 11, 2022.

41. "The Streets Belong to the People" leaflet, Workshop on Tactical Street Action, October 1968.

42. Osha Neumann, *Up Against the Wall, Motherfucker: A Memoir of the '60s, With Notes for Next Time* (New York: Seven Stories Press, 2008), 95.

43. David Farber, *Chicago '68* (Chicago: University of Chicago Press, 1988), 94.

44. Eldridge Cleaver, Stew Albert, Abbie Hoffman and Jerry Rubin, "Yipanther Pact," *Berkeley Barb*, October 4, 1968.

45. FBI Memorandum, "Disruption of Paul O'Dwyer at Trinity Church," October 19, 1968.

46. Clayton Knowles, "O'Dwyer Is Jeered by Antiwar Group," *New York Times*, October 21, 1968.

47. NYPD Memo, B.S.S. #898-M (first and final), October 21, 1968.

48. Michael D. Cohen, "Presidential Races Can Change Significantly as Election Day Approaches," Gallup.com, October 26, 2000.

49. Robert D. McFadden, "Naked Couple Disrupt a Humphrey Rally Here," *New York Times*, November 1, 1968, 34.

50. Sloman, *Steal This Dream*, 122.

51. "The Sane Bombers," *The Movement*, January 1970, 4.

52. Walter Teague, interview with the author, December 9, 2022.

53. FBI Memorandum, Vincent Alvino to Secret Service, April 26, 1969.

54. John Kenneth Galbraith, *A Life in Our Times* (New York: Random House Publishing Group, 1982).

55. "Flashing the Democrats," *American Heritage*, December 1989.

56. Palmer interview with Varon, October 25, 1994. Palmer's antics that night did raise his profile and credibility in the Movement, though. When a few weeks later he bumped into Mark Rudd—whom Palmer had met just once, during the Columbia siege—Rudd grinned and said, "Gee, Robin, I didn't recognize you with your clothes on!" Ibid.

57. NYPD Memo, "Election Day Demonstrations," B.S.S. #927-M (Final Report), November 6, 1968.

58. Neumann, *Up Against the Wall, Motherfucker,* 104.

59. Ben Morea, interview with the author, December 9, 2022.

60. "Graham Is Crackers or Try to Find the Wall," Liberation News Service, October 22, 1968.

61. Ibid.

62. Lita Eliseu, "Up Against the Wall, Bill Graham!" *East Village Other*, October 25, 1968, 9.

63. "Graham Is Crackers."

64. Bill Graham and Robert Greenfield, *Bill Graham Presents: My Life Inside Rock and Out*, (New York: Doubleday, 1990), 254.

65. FBI Memorandum, November 22, 1968.

66. Charlotte Polin, Letter to the Committee for Cultural Relations with Foreign Countries, June 7, 1967.

67. Alpert, *Growing Up Underground*, 122.

68. Ibid., 129.

69. Charles Merrill, "Re 'The Village Voice, Keeper of Downtown Cool, Will Shed Its Print Edition,'" *New York Times*, August 30, 2017.

70. Ronald Sukenick, *Down and In: Life in the Underground* (New York: Collier Books, 1987), 127.

71. Susan Sherman, interview with the author, January 8, 2023. When interviewed fifty-five years later Sherman was still living in the same East Village apartment among a lifetime's accumulation of documents, photos, and books, most relating to poetry and feminism.

72. FBI report, "Investigation Regarding Samuel Joseph Melville," File Number 117 506 H, Report Number NY 52-9441, December 1969, 108.

73. "Antiwar Parley Repairs a Split," *New York Times*, December 1, 1968.

74. Phoebe Hirsch, "Radical Caucuses Highlight Montreal Conference," *New Left Notes*, December 11, 1968, 7.

75. Tom Wodetzki, interview with the author, December 16, 2022.

76. Alpert, *Growing Up Underground*, 135.

77. Pat Swinton interview, "Here We Are," Brattleboro Community Television, February 3, 2020, https://www.brattleborotv.org/here-we-are/guest-shoshana-rihn

78. John Gerassi and Steve Weissman, "The Vietnamization of Latin America," reprinted in *The New Left: A Documentary History*, ed. Massimo Teodori (New York: Bobbs-Merrill Company, 1969), 269.

79. Advertisement in the *Rat Subterranean News*, October 1968.

80. Alpert, *Growing Up Underground*, 140.

81. Melville, *American Time Bomb*, 87–88.

82. Henry Raymont, "Sketches of 4 Seized as Bombing Suspects," *New York Times*, November 14, 1969.

83. Teague interview, December 9, 2022.

84. Carola Hoffman, interview with the author, December 10, 2020.

85. Richie Unterberger, *White Light/White Heat: The Velvet Underground Day by Day* (London: Jawbone Press, 2009), 217.

86. Wayne Kramer, "Riots I Have Known and Loved," 2002, http://makemyday.free.fr/wk1.htm.

87. Neumann, *Up Against the Wall, Motherfucker*, 110.

88. John Glatt, *Live at the Fillmore East and West: Getting Backstage and Personal with Rock's Greatest Legends* (Guildford, CT: Lyons Press, 2015), 189.

89. Dean Latimer, "Up Against the Mother, Fucker," *East Village Other*, January 10, 1969, 7.

90. Neumann, *Up Against the Wall, Motherfucker*, 11.

91. FBI Memorandum from Special Agent in Charge, New York, to FBI Director, December 3, 1968.

10. Sixty-Nine

1. Joseph R. Sahid, ed., *Rights in Concord: The Response to the Counter-Inaugural Pretest Activities in Washington D.C., January 18–20, 1969*, The Task Force on Law and Law Enforcement to the National Commission on the Causes and Prevention of Violence, 83.

2. Ibid., 85–86, 90, 93.

3. Ibid., 93.

4. Craig Simpson, "The 1969 Nixon Inauguration: Horse Manure, Rocks & Pigs," *Washington Spark*, January 9, 2009.

5. Sahid, *Rights in Concord*, 93–94.

6. Ibid.

7. FBI Memorandum, "Correlation Summary, Subject Richard Robin Palmer," March 2, 1972, 6.

8. FBI Memorandum, "Youth International Party," September 12, 1968.

9. Robin Palmer, interview with Jeremy Varon, December 4, 1994.

10. Sahid, *Rights in Concord*, 95.

11. Susan Faludi, "Death of a Revolutionary," *New Yorker*, April 8, 2013.

12. Todd Gitlin, *The Sixties: Years of Hope, Days of Rage* (New York: Bantam Books, 1987), 363, 373.

13. Faludi, "Death of a Revolutionary."

14. Alice Echols, *Daring to Be Bad: Radical Feminism 1967–1975* (Minneapolis: University of Minnesota Press, 1989), 116.

15. Faludi, "Death of a Revolutionary."

16. Echols, *Daring to Be Bad*, 119.

17. Sahid, *Rights of Concord*, 96.

18. Sahid, *Rights of Concord*, 97–98.

19. SDS Pre-Inauguration Planning Paper, https://omeka.library.kent.edu/special-collections/items/show/3163.

20. Sahid, *Rights in Concord*, 100–103.

21. FBI Memorandum, Demmerle Inauguration Report, January 18–20, 1969.

22. Joshua Melville, "American Time Bomb—Sam and Jane," sammelville.org/media/american-timebomb-sam-and-jane/.

23. Jane Alpert, *Growing Up Underground* (New York: Morrow, 1981), 146.

24. Sahid, *Rights in Concord*, 105.

25. Ibid., 106.

26. David Squires, " . . . And Counter-Inaugurated," *Campus*, January 22, 1969, 3.

27. Sahid, *Rights in Concord*, 106–107.

28. Ibid., 107.

29. J. R. Covert, "Nixon Inaugurated," *Campus*, January 22, 1969, 8.

30. Sahid, *Rights in Concord*, 107–109.

31. Timothy Denevi, "The Striking Contradictions of Richard Nixon's Inauguration 50 Years Ago," *Time*, December 19, 2019.

32. David Lewis Stein, *Living the Revolution: The Yippies in Chicago* (New York: Bobbs-Merrill, 1969), 3.

33. Ibid., 3.

34. Sahid, *Rights in Concord*, 111.

35. Stein, *Living the Revolution*, 3.

36. Ibid., 4.

37. Covert, "Nixon Inaugurated," 8.

38. FBI Memorandum, unknown date.

39. Ben A. Franklin, "Young Demonstrators at Parade Throw Smoke Bombs and Stones at Nixon's Car," *New York Times*, January 21, 1969.

40. "The Crazies," *Newsweek*, March 24, 1969, 88.

41. Carola Hoffman, email to the author, December 12, 2020.

42. FBI Memorandum, January 7, 1969.

43. FBI Memorandum, December 3, 1968.

44. Jan Cohen-Cruz, Ed. *Radical Street Performance: An International Anthology* (New York: Routledge, 1994), 190.

45. Abbie Hoffman, *The Autobiography of Abbie Hoffman* (New York: Four Windows Eight Walls, 1980), 113.

46. FBI Memorandum from Special Agent in Charge, New York, to FBI Director, February 13, 1969.

47. FBI Memorandum, NY 100-165630, February 16, 1969.

48. "Crazies," FBI Report, NY Summary Report, January 14, 1970, 197.

49. Antony Prisendorf, "Did the Crazies Fox the Army?" *New York Post*, January 4, 1971.

50. Lee Merrick, "Life with 'Crazie' George," Liberation News Service, January 24, 1970, 18.

51. Jerry Rubin, *We Are Everywhere* (New York: Harper & Row, 1971), 216.

52. Jay Levin, "The Wildest Radical," *New York Post*, May 25, 1970.

53. Ann Zimmer, "Yippie Spy," *Dallas Observer*, March 16, 1995.

54. "Provocation a la FBI," *Dissent*, July–August 1970, https://www.dissentmagazine.org/article/provocation-a-la-fbi.

55. Walter Teague, interview with the author, December 9, 2022.

56. Alpert, *Growing Up Underground*, 147, 150.

57. Carola Von Hoffmannstahl, "Robin Palmer: Weatherman Yippie Right Wing Rebel Forever," Blogger News Network, October 18, 2010.

58. Ronald Sukenick, *Down and In: Life in the Underground* (New York: Collier Books, 1987), 191.

59. Bellevue flyer, Demmerle Archives.

60. Carola Hoffman, interview with the author, December 11, 2022.

61. Stein, *Living the Revolution*, 13, 2.

62. Eric Darton, "Radio Tirane," *Conjunctions, 10th Anniversary Issue* (New York: Random House, 1991), 141.

63. Alice Widener, "Pig on a Peace Plate," *Human Events*, March 22, 1969, 11, reprinted in the *Congressional Record*, March 27, 1968, 7893.

64. Tom Wodetzki, interview with the author, December 16, 2022.

65. Ana Marie, "Protesters in Pig Masks Take the Mic from Senator Fulbright," WNYC, December 1, 2016.

66. Carola Hoffman, "Crazies Attack," *Ann Arbor Argus*, March 28, 1969, 6.

67. "Outbursts by Hecklers Silence Senator Fulbright at a Peace Luncheon Here," *New York Times*, March 6, 1969.

68. Hoffman, "Crazies Attack," 6.

69. Van Gosse, *Rethinking the New Left: An Interpretative History* (New York: Palgrave Macmillan, 2005), 91.

70. Marie, "Protesters in Pig Masks."

71. Hoffman, "Crazies Attack," 6.

72. "Outbursts by Hecklers Silence Senator Fulbright at a Peace Luncheon Here," *New York Times*, March 6, 1969.

73. Krassner, "The Crazies Are Coming," *Cavalier*, July 1969.

74. Ibid.

75. Ibid.

76. John Leo, "Pro-Vietcong Group Demonstrates at Meeting Here," *New York Times*, March 9, 1969.

77. Wodetzki interview, December 16, 2022.

78. FBI Memorandum, NY 100-150001, March 10, 1969.

79. FBI Memorandum, NY 100-163804, March 11, 1969.

80. Alpert, *Growing Up Underground*, 153.

81. Alpert, *Growing Up Underground*, 153, 156.

82. "Crazies Go to Church (And Take Their Friends)," *Rat Subterranean News*, March 1969.

83. Ibid.

84. Krassner, "The Crazies Are Coming."

85. "Crazies Go to Church."

86. Palmer interview with Varon, December 8, 1994.

87. NYPD Memo, B.S.S. #279-M (First and Final Report), March 23, 1969.

88. Krassner, "The Crazies Are Coming."

89. Ibid.

90. NYPD Memo, B.S.S. #279-M (First and Final Report).

91. The *Cavalier* article references Hoffman's arrest and claims that the drugs had been planted there.

92. Andrew Cornell, *Unruly Equality: U.S. Anarchism in the Twentieth Century* (Berkeley: University of California Press, 2016), 264.

93. NYPD Memorandum, B.S.S. #279-M (First and Final Report).

94. FBI Memorandum, April 2, 1969.

95. *Alternate U. Course Catalog*, Fall 1969.

96. Krassner, "The Crazies Are Coming."

97. Ibid.

98. FBI memorandum, NY-100-165630, March 29, 1969.

99. Krassner, "The Crazies Are Coming."

100. David C. Viola Jr., "Terrorism and the Response to Terrorism in New York City During the Long Sixties," PhD diss., City University of New York, 2017, 150. Viola says they met in Champlain, NY but Alpert says it was Montreal.

101. Alpert, *Growing Up Underground*, 162.

102. From FBI Memorandum, "Samuel J Melville," June 25, 1969, via Viola dissertation.

103. Alpert, *Growing Up Underground*, 162.

104. NYPD Memo, B.S.S. #330-M (First Report), April 4, 1969.

105. Murray Schumach, "Thousands March Here to Demand Withdrawal from Vietnam by U.S.," *New York Times*, April 6, 1969, 1.

106. "Kites, Fists Fly at 'Love-In, Be-In," *New York Times*, April 7, 1969.

107. FBI Memorandum, Vincent Alvino to Secret Service, August 12, 1969.

108. Committee on Internal Security Staff Study, October 6, 1970, 31.

109. *Rat Subterranean News*, date unknown, from Demmerle Archives.

110. FBI Memorandum from Special Agent in Charge, New York, to FBI Director, NY 100-150001, April 19, 1969.

111. "8 Seized with Forged Tickets to a Luncheon for Humphrey," *New York Times*, April 20, 1969.

112. FBI Memorandum, April 1969.

113. FBI Memorandum, Vincent Alvino to Secret Service, August 12, 1969.

114. FBI Memorandum, NY 100-161993, April 22, 1969; FBI Memorandum, "Meeting at Apt.," April 1969.

115. FBI Memorandum, NY 100-161993, April 22, 1969.

116. https://www.vietnamwar50th.com/1969-1971_vietnamization/Peak-U-S-Troop-Levels/.

117. Douglas Robinson, "Militants Protest at Arraignment of 12 Seized in Weapons Raid," *New York Times*, February 4, 1970.

118. "Prosecutor Says New York Lawyer Ordered the Slaying of Panther," *New York Times*, June 17, 1971.

119. "Lawyer Put on Probation for Assault in Maryland," *New York Times*, February 15, 1972.

120. FBI Memorandum, April 1969.

121. Lew Friedman, interview with the author, December 3, 2020.

122. FBI Memorandum, NY 100-161993, April 22, 1969.

123. Alpert, *Growing Up Underground*, 165. Alpert used aliases in her book, and these have been replaced with the actual names in this account.

124. Ibid., 167–168.

125. Palmer interview with Jeremy Varon, December 16, 1994.

126. Alpert, *Growing Up Underground*, 175.

127. Tom Robbins, "Why Mailer Matters," *Village Voice*, November 13, 2007.

128. FBI Memorandum, May 14, 1969.

129. "'Crazies' Break Up Mailer Rally," *New York Post*, May 15, 1968.

130. Robbins, "Why Mailer Matters."

131. "'Crazies' Break Up Mailer Rally."

132. FBI Memorandum, Vincent Alvino to Secret Service, August 12, 1969.

133. FBI Memorandum, "Crazies Disruption of Norman Mailer at PS 41," NY 100-165630, May 14, 1969.

134. Gerri Bradley, interview with the author, December 19, 2022.

135. FBI Memorandum, "Crazies Coalition Meeting," NY 100-165630, May 23, 1969.

136. Thomas R. Brooks, "The New Left Is Showing Its Age," *New York Times*, June 15, 1969.

137. Ben Morea, interview with author, December 9, 2022.

138. Larry Sloman, *Steal This Dream: Abbie Hoffman and the Countercultural Revolution in America* (New York: Doubleday, 1998), 184.

139. "People Against the Pestilence," *Crazie*, June/July 1969, 2–4.

140. Alpert, *Growing Up Underground*, 172.

141. Ibid., 176, 179, 181.

142. Carola Hoffman, email to the author, December 4, 2020.

143. *Crazie*, August 1969.

144. FBI Memorandum, NY 100-161993, June 1969.

145. FBI Memorandum, NY 100-165630, June 26, 1969.

146. FBI Memorandum, NY 100-165630, June 25, 1969.

147. Kopkind, *Weatherman*, from Harold Jacobs, ed., "Chronology of Events," *Weatherman* (Berkeley, CA: Ramparts Press, 1970), 4.

148. Jack Smith, "Two, Three, Many S.D.S.'s," *Ann Arbor Argus*, July 10, 1969, 7.

149. Paul Cronin, ed., *A Time to Stir: Columbia '68* (New York: Columbia University Press, 2018), 297–298.

150. Smith, "Two, Three, Many S.D.S.'s," 7.

151. Kirkpatrick Sale, *SDS* (New York: Random House, 1973), 559.

152. Gitlin, *The Sixties*, 385.

153. Bryan Burrough, *Days of Rage* (New York: Penguin Press, 2015), 67–68.

154. Smith, "Two, Three, Many S.D.S.'s," 7.

155. Gitlin, *The Sixties*, 388.

11. Point of No Return

1. Jane Alpert, *Growing Up Underground* (New York: Morrow, 1981), 59, 183.

2. Sam Melville, "American Timebomb—Sam and Jane," sammelville.org.

3. Robin Palmer, interview with Jeremy Varon, December 8, 1994.

4. Albert A. Seedman and Peter Hellman, *Chief! Classic Cases from the Files of the Chief of Detectives* (New York: Avon Books, 1975), 228.

5. Alpert, *Growing Up Underground*, 191–193.

6. Joshua Melville's account has Sam renting the apartment earlier, in June, and moving the dynamite the morning after the heist.

7. Todd Gitlin, *The Sixties: Years of Hope, Days of Rage* (New York: Bantam Books, 1987), 350.

8. Robin Palmer, interview with Jeremy Varon, October 25, 1994.

9. FBI Memorandum, NY 157-4226, July 17, 1969.

10. FBI Memorandum, First National Conference for a United Front Against Fascism, August 8, 1969.

11. FBI Memorandum, August 8, 1969.

12. Alpert, *Growing Up Underground*, 199.

13. "UFAF Conference," *Old Mole*, August 1, 1969.

14. Alpert, *Growing Up Underground*, 199.

15. Joshua Melville, *American Time Bomb: Attica, Sam Melville, and a Son's Search for Answers* (Chicago: Chicago Review Press, 2021), 129.

16. Jane Alpert says that the Panthers did this at the urging of the Revolutionary Youth Movement, a militant faction of SDS that morphed into the Weathermen. Alpert, *Growing Up Underground*, 199.

17. David Barber, "Leading the Vanguard: White New Leftists School the Panthers on Black Revolution," in *In Search of the Black Panther Party: New Perspectives on a Revolutionary Movement* (Durham, NC: Duke University Press, 2006), 231.

18. FBI Memorandum from Vincent Alvino to Secret Service re: Richard Robin Palmer, November 21, 1969.

19. Josh Melville writes that the Panther approval from Bobby Seale came via George Demmerle, but this is not corroborated by any FBI documents or first-person interviews for this book. If Demmerle knew about the Melville Collective's stash of explosives and bombing plans in July, that would make his subsequent infiltration seem more skillful than lucky. It would also raise the question of whether Demmerle purposefully did not tell the FBI this information or whether he did tell them, and they disposed of any record of it. Melville, *American Time Bomb*, 131.

20. Alpert, *Growing Up Underground*, 199.

21. Melville, *American Time Bomb*, 130.

12. Bombs Away

1. *Crazie*, August 1969, 2.

2. Jane Alpert, *Growing Up Underground* (New York: Morrow, 1981), 199–200.

3. Ibid., 201.

4. Robin Palmer, interview with Jeremy Varon, December 8, 1994.

5. "What's Coming Down," *Rat Subterranean News*, August 12, 1969, 6.

6. Albert A. Seedman and Peter Hellman, *Chief! Classic Cases from the Files of the Chief of Detectives* (New York: Avon Books, 1975), 222–224.

7. FBI Memorandum, File number NY 100-150001, "Meeting—Veterans and Reservists to End the War in Vietnam," July 28, 1969.

8. FBI Memorandum, "Demonstrations," August 5, 1969.

9. Walter Teague, interview with the author, December 9, 2022.

10. NYPD Memo, S.S.B. #651-M (Final Report), August 11, 1969.

11. Teague interview.

12. Teague's personal frustration with the Parade Committee went back to the march on the Pentagon in October 1967, when its members resisted his attempts to get a Vietnamese American speaker included in the program, relenting only when Teague provided them with a copy of the man's speech. Even then the organizers cut the speaker off after thirty seconds.

13. Claudia Dreifus, "Up Against the Wall, Crazies," *East Village Other*, August 10, 1969.

14. Ibid.

15. Claudia Dreifus, "George Demmerle: The Pig Wore a Dayglo Helmet," *East Village Other*, December 3, 1969, 3.

16. USCANLF Press Release, September 1, 1969.

17. Dreifus, "George Demmerle," 3.

18. USCANLF Press Release, September 1, 1969.

19. Joshua Bloom and Waldo E. Martin, *Black Against Empire: The History and Politics of the Black Panther Party* (Berkeley: University of California Press, 2016), 291.

20. Jakobi Williams, "We Need to Unite with as Many People as Possible: The Illinois Chapter of the Black Panther Party and the Young Lords Organization in Chicago," in *Civil Rights and Beyond: African American and Latino/a Activism in the Twentieth Century United States*, ed. Brian D. Behnken (Athens: University of Georgia Press, 2016), 110.

21. Darrel Enck-Wanzer, ed., *The Young Lords: A Reader* (New York: New York University Press, 2010), 30.

22. Williams, "We Need to Unite," 120.

23. Bloom and Martin, *Black Against Empire*, 293.

24. Judson Jeffries, "Gang-Bangers to Urban Revolutionaries: The Young Lords of Chicago," *Journal of the Illinois State Historical Society* 96, no. 3 (Autumn 2003): 292.

25. Johanna Fernandez, *The Young Lords: A Radical History* (Chapel Hill: University of North Carolina Press, 202), 81, 65–66.

26. Bloom and Martin, *Black Against Empire*, 294.

27. Enck-Wanzer, *The Young Lords*, 31.

28. FBI Memorandum, August 4, 1969.

29. Ibid.

30. In Joshua Melville's account, Sam decided to go to Woodstock specifically to size up Demmerle. Joshua Melville, *American Time Bomb: Attica, Sam Melville, and a Son's Search for Answers* (Chicago: Chicago Review Press, 2021), 133.

31. Alpert, *Growing Up Underground*, 204.

32. Tom Wodetzki, interview with the author, December 16, 2022.

33. "What Happened at Woodstock?" *Movement for a Democratic Society* newsletter, September 1969.

34. Wodetzki interview.

35. Abbie Hoffman, *The Autobiography of Abbie Hoffman* (New York: Four Windows Eight Walls, 1980), 182.

36. UNT interviews, 2002.

37. Alpert, *Growing Up Underground*, 205.

13. On the Case

1. Jane Alpert, *Growing Up Underground* (New York: Morrow, 1981), 207.

2. Albert A. Seedman and Peter Hellman, *Chief! Classic Cases from the Files of the Chief of Detectives* (New York: Avon Books, 1975), 224.

3. "Blast Rips Bank in Financial Area," *New York Times*, August 21, 1969, 18.

4. Seedman and Hellman, *Chief!*, 224, 226–227.

5. Martin Arnold, "Bank Blast Laid to Bomb; Clues to Motive Sought," *New York Times*, August 22, 1969.

6. Seedman and Hellman, *Chief!*, 225.

7. Martin Arnold, "Bank Blast Laid to Bomb."

8. Wolfe Lowenthal, *Gateway to the Miraculous: Further Explorations in the Tao of Cheng Man-ch'ing* (Berkeley, CA: Frog, Ltd., 1994), 44.

9. Seedman and Hellman, *Chief!*, 228.

10. Ibid., 229–231.

11. Cy Egan and Marvin Smilon, "One of Suspects Bares Bomb Plot," *New York Post*, November 15, 1969.

12. Seedman and Hellman, *Chief!*, 232.

13. UNT interviews, 2002.

14. FBI Memorandum, NY 100-165630, September 4, 1969.

15. FBI Memorandum, NY 100-163878, September 12, 1969.

16. Lynn Darling, "Coming of Age in the Season of Rage," *Washington Post*, November 22, 1981.

17. Alpert, *Growing Up Underground*, 213.

18. Thomas A. Johnson, "Explosion Wrecks U.S. Offices Here," *New York Times*, September 20, 1969, 46.

19. Joshua Melville, *American Time Bomb: Attica, Sam Melville, and a Son's Search for Answers* (Chicago: Chicago Review Press, 2021), 129.

20. "Letters Claim Blast in Federal Building Was a Time Bomb," *New York Times*, September 21, 1969, 80.

21. "15 Arrested for Disrupting N.Y.U. Meeting on Vietnam," *New York Times*, September 21, 1969.

22. FBI Memorandum from Vincent Alvino to Secret Service, "Richard Robin Palmer," November 21, 1969.

23. Robin Palmer, interview with Jeremy Varon, November 14, 1994.

24. Seedman and Hellman, *Chief!*, 236.

25. Ibid., 233; FBI Memorandum, NY 52-9441, Synopsis, November 17, 1969, 53.

26. Alpert, *Growing Up Underground*, 217.

27. UNT interviews, 2002.

28. FBI Memorandum, File number NY 157-3768, September 18, 1969; Joshua Bloom and Waldo E. Martin, *Black Against Empire: The History and Politics of the Black Panther Party* (Berkeley: University of California Press, 2016), 292.

29. Amy Sinnie and James Tracy, *Hillbilly Nationalists, Urban Race Rebels, and Black Power: Community Organizing in Radical Times* (New York: Melville House, 2011), 74–75.

30. James Carr, *Bad: The Autobiography of James Carr* (Oakland, CA: AK Press/Nabat, 2002), 232.

31. FBI Report, "Meeting, Young Patriots Organization," File number NY 100-167484, September 26, 1969.

32. FBI Report, "Young Patriots Organization," File number NY 100-167484, September 29, 1969.

33. FBI Report, "Meeting, Young Patriots Organization," File number NY 100-167484, October 1, 1969.

34. FBI Report, "Meeting, Young Patriots Organization," File number NY 100-167484, October 3, 1969.

35. Walter Teague, interview with the author, December 9, 2022.

36. Alpert, *Growing Up Underground*, 218–219.

37. "Draft Center Here Damaged by Blast," *New York Times*, October 8, 1969, 1.

38. FBI Memorandum, NY 52-9441, Synopsis, November 17, 1969, 53.

39. "Evidence Regarding Typewriters, Press Releases and Laboratory Examinations," FBI Report, File #NY 52-9441, October 9, 1969, 49.

40. Seedman and Hellman, *Chief!*, 236.

41. Tom Thomas, "The Second Battle of Chicago 1969" from Harold Jacobs, ed., *Weatherman* (Berkeley, CA: Ramparts Press, 1970), 196.

42. Bryan Burrough, *Days of Rage* (New York: Penguin Press, 2015), 73.

43. Jacobs, ed., *Weatherman*, 283.

44. Milton Viorst, *Fire in the Streets: America in the 1960's* (New York: Simon and & Schuster, 1979), 496.

45. Jacobs, ed., *Weatherman*, 227.

46. Burrough, *Days of Rage*, 80.

47. Mark Rudd, *Underground: My Life with SDS and the Weathermen* (New York: William Morrow, 2009), 187–188, 190.

48. Van Gosse, *Rethinking the New Left: An Interpretative History* (New York: Palgrave Macmillan, 2005), 101.

49. Seedman and Hellman, *Chief!*, 235–236.

50. Martin Arnold, "Tip from Canadian Police Led to Bombing Arrests," *New York Times*, November 15, 1969.

51. Alpert, *Growing Up Underground*, 219.

52. Melville, *American Time Bomb*, 176.

53. Alpert, *Growing Up Underground*, 220.

54. FBI Memorandum from Vincent Alvino to Secret Service, "Richard Robin Palmer," November 21, 1969.

55. FBI Airtel Memorandum from Special Agent in Charge, Chicago, to Special Agent in Charge, New York, January 30, 1970.

56. "Crazies," FBI Report, NY Summary Report, January 14, 1970, 201.

57. "Imprisoned Soldiers Rebelled During Vietnam War," *Workers World*, June 2, 2019.

58. "150 Riot at Ft. Dix Stockade; Fires Set and Windows Broken," *New York Times*, June 5, 1969.

59. William Borders, "Macy's Seeks Clues in 5 Bomb Blasts," *New York Times*, October 13, 1969.

60. Lindsy Van Gelder, "Leftists, Near and Far, Form the Co-Conspiracy," *New York Post*, October 30, 1969, 10.

61. Benefit flyer, November 1, 1969 (FBI files).

62. FBI Memorandum, "Benefit for Young Patriots by Rainbow Coalition," File number NY 100-167484, November 1, 1969.

63. Sinnie and Tracy, *Hillbilly Nationalists*, 92.

64. Rudd, *Underground*, 184.

65. UNT interviews, 2002.

14. Join the Conspiracy

1. Lee Merrick, "Life with 'Crazie' George," Liberation News Service, January 24, 1970, 18.
2. Interview with George Demmerle, Irving (TX) Community Television, March 29, 1999.
3. "Posing the Left for a Group Picture," *Combat*, January 15, 1970.
4. Judson Hand, "Photog Spy for FBI Now an Outcast," *Daily News*, March 29, 1970.
5. John Kifner, "F.B.I. Paid 'Friend' of the 'Chicago 8,'" *New York Times*, October 23, 1969, 28.
6. FBI Memorandum from the Special Agent in Charge, New York, to the FBI Director, November 7, 1969.
7. Larry Sloman, *Steal This Dream: Abbie Hoffman and the Countercultural Revolution in America* (New York: Doubleday, 1998), 154.
8. Demmerle interview, Irving (TX) Community Television.
9. FBI Memorandum, November 7, 1969.
10. FBI Memorandum from A. Rosen to Mr. Deloach, November 14, 1969.
11. Shoshana Rihn, interview with the author, January 20, 2021.
12. Demmerle interview, Irving (TX) Community Television.
13. UNT interviews, 2002.
14. Demmerle interview, Irving (TX) Community Television.
15. Sloman, *Steal This Dream*, 242.
16. Ann Zimmer, "Yippie Spy," *Dallas Observer*, March 16, 1995.
17. Twaddle identified as George's contact in Cross Examination of Special Agent John Robinson, December 30, 1969.
18. FBI Memorandum, dictated on November 12, released on November 15, 1969.
19. "United States of America v. George Demmerle," Nolle Prosequi, United State District Court, Southern District of New York, September 1971, 3.
20. FBI Memorandum, November 13, 1969.
21. Jane Alpert, *Growing Up Underground* (New York: Morrow, 1981), 224.
22. FBI Memorandum, NY 52-9441, Synopsis, November 17, 1969, 52–53.
23. "Bombs Go Off at G.M. Building, Rockefeller Center, Chase Plaza," *New York Times*, November 11, 1969, 1.
24. FBI Report, File #NY 52-9441, December 12, 1969, 82.
25. "Probe Tips on the Bombings," *New York Post*, November 11, 1969, 1.
26. Albert A. Seedman and Peter Hellman, *Chief! Classic Cases from the Files of the Chief of Detectives* (New York: Avon Books, 1975), 240.
27. FBI Memorandum from New York 52-9441 to Director, November 12, 1969.
28. Seedman and Hellman, *Chief!*, 243.
29. To be fair, Palmer had been busy with Mobe plans. On November 9, Palmer represented the Crazies at a meeting at Judson Church about the Mobe march coming up in Washington, DC, on November 15.
30. Seedman and Hellman, *Chief!*, 242.
31. "How He Helped FBI Nab 2," *Daily News*, November 14, 1969, 5.
32. FBI Memorandum, November 15, 1969.
33. Demmerle interview, Irving (TX) Community Television.
34. "Arrest Record of George Demmerle," FBI Report NY 52-9441, November 14.
35. Brian Burrough, *Days of Rage* (New York: Penguin Press, 2015), 22.

36. Demmerle interview, Irving (TX) Community Television.

37. "How Lawmen Stalked the Bomb Suspects," *Daily News*, November 14, 1969, 5.

38. "Arrest Record of George Demmerle," FBI Report NY 52-9441, November 14, 1969, and NY Summary Report, January 14, 1970, 6.

39. FBI Memorandum, NY 52-9441, Synopsis, November 17, 1969, 14.

40. "How Lawmen Stalked the Bomb Suspects," 5.

41. Seedman and Hellman, *Chief!*, 248; FBI Memorandum, NY 52-9441, Synopsis, November 17, 1969, 29. In a 2002 interview Demmerle confirmed both of their locations. "[Sam] got caught across the street and I was caught next to the trucks cause I was checking to make sure the doors were all open to place the explosives inside, on the floor board, under the steering column or in front of the steering column, to maximize [the impact]." UNT interviews, 2002.

42. FBI Memorandum, NY 52-9441, Synopsis, 29.

43. Seedman and Hellman, *Chief!*, 247. According to an FBI report, Melville said 4:00 a.m., not 2:00 a.m.

44. FBI Memorandum, NY 52-9441, Synopsis, 13.

45. "How Lawmen Stalked the Bomb Suspects," 5.

46. FBI Memorandum, NY 52-9441, Synopsis, 45.

47. Alpert, *Growing Up Underground*, 229.

48. FBI Memorandum, NY 52-9441, Synopsis, 27.

49. Shoshana Rihn, interview with the author, January 20, 2021.

15. The Trial

1. "Kaboom!" *Seed*, December 1969.

2. Martin Arnold, "F.B.I. Charges 4 with 8 Bombings Here Since July," *New York Times*, November 14, 1969.

3. Albert A. Seedman and Peter Hellman, *Chief! Classic Cases from the Files of the Chief of Detectives* (New York: Avon Books, 1975), 249.

4. *U.S. vs. Samuel Joseph Melville, George Demmerle, John David Hughey, III, Jane Lauren Alpert and Pat Swinton*, November 14, 1969, 15.

5. Ibid.

6. Jane Alpert, *Growing Up Underground* (New York: Morrow, 1981), 233.

7. "*U.S. vs. Samuel Joseph Melville* et al.," 35.

8. Henry Lee, "4 Bomb Suspects' Bail Cut Again—But," *New York Daily News*, November 16, 1969.

9. Carl J. Pelleck, "The Bomb Suspects—Their Backgrounds Are Murky," *New York Post*, November 15, 1969.

10. William E. Farrell, "Sketches of 4 Seized as Bombing Suspects," *New York Times*, November 14, 1969.

11. David Bird, "Sketches of 4 Seized as Bombing Suspects," *New York Times*, November 14, 1969.

12. "Terrorism: The House on Fourth Street," *Newsweek*, November 24, 1969, 37–38.

13. FBI Report, NY 52-9441, December 23, 1969.

14. John Herbers, "250,000 War Protesters Stage Peaceful Rally in Washington; Militants Stir Clashes Later," *New York Times*, November 16, 1969, 1.

15. Carl Davidson, "Four Arrested in New York Bombings," *Guardian*, November 20, 1969.

16. *United States of America v. Samuel Joseph Melville, George Demmerle, John David Hughey, III, and Jane Lauren Alpert*, Indictment 69 Cr. 811, United States District Court, Southern District of New York, November 18, 1969.

17. Emanuel Perlmutter, "Four Held in Series of Bombings in City Win a Reduction of 80% in Their Total Bail of $2-Million," *New York Times*, November 16, 1969, 37.

18. Alpert, *Growing Up Underground*, 234.

19. Carl Davidson, "Lawyers to File Motions in N.Y. Bomb Case," *The Guardian*, December 27, 1969, 3.

20. Jeff Shero, "Bomb Plot," *Rat Subterranean News*, November 19, 1969.

21. Jane Capellaro, "The Conspiracy," *5th Estate*, November 27, 1969, 8.

22. Charles Hightower, "Who or What Is George Demmerle?" *Daily World*, November 29, 1969.

23. "Bomb Suspect Is Sprung," *Daily News*, November 20, 1969, 32.

24. Alpert, *Growing Up Underground*, 235–236.

25. "350 Attend Benefit for Bomb Suspects," *New York Post*, November 24, 1969, 28.

26. "Five New Yorkers Charged with Political Bombings," Liberation News Service, November 20, 1969.

27. FBI Memorandum from Special Agent in Charge, New York, to the FBI Director, November 28, 1969, 4.

28. UNT interviews, 2002.

29. Hightower, "Who or What Is George Demmerle?"

30. Claudia Dreifus, "The Pig Wore a Dayglow Helmet," *East Village Other*, December 3, 1969.

31. Jay Levin, "The Wildest Radical," *New York Post*, May 25, 1970.

32. James A. Wechsler, "Prince Crazy," *New York Post*, May 28, 1970.

33. Allan Katzman, "Poor Paranoid's Almanac," *East Village Other*, November 29, 1969.

34. "Kaboom!"

35. Wechsler, "Prince Crazy," 37.

36. "Provocation a la FBI," *Dissent*, July–August 1970, https://www.dissentmagazine.org/article/provocation-a-la-fbi.

37. FBI Memorandum from Special Agent in Charge, New York, to the FBI Director, November 28, 1969, 5–6.

38. John Cohen, "Free Sam Melville!" *Rat Subterranean News*, December 25, 1969.

39. At an early meeting in his office Katz held up a piece of paper with a handwritten note: "Do you know where Pat is?" Jane shook her head and mouthed back, "Do you?" Katz put the paper down and wrote something else on it. "In USA." Alpert, *Growing Up Underground*, 238.

40. Lester Abelman, "$50,000 Bail Doubled in Bombing Plot," *Daily News*, December 30, 1969.

41. Agent Robinson Cross Examination by Mr. Katz, December 30, 1969.

42. "Dynamite 5 Facts," *Rat Subterranean News*, April 17, 1970.

43. Fred Loetterle, "High Bail Bid Stirs Rumpus in Bomb Case," *Daily News*, January 16, 1970.

44. Craig R. Whitney, "Bomb Suspect Calls Judge a Jackass," *New York Times*, February 21, 1970.

45. Lesley Oelsner, "City Judge Denies Bail in Bomb Case," *New York Times*, March 11, 1970.

46. Mike Pearl, "Bare Melville Escape Try," *New York Post*, March 11, 1970.

47. UNT interviews, 2002.

48. Richard Schwartz, "Undercover Man Highly Visible," *New York Post*, October 21, 1971.

49. Letter to George Demmerle, November 21, 1969 (FBI files).

50. FBI Memorandum, NY 100-167404, December 1, 1969.

51. Ann Zimmer, "Yippie Spy," *Dallas Observer*, March 16, 1995, 22.

52. Walter Teague, interview with the author, December 28, 2022.

53. *Combat*, unknown date and source; screenshot provided to author by email.

54. FBI Memorandum, January 3, 1969.

55. Zimmer, "Yippie Spy," 22.

56. Teague interview.

57. In three years of research for this book, Grell's name never came up in any other context, and according to a footnote in *Letters from Attica*, "Sam did not even know who he was." Jane Alpert, "Profile of Sam Melville," from Sam Melville, *Letters from Attica* (New York: William Morrow & Company, 1972), 40.

58. Norma Abrams and William Federici, "Mounties Hunt Bomb Case Girl," *Daily News*, March 28, 1970.

59. Kathy Mason, "Youth Charged in N.Y. Bombings," *Albuquerque Journal*, March 27, 1970.

60. "New Mexico Holds Teen in N.Y. Bombings," *Daily News*, March 27, 1970.

61. "Dynamite 5 Facts," *Rat Subterranean News*, April 17, 1970.

62. "Add Defendant for Bomb Trial," *Daily News*, April 3, 1970.

63. "Dynamite 5 Facts."

64. "Separate Trial Granted Grell," *Daily News*, May 1, 1970.

65. "Guilty Plea Was 'Package Deal': Jane Alpert," *Village Voice*, May 7, 1970.

66. Norma Abrams, "Warrant Out for Vanished Bomb Plot Girl," *Daily News*, May 15, 1970.

67. Mark Rudd, *Underground: My Life with SDS and the Weathermen* (New York: William Morrow, 2009), 194.

68. Robin Palmer, interview with Jeremy Varon, November 14, 1994.

69. Rudd, *Underground*, 194.

70. Bernadine Dohrn, "New Morning—Changing Weather," *Weather Underground Communique*, December 6, 1970, https://rozsixties.unl.edu/items/show/446.

71. Alpert, *Growing Up Underground*, 246.

72. Palmer interview with Varon.

73. FBI Memorandum from Special Agent in Charge, New York, to FBI Director, March 17, 1970.

74. UNT interviews, 2002.

75. FBI Memorandum from Special Agent in Charge, New York, to FBI Director, April 6, 1970.

76. Teague interview.

77. Alpert, *Growing Up Underground*, 249.

78. Anthony Mancini, "Three Admit They Plotted Bombings," *New York Post*, May 4, 1970.

79. Arnold H. Lubasch, "3 Plead Guilty in Conspiracy to Bomb," *New York Times*, May 5, 1970.

80. Lucinda Franks, "The 4-Year Odyssey of Jane Alpert, From Revolutionary Bomber to Feminist," *New York Times*, January 14, 1975, 14.

81. Lindsy Van Gelder, "Jane Alpert Jumps Bail," *New York Post*, May 8, 1970.

82. Jay Levin, "Bomb Informer Tells His Tale," *New York Post*, May 23, 1970
83. UNT interviews, 2002.
84. Kirkpatrick Sale, *SDS* (New York: Random House, 1973), 605.
85. Stuart Daniels, "The Weathermen," *Government and Opposition*, Autumn 1974, 442.
86. Vincent Butler, "13 Years for N.Y. Bomber," *Chicago Tribune*, June 20, 1970.
87. "Accused Bomber Goes to Jail for 13–18 Years," Liberation News Service, July 1, 1970.
88. Craig R. Whitney, "Melville Sentenced to 13 to 18 Years in Bombings Here," *New York Times*, June 20, 1970.
89. "Accused Bomber Goes to Jail for 13–18 Years," 24.
90. Whitney, "Melville Sentenced."
91. Butler, "13 Years for N.Y. Bomber."
92. Whitney, "Melville Sentenced."
93. FBI Memorandum from Special Agent in Charge, New York, to FBI Director, August 10, 1972.
94. Airtel from Special Agent in Charge, New York, to FBI Director, November 23, 1970.
95. Demmerle's total earnings of $5,735.96 are cited in an FBI memorandum from the FBI Director to the Special Agent in Charge, New York, November 18, 1971.

16. Aftermath

1. David Behrens, "Undercover: A Cop in the Weather Underground," *Newsday*, March 28, 1982.
2. Robin Palmer, interview with Jeremy Varon, November 14, 1994.
3. Behrens, "Undercover."
4. Ibid.
5. Ibid., 40.
6. Ibid., 43.
7. Ibid., 44.
8. Ibid.
9. "Bust," *Rat Subterranean News*, December 17, 1970, 19.
10. Palmer interview with Varon, November 14, 1994.
11. Vincent Lee, "500G Bail Holds Six in Bomb Conspiracy," *Daily News*, December 9, 1970.
12. Robin Palmer, interview with Jeremy Varon, December 16, 1994.
13. Juan M. Vasquez, "5 in Bomb Plot Here Sentenced; 3 Get Maximum 4-Year Terms," *New York Times*, May 8, 1971.
14. Jean Crafton, "Sentence Five in Plot to Bomb Bank," *Daily News*, May 8, 1971.
15. FBI Memorandum from Special Agent in Charge, New York, to FBI Director, August 25, 1971.
16. Lucinda Franks, "The 4-Year Odyssey of Jane Alpert, From Revolutionary Bomber to Feminist," *New York Times*, January 14, 1975, 14.
17. Jane Alpert, *Growing Up Underground* (New York: Morrow, 1981), 301, 303.
18. Michael T. Kaufman, "Bomb-Carrying Convict Killed by Sharpshooter," *New York Times*, September 14, 1971.
19. Jeremy Varon, conversation with the author, 2022.
20. Joshua Melville, *American Time Bomb: Attica, Sam Melville, and a Son's Search for Answers* (Chicago: Chicago Review Press, 2021), 264.

21. Prisoners Solidarity Committee, Second 8-Page Newsletter on Attica, September 30, 1971, 4.

22. John Mullane, "Melville's Funeral—Cops Were There Too," *New York Post*, September 21, 1971.

23. Alpert, *Growing Up Underground*, 304.

24. "Ex-Undercover Man for FBI To Be Honored," *Leader-Observer*, October 14, 1971.

25. FBI Memorandum from the FBI Director to the Special Agent in Charge, New York, November 18, 1971.

26. Allen W. Finger, Letter to Freedom's Foundation, November 23, 1971.

27. Ibid.

28. Robin Palmer, interview with Jeremy Varon, December 8, 1994.

29. "Leslie Bacon Indicted," *California Aggie*, April 11, 1972, 3.

30. FBI Memorandum from Special Agent in Charge, New York, to FBI Director, May 2, 1972.

31. Alpert, *Growing Up Underground*, 310.

32. Ibid., 315.

33. Franks, "The 4-Year Odyssey."

34. Mark Rudd, *Underground: My Life with SDS and the Weathermen* (New York: William Morrow, 2009), 244.

35. Ibid., 245, 248–249.

36. "Women Take Over Rat," *Rat Subterranean News*, February 6, 1970, 2.

37. "Goodbye," *Rat Subterranean News*, February 6, 1970, 6–7.

38. Jane Alpert, "Mother Right: A New Feminist Theory," *Off Our Backs*, May 1973.

39. Ibid.

40. Ibid.

41. Palmer interview with Varon, November 14, 1994.

42. Alpert, "Mother Right."

43. FBI Memorandum from Special Agent in Charge, New York, to FBI Director, August 10, 1972.

44. FBI Memorandum from Special Agent in Charge, New York, to FBI Director, August 15, 1972.

45. UNT interviews, 2002.

46. FBI Memorandum from Special Agent in Charge, New York, to FBI Director re: Richard Robin Palmer, June 21, 1973.

47. FBI Memorandum from Special Agent in Charge (NY) to FBI Director re: Richard Robin Palmer, November 29, 1973.

48. Franks, "The 4-Year Odyssey."

49. *United States v. Patricia Elizabeth Swinton*, Affidavit of David A. Cuttner, Assistant U.S. Attorney, 70 Cr. 230, May 12, 1975.

50. "Bomb Terrorist Sentenced," *Rochester Democrat and Chronicle*, January 14, 1975, 7A.

51. "Jane Alpert Interview," *Her-self*, March 1975, 6.

52. Susan Sherman, interview with the author, January 8, 2023.

53. "Petition #2: The Crisis in Feminism," *Majority Report*, March 5, 1975.

54. Sherman interview.

55. Susan Sherman, *The Color of the Heart: Writing from Struggle and Change, 1959–1990* (Willimantic, CT: Curbstone Press, 1990), 95.

56. "Petition #3: Vindication of the Rights of Feminists," *Majority Report*, March 5, 1975.

57. Palmer interview with Varon, November 14, 1994.

58. Alice Echols, *Daring to Be Bad: Radical Feminism in America 1967–1975* (Minneapolis: University of Minnesota Press, 2019), 260.

59. "Pat Swinton Trial Begins," Liberation News Service, September 24, 1975.

60. Alpert, *Growing Up Underground*, 315.

61. *United States v. Patricia Elizabeth Swinton*, Cuttner affidavit.

62. Grace Shinell, "Pat Swinton: Jane Taught Me Feminism," *Majority Report*, April 19, 1975.

63. Mary Moylan, "Moylan on Alpert," *Off Our Backs*, May–June 1975, 22.

64. Women of the Weather Underground Organization, "Weather Women," *Off Our Backs*, May–June 1975, 22–23.

65. "Shoshana (Pat Swinton): 'What You Do Matters,'" *Off Our Backs*, July 1975, 2–6.

66. "Pat Swinton Trial Begins."

67. Edith Evans Asbury, "Patricia Swinton Goes on Trial; 2 Witnesses Balk at Testifying," *New York Times*, September 23, 1975.

68. Ruth Shereff and Jeanne Cordova, "Underground Activist Acquitted," *LA Free Press*, October 3, 1975.

69. "Former FBI Informer Fails to Identify Patricia Swinton," *Brattleboro Reformer*, September 24, 1975.

70. "Pat Swinton Trial Begins."

71. Edith Evans Asbury, "Witness Links Mrs. Swinton to Leak to Press About 1969 Bombings," *New York Times*, September 24, 1975.

72. Edith Evans Asbury, "Jury Pondering Swinton Verdict in Bombing of Federal Buildings," *New York Times,* September 26, 1975.

73. Scott Latham, "Swinton Acquittal: A 'Contribution to Bicentennial,'" *Brattleboro Reformer*, September 27, 1975, 1.

74. William Poole, "Terror Seeking News Coverage," *Coshocton Tribune*, April 14, 1976, 13.

75. Richard Schwartz, "Undercover Man Highly Visible," *New York Post*, October 21, 1971.

Epilogue

1. David Behrens, "Undercover: A Cop in the Weather Underground," *Newsday*, March 28, 1982.

2. Judson Hand, "Photog Spy for FBI Now an Outcast," *Daily News*, March 29, 1970.

3. Michael Spector, email to the author, January 21, 2023.

4. Richard Schwartz, "Undercover Man Highly Visible," *New York Post*, October 21, 1971.

5. Behrens, "Undercover."

6. Richard Schwartz, "Undercover Man Highly Visible."

7. Undated typed note, Demmerle Archive.

8. Lew Friedman, interview with the author, December 3, 2020.

9. Ann Zimmer, "Yippie Spy," *Dallas Observer*, March 16, 1995, 24.

10. Judson Hand, "Photog Spy."

11. Behrens, "Undercover."

12. Jane Alpert, *Growing Up Underground* (New York: Morrow, 1981), 223.

13. David Bonner, "Remembering George Demmerle: Portrait of a Police Informer," *Counterpunch*, October 1–15, 2008, 7.

14. Lee Merrick, "Life with 'Crazie' George," Liberation News Service, January 24, 1970, 18.

15. Martin A. Lee and Bruce Shlain, *Acid Dreams: The Complete Social History of LSD—The CIA, The Sixties, and Beyond* (New York: Grove Press, 1985), 173.

16. Jerry Rubin, *We Are Everywhere* (New York: Harper & Row, 1971), 216.

17. Steve Aydt, email, December 2, 2002, Demmerle Archives.

INDEX

Jonathan Butler, a Brooklyn-based writer and entrepreneur, has made significant contributions to journalism, local culture, and the arts. His ventures include founding Brownstoner.com, the Brooklyn Flea, and Smorgasburg, all of which have attracted widespread attention and accolades. Featured in top publications like the *New York Times*, *Wall Street Journal*, and *New Yorker*, he has been honored with awards from the Municipal Art Society, New York Landmarks Conservancy, Brooklyn Historical Society, and others.